The UK Economy
A Manual of
Applied Economics

Second Edition

Edited by
A.R. Prest M.A. Ph.D

*Stanley Jevons Professor of Political Economy
and Cobden Lecturer, University of Manchester*

Weidenfeld and Nicolson

5 Winsley Street London W1

First published 1966
Second impression 1967
Third impression 1968
Second edition 1968
Second impression 1969

PRINTED BY Unwin Brothers Limited
THE GRESHAM PRESS OLD WOKING SURREY ENGLAND

A member of the Staples Printing Group

CONTRIBUTORS

Chapter 1
> M. C. Kennedy, *B.Sc. (Econ.) (London)*
> *Lecturer in Economics, University of Manchester*

Chapter 2
> N. J. Gibson, *B.Sc. (Econ.), Ph.D. (Belfast)*
> *Professor of Economics, The New University of Ulster*
> *(formerly Senior Lecturer, University of Manchester)*

Chapter 3
> D. J. Coppock, *B.A. (Econ.) (Manchester)*
> *Professor of Economics, University of Manchester*

Chapter 4
> J. R. Cable, *B.A. (Nottingham) M.A. (Econ.) (Manchester)*
> *Lecturer in Economics, University of Warwick*
> *(formerly Lecturer, University of Manchester)*

Chapter 5
> Shirley W. Lerner, *B.A. (Roosevelt), Ph.D. (London)*
> *Senior Lecturer in Industrial Relations, University of Manchester*

The UK Economy
A Manual of Applied Economics

Contents

TABLES

STATISTICAL APPENDIX

LIST OF ABBREVIATIONS

(1) Economic Terms

c.i.f.	Cost including Insurance and Freight
f.o.b.	Free on Board
GDP	Gross Domestic Product
GNP	Gross National Product
PAYE	Pay as you Earn
PDI	Personal Disposable Income
R and D	Research and Development
RPM	Resale Price Maintenance
SIC	Standard Industrial Classification
SITC	Standard Industrial Trade Classification
TFE	Total Final Expenditure at market prices

(2) Organisations etc.

CBI	Confederation of British Industry
CSO	Central Statistical Office (UK)
ECE	Economic Commission for Europe
ECSC	European Coal and Steel Community
EEC	European Economic Community
EFTA	European Free Trade Area
FAO	Food and Agriculture Organisation
GATT	General Agreement on Tariffs and Trade
IBRD	International Bank for Reconstruction and Development
IFC	International Finance Corporation
IMF	International Monetary Fund
IRC	Industrial Reorganisation Corporation
NEDC	National Economic Development Council
NBPI	National Board for Prices and Incomes
NRDC	National Research Development Corporation
OECD	Organisation for Economic Co-operation and Development
SIB	Shipbuilding Industry Board
TUC	Trades Union Congress
UN	United Nations
UNCTAD	United Nations Commission for Trade and Development

(3) Journals etc.

AAS	*Annual Abstract of Statistics* (HMSO)
BEQB	*Bank of England Quarterly Bulletin*
BJIR	*British Journal of Industrial Relations*
BTJ	*Board of Trade Journal* (HMSO)
DBR	*District Bank Review*
EJ	*Economic Journal*
ET	*Economic Trends* (HMSO)
FES	Ministry of Labour, *Family Expenditure Survey* (HMSO)
FS	*Financial Statistics* (HMSO)
IFS	*International Financial Statistics*

ILRR	*Industrial and Labour Relations Review*
IR	*Industrial Relations*
JIE	*Journal of Industrial Economics*
JRSS	*Journal of Royal Statistical Society*
LBR	*Lloyd's Bank Review*
LCEB	*London and Cambridge Economic Bulletin*
MDS	*Monthly Digest of Statistics* (HMSO)
MLG	*Ministry of Labour Gazette* (HMSO)
MS	*The Manchester School of Economic and Social Studies*
NIBB	*National Income Blue Book* (HMSO)
NIER	*National Institute Economic Review*
ROT	*Report on Overseas Trade* (HMSO)
SIPEP	*Statistics on Incomes, Prices, Employment and Production* (HMSO)
TER	*Treasury Economic Report* (HMSO)

Foreword to the Second Edition

THE foreword to the first edition of this book, published in 1966, began as follows:

> The central idea behind this book is to give an account of the main features and problems of the UK economy today. The hope is that it will fulfil two functions simultaneously, in that it will be as up to date as possible and yet will not be simply a bare catalogue of facts and figures. There are many sources of information, official and otherwise, about the structure and progress of the UK economy. There are also many authors to whom one can turn for subtle analyses of the problems before us. Our effort here is based on the belief that there is both room and need for an attempt to combine the functions of chronicler and analyst in the confines of a single book.
>
> The contributors to these pages subscribe rather firmly to the belief that economists should practise, as well as preach, the principle of the division of labour. The complexity of a modern economy is such that, whether one likes it or not, it is no longer possible for any single individual to be authoritative on all its aspects; so it is inevitable that the burden of producing a work of this kind should be spread among a number of people, each specialist in his or her particular field. Such a division carries with it the obvious dangers of overlap and inconsistency. It is hoped that some of the worst pitfalls of this kind have been avoided and there is a reasonable unity of purpose, treatment and layout. At the same time, it was wholly undesirable to impose a monolithic structure and it is just as apparent to the authors that there are differences in outlook and emphasis among them as it will be to the readers.
>
> The general intention was to base exposition on the assumption that the reader would have some elementary knowledge of economics—say, a student in the latter part of a typical first year course in economics in a British University. At the same time, it is hoped that most of the text will be intelligible to those without this degree of expertise. We may not have succeeded in this; if not, we shall try to do better in future.

As a statement of content and intent, these paragraphs still hold good. At the same time, it must be very strongly emphasised that this edition is in no sense a simple updated version of the previous one. Every chapter has been extensively re-written in the light of recent developments at both analytical and empirical levels. As a result, some topics previously dealt with at length are now omitted or only receive a brief mention, whilst others are introduced for the first time. Naturally, we hope that this edition is an improvement on the previous one in coverage and presentation; but, as economists, we must be prepared to accept the consumer's verdict on this.

Chapter 1, 'The Economy as a Whole' is primarily concerned with recent movements of total output and total demand in the economy. A good deal of time is spent on the short term movements in demand and output of the last few years and the measures for dealing with them. Various problems of inflation and growth are also discussed. The chapter ends with a short section on the economic prospects in the near future. Chapter 2, 'Monetary, Credit and Fiscal Policies' starts with a brief discussion of the general theoretical background and then analyses in detail the theory and practices of monetary, credit and fiscal policies in the UK in recent years. The final section discusses the various trends in policy over the period. Chapter 3, 'Foreign Trade and the Balance of Payments', deals with the importance of foreign trade and payments to the UK economy, concepts of equilibrium in the balance of payments and an assessment of recent performance, trends in visible and invisible trade and problems of policy in the context of international co-operation and agreements. Chapter 4, 'Industry and Commerce', starts with an analysis of recent trends and discusses some of the reasons for these changes. After discussing problems of size structure and business objectives, the author has a long final section on the various ways in which government actions, in one form or another, impinge on the operation of industry and commerce. The last chapter is devoted to 'Social Problems'. Various aspects of income distribution are looked at first and this leads on to social security arrangements and proposals for reducing poverty. The second main topic is collective bargaining and incomes policy, covering recent developments such as the pronouncements of the National Board for Prices and Incomes as well as more traditional fare. The last subject is housing and rents.

Each chapter is accompanied by a list of references and further reading. The Statistical Appendix has twelve tables dealing with different aspects of the UK Economy. Finally, we have on this occasion provided an index as well as the detailed list of headings and sub-headings given in the Contents pages.

We acknowledge the great help given to us by Mr M. G. Cooper in preparing the Statistical Appendix. We are also heavily indebted to the secretarial and computing staff of the Faculty of Economics for further invaluable assistance.

University of Manchester   A. R. PREST
April 1968

1

The economy as a whole

I. INTRODUCTION

I.1 Facts, Hypotheses and Priorities

THIS chapter is meant as an introduction to applied macroeconomics. It discusses such matters as the determination of the level of economic activity in the short run, the pace of inflation and the long-term rate of economic growth. Although it contains a great deal of factual material it is not intended as a work of pure description. Rather, the intention is to make some progress towards explaining the way in which the economy works.

To do this for such a complex economy as that of Britain is, of course, a difficult task. But it is the author's firm conviction that it cannot be accomplished without the help of theories or hypotheses that are for the most part similar to those found in textbooks and articles dealing with economic theory. An event can be said to be explained when it can be predicted from some law or hypothesis; it certainly cannot be explained by a description.[1] We can, for example, explain the high level of UK imports in early 1967 by the removal of the import surcharge, perhaps by a high level of national output; we cannot explain it by simply enumerating the main categories of imports. It is essential, then, in the field of applied economics to combine theories and facts together. One without the other gets us nowhere.

In asserting the importance of theory we should perhaps guard against the idea that a 'real world' economy, such as that of modern Britain, moves in exact accordance with the assertions of a first year textbook of macroeconomics. Such an assumption would not only be false but unfair to the textbook. Textbook theory must often make simple premises in order to facilitate the analysis of complex problems. We must be prepared, then, in this chapter and elsewhere in applied economics, for hypotheses that are considerably modified versions of the textbook form: the multiplier concept discussed below[2] is one example. Some of our hypotheses, moreover, may be completely unfamiliar. It will be suggested, for example, that one of the influences on the level of imports is investment in stocks, yet this is seldom, if ever, mentioned in a textbook. This relationship is one example of the kind of *ad hoc* hypothesis which a working economist may discover without the aid of textbook theory, which may be intellectually unsatisfactory in that there is no body of *a priori* reasoning in support of it, but which, nonetheless, may furnish good predictions of economic events. The fact that such hypotheses exist serves as a reminder of the undeveloped state of economics and as a challenge to theorist and applied economist alike.

Besides trying to explain our subject matter with the aid of theories supported by facts we are also interested in many controversial matters of economic policy. This means that we must recognise a third type of concept: the value judgment. Value judgments, as is well known, can vary from person to person and also from time to time. Fortunately, this does not mean that, as economists, we are forbidden to make appraisals of economic policy. But it does mean that we should exercise a degree of caution in doing so, and that

---

[1] For a discussion of the methodology of economics see: R. G. Lipsey, *An Introduction to Positive Economics,* Weidenfeld and Nicolson, 1966, chapter 1; Milton Friedman, 'The Methodology of Positive Economics', *Essays in Positive Economics,* University of Chicago Press, 1953; K. R. Popper, *The Poverty of Historicism,* Routledge and Kegan Paul, 1961

[2] See section 1.3 of this chapter.

we should try to recognise where the policy-maker's scale of priorities differs from our own.

The economist's main functions as a policy adviser are to point out the probable consequences of various lines of action and the alternative means of achieving a given set of objectives. As a general rule he is better equipped by his specialist knowledge to do this than the policy-maker himself, although the economist may feel limited by the tentative nature of the hypotheses that make up the tools of his trade. Very often he can be positively helpful to the policy-maker by warning that the pursuit of one objective may put limitations on the achievement of another. The pursuit of fuller and fuller employment may, for example, mean the achievement of less and less price stability. What he cannot do, however, is to say where the line should be drawn between the pursuit of one of these objectives and the other. For this implies that he knows the policy-maker's preferences and priorities with respect to all the objectives with which he is concerned; and only the policy-maker knows this. The economist can help the policy-maker by providing information about the costs of various lines of action in terms of opportunities foregone; but he exceeds his role as an expert if he tries to dictate policy without taking due notice of the policy-maker's own preferences.

The temptation for philosophers to be kings is an ancient one, and nobody would claim that it has been resisted by economists. But it is left to the reader of this chapter to judge where this particular sin has been committed, and to draw his own conclusions.

1.2   Domestic Income and Output

Most of the topics discussed in this chapter require some knowledge of the national accounts statistics. A full explanation of what these are and of how they are put together would require a great deal more space than we can afford and is, in any case, available elsewhere.[1] It may be useful, however, in the next few pages to remind the reader of the main national accounting categories in so far as they affect this chapter.

The most important of these concepts is that of gross domestic product, or GDP for short. Perhaps the easiest approach to understanding GDP is to think first of a single, simple production unit, such as a farm. Suppose that a farm produces 100 bushels of wheat a year at a price of £1 each. The value of its output is £100 and is divided between the incomes of various factors of production in the form of wages, rent and profits. Only 95 bushels are sold for current consumption by households (including the farmer's own household). The remaining 5 bushels accumulate as stocks of unsold output and are regarded as investment expenditure by the farmer. Thus the total income, output and expenditure of the farm are all identically equal.

The UK domestic income, by analogy with the simple production unit, can also be added up in three different ways: from the sides of income, output and expenditure. The first of these, gross domestic income, measures the sum of all the income of the residents of the UK earned in the production of goods and services in the UK during a stated period. It divides into income from employment, income from self-employment and profit, and income from rent. These are all factor incomes earned in the process of production and are distinct from transfer incomes, such as pensions and sickness benefits, which are not earned from production and which, therefore, are excluded from the total. The breakdown of factor incomes is illustrated for 1966 in Table 1.1 (page 5).

As with the simple production unit the value of output accruing in the form of accumulated stocks is included in total factor output. But a problem arises when the prices at which stocks are valued in the national accounts vary during the course of the accounting period. When this happens the value of stocks held at the beginning and end of the period will have been reported at two different prices, and it is then necessary to

---

[1]   See, for example, R. and G. Stone, *National Income and Expenditure,* Bowes and Bowes, 1964;
H. C. Edey and A. T. Peacock, *National Income and Social Accounting* (2nd ed.), Hutchinson,
1959; or the official handbook *National Income Statistics. Sources and Methods,* HMSO, 1956.

make a special valuation adjustment known as the 'adjustment for stock appreciation'. A firm holding stocks of lead, for example, may increase its holding from 100 tons on 1st January to 200 tons on 31st December. If the price of lead was £100 a ton at the beginning of the year and £120 at the end of the year the increase in the value of stocks will show up as (£120 × 200) - (£100 × 100), which equals £14,000. This figure is inflated by the amount of the price increase and fails, therefore, to give an adequate record of what the CSO calls 'the value of the physical increase in stocks'. In order to rectify this the CSO tries to value physical changes in stocks by the average price level prevailing during the period. If, in the example, the price averaged £110 over the period then the amount of stock investment would be shown as £110(200-100) which equals £11,000. The difference of £3,000 between this and the previous total is called the 'adjustment for stock appreciation'.

Gross domestic product is identically equal to gross domestic income but is measured by adding up the value of production by the various firms and public enterprises in the country. This procedure presents two types of problem. First, the production of goods and services by one domestic firm may form part of the output of some other firm. Wheat produced on a farm, for example, is entered as farm output, but it may also be used by a bakery to produce bread in which case it will be entered as bread output too. Thus the addition of the farm's output to that of the bakery will result in some double-counting. This means that a distinction must be drawn in the production accounts between output sold to final buyers as total final output and intermediate output sold to other productive units. Intermediate output must be excluded before arriving at a firm's contribution to gross domestic product. Secondly, imports are a form of intermediate output which are not produced by UK firms at all, so that their value must be subtracted from the value of total final output in order to derive domestic output. In Table 1.1 the various categories of output are all measured net of intermediate output and of the import content of final output.

Gross domestic product (GDP) can also be measured from the side of expenditure. Conceptually this total is identical to the income and output total; but in practice the statistics are collected from independent sources and do not lead to exactly the same figure. The difference is called the residual error and is sometimes quite large. In 1966 it was 0.5 per cent of the total. The expenditure estimate is the most frequently quoted version of GDP and the one which we shall use as the standard total throughout this chapter.

The breakdown of the expenditure total is especially important in the analysis of aggregate demand. Expenditures are undertaken by four types of spending unit: households, public authorities, firms and foreign residents. Purchases by households are described as consumers' expenditure, or more loosely, as consumption. The latter description, however, may be slightly misleading when applied to expenditure on durable goods such as motor cars and refrigerators, the services of which are consumed over several years and not solely in the year when they are purchased. We shall see later that the forces determining durable goods expenditure sales are not quite the same as those determining non-durable consumption. One form of personal expenditure, however, which is not classed as such is the purchase of new houses. These are deemed to have been sold initially to 'firms' and are included under the broad heading of domestic capital formation or gross investment. Fixed investment other than housing represents the purchases by firms of physical assets which are not completely used up in current production but which accrue as additions to the nation's capital stock. The preface 'gross', however, warns us that a year's gross investment does not measure the change in the size of the capital stock during the year because it does not allow for withdrawals from the capital stock due to wear and tear or scrapping. The gross concept of capital formation is also carried through into the definition of domestic product itself. Net domestic product would include additions to the capital stock net of capital consumption.

The sum of exports, consumers' expenditure, government current consumption and gross investment is denoted as total final expenditure (TFE) and not as gross domestic product. This is because each of the four components contains two elements which must be subtracted before arriving at GDP at factor cost. The first of these elements is the import content of the expenditure which must, of course, be classified as foreign rather than domestic output. The simplest way of dealing with imports is to take the import total as given by the balance of payments accounts and subtract it from TFE; this is the usual method. Estimates do exist, however, for the import content of the separate components of final expenditure in the input-output tables,[1] but they are drawn up a great deal less frequently than the national accounts. The second element of TFE which must be excluded from GDP at factor cost is the indirect tax content (net of subsidies) of the various expenditures. This is present for the simple reason that the most readily available value for any commodity is the price it commands in the market. This price, however, will overstate the factor incomes earned from producing the commodity if it contains an element of purchase tax or other indirect tax; and it will understate factor income if the price is subsidised. Thus the sum of indirect taxes, net of subsidies, must be deducted from the market price total in order to arrive at GDP at factor cost. This deduction, known as the factor cost adjustment, is most conveniently made globally since it can be found from the government's records of tax proceeds and subsidy payments. But estimates of its incidence on the components of TFE such as consumers' expenditure and exports, are available annually in the National Income *Blue Book.*[2]

Gross domestic product from the expenditure side is thus reached by adding up the components of TFE at market prices, and by subtracting imports of goods and services together with the factor cost adjustment. GDP is the concept of total output which we shall use throughout most of this chapter and it relates to the total production in the UK of the residents of the United Kingdom. It differs from the other aggregate concept, gross national product (GNP), in that it does not include interest, profits and dividends earned by UK residents from productive activity that is carried out overseas, and it does not exclude the profits of foreign-owned enterprises producing in the UK. The balance of these two amounts is known as net property income from abroad and must be added to GDP in order to obtain GNP. It is fairly small and does not fluctuate much from one year to another.

Gross Domestic Product at Constant Prices

Table 1.1 summarises the national accounts for 1966 at the prices obtaining in 1966. As such it is a useful source of information as to the way in which domestic income was divided in a particular year. If, however, we want to know something about how the quantity of goods produced has varied from one year to another we must use a different set of figures. These are the estimates of GDP in constant prices, and they are presented in the Statistical Appendix, Table A-2. They show the value of GDP for each year since 1950 in terms of the prices ruling in 1958, and are computed by the CSO for both the production and expenditure sides of GDP. They are derived almost entirely from movements in quantities, and the various quantities for each year are added together by means of the value weights obtaining for 1958. The result is two conceptually equal sets of estimates of real domestic output but, as with the current price series, there is often a large residual error between the two. For convenience we shall adhere in this chapter to the expenditure estimate.

Gross domestic product is an important category in its own right and changes in its real amount are the best estimates available of changes in total UK production. But it does not measure national well-being or utility and should not be interpreted as a

---

[1] 'Provisional Summary Input-Output Tables for 1963', *ET,* August 1964; HMSO, Table 8.
[2] *NIBB.* 1967, Table 12.

TABLE 1.1

Gross Domestic and Gross National Product, UK, 1966

(a) From income

	£ m. at current prices	Per cent of GDP
Income from employment	22,437	69.8
Income from self-employment	2,470	7.7
Income from rent	1,949	6.1
Gross trading profits of companies	4,646	14.5
Gross trading surpluses of public corporations and profits of other public enterprises	1,046	3.3
Less Stock appreciation	−351	−1.1
Gross domestic product from income	32,287	100.5
Residual error	−160	−0.5
Gross domestic product at factor cost	32,127	100

(b) From output

	£ m. at current prices	Per cent of GDP
Agriculture, forestry and fishing	1,053	3.3
Mining and quarrying	701	2.2
Manufacturing	11,139	35.0
Construction	2,288	7.4
Services and distributions	17,457	
less Stock appreciation	−351	−1.1
Gross domestic product from output	32,287	100.5
Residual error	−160	−0.5
Gross domestic product at factor cost	32,127	100

(c) From expenditure

	£ m. at current prices	Per cent of TFE
Consumers' expenditure	24,116	54.4
Public authorities' current expenditure	6,391	14.4
Gross fixed investment in dwellings	1,309	3.0
Gross fixed investment other than dwellings	5,326	12.0
Investment in stocks	209	0.5
Exports of goods and services	6,939	15.1
Total final expenditure on goods & services	44,290	100.0
less Imports of goods & services	−7,125	
less Taxes on expenditure	−5,596	
plus Subsidies	558	
Gross domestic product at factor cost	32,127	
Net property income from abroad	371	
Gross national product at factor cost	32,498	

Source: NIBB, 1967, Tables 1, 10 and 12.

Detail does not add to totals because of rounding.

measure of such. Even as a production indicator it leaves a good deal out of the picture by excluding practically all productive work that is not sold for money. The activities of the housewife and home gardener are completely neglected by the national income statistician. GDP is the total level of expenditure on domestic production, and therefore includes expenditure by foreigners (i.e. exports) and excludes the expenditure of UK residents on imports. A closer approximation to the level of national welfare would be expenditure by UK residents. This is the sum of consumption, government expenditure and investment or, what amounts to the same thing, the level of GDP *minus* exports *plus* imports. This would certainly be better than GDP as a measure of the UK's use of total resources although it would still exclude the enjoyment of household services, leisure, and other activities for which the CSO does not have records.

I.3   National Accounts and the Multiplier Hypothesis[1]

As an illustration of the use of the national accounts in suggesting answers to questions of practical importance we may begin by asking about the likely value of the multiplier in the UK economy. To reach an answer we shall have to make a number of assumptions about the way in which domestic output is divided among income recipients, and the extent to which the income is saved, taxed or spent on new domestic output. The problem of quantifying these assumptions will, we shall see, be made very much easier by the existence of a well-organised set of national accounts.

At the outset it may be supposed that total final expenditure at market prices (TFE) rises by enough to raise GDP by £100 million. The increase in TFE needed for this result will depend upon its domestic output content. In the cases of fixed investment expenditure and exports of goods and services the increase in the market price amount would have to be of the order of £125 million since imports and indirect taxes are, together, likely to absorb about one-fifth of the expenditure increase.[2] Investment in stocks is thought to have a very large import content and might have to rise by as much as £200 million to secure an increase in GDP of £100 million (see section II.4 below). Public authorities expenditure, on the other hand, has a high domestic output content and would probably have to rise by only about £115 million in order to secure the assumed rise in GDP.

We must now ask how the additional £100 million of domestic output and income is going to be distributed between income recipients. At this point we can consult the *Blue Book*[3] and its counterpart in Table 1.1. It may be assumed that none of the new income is income from rent and that the residual error and stock appreciation can be ignored. Thus the £100 million will divide between income from employment and self-employment, the trading surpluses of public enterprises, and the profits of private enterprises. From the *Blue Book* it is evident that the proportionate shares of these three classes of income recipients do not vary greatly from one year to another so that the proportions ruling in 1966 may be assumed for our purposes. This means that the bulk of the £100 million (see Figure 1.1, page 8) will become income from employment or self-employment, and as such will form part of personal income. The small fraction that is likely to leak into the trading surpluses of public enterprises, however, will be completely neutralised since these enterprises do not pay dividends. The £15 million or so which enters company profits, on the other hand, will not be completely lost. To judge from the appropriation accounts[4] for such companies the average proportion of gross profits to be distributed in the form of dividends has been fairly

---

[1] This section has been helped by W. A. B. Hopkin and W. A. H. Godley, 'An Analysis of Tax Changes', *NIER,* May 1965, which the reader might usefully consult.

[2] See Table 8 of 'Provisional Summary Input-Output Tables for 1963', *opus cit.,* and Table 1.6 below.

[3] *NIBB,* 1967, Table 1. The reader may find that it helps to read this section with the *Blue Book* alongside.

[4] *NIBB,* 1967, Table 34.

steady at one fifth over the last four or five years. Thus it may be assumed that £3 million is accredited to persons as dividends, gross of income tax. Of the £12 million that is not passed on to personal income recipients about £5 million will go into corporation tax receipts, £1½ million in selective employment tax, and the rest will remain as undistributed profits.

The result of the assumptions made so far is that a rise in domestic income of £100 million leads to a rise in person income of £84 million, of which £81 million comes as income from employment and the remainder as dividends. It is now necessary to estimate how much of this amount is lost as income tax. This means that we must find out what the marginal rate of direct taxation is likely to be for an average recipient of personal income. This sort of question is not easily answered without expert knowledge but the rate cannot be far off 29 per cent which is the marginal rate for a married man with two children earning £1,000 a year and paying the standard rate of 8/3d in the £, less an earned income allowance of two-ninths.[1]

Deduction of income tax at this rate leaves an increase in personal disposable income of £59 million. If we assume that the marginal propensity to consume is nine-tenths (we are anticipating the next section of this chapter), then the addition to consumers' expenditure will be roughly £53 million. This, of course, is consumers' expenditure on all goods and services at market prices, so that it is now necessary to deduct indirect taxes and the import-content of consumption in order to arrive at the addition to domestic output. The most recent estimate in the *Blue Book*[2] is that indirect taxes constitute some 17 per cent of consumers' expenditure whilst imports[3] take a further 19 per cent. These two fractions, taken together, amount to 36 per cent so that the rise in consumers' expenditure on domestic goods and services at factor cost comes to about £34 million.

Thus our first conclusion is that an initial increase in GDP of £100 million is likely through the operation of the consumption function and a number of other leakages such as marginal tax rates, the rate of distribution of dividends, and the marginal import propensity, to lead to a secondary rise in GDP of £34 million. This is a hypothetical conclusion, but its derivation has been greatly helped by the information available in the national accounts.

It is now only a short-step from this conclusion to an estimate of the value of the multiplier. At the end of the first round of the income-flow GDP is higher than its original level by its initial increase of £100 million, plus a secondary increase of £34 million. The secondary increase is 34 per cent higher than the initial increase, and if we make the defensible assumptions that the marginal propensities to divide domestic income, to consume, pay taxes, etc. all remain unchanged during the multiplier process, then the secondary increase in GDP must lead in turn to a tertiary rise of 34 per cent of £34 million. Each successive rise in GDP leads to a new rise 34 per cent as large as the previous one so that the full increase in GDP is given as the initial injection plus the sum of all round-to-round increases. This sum is represented by the following series:

i.e. £100 $[1 + 0.34 + (0.34)^2 + (0.34)^3 \ldots \ldots + (0.34)^n]$ million, or, approximately, as:

£100 + 34 + 11.1 + 3.8 + 1.3 + 0.4 + 0.1 = £151 million

The successive spending of income, therefore, is likely to raise an initial increase in GDP of £100 million into an eventual increase of about £151 million, so that the multiplier on

---

[1]   A more elaborate calculation using the frequency distribution of personal income given in *NIBB*, 1967, Table 26, produces an almost identical answer (29½ per cent). This involved finding marginal tax rates at different income levels and weighting each of these rates by the relative importance of the income level in total personal income.

[2]   *NIBB*, 1967, Table 12.

[3]   'Provisional Summary Input-Output Tables for 1963', *ibid.*

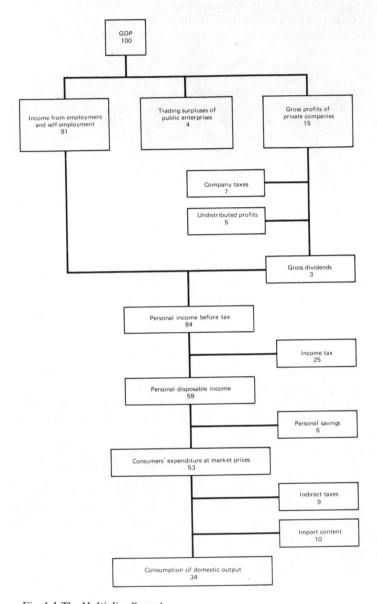

Fig. 1.1 The Multiplier Round

these calculations may be estimated at 1½. This figure is asserted not as an item of
revealed truth, but as a hypothesis estimated from data in the national accounts. The
reader is free to disagree with some of the assumptions and to substitute his own if he
has grounds for doing so.

In conclusion it is worth noting, perhaps, that this rather complicated multiplier
hypothesis bears a close relationship to the simpler textbook case where national
income (Y) is divided into consumption and investment (I), and the multiplier is
expressed as the reciprocal of the marginal propensity to save, i.e.

$$\frac{\triangle Y}{\triangle I} = \frac{1}{1 - \text{marginal propensity to consume}} = \frac{1}{\text{marginal propensity to save}}$$

In the more complex case there are a number of other leakages in the system besides personal savings so that neither of the expressions above are adequate. Furthermore, the existence of the indirect tax and import contents of investment means that it is no longer possible to look upon a rise in investment expenditure as being equivalent to so much domestic output. Thus the equivalent expressions in the more complex case we have discussed are:

$$\frac{\triangle Y \text{ (final)}}{\triangle Y \text{ (initial)}} = \frac{1}{1 - \text{marginal propensity to re-spend domestic output}} = \frac{1}{\text{marginal propensity to leak}}$$

$$= \frac{1}{1 - 0.34} = 1.51$$

Here the marginal propensity to consume out of personal income has to be replaced by a 'marginal propensity to re-spend upon domestic output' with respect to domestic output. Similarly, the marginal propensity to save becomes a 'marginal propensity to leak' or a marginal propensity for domestic output *not* to be re-spent upon itself. The difference between the simpler textbook case and the more complicated 'real world' situation is that there are far more opportunities in the latter for not re-spending income. Both are subject to the further assumptions that sufficient spare capacity exists for the multiplier to work itself out and that this process is not disturbed by other mechanisms such as the capital-stock adjustment principle (referred to on page 17) or the profits theory of investment (page 15).

II   THE COMPONENTS OF AGGREGATE DEMAND

It is now widely accepted that within the limits set by full employment of productive resources the level of domestic output in the short run is determined along Keynesian lines by the level of aggregate demand. The relevant demand total is the sum of all demands for domestic output whether from consumers, business, the public authorities or foreigners. The total is an *ex ante* concept. It represents desired spending on all goods and services produced by the domestic economy, and, as such, it is only equal to actual spending, or GDP *ex post*, in a state of full demand equilibrium. This means that, strictly speaking, it is not correct to use statistically recorded GDP as an indicator of aggregate demand since full equilibrium is unlikely ever to obtain in practice. Nevertheless, GDP has to be used in this way because it is the only available approximation to total demand. Similarly, the components of GDP, such as consumers' expenditure and investment are generally taken as indicating their own respective demand levels. In making such approximations, however, we should bear in mind the possibility that in periods of very intense use of resources the demand for some classes of commodity may well be in excess of actual expenditure. When this is the case we must hope that some independent statistics, such as large unfilled orders will prevent misunderstanding.

Aggregate demand may now be divided into the main expenditure categories, and each one discussed separately.

II.1   Consumers' Expenditure

Consumers' expenditure is the largest single element in aggregate demand. It accounts for nearly half of TFE (see Table 1.1), and when stripped of its import and indirect tax

content for about the same proportion of GDP at factor cost.[1] It is generally regarded
as one of the more stable elements in total demand and this is true in the sense that
fluctuations in consumption are small when measured as percentages of its own total.
The total itself, however, is so large in relation to GDP that even fairly small percentage
variations can have important repercussions for output and employment. An understanding of consumption behaviour, therefore, as well as an ability to predict it, are important
objectives for economic analysis. A great deal of attention has, in fact, been given to
consumption, both in theory and statistically, although unfortunately this work has
been more heavily concentrated upon consumption in the United States than in the
United Kingdom.[2]

The starting point for most studies of consumer behaviour is the well-known theory
of Lord Keynes, whereby the level of spending is taken to be largely determined by the
level of current personal income after tax. 'The fundamental psychological law', wrote
Keynes,[3] 'upon which we are entitled to depend with great confidence both *a priori*
and from the detailed facts of experience, is that men are disposed, as a rule and on the
average, to increase their consumption as their income increases, but not by as much
as the increase in their incomes'. Keynes believed that the marginal propensity to
consume (i.e. the ratio of additional consumption to additional income) was positive,
fractional, and reasonably stable over the short run. The extent to which these
assumptions are borne out in practice is a question of some relevance if we are to use
the Keynesian theory for prediction, and some evidence on this point is set out in
Table 1.2 (page 11). This shows the marginal propensity to consume (MPC for short)
as inferred from statistical changes in income and consumption over the last sixteen
years. Two features are disturbing. First, it seems clear that the MPC measured in this
way has been anything but stable over the period, and has in fact varied from a lower
value of 0.6 to an upper value of 1.2. Secondly, the fractional value expected of the
MPC is found to obtain only 9 times out of 16 and the MPC is greater than unity in
the other seven years.

By disputing the Keynesian assumptions in these two ways the data in Table 1.2
may be taken as something of a challenge to accepted theory. But before the theory is
thrown overboard it is wise to check whether the falsity of the assumptions leads to
inaccurate predictions. To do this we can, for example, adopt a rule of thumb whereby
the average of the marginal propensities over a run of years is assumed as a norm to be
predicted for the following year, and we may then check how well or badly this
prediction turns out. Taking five years as the norm period this would mean that the
average of the observed MPC's for 1951-55 is taken in order to predict 1956; that for
1952-56 to predict 1957; and so on. The result of doing this for every year from 1955 to
1965 is shown in the right hand columns of the table, which confirm that the method
leads to errors. The predicted MPC for 1955-56, for example, turns out to be 0.18 higher
than the actual MPC and that for 1956-57 is 0.20 below the actual. For the whole period
the errors range, disregarding their signs, from 0.07 to 0.35 and the average error in the
predicted MPC is 0.17. If this size of error is applied to an annual income change of the
order experienced over recent years, say £1500 million, the resulting error in predicting
consumers' expenditure is £260 million (nearly 1.0 per cent of total consumption). The
question we must now ask is whether errors of this magnitude, together with the
possibility of errors larger than average, are sufficiently serious to oblige us to reject
the whole approach. The answer will depend a good deal upon the purpose in hand. If,
for example, we are interested in forecasting the level of GDP in order to recommend

---

[1] It is misleading, although not uncommon, to compare expenditures at market prices, inclusive
of their import contents, with GDP at factor cost.

[2] See, however, the article by R. Stone 'Private Saving in Britain, Past, Present and Future',
MS, May 1964.

[3] J. M. Keynes, *The General Theory of Employment, Interest and Money,* Macmillan, 1936, p. 96.

measures to maintain full employment then we have to accept that, on the average, our method results in errors in predicting consumption equal to about 1.0 per cent of consumers' expenditure, and, taking its domestic output content, to about 0.6 per cent of GDP. An error in GDP of this size is certainly appreciable but it may not be so disastrous for stabilisation policy that we should want to dismiss the whole approach. Perhaps the most sensible conclusion is that the simple Keynesian principle which we have adopted works with a modest degree of success but is in need of further refinement.

TABLE 1.2

Observations and Predictions of the Marginal Propensity to Consume, UK, 1950–66

	Change in consumers' expenditure (£ million, current prices)	Change in personal disposable income (£ million, current prices)	Observed MPC	Predicted MPC (equals average of observed values in 5 previous years)	Error (equals predicted MPC less observed MPC)
1950-51	754	699	1.08	–	–
1951-52	551	894	.62	–	–
1952-53	709	748	.95	–	–
1953-54	689	669	1.03	–	–
1954-55	949	1,078	.88	–	–
1955-56	716	985	.73	.91	+ 0.18
1956-57	770	740	1.04	.84	– 0.20
1957-58	787	686	1.15	.93	– 0.22
1958-59	810	966	.84	.97	+ 0.13
1959-60	810	1,207	.67	.93	+ 0.26
1960-61	911	1,313	.69	.89	+ 0.20
1961-62	1,049	853	1.23	.88	– 0.35
1962-63	1,175	1,123	1.05	.92	– 0.13
1963-64	1,351	1,756	.77	.90	+ 0.13
1964-65	1,359	1,428	.95	.88	– 0.07
1965-66	1,265	1,249	1.01	.94	– 0.07

Source: NIBB

Another and more sophisticated reply to the challenge of Table 1.2 is to argue that the recorded marginal propensities are mere statistical ratios, and that they will deviate from the 'true' marginal propensity to consume if other factors enter into the determination of consumption besides annual current income. If consumption is influenced both by income and by wealth, and if both alter in a particular year, then the statistical ratio of that year will not measure the influence of income alone, and will not be a 'true' MPC. Moreover the averaging of five statistical MPC's in order to estimate a 'true' MPC is not really satisfactory since five years is too short a period for much faith to be put in the implicit assumption that non-income factors cancel each other out.

The presence of other factors besides current income can hardly be disputed and there is much to be said for an attempt to estimate their influences separately. This, however, would require techniques which are beyond the scope of this chapter. We can, nevertheless, recognise what some of these factors are likely to be. One, undoubtedly, is the availability of credit to finance purchases of durable consumer goods. These goods are more of the nature of capital than of consumption in that they yield a flow of income over time, and as such it is natural that they should be bought on credit. Over the last

few years durable goods expenditure[1] has accounted for 7-8 per cent of total consumers'
expenditure, and to judge from the statistics of hire purchase credit something like half
of this expenditure has been financed by borrowing. The availability of hire-purchase
facilities and of other types of consumer credit, such as personal loans, is therefore
likely to be an important influence upon durable goods expenditure. The influence is
especially felt in Britain where the government has powers to regulate hire-purchase
agreements and has used these powers actively over a number of years. The controls take
two forms: first, the specification of the minimum percentage downpayment; and,
secondly, the stipulation of a maximum period for repaying the loan. These regulations
can be enforced swiftly, and without legislative delay, and they have been altered no less
than twenty times in the period from 1952 to 1967. Their influence upon durable goods
consumption can be gauged from Figure 1.2 where the direction of impact of HP
regulations is charted on a graph of durables' expenditure as a percentage of personal
income. It can be seen that the trend of spending was upwards in the 1950's but that
changes in its direction were frequently associated with changes in the controls. The
uptrend was checked, for example, by the restrictions of 1955-56, and reinforced by
their easing in 1957-58. More recently, in 1965-67, a series of restrictive moves has led
to some decline in durables spending in relation to income. This evidence, although not
conclusive, is strongly indicative of the short-term effectiveness of HP controls in
influencing consumers' expenditure.

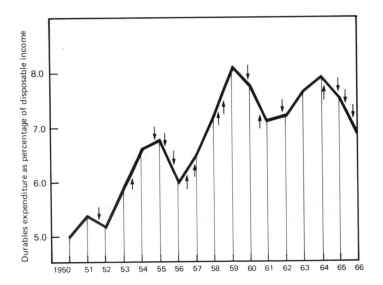

Figure 1.2   Hire purchase restrictions and consumers' durable goods expenditure as a percentage
of disposable income, UK, 1950-65.

(Note: arrows indicate direction of effect e.g. ↑ indicates removal or easing of restrictions, ↓ imposition
or tightening).

---

[1]   It should be noted that the *Blue Book* definition of durable goods includes cars, motor cycles,
furniture, carpets and electrical goods but, perhaps arbitrarily, does not include clothing,
curtains, pots and pans or expenditure on house repairs and maintenance.

Whether interest rates exert much influence on consumers' demand is not so easy to say. Traditionally, it has been argued that high interest rates discourage spending by making saving more profitable, but their effect on the terms of HP agreements may be still more important now that durables expenditure is a significant part of the total. Unfortunately, the timing of interest rate changes has coincided fairly closely with that of alterations in the HP controls so that it is more or less impossible, even with sophisticated techniques, to separate one effect from the other. Indeed, it could be argued that the effects we have attributed to HP controls are really due to coincident changes in interest rates. On the whole we suspect that direct controls over hire-purchase transactions and the rationing of personal loans by the banks are more effective in regulating expenditure on durables than interest rates.

There are undoubtedly other factors and other theories[1] to be discussed in relation to consumers' expenditure and accounts of these may be found in more advanced readings. What we have sought to establish in this section is that the simple theory of consumption based on current disposable income is not without application in the UK and that one other factor of importance is the availability of consumer credit. It is worth mentioning that, to judge by the official account,[2] these used to be the two main factors considered by the government in its short-term forecasts of the economy.

II.2 Public Consumption

Public authorities' current expenditure on goods and services includes spending by both central and local government. Its main constituents in 1966 are shown in Table 1.3.

TABLE 1.3

Public Current Expenditure, UK, 1966   *£ million current prices*
                                                      Local government

Central government		Local government	
Military defence	2,162	Education	1,151
National health service	1,158	Civil defence	178
Social security benefits	118	Sewerage and refuse disposal	152
Finance and tax collection	144	Police	203
All other current expenditure on goods	529	National health service	127
		All other current goods and services	469
Total	4,111	Total	2,280

Source: NIBB, 1967, Tables 41 and 45.

The determination of central government expenditure is a matter for the government of the day and there is little that macroeconomics can do by way of explaining it. This admission, however, does not remove government expenditure from the realm of economics, for there is a great deal of scope for appraising the costs and benefits of the

[1] Notably, the permanent income and 'life cycle' hypotheses. See Stone, op. cit., and the account and bibliography in R. Ferber, 'Research on Household Behaviour', *Surveys of Economic Theory,* Volume 3, Macmillan, 1966.

[2] 'Short-term economic forecasting in the United Kingdom', reprinted from ET, August 1964, in *New Contributions to Economic Statistics,* Fourth Series, CSO, 1967. More recently the real level of wealth and the lagged value of consumption have also been taken into account—see House of Commons, *Government Statistical Services,* (Fourth Report from the Estimates Committee together with Minutes of Evidence, Session 1966-67), HMSO, 6th December 1967, page 477.

various types of expenditure in the light of political and social preferences. But this is essentially a microeconomic task.

It might be thought, in the light of Keynesian economics, that the level of government expenditure would be varied as part of the government's policy to maintain full employment. In fact, it is rare for government spending to be used in this way. The main reason for this is that most government activities are undertaken in response to a political or social need which is felt to be independent of the cyclical state of the economy. Expenditure on schools and health, for example, cannot be readily subjected to the whims of the business cycle. Another reason for not using government current or capital expenditure as a cyclical instrument is that the administrative machine is too sluggish to bring about rapid changes in its spending. In these days of short business cycles, therefore, there is the danger that the increase or decrease in expenditure might come too late for the job for which it was intended and, indeed, that it might add to demand (or reduce it) at a time when the opposite effect was needed.

Occasions do arise, however, when substantial changes—generally cuts—are made in government expenditure programmes. These tend to occur as results of reassessments of the size of the public sector in relation to the whole economy. They will occur, for example, if over-optimistic forecasts of the growth of GDP, and therefore of government revenues, have misled ministers into believing that a certain level of expenditure can be sustained without higher tax rates or unwanted inflationary pressure. They will also occur if the government decides to put a higher priority than previously on some aspect of private spending, such as exports or fixed investment. The cuts in government expenditure announced in January 1968 were a case in point. The government's programmes had been based on the over-optimistic GDP predictions of the 1965 National Plan, and were clearly implying higher taxation or more inflation at a realistic growth of output. Secondly, the devaluation of the pound in November 1967 could not be expected to work unless more resources were made available to the industries producing exports and competing with imports.[1] Thus on both scores it was deemed necessary to curtail government expenditure programmes over the longer run.

II.3   Gross Fixed Investment

Fixed investment expenditure is a more amorphous total than is usually supposed. Its division by sector and by type of asset purchased is set out in Table 1.4 (below).

TABLE 1.4

Gross Fixed Capital Formation, UK, 1966   £ million at current prices

	Dwellings	Other building	Vehicles, ships, aircraft, plant and equipment	Total
Private	673	766	2,078	3,517
Public sector	636	1,286	1,196	3,118
Total	1,309	2,052	3,274	6,635

Source: NIBB, Table 54.

Investment in dwellings comprises something like one fifth of gross fixed capital formation. Nearly half of it is undertaken by local authorities and is financed partly out of rates and partly from central government grants. Private housing is likely to be determined by a complex of factors which can only be discussed in general terms. Practically all new houses are bought on mortgage so that one factor determining the demand is the level of current income and its expected future value. Most building

---

[1]   See Chapter 3 for a full discussion.

societies require a down-payment, and the ability to make this will depend upon the
accumulated savings, and therefore incomes, of the intending purchaser over a run
of several past years. Other things being equal it is to be presumed that periods of
rapidly rising incomes are likely to be followed by periods of high demand for housing.
It is often suggested that interest rates are more influential in the determination of
housing expenditure than of other kinds of investment. This may well be true although
the main influence is likely to be indirect. Higher interest rates will drive down the
values of securities held by building societies and lead them to restrict their mortgage
lending. Thus the availability rather than the cost of mortgage credit is the main factor
at work. Other factors affecting the demand for housing include the number of
marriages and first births, and the rate at which older houses are knocked down. The
amount of housebuilding undertaken is sometimes limited by capacity factors, such as
the supply of bricks and cement and the number of skilled workers. Exceptionally cold
weather, such as the winter of 1962-63, can hold up building activity and create back-
logs of unsatisfied demand which may take months to work off.

The remaining component of gross domestic fixed capital formation is *investment,
other than dwellings,* by both the private and public sectors. Both are likely to be
determined by factors of a commercial nature: the expected rate of return, expected
costs, long run expectations about demand, and by attempts to allow for risk and
uncertainty. None of these determinants are at all easy to identify statistically and
several of them are extremely difficult to fit into a macroeconomic theory of
investment. This means that the explanation of investment in aggregative terms is
something of a hit-or-miss affair where resort is made to rules of thumb and to various
over-simplified hypotheses.

One such hypothesis is the acceleration principle whereby the level of investment in
a particular period is assumed to be related to the rate of change of total sales. It is
sometimes argued in support of this hypothesis that businessmen will regard the change
in sales as an indicator of their future rate of expansion and that this will determine
the extent to which they are willing to expand or modernise productive capacity. This
could have been the case before the war when cycles in activity were much longer and
more severe than they are today. In these circumstances the first decline in total sales,
for example, could have been taken quite reliably as signifying a period of stagnation for
several years. Under these conditions there is nothing very implausible about this sort
of reaction.

An alternative hypothesis to the acceleration principle is the profits theory, according
to which the level of business investment is assumed to be governed mainly by the size
of business profits. This theory presupposes that investment is largely financed from
internal funds and that the full amount of after-tax profits does not have to be
distributed as dividends. Both these propositions apply fairly well in the case of the
United Kingdom. External sources of finance have been found to contribute only
10 - 30 per cent of company investment over the period 1954-63,[1] and dividends do not
vary much in relation to the size of total profits. In these conditions it might be
expected, unless there are substantial changes in the long-term economic outlook, that
the level of investment planned for a particular year might depend, in the absence of
substantial changes in the long-term economic outlook, upon the current level of
company savings (undistributed profits). It is interesting to check from Table 1.5 (page 16)
whether there is any truth in this suggestion.

---

[1]   See 'Internal and external sources of company finance', reprinted from *ET,* February 1966, in
New Contributions to Economic Statistics, Fourth Series, CSO, 1967.

TABLE 1.5

Company Savings Investment, UK, 1957–66

	Savings[1] (undistributed profits)	Gross fixed Investment	Investment as a proportion of the previous year's savings
	£million at current prices		
1957	2044	1411	.74
1958	2037	1457	.71
1959	2220	1525	.75
1960	2357	1732	.78
1961	2337	1982	.84
1962	2357	1991	.85
1963	2703	1942	.83
1964	2923	2373	.88
1965	3478	2557	.87
1966	2878	2601	.75

Source: NIBB, 1967, Table 6.

[1] Before providing for depreciation and stock appreciation.

Table 1.5 does seem to provide some support for the profits theory although it is noticeable that the ratio of investment to the previous year's savings has shown a fairly strong upwards trend. It can be seen that it would be possible to predict investment in current prices from the company savings within a fairly small margin of error. Nevertheless, it has to be admitted that a great deal more work needs to be carried out before a satisfactory theory of investment emerges.

II.4   Stocks and Stockbuilding

Stockbuilding, or investment in stocks, is the addition to final expenditure brought about by a change in the level of stocks between the beginning and end of the period. To understand the nature of stock investment we must therefore examine the reasons for holding stocks.

Stocks consist of unsold finished goods, work in process of production, and stocks of materials and fuel for further processing. Of these, stocks of work in process are a technical necessity of production and can be assumed to bear a more or less proportionate relationship to it. Stocks of materials and fuels, and stocks of finished goods, are not immediately necessary for production. They are held because businessmen can never be completely sure that the current level of production will precisely coincide with sales of the product or deliveries of raw materials. On these grounds it is reasonable for business-men to hold stocks in order to guard against the danger of running short of materials or of finished goods. This suggests that they might carry in their minds the notion of a certain desired ratio, k, of stocks to future output. Thus the desired level of stocks at the end of the period will be equal to k times the expected level of output in that period.

If future output is known, or if it can be approximated by current output, then the desired level of stocks is determined, and desired investment in stocks is the difference between desired stocks and current actual stocks. It follows from this hypothesis, which is known as the stock-adjustment principle, that the amount of stock investment is likely to be inversely related to the stock-output ratio,[1] so that when the ratio is high stockbuilding tends to be on the small side and when the ratio is low stockbuilding tends to be large. Some evidence for this view is given by the data for manufacturing stocks plotted in Figure 1.3. It can be seen from the figure that the stockbuilding peaks in 1956, 1960 and 1964 all coincided with low values of the stock-output ratio; and the troughs of 1958 and 1962 with high values.

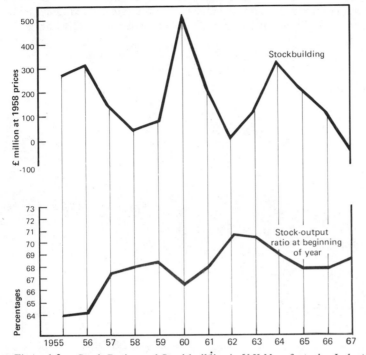

Figure 1.3   Stock Ratios and Stockbuilding in U.K Manufacturing Industry, 1955–67.

II.5   Exports of Goods and Services

The behaviour of exports is much more fully discussed in chapter 3. Their volume can be expected to depend largely upon two factors: the state of overseas demand, as indicated by the volume of world trade, and their prices relative to those of competing commodities. In the short run we should not expect changes in relative prices to be sufficiently large to bring about substantial changes in the export volume, although devaluation is likely to exert a powerful effect during the next year or two. Over the longer run, however, a rise in UK prices relative to other countries has probably been responsible for much of the long-term decline in the UK share of world trade.

---

[1]   In symbols

$$S^*_{t+1} = k.Y_{t+1} = k.Y_t$$

$$I^*_{t+1} = S^*_{t+1} - S_t$$

$$= k.Y_t - S_t$$

$$= k.Y_t - r.Y_t$$

where S^*_{t+1} is the desired stock level; Y^*_{t+1} expected output; I^*_{t+1} desired investment in stocks; k, the desired stock-output ratio; and r, the actual stock-output ratio at the end of the previous period.

Besides these two factors there is probably room for a third influence in the form of the pressure of demand upon UK resources. When domestic demand is high in relation to resources we should expect firms to experience difficulties in obtaining materials and in meeting demand both at home and abroad. When domestic demand is lower, however, the firm is likely to find it a lot easier to supply the export market, and there may well be a direct incentive to search for new overseas customers. In the short run, therefore, we should expect the pressure of home demand, as indicated by the rate of unemployment, to be inversely related to the UK share of world trade. Some evidence for this view is presented in Figure 1.4 below.[1]

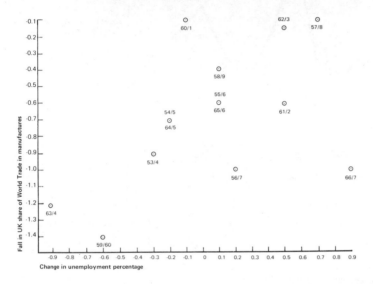

Figure 1.4   Movements in U.K share of World Trade in relation to changes in
              unemployment, 1953–66

As Figure 1.4 shows, movements in the UK share of world trade have been downward in every year since 1964, and the extent of these declines has been loosely related to the change in the unemployment rate.[2] In interpreting this result, however, we must bear in mind that the demand for exports is one of the determinants of unemployment so that the causal relationship could run both ways. Nevertheless, changes in export demand have not been the predominant influence on the economy over this period so that it is probably safe to assume that most of the correlation shown is the result of the influence of the pressure of demand on exports, and not vice versa. But the question of whether exports in the long run thrive best in conditions of low demand pressure in the home market is another matter, and depends a good deal on the way in which the growth of productivity is influenced by home demand. These matters are discussed later in this chapter.

II.6   From TFE to GDP

The categories of final expenditure discussed above have all been valued at their market prices. If we are interested in the rewards of factors of production then we must, as explained in section 1.2 above, subtract indirect taxes from the market price and add in

---

[1] See also R. J. Ball, J. R. Eaton and M. D. Steuer 'The Relationship between United Kingdom
     Export Performance in Manufactures and the Internal Pressure of Demand', *EJ*, September 1966;
     and for a contrary view W. Beckerman and associates, *The British Economy in 1975*, Cambridge
     University Press, 1965, pp.60-64.

[2] The large decline in the UK share of trade in 1966-67 must be associated with the dock strikes.

subsidies. The 'factor cost adjustment' is the net amount of these two elements and comes to about 11 per cent of TFE.[1] Indirect taxes are levied mainly on consumer goods such as cars, beer, cigarettes and household appliances and the subsidy element in market prices is relatively small. Hence the factor cost adjustment is proportionately larger for consumers' expenditure than it is for the other categories of final expenditure. The proportions are set out in Table 1.6 (below).

TABLE 1.6

Domestic Output Content of Total Final Expenditure at Market Prices, UK, 1966

	Percentages of market price totals				
	Consumers' expenditure	Government current expenditure	Gross domestic fixed investment	Exports of goods and services	Total final expenditure
Indirect taxes less subsidies	17	4	7	2	11
Imports of goods and services	19	8	15	17	16
Domestic output content	64	88	78	81	73

Source: NIBB, 1967, Table 12. 'Provisional Summary Input-Output Tables for 1963'.

Imports

Finally, to arrive at demand for domestic output we must subtract the imported component of each category of final expenditure. This is also illustrated in Table 1.6 where it can be seen that the import content of consumers' expenditure is higher than for other categories of expenditure.

The ratio of imports to final expenditure was about 18 per cent in 1966.[2] The ratio has shown a long-term tendency to rise, which may be explained by factors such as trade liberalisation and the tendency for the prices of UK manufactures to rise faster than those of foreign manufactures. These are discussed in chapter 3. But superimposed on the long-term upward trend are short, sharp, year-to-year variations. The ratio rose by 1 per cent in 1954-55, for example, and again in 1959-60, and in 1963-64 it rose by about ½ per cent. Fluctuations as large as this have important repercussions on the balance of payments: a 1 per cent rise today would add about £400 million to the balance of payments deficit.

Short-term movements in the import ratio can be explained by movements in stocks, movements in the pressure of demand, or by a mixture of the two. The first is the more widely accepted explanation. Sharp movements in stockbuilding involve sharp increases in the rate at which raw materials and fuels are imported from abroad so that years of high stockbuilding are likely to be years in which imports are high in relation to final expenditure. This has nearly always been the case, as can be seen from Figure 1.5. Other things being equal, a change in stocks of £100 million is normally associated with a change in imports of about £50 million.[3] An implication of this estimate is that movements in stockbuilding will have a much less pronounced effect on domestic output than movements in other types of final expenditure. A rise in stockbuilding will be met as to only one-half by domestic production whilst increases in other expenditure will generate output increases of something more like three-quarters depending on the type of expenditure (see Table 1.6).

---

[1]   For details see chapter 2.
[2]   This figure differs from the one shown in Table 1.6 because it is based on data expressed in 1958 prices.
[3]   See W. A. H. Godley and J. R. Shepherd, 'Forecasting Imports', *NIER,* August 1965.

Changes in the import-ratio are also likely to be associated with changes in the pressure of demand. When pressure is high producers in the home market experience difficulties in meeting new orders because of shortages of particular types of labour and materials. Delays will occur and buyers are likely to look overseas for their supplies. This factor is not likely to be important in the case of raw materials since these are almost entirely imported. But in the case of finished and semi-finished manufactures imported articles are frequently close substitutes for home products. The fact that movements in the pressure of demand have tended to coincide with movements in stockbuilding makes it difficult in practice to distinguish the one influence from the other. But it may be misleading to think in terms of a stable and precise 'import-content of stockbuilding' even though this assumption fits the facts quite well.

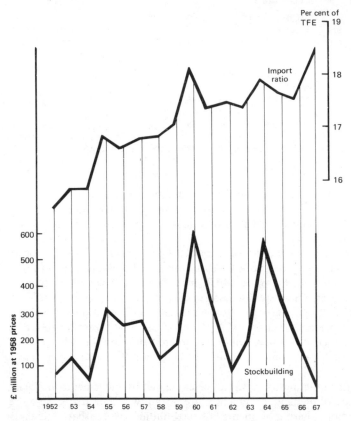

Figure 1.5   The Import Ratio in relation to Stockbuilding, U.K, 1952–67

III   ECONOMIC ACTIVITY AND ITS REGULATION

III.1 Fluctuations in Economic Activity

Cycles in national output and employment with a peak-to-peak duration of 7-10 years were a regular feature of British economic history in the nineteenth century. Full employment, or something like it, obtained only at the cyclical peaks, and there was generally a substantial amount of unemployment in the recession. This pattern changed after the end of the First World War, when for two decades unemployment was massive not only during the recession but also at the peak of each cycle. Economic activity fluctuated well short of full employment, and unemployment did not fall below 9 per cent of the labour force in any single year from 1921 to 1939. The worst year was 1932, when unemployment reached 22 per cent (2.8 million people), and the rate was above 15 per cent from 1930 to 1935.

Large-scale unemployment has been largely eliminated in the post-war period although it is still a serious problem in a few areas, most notably in Northern Ireland. The pre-war sequence of ups and downs in GDP has also disappeared, and since 1947 there has been only one decline in GDP between two full years—a fall of less than ½ per cent between 1957 and 1958. This makes it difficult to detect a cyclical pattern in the GDP figures alone, although an examination of their rates of change from one year to the next reveals a fairly regular sequence of slow and fast increases. The numbers unemployed, however, have moved up and down in a typically cyclical fashion, and these now serve as the best single indicator of cyclical performance in the post-war period (see Table 1.7 below).

TABLE 1.7

Unemployment Rates in Post-War Cycles

1951-55		1955-61		1961-65		1965-67	
1951	1.2	1955	1.1	1961	1.5	1965	1.4
1952	2.0	1956	1.2	1962	2.0	1966	1.5
1953	1.6	1957	1.4	1963	2.5	1967	2.4
1954	1.3	1958	2.1	1964	1.6		
1955	1.1	1959	2.2	1965	1.4		
		1960	1.6				
		1961	1.5				
Average	1.5	Average	1.6	Average	1.8		

Source: SIPEP (registered unemployment).

The table shows three complete cycles during the period from 1951 to 1965. It is interesting to note that both the highest and the average rates of unemployment during each complete cycle have tended to increase from one cycle to the next. Whether this trend trend will continue in the fourth cycle, which began in 1965 remains to be seen, and depends almost entirely on government policy.

Movements in unemployment have been accompanied, as might be expected, by a succession of slow and fast increases in GDP and the level of employment. More surprisingly, they have also been accompanied by slow and fast movements in the ratio of GDP to employment—output-per-employee or 'productivity' for short. This cyclical pattern of productivity change is illustrated in Figure 1.6 (page 22). It can be seen that the increases in productivity in boom years were well above the average rise, whilst in periods of very slow expansion productivity rose hardly at all. For example in the 1963-64 boom productivity increased by 4.7 per cent whilst in the slack period of 1960-1961 it rose by only 0.3 per cent. The reasons for this pattern appear to be threefold. First, a rising pressure of demand on manpower resources leads to the working of more overtime and to some setback in the generally downwards trend of the average working week: thus employment-hours generally rise faster than employment, and output per man-hour goes up less rapidly than the crude productivity measure shown in the figure. A second reason is believed to be that employers hold on to skilled labour during recessions for fear of being caught short-staffed in the ensuing boom. The result is that the skilled men are shown as being in employment in the Ministry of Labour's statistics, although they are being paid for little or no work. This means that the figures of output per man will be depressed when there is substantial 'labour-hoarding', as it is called, but will rise again when the hoarded labour is given work to do. A third reason, which perhaps is more conjectural, is that the most efficient combination of capital and labour is one in which the machinery is being fully utilised at full capacity, so that when demand falls below the

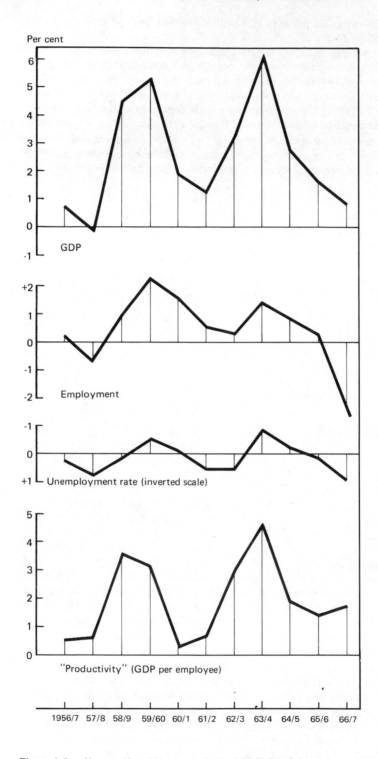

Figure 1.6   Year-to-Year Movements in Real GDP, Employment, the Rate of Unemployment
              and GDP per man (per cent), UK, 1956–67.

full capacity rate output-per-man will decline. The implication of these considerations is that short-term changes in productivity have to be interpreted as reflections of the way in which business employment policies react to cyclical change and not as indicators of productive efficiency at optimal levels of output. In particular, it is extremely hazardous to draw conclusions for the growth of productivity in the long run from changes between one year and the next.

Another relationship brought out by Figure 1.6 is that between employment and unemployment. It will be noticed that the changes in unemployment as a percentage of the labour force are by no means large enough to match the changes in employment. In 1963-64, for example, employment rose by 1.4 per cent whilst the unemployment rate came down by only 0.9 per cent. The implication is that the labour force itself (i.e. employment plus unemployment) tends to fluctuate during the cycle. In the recovery phase of the cycle marginal workers, such as married women who have not previously been registered as unemployed, enter the labour force and remain in it whilst demand remains high. Similarly, workers who have reached retiring age are pressed to remain in their jobs during periods of high demand, whilst in periods of recession they are retired early. Thus, we can conclude that the phase of the cycle has an important influence on the size of the labour force and the level of output-per-man, as well as on the more obvious figures such as GDP itself, employment and unemployment.[1]

The causes of cyclical changes in total production and employment must be sought in the behaviour of aggregate demand as described in section II above. Theoretical models of the cycle, such as the multiplier-accelerator model, tend to emphasise the inter-relationships of consumption and investment behaviour. A theory of the post-war cycle, however, would have to take account of the other sectors of demand, such as exports and government expenditure, and also of the actions of the government in stimulating and retarding the level of consumers' expenditure. Some consideration of these actions is given in sections III.2 and III.3 below, but meanwhile it is useful to bear in mind the way in which the various demand categories have moved during recent cycles. These movements are set out for the period from 1956 to 1967 in Figure 1.7 (page 24). The object of this figure is to represent the importance to economic activity in general of movements in the various expenditure categories. For this reason the movements in expenditure have been expressed as percentage of total final expenditure. Consumption has not shown a single decline during the period but its annual increases have varied from 0.8 per cent of TFE to 2.9 per cent, and this variation has exerted an important influence upon the rate of increase of GDP. Fixed investment and stockbuilding have been of roughly equal influence in governing the rate of change of GDP. Changes in fixed investment have varied from − 0.1 to +2.3 per cent of TFE and changes in stockbuilding from −0.9 to +1.1 per cent. In contrast to these three rather unstable categories of demand exports and public current expenditure have been much more stable. The changes in exports have varied from −0.3 to +1.0 per cent of TFE and the changes in public expenditure have been within the even narrower range −0.3 to +0.4 per cent of TFE.

III.2 The Management of Aggregate Demand

It is a moot point whether or not the economic fluctuations we have just described should have been allowed to occur. For, since 1944, successive governments have accepted the responsibility, set out in the White Paper on Employment Policy,[2] of maintaining 'a high and stable level of employment'. The White Paper, however, did not attempt to define the target level of employment at all precisely, and individual governments have interpreted the wording according to their own particular wishes and priorities. There is, of course, no unique definition of full employment and very few

---

[1] For a further discussion see W. A. H. Godley and J. R. Shepherd, 'Long-term growth and Short-term policy', *NIER*, August 1964.
[2] Cmnd. 6527, HMSO, 1944.

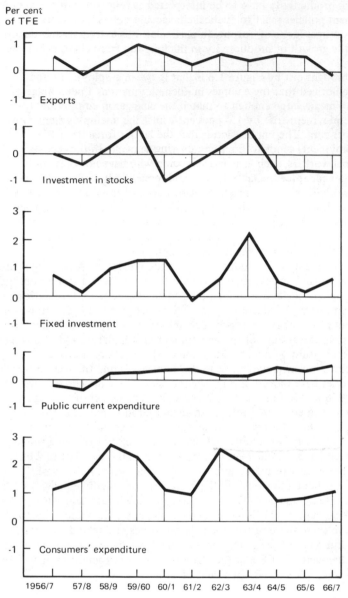

Per cent
of TFE

Figure 1.7   Year-to-Year Movements in Expenditure as percentages of
                TFE at constant prices, UK, 1956−67.

governments have disclosed their intentions in this respect to Parliament or to the
electorate. It must be presumed, however, that some target level of employment, or, as
seems more relevant, of unemployment is secretly entertained by every Chancellor of the
Exchequer, and that this target together with the forecast of prospective GDP and
employment determine the amount of additional or reduced taxation at the time of the
Budget. Indeed, the activity of demand management can, on these lines, be divided into
three main stages: first, the normative stage of selecting targets for employment,
unemployment or GDP; second, a forecast of the prospective level of economic activity

in the absence of government efforts to regulate it; third, governmental action to close
the gap between target and prospective levels of activity. We shall discuss these stages in
sequence.

The Policy Target

The first stage, then, is to select the target level of economic activity. On some considerations this would be taken to be the highest level of output and the lowest level of
unemployment which was physically possible. This would not be an unemployment
rate of zero because a number of workers, the so-called 'unemployables', have little
prospect of being taken on even in periods of acute labour shortage. Some allowance,
moreover, must be made for the fact that workers are not perfectly mobile between jobs,
so that some unemployment is likely to occur as workers take time to move from one job
to another and time to train for new kinds of work. Even aside from these considerations,
however, there are reasons for doubting whether a physical minimum for the unemployment rate is likely to be accepted by any government as the optimum to which policy
should be directed. The most potent reason for opting for something more than the
minimum is the assumption that the rate of inflation and the level of unemployment are
inversely related. This relationship, which is discussed in section IV, suggests that
governments are likely to make some compromise between the conflicting demands of
full employment and price stability. Another consideration is that low levels of economic
activity and low rates of inflation are conducive to balance of payments equilibrium, and
there is little doubt that there have been periods over the last eight years when the
desired level of employment has been governed very largely by balance of payments
considerations.

Having selected such a target for unemployment there is the technical problem of
translating it into a desired level of GDP. This has to be done by reference to the
considerations set out in section III.1 above. The problem is simplest when the current
level of unemployment and the desired level of unemployment in, say, eighteen months
time are one and the same thing. When this is the case the desired increase in GDP will be
equal to the demographic change in the labour force plus the so-called 'underlying
increase in output per man'. The latter is determined by changes in the amount and the
increase in quality of productive factors (see section V) but for short periods is generally
taken as the trend increase over the last few years, which is currently thought to be some
3 per cent per annum.[1] Therefore, if the labour force is growing by 0.2 per cent a year
for purely demographic reasons, the desired rise in GDP, with no change in unemployment,
will be 3.2 per cent a year.

More often, however, the desired level of unemployment is different from the current
level, and the required increase in GDP has to be either more or less than the sum of the
underlying increases in productivity and employment. An example is the period between
the second quarter of 1963 and the second quarter of 1964. The main changes during this
period were as follows:

change in unemployment rate	−0.8 per cent
change in employment	+1.1 per cent
change in productivity	+4.9 per cent
change in GDP	+6.0 per cent

The unemployment rate in the second quarter of 1963 was 2.4 per cent, seasonally
adjusted, for the wholly unemployed. If the government's aim was to reach an
unemployment rate of 1.6 per cent in twelve months time (as in fact happened) then it
would have been necessary to translate this into a required rise in GDP of 6 per cent. With
some knowledge[2] of the underlying trends in productivity and the labour force, and of the

---

[1]   *NIER*, February 1968, p.19.
[2]   Godley and Shepherd, 'Long-term growth and short-term policy'.

way in which short-term changes can deviate from trend, it should have been possible to
arrive at something like the correct figure. It would be wrong, however, to underestimate
the difficulties of such calculations in practice. As already explained the statistics of GDP
can often be ambiguous, and the figures for employment are notoriously subject to
revision.

Forecasts of National Income

The second stage in the management of aggregate demand is a forecast of the likely course
of GDP over the next twelve to eighteen months. The comparison of the prospective and
required paths of GDP can then be used to decide the appropriate magnitude of government stabilising action.

   National income forecasts are prepared in the Treasury three times a year. The timing
of the three main forecasts is geared to the Budget which is normally in the first half of
April. A preliminary assessment of next year's prospects is generally made in late autumn,
and this is brought up to date and extended a further six months in February and March.
A third forecast is made in early summer.

   From a policy point of view the most important forecast is the one made in February
and March. This extends from the last known figures for GDP (which relate to the third
quarter of the previous year) as far as the second quarter of the following year. This
period covers seven quarters altogether, of which the last five quarters, from April of this
year to June of next, are genuinely in the future. The first two quarters, from last October
to March of the current year, represent a sort of no-man's land between the relatively well-
known past and the unknown future. The problem for this period is one of piecing together bits of statistical information, such as the monthly figures of exports, imports,
retail sales and industrial production, into a reasonably coherent picture of the base period.
This is always difficult because there is very little monthly information about investment
or government expenditure, and the difficulties are sometimes made worse by apparent
contradictions between the available monthly figures of production and sales.

   Once the base period for the forecast is established the forecast proper (i.e. the part
relating to the future) can be begun. The method by which this is done is difficult to
describe in detail[1] but the general approach is to combine the maximum use of direct
information from business firms and government departments with macroeconomic
relationships of the simple type found in sections I and II of this chapter. Government
current expenditure and the government component of fixed investment for example can,
or should, be quite easily predicted from information provided by the nationalised
industries and the government departments. The forecast of business fixed investment
(excluding housing) is made on the basis of the sample enquiries into investment
intentions conducted by the Board of Trade. These enquiries have been found to be
reasonably reliable predictors of reality, although their value is limited by the fact that
they relate only to annual periods, so that the forecaster still has the problem of spreading
the total over the four quarters of the year. A further difficulty is that the enquiry
available for the pre-Budget forecast covers only the calendar year, so that quite
separate considerations are needed to predict the investment levels for the first half of
the following year. There is little doubt, however, that these sample surveys are invaluable
aid to the national income forecaster. Forecasts of housing investment are derived largely
from figures of housing starts and an assumption about the average period of house
construction.

   Exports present a rather more difficult problem for the national income forecaster

---

[1]   The student who is interested in a fuller discussion is advised to read through one of the recent
   forecasts by the National Institute of Economic Research (and *NIER*) since the methods are
   probably very similar to those used by the Treasury. Also useful is the official account, 'Short-
   term economic forecasting in the United Kingdom', and the *Fourth Report of the Estimates
   Committee,* pp.474-480.

since they depend predominantly upon the volume of world trade and production. It follows that a full set of assumptions has to be made about the world economy before a forecast of exports can be made. In 1968, moreover, the problem of forecasting exports has been made particularly difficult by the sharp change in price competitiveness due to the devaluation of the pound.

Exports, fixed investment and government current expenditure are the main 'autonomous' parts of the national income forecast in the sense that they are not in the short run thought to depend much upon the level of GDP.[1] The dependent components are stockbuilding, consumers' expenditure, imports and the factor cost adjustment. In sections I and II we have suggested various hypotheses, such as the stock-adjustment principle, the multiplier and marginal propensity to consume, and the relationship of imports to GDP and stockbuilding, which might be used to forecast these categories. Some of these relationships, to judge from the published accounts, are indeed used by the government forecasters, albeit in somewhat modified forms. But the government has a rather more complicated and indirect method of forecasting consumer's expenditure, and on this the reader is referred to the official account of government forecasting.

The main upshot of the government forecasting work is a table in considerable detail of the course of GDP and its components, quarter-by-quarter, over a 12-18 month year. In the case of the pre-Budget forecast it will extend to the middle of the calendar year after the Budget.

The Instruments of Demand Management

The final stage of short-term economic management is the action that is taken to close the gap between the prospective increase in GDP, as given by the national income forecast, and the required increase, as determined by government priorities. If the forecast increase over the next twelve months is 2 per cent, for example, and the increase required to achieve the employment objective is 3 per cent, then the Chancellor of the Exchequer has to find ways and means of raising aggregate demand for GDP by 1 per cent more than it would otherwise be. His choice of instruments for achieving such a result ranges, in principle, over the whole paraphernalia of government expenditures, subsidies, grants, transfer payments, taxes and credit instruments. In practice, however, his choice is more limited since government expenditure, as we have already noted, is difficult to change quickly, for both administrative and political reasons. Alterations in the scale of investment grants to the private sector are also unlikely to be changed for short-term purposes, chiefly, it seems, because investment plans are difficult to alter at short notice and the effect, therefore, is largely on company savings. The exclusion of fixed investment and government expenditure from the domain of short-term economic management means in effect that the main brunt of it must be borne by personal consumption. A variety of instruments are available for this purpose, of which the ones most commonly used have been income tax, the indirect tax regulator, and hire-purchase restrictions. The introduction of the selective employment tax in April 1966 added another possible weapon to the Chancellor's armoury.

The effect of a rise in personal income tax is to bring an immediate decrease in personal disposable income which, via the marginal propensity to consume, leads to a fall in consumers' expenditure at market prices.[2] The initial change in GDP is the fall in consumption after deduction of its import and indirect tax content. For a rise of 6d. in the standard rate, together with proportionate increases for the various reduced rates of tax, the initial effect on GDP, which we may assume is felt in the first or second quarters after the tax change, is to reduce it by about 0.3 per cent. Allowing for a multiplier of 1½ the final effect will be something between 0.4 and 0.5 per cent of GDP. The time-lag

---

[1]   Not strictly true in the case of exports since these are thought to be partly dependent upon the pressure of home demand—see section II.

[2]   The reader may at this point wish to refer back to the multiplier diagram in Figure 1.1

between the initial and final effects on GDP is not at all easy to estimate, and it seems that the only guide, in the absence of highly sensitive statistical techniques, is the time-honoured procedure of guesswork. Most estimates allow something between one and two years for the bulk of the multiplier process to work itself out.[1]

The most expedient tax instrument for short-term stabilisation purposes is the 'regulator'. This is the power given to the government by Parliament to vary, by up to 10 per cent in either direction, the rates of purchase tax and the customs and excise duties on drink, tobacco and petrol. The effect of increasing indirect taxes in this way is partly to divert expenditure into other directions, but mainly to cause higher prices and lower real disposable incomes. This leads to reduced consumption and GDP in the same way as a rise in income tax. It is estimated (see Table 1.8) that the initial fall in GDP for the full 10 per cent addition to indirect tax rates is about 0.5 per cent, and this becomes 0.7 per cent after the operation of the multiplier process.

The selective employment tax, which is explained more fully in chapter 2, is a levy on employers related to the size of their labour force. The National Institute[1] has estimated that an additional 5 shillings per employee would reduce consumption by 0.5 per cent. This implies an initial fall in GDP of 0.2 per cent, and a multiplied fall of 0.3 per cent.

Alterations in the statutory minimum deposit on hire purchase transactions and in the maximum repayment period have, as we saw in section II.1, been used frequently as stabilisation instruments over the last ten years. The most recent example was at the time of devaluation in November 1967 when the minimum deposit on cars was raised to $33\frac{1}{3}$ per cent and the maximum period of repayment was shortened by twenty-seven months. The effect of raising the minimum down-payment is to choke off purchases until consumers have managed to save the increase in deposit, whilst a shortening of the repayment period is intended to deter purchasers from buying until they are satisfied that their current income will cover the higher monthly payments. These restrictions cannot be expected to be effective if consumers have access to alternative sources of finance, but the presumption is that a good many of them have no such alternative and a tighter control over personal bank advances can always be arranged to take care of the few that do. The main objection to the use of HP controls is not so much that they are not effective (indeed Figure 1.2 suggests the contrary) but rather that their effects are temporary. The estimate in Table 1.8 (page 29) of a 0.5 per cent decline in personal consumption as a result of changes in HP restrictions represents savings worth roughly £27 million a quarter (in 1958 prices), and it may take only a few months' savings out of rising incomes for consumers to be able to afford the increase in HP deposits. The effect of the restrictions, therefore, is to postpone rather than to reduce personal spending, and there is a possibility that the period of postponement may be too short for the purposes of government policy.[2]

Monetary measures are discussed more fully in chapter 2. Alterations in interest rates of the small size normally encountered in post-war Britain are generally thought to have a somewhat feeble effect on fixed investment other than housebuilding, and even the effect on housebuilding is likely to be delayed. The restriction of bank advances and other direct reductions in the quantity of money may, however, have significant effects on fixed investment by small business, and possibly on the buying of consumer durables. Perhaps the main reason why so little emphasis is placed on monetary policy in the management of domestic demand is that so little is known about its effects. With fiscal changes it is possible to calculate, admittedly within fairly wide margins of error, the initial effects on disposable income, consumption and GDP. With monetary changes, however, a far wider range of uncertainty attaches to these initial effects, and until the

---

[1] *NIER*, February 1968, Table 5, p.18.

[2] It is this possibility which appears to lie behind the Chancellor's decision not to tighten HP in his Budget of March 1968.

means are found of removing such uncertainty it seems likely that the main emphasis in demand management will continue to be placed upon fiscal instruments.

TABLE 1.8

Estimated Effects of Certain Tax and HP Changes on Consumption and GDP

	Percentage changes in:		
	Consumption (initial)	GDP (initial)	GDP (final)
6d. on standard rate of income tax	−0.2	−0.1	−0.2
6d. on standard rate and proportional changes in reduced rates	−0.6	−0.3	−0.4
Use of regulator (10 per cent on all indirect taxes)	−1.0	−0.5	−0.7
Tightening of HP restrictions (repayment term from 27 to 24 months on cars and 30 to 24 months on domestic appliances; minimum deposit $33\frac{1}{3}$ to 40 per cent on cars and 25 to 33½ per cent on domestic appliances)	−0.5	−0.3	−
Additional 5s. per head on selective employment tax	−0.5	−0.2	−0.3

Source: the left hand column is taken from *NIER,* February 1968, Table 5, p.18, and the remaining columns are calculated from the multiplier relationships in Figure 1.1 of this chapter.

III.3 The Pathology of Short-term Policy

In setting out the approach to economic management adopted in the UK we have deliberately glossed over the fact that the course of the economy over the last ten years has been anything but a smooth one. GDP, as is shown in Figure 1.6 above, has increased in a series of slow and fast phases whilst unemployment has fluctuated in cycles of roughly constant duration and increasing amplitude. We must now ask why it is that the government with its equipment of forecasts and stabilisation instruments, has allowed the economy to pursue such a patently unstable course?

One attempt to answer this question is to postulate that the 'stop-go' pattern of movements in economic activity reflect a 'stop-go' attitude on the part of those in control of the economy. This interpretation of events rests on the analogy with the inexperienced driver whose actions result from a failure to look beyond his front bumper. The implication seems to be that the government does not look ahead, but this is flatly belied by the system of economic forecasting described above. Economic forecasts for a period of from twelve to eighteen months ahead have been made ever since the White Paper of 1944.

An alternative suggestion is that economic policy has gone wrong not through any lack of forecasts but because the forecasts have been bad ones. If, for example, the forecasts of 1959 and 1964 had underestimated the increases in aggregate demand then this would have gone some way to explaining why the rapid expansion which took place was not contained by sterner measures of demand regulation. Similarly, the high unemployment rates of 1962, 1963 and 1967 could, conceivably, have been due to over-optimistic forecasts at the time of the Budgets. Two difficulties arise in advancing such an explanation of 'stop-go'. The first is that if bad forecasting was the whole explanation then the actual error in the forecasts would itself have had to be cyclical, and this seems unlikely. Nobody denies that economic forecasts are imprecise and sometimes prone to large errors, but it would be very surprising if the difference between forecast and actual was regularly positive in the recession and negative in the boom. The second difficulty about the forecasting explanation is that it cannot be checked since the forecasts have not been published and only the vaguest indications of them are available in public pronouncements such as the annual Budget speech.[1] An attempt to infer forecasts from Budget speeches has, nonetheless, been made by Mr. J. C. R. Dow,[2] and his conclusion for the GDP forecasts from 1951 to 1960 was that they had been seriously wrong on only three occasions, of which 1959 was one. Unfortunately his work does not cover the period from 1960 to 1967 when the course of the economy has been still more erratic, but it is reasonable to suppose that improvements in national statistics together with several more years of forecasting experience should, if anything, have reduced the likelihood of forecasting errors.

Another possibility is that the government has not properly understood its stabilisation instruments. If, for example, its notions of the effect of income and indirect tax changes are seriously astray, then this could be a reason for the course of economic activity. On this it is difficult to say a great deal except to argue that the same knowledge of the way the economy works is required to estimate the effects of these instruments as is required for making economic forecasts. It is difficult, therefore, to separate this suggestion from the argument that the forecasts are to blame, and our inclination is to reject both.

The diagnosis which seems most acceptable has little to do with 'stop-go' attitudes, bad forecasts or misunderstood instruments of policy, but simply assumes that the path taken by the economy has been very close to what the government has intended. This diagnosis upholds the efficacy of the techniques of economic management and puts the blame for fluctuations in the economy upon fluctuations in the government's own priorities. In particular it blames the competing demands of the balance of payments and the ballot box. It explains the expansionary booms before the general elections of 1959 and 1964, together with the high level of economic activity in early 1966 by the desire of the government to be re-elected into power. The ensuing bouts of deflation can, at least in part, be blamed upon the balance of payments crises that have been associated with high levels of domestic activity. The progressive deterioration in the balance of payments since the mid-1950s, moreover, has meant that each deflationary bout has had to be sterner than the previous one, with the result that the amplitude of the cycle has gradually increased.

This diagnosis of the 'stop-go' cycle implies that the devaluation of the pound in November 1967, assuming it to be effective, should mean some amelioration of the recession phase of the cycle. But the power to influence votes through the manipulation of aggregate demand will not disappear until the electorate itself is able to perceive what is going on. Until this happens the techniques of economic management will continue to bestow an unfair advantage on the party in power, a state of affairs which is injurious to the democratic system as well as to the economy.

IV   Inflation

IV.1   Post-War Inflation

Post-war economic policy, whatever its limitations, can at least claim to have been successful in avoiding heavy unemployment. The same thing cannot be said of post-war efforts to avoid inflation. Prices, which in the inter-war period were tending slowly downwards, have since 1940 shown a continuous and relentless increase. The rate of increase since the end of the Second World War has been somewhat in excess of the rate of decline between the wars. The contrast between the two periods is illustrated in Table 1.9 (page 31).

---

[1]   1968 is a welcome exception since a reasonably complete forecast has been incorporated in the Financial Statement. See section II.
[2]   J. C. R. Dow, *The Management of the British Economy 1945-60*, Cambridge University Press, 1964, chapter 5.

TABLE 1.9

Average Annual Changes in Retail Prices, UK, 1919-67

	Per cent per annum
1919-29	−2.6
1929-39	−0.3
1939-47	+5.9
1947-55	+4.9
1955-67	+2.9

Sources: London and Cambridge Economic Service: *The British Economy, Key Statistics 1900-66.* MLG.

The index of retail prices (or 'cost of living index' as it is often called) is but one of several indicators of the rate of inflation. It registers the prices of a collection of goods entering into a typical retail shopping basket. It is a 'true' price index in that it is collected directly from the data of actual prices. In this respect it differs from an average value index, such as the index of consumer prices, in which the 'prices' are derived by the division of consumers' expenditure at constant prices into consumers' expenditure at current prices. The effect of doing this is to arrive at a current-weighted index, changes in which can be brought about by changes in the pattern of expenditure as well as by changes in actual prices. The consumer price index, along with similar indices for investment goods, exports, and goods and services bought by the public authorities, forms part of the index of final prices. The recent rates of change in the final price index and its components are shown for the last ten years in Table 1.10 (below).

TABLE 1.10

Increases in Average Value Indices, UK, 1956-66

	Overall increase 1956-66 per cent.	Average annual increase, per cent.
1. Consumer goods and services	30	2.6
2. Government expenditure on goods and services	57	4.6
3. Gross domestic capital formation	26	2.3
4. Final goods sold on the home market (1 + 2 + 3)	33	2.9
5. Exports of goods and services	11	1.1
6. Total final expenditure (1 + 2 + 3 + 5)	29	2.6
7. Imports of goods and services	7	0.7

Source: NIBB, 1967, Tables 12, 14, 16.

As Table 1.10 shows, there has been a fairly wide variation over the last ten years in the rates of price increase for the various categories of expenditure. The fastest increase of all has been that for government expenditure on goods and services, and this may be because of the relatively high service content compared with other types of domestic expenditure. The indices for consumers' and investment expenditure have both increased at about 2½ per cent per annum, and the increase shown for exports is barely 1 per cent a year. This rather slow increase in export prices could well be a reflection of the harsher competitive conditions in the export than in the home market. One of its consequences has been to squeeze profit margins on exported goods relative to those on goods sold in the home market, thereby discouraging firms from remaining in the export market. The very slow rise in import prices is sufficient to scotch the idea that the bulk of our inflationary problem has been imported. With imports accounting for only about one quarter of final prices, it is difficult to see how more than about 0.2 per cent out of the total rise in final prices of 2.7 per cent can be attributed to higher import costs. Import prices were, however, an important ingredient in the inflation following the Korean War, and they will be important again following the devaluation of the pound in 1967.

It is sometimes forgotten that inflation in the post-war period has by no means been confined to Britain, but has been common throughout the industrial countries. In a number of countries, notably France, Japan, Sweden, the Netherlands and Italy, the increase in consumer prices in the period from 1956 to 1966 has been larger than the 30 per cent rise recorded for Britain. The price increases in these countries have ranged from 38 to 60 per cent; German prices have increased by 27 and Belgian prices by 25 per cent in this period, and only the United States and Canada have had noticeably less inflation than in Britain (19 and 22 per cent respectively).[1] Inflation has been as universal in the post-war period as was unemployment between the wars.

IV.2 The Generation of Inflation

The most widely accepted hypothesis to account for inflation is the view that it arises from a high pressure of demand on available resources. This view sees inflation as originating in the labour market, where the pressure of demand is indicated by the unemployment percentage or the ratio of unemployment to unfilled vacancies. The argument is that the rate of change of wage rates is positively related to the pressure of demand for labour, and this in turn is inversely related to the rate of unemployment. Thus the rate of change of wage rates is determined by the level of unemployment. When unemployment is high, as in the 1930s, the rate of wage inflation is expected to be low, or even negative, and when unemployment is low, as in the post-war period, a much faster rate of wage increase is to be expected.

The next step in the argument is the hypothesis that the level of prices is determined, by and large, by the level of costs. This conclusion is the same whether we assume the full-cost pricing hypothesis or marginal-cost pricing. In either case a rise in wages, which is not offset by higher productivity or lower import prices, can be expected to give rise to an increase in prices. The fact that firms are in competition with each other does not seriously alter the conclusion, since cost increases for firms in the same industry are likely to be very similar, and the squeeze on profit margins is likely to affect all firms equally.

A considerable amount of evidence has been collected in support of this hypothesis, of which the observations recorded in Table 1.11 (page 33) and Figure 1.8 (page 34) are an example. These show that the periods of high unemployment have invariably been associated with periods of low wage increase, and that wages and prices have generally moved together. An impressive series of econometric studies has been concerned with the problem of quantifying such relationships.[2]

---

[1] These figures are taken from *NIER,* February 1968, Table 20.

[2] Notably A. W. Phillips, 'The Relation between Unemployment and the Rate of Change of Money Wage Rates in the United Kingdom, 1861-1957', *Economica,* November 1958; R. G. Lipsey 'The Relation between Unemployment and the Rate of Change of Money Wage Rates in the United Kingdom 1862-1957', *Economica,* February 1960; L. A. Dicks-Mireaux 'The Inter-relationship Between Cost and Price Changes 1946-1959', *Oxford Economic Papers,* October 1961.

TABLE 1.11

Unemployment, Wage Rates and Final Prices, UK, 1956-66

	Unemployment Percentage	Percentage change in wage rates[1]	Percentage change in final prices[2]
1956	1.2	5.0	3.5
1957	1.4	5.2	4.0
1958	2.1	3.6	1.3
1959	2.2	2.9	0.3
1960	1.6	5.9	2.3
1961	1.5	5.2	3.4
1962	2.0	3.9	1.7
1963	2.5	3.1	1.8
1964	1.6	5.5	3.7
1965	1.4	7.7	3.7
1966	1.5	4.2	3.7

Source: MLG; ET, October 1967, January 1968.

[1] Percentage annual change in average hourly wage rates to December of year shown as interpolated from October and April data in the Ministry of Labour's half-yearly enquiry.
[2] Percentage change in index of final prices from 1st quarter of year shown to 1st quarter of following year.

One problem which arises with this explanation of wage and price changes is that it may not allow sufficiently for the interrelationships between them. Higher wages can lead to higher prices, but this may not be the end of the story since the rise in the cost of living will lead trade unions to bid for higher wages. If this is the case then unemployment ceases to be the sole determinant of the wage change and allowance must be made for a wage-price spiral which is superimposed upon the pressure of demand for labour.[1]

The unemployment explanation of inflation and its variant in terms of a superimposed wage-price spiral both seem to furnish fairly satisfactory accounts of the rate of wage and price change. Some extraneous allowance must also be made for the influence of import costs, and it is interesting to note that Mr Dicks-Mireaux' study arrived at an elasticity of one-fifth between final prices and import costs, a result which coincides fairly closely with the size of the import content of final expenditure (see Table 1.6). The influence of productivity changes must also be taken into account, although it is not certain whether the short-term change in productivity, which as we have seen is strongly influenced by cyclical factors, is the most appropriate variable.

The explanation of inflation which we have given avoids the use of the terms cost or demand inflation, since either description seems to apply. The association between the pressure of demand and the rate of wage increase could for example be described as demand inflation, since different levels of demand imply different rates of wage and price increase. On the other hand the origin of the wage increase in the labour market, and its subsequent 'cost-push' effect on prices could equally well be described as cost inflation. This ambiguity might not arise if the terms cost and demand inflation were precisely defined and understood at the outset, but in the absence of any general consensus it seems best to avoid them altogether.

---

[1] As in Dicks-Mireaux, *op. cit.*

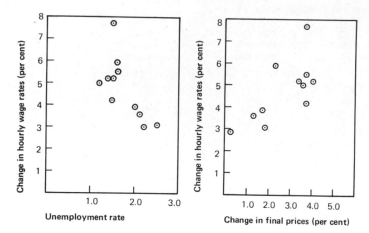

Figure 1.8 Unemployment and Changes in Wage Rates and Prices, UK, 1956–66.

IV.3 The Control of Inflation

The avoidance of inflation has been a goal of economic policy for a great deal longer than the maintenance of full employment. The consequence of inflation that is judged to be most unfortunate is the arbitrary and uncontrollable manner in which it redistributes real income. The retired person living on a pension that is fixed in monetary terms is liable, under conditions of fast inflation, to face a considerable erosion of his real standard of living. The fall in his real income is matched by a rise in that of the government or institution responsible for paying the pension. Inflation redistributes income between borrowers and lenders, and between those who belong to strong trade unions and those who belong to weak ones. Such redistribution is extremely difficult for the government to control except by introducing a universal cost of living clause, the effect of which would be to make the inflation still faster. The other consequence of inflation that seems most feared by governments is its effect upon the balance of payments, although this effect can in principle be neutralised by an appropriate adjustment of the exchange rate.

For these and other reasons government policy aims to curb the inflationary process. Policies to raise the non-cyclical rate of growth of productivity, or to eliminate restrictive practices in trade unions, would tend to be anti-inflationary in so far as they alleviate increases in money costs by lowering real costs of production. Something could also be claimed for policies to encourage price competition among producers and retail shops. But the two main approaches to the problem of inflation aim either to reduce demand by deflationary action or to restrain wage and price increases by direct government intervention.

The traditional remedy for countering inflation derives from the view, stated directly above, that its speed is related to the level of unemployment. This means that inflation can be brought under control by the exercise of the demand-management functions set out in section III of this chapter. A direct conflict, however, arises between the desirability of high employment and price stability, and some compromise has to be struck between the two goals. Thus the level of unemployment that is thought to be optimal depends both on a person's subjective assessment of the extent to which price stability should be sacrificed for full employment, and on his objective view of the strength of the causal relationship between them. There is room for argument about both and it is not surprising to find that different writers prescribe or imply different levels of unemployment

as the long-term policy target. Professor Paish,[1] for example, has stood out for an unemployment percentage of 2¼ per cent on the grounds that this would permit price
stability through an increase in wages of the same magnitude as the long-term rise in
productivity. It may be remarked, however, that unemployment averaged 2¼ per cent in
1962-63 but that prices still rose appreciably, the final price increase during these two
years being an average of 2.4 per cent per annum. This experience fits better with the
econometric estimates of Mr Dicks-Mireaux, which imply a substantially larger volume of
unemployment for the achievement of complete price stability.

Whilst the various estimates may differ there does not seem to be a great deal of
doubt that a policy of running the economy at a low pressure of demand will be less
inflationary than one which allows unemployment to fall to very low levels. But this
observation does not remove the dilemma for the policy maker. An increase in the unemployment level of 0.2 per cent, for example, has been associated in the past (see
Figure 1.6) with a fall of about 1 per cent in GDP, and this corresponds to a loss of
production of something like £350 million at current prices. When we recall how strong
the pressure is for more and better hospitals, schools, business equipment, not to mention
private consumption, it is not difficult to see why governments have been reluctant to
adhere to a policy of high and stable unemployment as a way of stopping inflation.

An alternative with fewer unattractive features is to attempt to even out regional
differences in unemployment without necessarily altering the national rate. The reasoning
behind this policy is that the sensitivity of wages to the pressure of demand increases as
unemployment falls. It follows from this that the additional wage inflation which arises
from a unit fall in unemployment in one of the depressed areas is of small significance
compared with the abatement of inflation which follows from an equal rise in unemployment in one of the areas of high pressure of demand. Therefore a policy of transferring unemployment from areas like Northern Ireland and the north to high pressure
regions such as London, the midlands and the south-east would tend to reduce the rate of
inflation to be expected from any given national rate of unemployment. The difficulty
with such a policy is one of finding ways and means of effecting such a transfer, and it is
doubtful whether the very small amount of regional selectivity in the system of investment grants and selective employment tax[2] is sufficient to achieve much result.

The third method of approaching the control of inflation is incomes policy.[3] Hence,
the aim is to break out of the inflation-unemployment dilemma by altering the whole basis
of wage settlements. Incomes policy has many adherents and a great deal was expected
from it in the early days of the present government. Up to now, however, it appears to
have been remarkably ineffective except during the 'incomes standstill' in the second half
of 1966 and the 'period of severe restraint' in the ensuing six months. Even these effects,
however, were temporary and the return to a voluntary incomes policy in the second half
of 1967 was accompanied by a much faster rate of wage increase than would normally
have been associated with such a high level of unemployment.

The conclusion we reach is that the one effective method of avoiding inflation is the
highly unpleasant one of creating unemployment. Ancillary policies, such as the regional
reorientation of demand and incomes policy, are both in their infancy, and it may be
expecting too much of them for effects to be immediately visible. But until these effects
show up there is likely to be a continuing conflict between the objectives of price
stability and full employment.

---

[1] F. W. Paish and J. Hennessy, 'Policy for Incomes', Hobart Paper No. 29 (3rd edition), 1967.
[2] See chapter 2.
[3] Discussed much more fully in chapters 4 and 5.

V   ECONOMIC GROWTH

V.1   The Growth of Productive Potential

We have acknowledged in section III that movements in domestic output can be determined by the behaviour of aggregate demand. This principle, which lies at the heart of
Keynesian economic theory, holds when there are ample reserves of unused resources.
It implies that the rate of expansion of GDP can, under these conditions, be governed by
the rate of increase of total demand. A fast rate of expansion can be sustained for so
long as there are unused resources of labour and capital. It will be accompanied by a
decline in the percentage rate of unemployment and the margin of unused capacity.

The economics of growth is concerned with a different sort of problem. It asks what
rate of growth is sustainable at full employment or at some definable margin of unused
resources. For this purpose it requires the concept of 'the growth of productive potential'
and 'the underlying trend of productivity'. The first of these is defined as the rate at
which GDP could grow without any change in either direction in the pressure of demand
on productive resources. The underlying trend in productivity is similarly defined as the
growth of output per man, or sometimes per man-hour, between periods of identical
demand pressure. For all practical purposes identical demand pressure can be indicated
by equal or closely similar rates of unemployment. The periods 1900-13, 1922-38, 1950-
57 and 1957-65 all began and ended with the same or similar unemployment rates, so
that growth rates of GDP and productivity in these periods should be in reasonable con-
formity with the definitions above. They are shown in Table 1.12 (below)

TABLE 1.12

Economic Growth, UK, 1900-65

| | | Percentage increase per annum in: | | |
	GDP	GDP per man	Civilian labour force	Capital stock excluding dwellings
1900-13	0.9	−0.1	1.0	1.9
1922-38	2.2	1.0	1.2	1.1
1950-57	2.7	1.9	0.8	2.6
1957-65	3.1	2.3	0.8	3.4

Source: London and Cambridge Economic Service. *The British Economy, Key statistics 1900–66.*

As the table shows both the growth rates of productive potential and the underlying
trend in productivity seem to have increased fairly steadily since the beginning of this
century.

Calculations of the underlying growth rate have to be treated with a considerable
amount of caution. In the first place they tell us little or nothing about the causes of
underlying growth but simply state what kind of time-trend has fitted most closely with
past data. An extrapolation of the growth of potential output for any distance into the
future could easily turn out wrong if, as is likely for the next few years, the work force is
not going to increase at the same rate as in the past. In extrapolating the underlying
productivity trend, moreover, we make the implicit assumption either that all the
factors that influenced it during the past period will be present to the same degree in
future, or that alterations in them are mutually offsetting. As we do not know what all
these factors are and as we are unable to quantify them separately an extrapolation of the
past growth rate is extremely hazardous.

A second reservation concerns the interpretation of growth rates generally and their

relation to levels. In calculating growth from 1957 to 1965, for example, we calculate
what compound rate of increase will transform the level of GDP in 1957 into that of 1965.
This tells us nothing about what happens in the intervening years so that the growth rate
so obtained is no guide to the average level of output over the intervening period. So far
as the calculation is concerned we could have experienced a huge increase or decrease in
output between 1957 and the middle of the period. In fact what happened was that the
growth of actual output was below the 3.1 per cent rise in potential from 1960 to 1962
and again in 1964-65. An allied point is that the *level* of potential output in this case is
quite arbitrarily defined as being consistent with an unemployment rate of 1.6 per cent
and does not represent the maximum attainable level. A whole series of levels each
corresponding to a different unemployment rate can be drawn for any given growth rate.

V.2   An International Comparison

A number of studies of the causes of economic growth start from what has been called a
'league table' showing growth rates for different countries. They then go on to ask why
some countries have managed to grow so much faster than others. Table 1.13 (below) is
an example.

The table shows the growth of total output, output per head of population, output per
worker and output per man-hour in the UK and eleven other industrial countries during
the 1950s. It will be seen that the UK growth rate, however measured, was slower than
that of nearly every other country in the table. Belgium, the United States, Canada and
Denmark were the only countries to show similar growth rates to that of the UK.

TABLE 1.13

Annual Average Percentage Rates of Growth, 1950–60

	GDP	GDP per head of population	GDP per man	GDP per man-hour
Belgium	2.9	2.3	2.5	2.5
Denmark	3.3	2.6	2.3	2.9
France	4.4	3.5	3.8	3.9
Germany	7.6	6.5	5.3	6.0
Italy	5.9	5.3	4.1	4.1
Netherlands	4.9	3.6	3.7	3.7
Norway	3.5	2.6	3.2	3.9
Sweden	3.3	2.6	2.7	3.5
Switzerland	5.1	3.7	3.8	4.2
United Kingdom	2.6	2.2	1.9	2.0
Canada	3.9	1.2	2.0	2.5
United States	3.2	1.6	2.1	2.4
Average	4.2	3.1	3.2	3.5

Source: A. Maddison, *Economic Growth in the West,* Allen and Unwin, 1964.

Comparisons such as this have to be interpreted with a number of reservations in mind.
In the first place, the pressure of demand in the UK was much the same in 1960 as it was
in 1950, but for Germany, Italy and the Netherlands[1] it was considerably higher. This
means that the comparison of the UK with these countries is somewhat biased in their

---

[1]   Maddison, *Economic Growth in the West,* gives the following unemployment rates for these
      countries:

	1950	1960
Germany	7.2	0.9
Italy	8.7	4.0
Netherlands	2.0	1.1

favour although there is little doubt that adjustment for this bias would not greatly alter the picture. Secondly, we have already seen in the previous Table that the underlying trend of potential output and productivity in the UK increased over the period so that the comparison with other countries may be misleading as an indication of more recent trends.

These reservations, however, are not likely to be serious enough to alter the general conclusion that growth in the UK in recent years has been a great deal slower than in a number of other industrial countries, and this observation raises the important question of why this has been so.

V.3   The Causes of Economic Growth

The causes of 'increasing opulence' have been discussed by economists since the time of Adam Smith. At the outset it is helpful to divide the various influences at work into factors operating from the side of supply and factors operating from the side of demand. On the supply side we have the various forces determining the quantity, quality and economic efficiency of the factors of production. On the demand side we discuss the pressure of demand, its rate of increase, fluctuations in demand, and demand expectations. In making these distinctions, however, we must remember that the growth process arises out of the interaction of both the supply and demand sides of the equation and that neither side is completely independent of the other.

The supply of labour is a largely autonomous entity dependent on the evolution of the population of working age, its distribution by age and sex, the secular decline in hours worked and the increase in the length of annual and national holidays. Changes in the pressure of demand, however, exert an influence on the size of the labour force and the number of hours worked. It is possible that such tendencies, which we have observed during periods of cyclical change, would also operate over longer periods.

The quality of labour must in large degree depend upon the facilities available for education and training, the opportunities taken of them, and the degree to which they match the changing demands for skill arising out of changes in technology and the structure of aggregate demand. Measurement of these influences, however, is difficult and there is little evidence to show which way, if at all, they have affected the international comparison in Table 1.13. The mobility of labour from job to job and from area to area is probably an important factor in economic growth in so far as it reflects the degree to which the labour force can adjust to economic change. Evidence has been found in support of the view that a part of the relatively fast growth of the German, Italian and French economies can be attributed to the movement of labour from the agricultural to the industrial sectors.[1]

One of the most potent influences on the growth of labour productivity is the rate of increases in the nation's stock of capital, both in quantity and in quality. Some indications of the growth of the UK capital stock are given in Table 1.12, where it can be seen that the rate of increase, like that of productivity, has tended to rise during the course of this century. The stock of capital, however, is an extremely difficult thing to measure. This is chiefly because the figures of depreciation in the national accounts are based on data for tax purposes and do not serve as an indication of the rates of scrapping and deterioration of existing capital. Estimates of the capital stock, therefore, must be treated with a good deal of reserve.

The quality of the capital stock is perhaps even more important and even more difficult to measure. According to one widely accepted view the quality of capital depends, by and large, upon its age-structure. This view looks upon the capital stock as a series of vintages of gross investment, each new vintage containing machines of higher quality than the previous one. Scientific and technical progress are embodied in new machines, not old ones,

---

[1]   Maddison, *Economic Growth in the West*, pp.59–60.

so that the most recent capital equipment is likely to be the most efficient. This view, together with the difficulties of measuring the quantity of capital, has led a number of economists to emphasise gross rather than net capital formation in a period as the better indicator of the extent to which capital resources have been enhanced. A high rate of gross investment, even if it is entirely for replacement purposes, will reduce the age of the capital stock and increase its quality.[1]

Turning now to the demand elements in economic growth we can distinguish three possible influences: the change in the pressure of demand over the period in question; the average level of the pressure of demand; and the size of fluctuations around the average. The first of these is hardly relevant to the growth of productive potential which is concerned with changes between periods of equal demand pressure. The average level of demand pressure can, however, be expected to influence growth in a number of ways. A transition from one unemployment rate in one decade to a different rate in the next could, on the assumption that productivity schedules are bell-shaped, lead to machinery being worked at less than the maximum productivity level for more of the time. This would happen whether the pressure of demand was raised or lowered but it would be a transitional effect only, and one which would gradually disappear as new machinery was introduced. If the transition was to a higher pressure of demand it would tend to stimulate investment which should itself raise labour productivity. It might also encourage managers and workers to learn more efficient methods of production since slack levels of economic activity, although they may stimulate competition between firms, do not provide the same intensity of experience as do periods of high pressure. The experience gained from the activity of production has been called 'learning by doing'. Its quantitative importance is difficult to assess, but it might emerge as a large bonus if, say, it was decided to run the UK economy at a higher long-term pressure of demand.

The other question is whether the amplitude of fluctuations tends to impede economic growth. It seems probable that the expectation of fluctuations will retard capital formation because profitability will be held down in periods of recession. It may also be the case that expectations of cycles lead to the installation of machinery which can be adapted to use in periods of both high and low sales whereas the prospect of steady growth could enable the introduction of machinery which would be specially designed to produce at some given level of sales. In this case it seems probable that the loss of adaptability would mean a gain in the efficiency of capital, and growth would be stimulated. It may be no coincidence, therefore, that three countries with some of the lowest growth rates—the UK, the United States and Belgium—have been subject to sharper fluctuations in unemployment than others.[1] Thus a policy of running the economy at a steady pressure of demand could turn out to be an effective way of increasing the rate of economic growth. Attempts to do this in the UK, as we have seen above, are liable to be undermined by the periodicity of general elections. Perhaps all we can do is to hope that experience of what is described as the 'stop-go' cycle will ultimately lead the electorate to distinguish between rampant expansion and steady growth, and to prefer the latter.

V.4   Economic Growth as a Policy Objective

Economic growth has become an objective of economic policy. In one sense it always was an objective since it was implied by the goal of maintaining full employment. In the last few years, however, the emphasis of policy has shifted to one of raising the rate of growth of productive potential above what it would otherwise have been. Fast growth is enticing to politicians because it raises the yield of taxes and allows the government to choose between the attractive alternatives of an increased scale of government expenditure and a reduction in rates of taxation.

---

[1]   Ibid., pp.43-56.

The problem up to now has been how to obtain faster growth. The National Economic Development Office was set up by Mr Selwyn Lloyd in 1962 with the object of exploring the possibilities of faster growth. It set a target rate of 4.0 per cent for the period of 1961-66 but the actual growth rate in this period was 3.0 per cent and there was a recession in 1962 and 1963. The NEDO, however, was a semi-official institution and its growth rate did not receive official blessing until the election campaign of 1964. The National Plan, by contrast, was prepared by a new ministry, the Department of Economic Affairs, with the prime functions of raising the growth rate. Published in the autumn of 1965 the National Plan looked to a growth rate of GDP of 3.8 per cent per annum from 1964 to 1970, and to an annual productivity increase of 3.4 per cent. The actual growth rate over the first three years of the Plan period, however, was a miserable 1.8 per cent per annum, and GDP would have to grow at nearly 6 per cent a year from 1967 to 1970 to realise the Plan target.

These projections of economic growth have been wrong for several reasons. The first mistake, which was made both by NEDO and the National Plan, was to pick a growth rate as an assumption without properly examining the means of achieving it. The Plan's choice of an overall increase in GDP of 25 per cent from 1964 to 1970 appears to have been made without any attempt to relate the growth of output to the growth of productive resources.[1] Its underlying productivity increase of 3.4 per cent per annum was substantially in excess of the 1960-64 increase of 2.7 per cent, yet very little justification was given for it. It must be asked, however, whether enough is known about the causes of growth to establish the conditions under which an increase of this order can be expected. The answer is probably that not enough is yet known. Over the years a great deal has been learned about the techniques of short-term demand management, but this knowledge has accrued as a result of continual experimentation in budgeting and forecasting. The same is not true of efforts to speed up economic growth, partly because these efforts have only recently been made, but also because the time needed to check such experiments against reality and to learn from them, is considerably longer than in the case of demand management. Thus it may be several decades before governments are in a position to say that particular policies will be sufficient to raise the growth rate by so-much per cent. Until this happens it may be safer to adhere to a policy of steady growth, and to avoid making projections of long-term growth that are significantly more optimistic than what has been achieved already.

The other reason that is often advanced for the failure of the National Plan was that it was wrecked by the balance of payments situation and the deflationary measures of July 1966. If this means that the Plan could have been achieved in the absence of these measures we must beg to differ, but we cannot refute it until it is shown that the growth of productive potential for 1964-70, or even 1967-70, is less than 3.8 per cent a year. The significance of the balance of payments measures was not so much to reduce the underlying growth rate as to question why the planners had not foreseen and forestalled this eventuality. The object of planning is not to tell the world what a lovely place it would be if there were no problems, but to look for the problems and solve them. In this respect the National Plan of 1965 must be judged a notable flop.

---

[1] 'In practice, given the comparatively short period we had to produce this document and do all this very large amount of work, we decided to tackle it by taking as a starting assumption a growth of the economy which was slightly higher than you would expect if past trends and policies had been pursued, but not so much higher that it was unrealistic. This figure came out at around 25 per cent.' (DEA witness, Minutes of Evidence taken before the sub-Committee on Economic Affairs, pages 320-21, *Fourth Report from the Estimates Committee*, Session 1966-1967, House of Commons, 6th December 1966).

VI   ECONOMIC PROSPECTS, 1968-71

In section III we discussed the failures of short-term economic management and in section V we touched briefly on the failures of planning for growth. It remains to ask what will happen to economic policy and to the economy in the next two or three years.

There is one respect in which the government made a welcome and significant step forward. It published its national income forecasts for the coming period in March 1968, the first time such forecasts have been made public since 1951. These are summarised in Table 1.14 (page 42) and show the expected increase in GDP, after the Budget changes, to be at a rate of just over 3 per cent a year.

The bulk of the increase in GDP was expected to arise from an increase in exports of £500 million between the second half of 1967 and the first half of 1969. Of this, about one quarter was attributed to a recovery of shipments from the strikes at the London and Liverpool docks during 1967. This left an increase in the export volume of 7.4 per cent a year, the main causes of which were the devaluation of the pound in November 1967 and the expansion expected in world income and trade. Clearly, it was extremely difficult to estimate the effects of devaluation upon exports, and an alternative official forecast of an increase of 9.2 per cent was also given in the Financial Statement. The exact amount of these increases which was assumed to follow from devaluation was not stated, but it looks as if the lower assumption may have been in the region of 4—5 per cent and the higher something like 6—7 per cent. The National Institute of Economic and Social Research put the rise in exports attributable to devaluation at 4½ per cent in their forecast of the out-look.[1] But all these estimates were extremely tentative and, unfortunately, it looks as if the level of exports in the first half of 1968 was rather less than either the National Institute or the government had expected.

The remainder of the increase foreseen in TFE was made up of additional expenditure on investment and public consumption. Private consumption was put as falling at an annual rate of about 1 per cent on a post-Budget basis, the effect of the Budget being to reduce it by 2 per cent, or some £500 million at current prices, from what it would other-wise have been. The size of this reduction was altogether exceptional as, indeed, was the estimate of a £920 million increase in revenue due to the Budget changes. If anything these changes, which affected mainly indirect taxes, corporation tax, SET and motor vehicle tax, looked too large for the job they were supposed to do—even allowing that some of them would fall more substantially on savings than on consumption. But it remains to be seen whether this will have been the case.

---

[1] *NIER*, February 1968. The 4½ per cent rise applies to the volume of merchandise exports from the 4th quarter of 1967 to the 4th quarter of 1968.

TABLE 1.14

Official National Income Forecast, UK, 1967-69

£ million at 1958 prices

	1967 2nd half	Change to 1969 1st half	Percentage change (annual rate)	Higher export forecast
Consumers' expenditure	10,170	−170	−1.1	
Government expenditure	2,370	80	2.2	
Fixed investment	2,990	200	4.4	
Exports	2,980	500	10.9(7.4)	12.8(9.2)
Investment in stocks	120	40	−	
TFE	18,630	650	2.3	
Imports	3,450	40	0.8	
Factor cost adjustment	1,860	− 10	−0.4	
GDP	13,320	620	3.1	3.6

Note: Bracketed figures refer to export increase attributed to the dock strike in 1967.
Source: Financial Statement 1968-69, HMSO, 1968, H. of C.151

The forecast of a 3 per cent rate of increase in GDP was about equal to the government's own estimate of the growth rate of productive potential. It may be surmised, then, that the official target for unemployment for the first half of 1969 was a rate of 2.3 per cent for the wholly unemployed. This rate, which represents about 540,000 unemployed workers, was the same as had obtained in the second half of 1967. It seems probable, however, that it was conceived as a temporary target by a government which was deliberately erring on the side of caution in its attempt to get more resources devoted to the export market. If the forecast increase in exports materialises towards the end of 1968 then it seems possible that the government will relax its hold on the economy and allow a modicum of reflation in the Budget of April 1969. Once the balance of payments position becomes reasonably secure it is to be hoped that a gradual return to a lower unemployment rate will be permitted.

The risks facing the economy are twofold. The first is that the government's failure to initiate an absolute wage freeze in the exceptional circumstances of 1968 will lead to a scramble for wage increases which will undermine the effects of devaluation. This seems unlikely, but it cannot be completely overlooked as a possibility. The opposite risk is that a successful outcome for the balance of payments, together with the increased unpopularity that will result from the continuation of high levels of unemployment, will lead the government to reflate too rapidly in the hopes of influencing the outcome of the next general election. The technical problem of avoiding both dangers, and the political strains of having to do so in a pre-election period, promise an extremely interesting and very tense three years for the UK economy.

SUGGESTIONS FOR FURTHER READING

W. Beckerman et.al., *The British Economy in 1975,* Cambridge University Press, 1965.
F. Blackaby and M. Artis, 'On Incomes Policy', *District Bank Review,* March 1968.
S. Brittan, *The Treasury under the Tories 1951-1964,* Penguin Books, 1964.
L. A. Dicks-Mireaux, *Cost or Demand Inflation,* Woolwich Economic Papers, 1965.
L. A. Dicks-Mireaux, 'The Interrelationship between Cost and Price Changes 1946-1959', *Oxford Economic Papers,* October 1961.
J. C. R. Dow, *The Management of the British Economy 1945-60,* Cambridge University Press, 1964.
W. A. H. Godley and J. R. Shepherd, 'Long-term growth and short-term policy', *NIER,*

August 1964.

W. A. B. Hopkin and W. A. H. Godley, 'An analysis of tax changes', *NIER*, May 1965.

R. G. Lipsey, 'The Relation between Unemployment and the Rate of Change of Money Wage Rates in the United Kingdom 1862-1957', *Economica*, February 1960.

A. Maddison, *Economic Growth in the West*, Allen and Unwin, 1964.

R. C. O. Matthews, 'Some Aspects of the Post-War Growth in the British Economy in Relation to Historical Experience', *Manchester Statistical Society*, 11th November 1964.

NIER, February 1968, and earlier issues.

F. W. Paish and J. Hennessy, 'Policy for Incomes?', Hobart Paper No. 29 (3rd edition), 1967.

A. W. Phillips, 'The Relation between Unemployment and the Rate of Change of Money Wage Rates in the United Kingdom 1861-1957', *Economica*, November 1958.

R. Stone, 'Private saving in Britain, Past, Present and Future', *MS*, May 1964.

House of Commons, *Government Statistical Services,* (Fourth Report from the Estimates Committee together with Minutes of Evidence, Session 1966-67), HMSO, London, 6th December 1966.

'Short-term economic forecasting in the United Kingdom', *ET*, August 1964.

2

Monetary, credit and fiscal policies

I INTRODUCTION

THE previous chapter attempts to convey an overall picture of the operation of the UK economy since the early 1950s, paying particular attention to fluctuations in economic activity, the behaviour of prices and economic growth. This chapter concentrates on a narrower area, the monetary, credit and fiscal policies of the authorities, that is, the UK government and the Bank of England.

The term policy implies the existence of both goals and a strategy or instruments to achieve them. The official policy goals most frequently cited in the UK since the Second World War are full employment, price stability, economic growth, fixed exchange rates and a 'satisfactory' balance of payments position.[1] But in addition to this there have been many other official goals, such as 'free' health, welfare and education services and, at least until recently, a strong defence posture at home and abroad.

Once a set of goals is chosen a host of questions arise. Are they mutually compatible within the particular economic system, given the usual policy instruments at the disposal of the authorities? If they are not, which goals should be sacrificed or modified? Are there alternative policy instruments that might be used to achieve one or more of the policy goals? Have the authorities, or for that matter any one else, the necessary knowledge about the relationships between instruments and goals? Do they know exactly when and by how much to manipulate the policy instruments or even how many instruments they need?

Implicit in the foregoing discussion of goals and instruments are questions concerning both value judgments and how an economic system works. Both of these questions are recurring themes in this chapter. Section II looks briefly at the theoretical basis of monetary and fiscal policy. Section III discusses the structure of the banking and financial system and examines some money and credit theories. The taxation system is considered in section IV. Finally, the whole policy record since the early 1950s is described and assessed in section V.

II SOME THEORETICAL BACKGROUND

II.1 Theoretical Basis of Monetary and Fiscal Policy

How do changes in the money supply or interest rates or changes in taxation and government expenditure affect the operation of an economic system? The use of monetary and fiscal policy implies some knowledge about the answers to these questions. However, the answers are highly controversial. One extreme viewpoint would argue that monetary policy is by and large ineffective and that, say, increases in the money supply and reductions in interest rates will have little or no effect as an encouragement to expenditure. Another, extreme view, but this time applied to fiscal policy, would argue that an increase in government expenditure will not stimulate an expansion of output and employment but will only substitute government expenditure for private expenditure. And, similarly, that a reduction in taxation will have no net expansionary effect on expenditure and hence output and employment.

The evidence is far from conclusive but there is a formidable body of research suggest-

---

[1] See chapter 3 for an extensive explanation and discussion of the balance of payments concept.

ing that these extreme positions are ill-founded and that both fiscal and monetary policy have an important influence on economic activity. In other words reductions in interest rates and increases in the money supply are expansionary and so also are increases in government expenditure and reductions in taxation. It is these latter views that underly the analysis of this chapter.

II.2 The Monetary-Fiscal Policy Mix

If both kinds of policy may be used to influence the economic system then the question arises what emphasis should be placed on each. Suppose it is desired to curtail the level of economic activity. One way of doing this might be to restrict the growth of the money supply. But this may tend to make money scarcer and hence more expensive and so increase interest rates. In so far as these are relevant to investment its volume may be reduced. The authorities may, however, be opposed to affecting investment adversely because they believe that its slowing down will retard economic growth. They might therefore prefer to increase taxation, especially of consumer goods, or reduce government expenditure in the expectation that these measures would reduce the level of economic activity without seriously upsetting the rate of investment. Thus the choice of policy to pursue is influenced by the side effects it might have on other goals. The value judgments of the authorities enter into the decision. In the example above they prefer to reduce consumption rather than investment because of their predilection for economic growth.

Suppose, however, that the situation is complicated by political considerations. It may be that the authorities on the whole emphasise fiscal policy, reducing taxation and increasing government expenditure when the economy is thought to need a stimulus, since these measures are considered to be popular with the electorate. On the other hand, if the economy has to be restrained it may be politically preferable to follow a restrictive monetary rather than fiscal policy. If this combination of expansionary fiscal and restrictive monetary policies was broadly pursued over a substantial period of years it would tend to raise interest rates to increasingly higher levels. Some observers have suggested that this is the kind of thing that has happened under successive governments in the UK in the post-war years. The reader will it is hoped be in a slightly better position to judge for himself as policy since the early 1950s is reviewed below.

III THE BANKING AND FINANCIAL STRUCTURE AND MONEY AND CREDIT THEORIES

III.1 The Bank of England and the Cash Base Theory

The Bank of England is the central bank of the UK; it has an overall responsibility for the management and control of the monetary and financial system and for its relations with the rest of the world. It acts as banker to the government, plays a basic role in smoothing government cash transactions, and in administering and managing the national debt, broadly speaking the debt liabilities of the state to its nationals, to its own agencies and to overseas holders. As agent of the government the Bank helps to regulate and control foreign exchange transactions and manages the Exchange Equalisation Account, which controls the official gold and foreign exchange reserves of the UK.

The Bank is divided into two parts for accounting purposes; it produces two balance sheets, one for the Issue Department and one for the Banking Department. The origin of the double balance sheet system is to be found in monetary controversies of the first half of the nineteenth century. But the two balance sheets still retain a certain, if somewhat artificial significance in that the Issue Department is classified in the national accounts of the UK as belonging to the public or government sector whilst the Banking Department is classified with the banking and financial sector. The position of the Issue Department on December 1967 is shown in Table 2.1.

TABLE 2.1

Issue Department (Selected Items) December 1967.

£ million

Liabilities			*Assets*	
Notes issued:				
	In circulation	3,160		
	To Banking Dept.	40	Government securities	3,199
		3,200		3,199

Source: BEQB

Note: The balance sheet does not exactly balance because certain subsidiary items have been omitted. This is also true of other balance sheets summarised in this chapter.

The notes in circulation are necessarily held by persons, companies and financial institutions. Notes in the Banking Department would, of course, disappear from the accounts if the two balance sheets were amalgamated. The assets of the Issue Department are almost entirely government securities and any increase in the note issue implies an equal addition to holdings of government securities. In other words, when the Issue Department issues additional notes it obtains interest earning government securities in exchange. Indeed the note issue may be looked upon as a gift which helps to finance the expenditure of the ˙Exchequer.

The assets of the Issue Department are a means of helping the government to organise its finances in another way. The government is continuously concerned with the issue and redemption of its debt; it may need to borrow new funds or pay off maturing obligations. The government, and indeed the Bank of England also, is generally anxious to avoid large transactions, perhaps involving hundreds of millions of pounds, that might temporarily upset the securities market. They do this by arranging for the Issue Department to purchase new issues of securities that are not taken up by the public on the day of issue. Subsequently the Issue Department gradually sells to the public the stock it took up. Similarly, the Issue Department purchases stocks nearing redemption, avoiding large cash payments to the public when the actual redemption dates arrive. The Issue Department may in fact be in the market as a buyer or seller of government securities or both almost continuously. That is, it engages extensively in open market operations.

The balance sheet of the Banking Department is shown in Table 2.2.

TABLE 2.2

Banking Department (Selected Items) December 1967.

£ million

Liabilities		*Assets*	
Deposits:			
Public	12	Government securities	454
Bankers	259	Discounts and advances	97
Other accounts	118	Other securities	29
Special deposits	213	Notes and coin	41
	602		621

Source: BEQB.

Public deposits are all government balances. They include those of the Exchequer, the Paymaster General, the Post Office and Trustee Savings Banks, the National Debt Commissioners, Dividend Accounts, and balances of the Revenue departments. The total amount involved is relatively small by comparison with bankers' deposits despite the enormous scale of government transactions. The main reason for this is that the government attempts to keep these balances as low as possible, consistently with carrying out its operations. Any so-called surplus balances are used to retire government debt in an attempt to keep down costs. Net payments from the government to the community will have an immediate effect on bankers' deposits, increasing the cash holdings of the banking system. The reverse is, of course, also true and smoothing out movements of funds between public and bankers' deposits is a major preoccupation of the Bank day by day.

Bankers' deposits belong almost entirely to the clearing banks, though the total also includes deposits of the Scottish and Northern Ireland banks and deposits of accepting houses and the discount market. As bankers' deposits necessarily appear as assets in the balance sheets of these financial institutions and will therefore be discussed later, nothing more is said about them at this point.[1]

Other accounts include balances of overseas central banks and overseas governments and certain dividend accounts which are not *direct* obligations of the British government. The accounts of the Bank's remaining private customers are also included here. These accounts are not without importance but they are not central to this chapter and so are not discussed further.

Special deposits are a relatively new category of deposit that the clearing banks and Scottish banks are from time to time obliged to transfer to the Bank as an aid to monetary policy. These deposits also necessarily appear in the balance sheets of the respective banks and for convenience their further discussion is postponed until later.[2]

Government securities introduce the assets of the Banking Department and includes Treasury bills and longer dated government securities and Ways and Means Advances to the Exchequer.[3] These advances occur if the Exchequer finds itself short of funds at the end of the day and wishes to make up its balance; the advances are generally only overnight loans, being repaid the following day.

The Banking Department through sales and purchases of government securities affects the volume of bankers' deposits and hence the cash holdings of the banking system. In general, government securities in the Banking Department can be used in much the same way as those in the Issue Department to facilitate debt management and monetary policy. However, the assets at the disposal of the Banking Department are much smaller than those available to the Issue Department.

Discounts and advances are of two types, discounts and advances to the discount houses and to the remaining private customers of the Bank. The first are by far the most important to the operation of the monetary and financial system and attention is concentrated entirely on them. They are discussed in the next section dealing with the discount houses.

Other securities and notes and coin can be dealt with briefly. Other securities are non-government securities and include bills purchased by the Bank in order to keep a watch on the quality of bills circulating in the London market. The Bank will not purchase bills of which they disapprove and this acts as a deterrent to their circulation. Other securities also include certain securities acquired by the Bank in the 1930s. Notes are the counterpart of the item in the Issue Department and some coin is held for ordinary business purposes.

Those notes and deposits of the Bank which are held by the commercial banks constitute, except for a small amount of coin, the cash base of the banking system. The London clearing banks, which account for the greater part of commercial bank activity, maintain an essentially fixed proportion of 8:100 of Bank of England notes and deposits

---

[1] See below, p. 50.
[2] See below, pp. 52-4.
[3] See below, p. 48 for a definition of 'bills'.

C

in relation to their own deposits. Now if the clearing banks were the only holders of Bank of England notes and deposits it would be very easy to see how a cash base theory of the volume of bank deposits might arise. For, given this fixed proportion or fixed cash ratio as it is generally called, all that the Bank of England would have to do to determine the volume of bank deposits would be to vary the amount of its own deposits and notes outstanding.[1] However, it is not so simple either in theory or practice.

For one thing Bank notes are held by the general public and other institutions besides the clearing banks. Thus if the Bank increases the cash base the non-clearing bank holders might absorb the whole increase, and hence there would be no increase in clearing bank deposits. The simple cash base theory outlined above would no longer hold. But if the non-clearing bank holders also held Bank notes in a fixed proportion to their deposits with the clearing banks the cash base theory would hold once more, though in a slightly more complicated form. For every change in the cash base would be distributed between the clearing banks and other holders in such a way as to preserve a fixed ratio between the cash base and the money supply, defined to include clearing bank deposits and notes held by others.[2]

However, the facts also do not support this version of the cash base theory. The non-clearing bank holders of Bank of England notes do not hold them in a fixed proportion to their deposits with the clearing banks. Furthermore, it is not at all clear that the Bank of England determines the amount of its notes and deposits outstanding in the way required by the theory. Alternative theories, based on the clearing banks' liquid assets and their liquid assets ratio, have been much more in vogue in recent years. But before considering these it is useful to look at the activities of the discount houses.

III.2 Discount Houses

The discount houses are a special type of financial institution which borrow a substantial proportion of their funds from the clearing banks and other institutional lenders. Most of these funds are at call or short notice in the sense that these lenders may demand their repayment immediately or subject to very short notice. The discount houses use these borrowed funds to acquire short-dated assets such as Treasury bills, commercial bills and other short-dated government securities.[3] If the clearing banks or other lenders demand repayment of their loans by the discount houses and cannot borrow elsewhere or otherwise obtain funds they turn to the Bank of England which makes funds available to them against suitable collateral. The discount houses are the only financial institutions which have access to the Bank in this way. It is in this sense and by this means that the Bank acts as lender of last resort to the monetary and financial system.

When the Bank lends in this way to the discount houses it usually charges at or above

---

[1]   The Bank could do this in a number of ways, the most important being open-market operations. See p. 46.

[2]   A little arithmetic may help to clarify this. Suppose deposits of the clearing banks equal 100 and they hold 8 Bank of England notes and deposits, whilst other holders have 2 Bank notes and the 100 clearing bank deposits. Thus the money supply, Bank notes and deposits held by other holders totals 102 and the cash base is 10. If the Bank increases the cash base to 15 the money supply must increase to 153, made up of 150 deposits and 3 Bank notes, with the clearing banks holding 12 of the cash base. The ratio 10:102 is the same as 15:153.

[3]   A 'bill' in the sense used here is a piece of paper which is evidence of indebtedness on the part of the person or body on whom it is drawn. The bill is said to be 'discounted' when it is purchased at a price below its value on maturity. Hence Treasury bills are evidence of indebtedness of the Treasury. These bills have usually ninety days to run to maturity and might be acquired by the discount houses at, say, £98 10s. 0d. per £100 which would represent a discount of 6 per cent on the value at maturity.

a rate called Bank rate.[1] This rate is often described as a *penal* rate as it is above the rates ruling in the market for the Treasury bills and commercial bills. It is then argued that if the discount houses are borrowing at Bank rate they are therefore making losses and will hasten to pay off their debts to the Bank. However, there have been periods when short-dated government securities of the kind held by the discount houses have yielded more than Bank rate. Thus the penal rate argument would not be valid for borrowings from the Bank against these securities. Moreover, it is conceivable that if the discount houses were expecting a reduction in interest rates they might be prepared to borrow for a time at the so called penal rates to take advantage of capital appreciation and high running yields on some or all of their asset holdings. The Bank, of course, has the option which it may or may not choose to use to charge more than Bank rate or to raise it.

The discount houses occupy a very special position in the market for Treasury bills. Each week as the Treasury issues new bills the discount houses tender as a syndicate at a single rate for the whole issue, except that individual houses may tender for some bills at rates above the syndicated rate. The joint bid of the discount houses is usually lower than outside bids. These higher bids are satisfied first and so the discount houses obtain the residual amount on offer.

The syndicated bid procedure has the merit from the point of view of the Treasury that it guarantees them the funds they need and probably helps to stabilise Treasury bill and other short-term rates. However, from another point of view the procedure is an odd one and perhaps has the danger of hiding what is really happening.

In the final analysis the discount houses are able to tender for the whole issue of Treasury bills because, as already explained, the Bank stands behind them. Moreover, they would presumably become concerned if they could only cover the tender over a sustained period by borrowing at Bank rate. To avoid this the Bank may have to enter the open-market and make purchases of securities which directly or indirectly will put funds at the disposal of the discount houses and allow them to take up Treasury bills.[2] But this is tantamount to the Bank lending directly to the Treasury, a potentially highly inflationary procedure.

III.3 The Clearing Banks

The London clearing banks are so named because they are all members of the London Bankers' Clearing House, the place where their representatives meet to settle interbank indebtedness. Eleven clearing banks may be identified, though the individual identities of most of them may disappear under the influence of the mergers early in 1968. Between them the clearing banks dominate the ordinary commercial banking business in England and Wales. However, in the last ten years or so the non-clearing banks have expanded rapidly and are now of considerable importance. Their activities are briefly touched on in the next section.

Deposits are the main liabilities of the clearing banks and may be seen, together with other items of the balance sheet for December 1967 in Table 2.3 (page 50). Gross deposits are made up of current, deposit and other accounts, and are practically all domestic liabilities. Current accounts or demand deposits are withdrawable on demand and transferable by cheque; they are the most important means of payment in the economy. Demand deposits do not generally earn an explicit rate of interest though the

---

[1] Bank rate is a key rate in the whole structure of interest rates in the UK. When it moves many other rates move. This is especially true of rates on bank deposits and rates in the London money markets.

   In June 1966 the Bank introduced an important modification in its lending practices. Previously loans to the market had been for a minimum period, usually of seven days. It is now prepared to lend overnight and may charge *less than* Bank rate, 'probably at a rate broadly reflecting the level of overnight rates in the market'. *BEQB,* September 1966, Vol. VI, No. 3, pp. 215-16.

[2] Alternatively the Bank might make use of one variant of its new procedure and lend overnight for a period to the discount houses at market rates.

size of the credit balance may be taken into consideration in determining the charge for managing the account. Deposit accounts or time deposits do earn interest and are subject to notice of withdrawal--at present seven days--and are not ordinarily transferable by cheque. However, these conditions can be waived, though usually with some loss of interest. Other accounts include credit items in course of transmission, contingency reserves and other internal accounts of the banks.

Coin, notes and balances with the Bank of England have already been encountered. The notes and coin are used by the banks for their day-to-day business and balances with the Bank to settle inter-bank indebtedness and for making payments to the authorities.

TABLE 2.3

London Clearing Banks (selected Items). 15 December 1967. £ million.

(i) *LIABILITIES*

Gross Deposits:

Current accounts		5,298
Deposit accounts		3,963
Other accounts		1,001
	TOTAL	10,262

(ii) *ASSETS*

Coin, notes and balances with Bank of England	822	
Money at call and short notice	1,366	
Treasury bills	450	
Other bills	489	
Total liquid assets		3,127
Investments		1,405
Advances to customers and other accounts		4,862
Special deposits with Bank of England		203
	TOTAL	9,597

Source: BEQB.

If for some reason a bank, or the banks as a whole, find that their cash holdings are tending to fall below 8 per cent of deposits something must be done to rectify the position. It may be possible for the individual bank to sell or exchange some of its assets for cash, perhaps by recalling some of its money at call and short notice from the discount market, which, as already explained may have to turn to the Bank of England. This will generally happen if the banks as a whole are short of cash. If the Bank does not wish to lend at Bank rate, perhaps because it is anxious to keep interest rates from rising, then it will normally enter the open market and purchase securities at market rates, paying for them with cheques drawn on the Bank and so relieving the cash shortage. However, if the Bank wishes to see some upward pressure on interest rates it will wait for the discount houses to come to the Bank and only make cash available at Bank rate or possibly even above.

Recalling money at call and short notice from the discount houses is not the only way the banks may attempt to restore their cash ratio. For one thing, as is explained below some of the money at call and short notice is a liability of financial institutions other than the discount market. But apart from this the banks may attempt to sell some of their investments and negotiate repayment of advances that they themselves have made to their customers. But by and large the banks as a whole can succeed in selling investments and having advances repaid only by engineering a reduction in their deposits. For if purchases by the authorities are ruled out then the non-bank private sector can only acquire bank assets or reduce its indebtedness to the banks by exchanging bank deposits for investments and advances.[1] Once deposits are reduced the necessary cash holdings to satisfy the cash ratio are also reduced. Thus the banks may restore their cash ratio in a variety of ways, the exact pattern of events depending to a large degree on the policy followed by the authorities. In the end it is they who determine the ease or difficulty of the adjustment process.

Money at call and short notice is made up of two main parts. The most important is loans to the discount houses, but of growing importance in recent years have been loans, for periods up to one month, to members of the stock exchange, with easily marketable stocks and shares being used as collateral, and loans to bullion brokers, and to money markets in other centres. Balances in sterling and in certain foreign currencies with other banks in the UK and overseas are also counted as money at call and short notice.

The clearing banks buy their Treasury bills in the market and do not bid for bills at the weekly tender, at least not for themselves, though they may do so on behalf of their customers. Bills bought on their own account by the clearing banks are usually held to maturity, though they are, on occasion, sold to the Bank if the latter is looking for maturities that are no longer held by the discount houses. The purchase of bills by the Bank from the clearing banks is one of the ways by which the Bank may relieve pressure on the discount houses and obviate their need to borrow at Bank rate or above. This is described as 'indirect help' to the discount houses as opposed to 'direct help' by means of purchases from the houses themselves. From the point of view of monetary management the Treasury bill is the most important instrument in the London money market.

Other bills are a composite item that includes commercial bills drawn on UK residents, various other bills such as Treasury bills of Commonwealth and foreign governments and, since February 1961, certain export credits which the banks may re-finance or obtain funds for from the Bank. These export credits arise from the banks' financing of exports on a medium-term lending basis and, in the first instance, generally run for some three to five years and are payable by instalments. The Bank, as an encouragement to the granting of finance for exports, is willing to refinance these credits when they have no more than eighteen months to go to final repayment. This clearly makes them a highly liquid asset from the point of view of the banks and the Bank specifically gave them permission to include these re-financeable export credits as part of their liquid assets. The significance of this will become clear shortly.

Investments consist of securities of the British government, Commonwealth governments, local authorities and mostly fixed interest securities of public companies. The British government securities are the most important and are so arranged that some of them mature each year and the major proportion of them within ten years. These securities give the banks additional flexibility in meeting demands for private credit because they are highly marketable and those close to maturity can generally be disposed of without serious capital loss. The banks do not aim, at any rate in the short run, at a specific ratio of investments to deposits.

Advances are of two main types, loans and overdrafts. With the loan the customer's account is credited with the amount whereas the overdraft is literally an overdrawing of a current account which is debited accordingly. Advances are generally assumed to be the most lucrative of the banks' assets. The rates payable are Bank rate, with a minimum of 4 per cent, for the nationalised industries, and for most other customers one per cent above Bank rate with a minimum of 5 per cent. As in the case of investments the banks do not maintain a fixed ratio of advances to deposits, though in ordinary circumstances there is probably some ratio around 55 per cent that they would not wish to exceed.[2]

---

[1] Strictly speaking, the private sector could purchase bank assets with notes. But this possibility is quantitatively unimportant and has been ignored in the text.
[2] The ratio of the clearing banks for 1967 averaged 48.4 per cent and under present credit restrictions they are not free to approach a 55 per cent ratio.

The authorities have shown a recurring interest in advances ever since the outbreak of the Second World War and, as will be seen below, on numerous occasions have requested the banks to restrict or even reduce their advances in the interest of economic policy.[1] The authorities consider advances to be particularly inflationary as they put immediate purchasing power in the hands of potential spenders. This purchasing power might not be all that important if the authorities were prepared to see interest rates rising as the banks sold securities in order to enable them to make additional advances. For the rising rates might be expected to have some, if not a complete, dampening effect on expenditure. But in fact the authorities have generally been unwilling to permit interest rates to rise as a consequence of the balance sheet adjustments of the banks. Thus the authorities' concern about advances reflects, at least in part, a preference for particular interest rate structures. However, the whole problem has been complicated by the historically low percentages advances bore to deposits for most of the post-war period and the banks' evident desire to raise them.[2]

III.4 Liquid Asset Theories and Special Deposits

From the point of view of recent theories of the money supply the most important aspect of the clearing banks' activities is the behaviour of their liquid assets and the liquid assets ratio. Their liquid assets are defined to include currency—mainly Bank of England notes— balances or deposits with the Bank, money at call and short notice—mostly but not entirely to the discount houses—Treasury bills and other bills. At present the banks are expected to maintain a *minimum* liquid assets ratio equivalent to 28 per cent of their gross deposits. When the ratio first emerged in the early 1950s it was not fixed, but in 1956 the Bank insisted on a minimum ratio of 30 per cent.[3]

By analogy with the cash base theory if there was only one kind of liquid asset supplied by, say, the Treasury and held only by the clearing banks, it would be reasonable to postulate a liquid assets theory of deposit determination. These circumstances have never existed. But there was a period after the Second World War when Treasury bills were far and away the most important component of the banks liquid assets. It was then plausible to argue that the volume of deposits was determined by the supply of Treasury bills.

The argument never appeared in this precise form. At its simplest it assumed that *all* Treasury bills were held by the Bank of England, the clearing banks and the discount houses, with the latter financing their holdings by money at call and short notice from the clearing banks. The cash holdings of the clearing banks—the notes and deposits of the Bank of England— might be thought of as being covered by Treasury bills held by the Bank. Thus on this argument any change in the supply of Treasury bills would be reflected in the liquid asset holdings of the clearing banks and, given the liquid assets ratio, would permit a multiple change in the same direction in the volume of deposits.[4]

Another version of the theory, which owes much to Professor Sayers and the Radcliffe Committee, emphasises, in addition to the role of the Treasury bill, the importance the authorities attach to maintaining short-run stability of the Treasury bill rate.[5]

---

[1] See section V of this chapter.
[2] As late as 1958 advances of the clearing banks were the equivalent of only 29 per cent of their deposits.
[3] In 1951 the Governor of the Bank of England indicated to the (clearing) banks that a liquidity ratio of from 32% to 28% would be regarded as normal but that it would be undesirable for the Ratio to be allowed to fall below 25% as an extreme limit'. From, 'Bank Liquidity in the United Kingdom', *BEQB*, December 1962, Vol. II, No. 4, p. 252.
[4] W. Manning Dacey, 'The Floating Debt Problem', *Lloyds Bank Review*, April 1956.
[5] R. S. Sayers, 'The determination of the Volume of Bank Deposits: England 1955-6', in his *Central Banking after Bagehot*, Oxford, 1957. Radcliffe Committee, *Committee on the Working of the Monetary System* (Chairman, Lord Radcliffe). See *Report*, Cmnd. 827, paras. 375 and 583-90.

Perhaps the most straightforward way to see some of the implications of this is to suppose that the authorities want to keep the rate completely stable but at the same time there occurs an increase in the supply of Treasury bills. If the discount houses buy these with additional money at call from the banks and the Treasury immediately spends the funds these will accrue as deposits to the customers of the banks. In other words the banks' deposits and their liquid assets will have increased but not, at this stage, their cash holdings. As far as liquid assets are concerned the banks are in a position to permit an expansion of their deposits. But if the 8 per cent cash ratio was exactly satisfied before the above transactions took place it will now no longer hold. The banks will have to take appropriate action. The traditional argument would be that the banks would attempt to obtain funds from the Bank via the discount houses. But if this happened interest rates would tend to rise. However, this suggestion does not make much sense as the banks are assumed above to have just extended additional call money to the discount houses. The point is that if the authorities are adamant in their determination to maintain stable rates they cannot stand idly by and allow the banks to experience any difficulties over their cash ratio. For any pressure on the cash ratios of the banks will tend to result in higher rates unless the situation is relieved by the Bank. The Bank, if it is to maintain rate stability, must provide the necessary cash thus permitting the banks to exploit the addition to their liquid assets.

In a simplified form this version of the liquid assets theory implies that if the authorities reduce the supply of Treasury bills but at the same time keep their interest rate constant, the volume of deposits will decline. The reason is that with the interest rate held constant the non-bank public hold the same amount of bills, hence leaving less for the banks to hold, and so with a fixed liquid assets ratio the banks deposits must decline. Alternatively, if the Treasury allows the interest rate to rise, but keeps the supply of bills constant, the non-bank public will demand more of the bills available, again leaving less for the banks, and once more leading to a reduction in the volume of deposits. Neither formulation of the liquid assets theory is supported by the facts, or at least not consistently so. The supply of Treasury bills has declined and the Treasury bill rate has increased without the volume of deposits decreasing.

If the volume of deposits can increase without an increase in the supply of Treasury bills and yet the banks maintain their liquid assets ratio then clearly the banks must be able to obtain other liquid assets besides Treasury bills and cash reserves. In fact, their commercial and other bill holdings and money at call and short notice have risen rapidly.

Thus these formulations of the liquid assets theory have been discredited. However, the authorities, whilst recognising that controlling the supply of Treasury bills is not a sufficient condition for controlling the volume of deposits, still give great attention to the volume of liquid assets as a whole.[1] There appears to linger in the minds of the authorities the belief that if they could effectively control the supply of liquid assets to the clearing banks they would be able to control the volume of deposits and the granting of credit by the banks. However, it will be argued below that the authorities are not prepared to accept the implications of maintaining tight control over the availability of liquid assets to the clearing banks.[2] For one of the implications would be that interest rates would have to be permitted to move more freely and this would conflict with their approach to the management of the national debt.

If these last statements are accepted then it follows that it is not the liquid assets ratio nor the cash ratio that have been of basic importance in relation to the volume of deposits, but the interest rate policy of the authorities and the factors that have influenced this policy. This, in turn, implies a much more complex approach to explaining the determination of money supply than a simple cash base or liquid assets theory, though

---

[1]   'Bank Liquidity in the United Kingdom', BEQB, December 1960, Vol. 1, No. 1, pp.248-55. See
      also the discussion of special deposits below, p. 54.
[2]   See below, pp. 87-8.

both ratios will necessarily appear in the explanation.[1]

Special deposits were defined earlier as a type of deposit that the clearing banks and Scottish banks are from time to time obliged to transfer to the Bank as an aid to monetary policy. The banks cannot draw cheques on special deposits or include them as part of their cash or liquid assets. The Bank first called for special deposits in April 1960. The calls are expressed as a percentage of total deposits with the calls from the Scottish banks being at one half the rate of those from the clearing banks. The Bank pays interest on special deposits at approximately the current rate on the latest issue of Treasury bills. Special deposits were designed by the authorities to reduce the amount of liquid assets such as Treasury bills at the disposal of the banks. The authorities hoped that the introduction of special deposits would make it more difficult for the banks to expand their deposits and to grant additional credit to borrowers. The scheme is obviously an offspring of the liquid assets theory of deposit determination.

From what was said above about these theories it will come as no surprise to find that it is concluded here that special deposits are a rather ineffective policy instrument. This can perhaps be seen as follows. Special deposits are really a compulsory loan by the banks to the authorities made in such a way that it is not allowed to reduce the cash holdings of the banks. For if the loan were allowed to reduce their cash holdings there would have to be a fall in the volume of deposits and an increase in interest rates. The authorities might like the first but generally do not want the second, though there have been times when interest rates have risen simultaneously with, but not primarily because of, calls for special deposits. Thus when a call for special deposits is made the banks must find the cash for payment by selling bills and/or securities directly or indirectly to the authorities. It will probably be in the banks' interest to sell securities and affect their liquid assets as little as possible. In so far as they feel obliged to sell liquid assets they can almost certainly manage to replace these fairly quickly. There is no reason to believe that special deposits which have no effect on the volume of the banks' deposits will reduce advances. On the contrary, special deposits may encourage an increase, if they earn less than the assets they replace and the banks are anxious to make good the difference by acquiring larger holdings of their most lucrative assets. The fact that the authorities have now introduced direct quantitative control of advances would seem to bear out the previous argument, leaving special deposits as a form of compulsory and relatively cheap lending to the authorities.[2]

III.5 Other Banks and the Money Supply

Until recently it has been common when discussing the money supply to concentrate on the deposits of the clearing banks, neglecting various other banks, including the Scottish and Northern Ireland banks, the accepting houses and overseas banks.

It was possible to make a case for this procedure as the deposits of the clearing banks dwarfed those of the other banks. Furthermore, the growth of the Scottish and Northern Ireland banks tended to be similar to that of the clearing banks. This feature still holds, and for that reason they are only treated incidentally to the main discussion here. But since about 1957-58, when exchange control restrictions were substantially relaxed and funds could move more freely between international financial centres, the accepting houses and overseas banks have expanded far more rapidly than the clearing banks and can no longer be neglected in discussions of the money supply.

The term accepting house arose because of the important role the houses played and still play in 'accepting' bills of exchange, the commercial or financial bill already encountered in the discussion of the discount houses and the clearing banks. A bill is accepted by signing it and in so doing the acceptor becomes liable for payment of the bill on

---

[1]   For a study along these lines, see W. E. Norton, 'An Econometric study of the United Kingdom Monetary Sector 1955-66', unpublished Ph.D. thesis, *University of Manchester,* December 1967.

[2]   See below, p. 83. Norton, p.277, concludes that 'an increase in special deposits is expected to have no significant effect on advances, the money stock or expenditures'.

maturity. The accepting houses accept bills on behalf of clients and in this way earn
commissions.

Accepting houses are also known as merchant banks. The name correctly implies that
some of these houses carry on both a merchanting and banking business. Indeed the title
suggests their origin, for the banking side of their activities generally emerged as a consequence of their business as merchants, particularly in overseas trade. Even today some
merchant banks maintain both a merchanting and a banking business. One owns a refinery,
others are concerned with the marketing and production of timber, trading in rubber and
coffee and in the export trade. A number are active in the gold and silver bullion markets
and the foreign exchange market, engage in making new issues of both domestic and overseas securities, advise and manage investments on behalf of clients and act as trustees. In
fact, the activities of the merchant banks are excitingly diverse.

There are over a hundred overseas and foreign banks, the major part of whose business
is carried on overseas, but at the same time they pursue an active banking business in
London. It is the latter that is of interest here.

In the ten years since 1957 the total deposits of the accepting houses and overseas
banks have grown from some £850 million to around £9,000 million. This is an extra-
ordinary rate of growth, but it is to some extent misleading. For the figures include a
substantial amount of inter-bank lending and a large amount of deposits of overseas
residents which cannot be considered as part of the domestic money supply. If these
categories are deducted the £9,000 million would be reduced to less than £2,000 million,
which compares with the £9,400 million of net deposits of the clearing banks.

These banks are extremely active in what are called the new money markets which in
recent years have developed in London and are distinct from the traditional money
market of the discount houses, though a number of these are involved in the new markets
through subsidiaries and by other means. The inter-bank money market refers to the
practice where the banks make sterling deposits with or grant loans to one another. The
deposits are usually for very short periods and may enable the participating banks to
adjust their liquidity positions without recourse to the discount houses. The banks are
also active in the local authority temporary money market, that is, the lending and
channelling of funds for periods of as little as seven days and as long as twelve months to
local authorities. A further market in which they are active is foreign currency deposits,
often called the Euro-dollar market, since many of the depositors are located in Western
Europe and the deposits are denominated in United States dollars.[1]

The accepting houses and overseas banks (and also the Scottish and Northern Ireland
banks) are not at the moment requested to maintain cash and liquid asset ratios as are the
clearing banks. [2]

III.6 Money versus 'General Liquidity'

The discussion so far indicates that the term 'money' is somewhat ambiguous. Traditionally one of the major attributes of money is the means of payment function. But if this
criterion is applied to British conditions then deposit accounts that ordinarily require
notice of withdrawal and cannot be transferred by cheque should be excluded from the

[1]   For further information on these money markets, see,'UK Banks' External Liabilities and Claims
      in Foreign Currencies', *BEQB*, June 1964, Vol. 4, No. 2 pp 100-08, and Overseas and Foreign Banks in
      London: 1962-68 *ibid*, June 1968, Vol. 8, No. 2 pp 156-65, also, W. M. Clarke, 'The City in the World
      Economy', *Institute of Economic Affairs*, 1965, and 'London's New Markets for Money', *Midland Bank
      Review*, August, 1966.
[2]   However, the Bank of England has recently announced a 'cash deposits' scheme for these institutions.
      (cf. 'Control of Bank Lending: the Cash Deposits Scheme', BEQB, June1968, Vol.8, No. 2 pp
      166-170.) Broadly speaking it allows the Bank to call for, as a further instrument of credit control,
      cash deposits from them. On first examination this new instrument promises to be just as ineffectual
      as the analogous special deposits one, unless the Bank implements it in such a way as to reduce the
      cash base of the total banking system. But if the Bank does this then the brunt of the adjustment will
      fall on the clearing banks and not on the banks which are party to the new scheme. The Bank can
      hardly intend that it should operate in this way.

money stock. Nevertheless, the previous discussion followed the usual British practice of including deposit accounts. But if deposit accounts are included then why not building society deposits and shares, Post Office deposits and so on?

This is essentially the approach of the Radcliffe Committee. They start with the common definition of money used in Britain but proceed to argue in favour of a broader concept of 'liquidity'. 'It is the whole liquidity position that is relevant to spending decisions, and our interest in the supply of money is due to its significance in the whole liquidity picture.'[1] By 'liquidity picture' they appear to have had in mind a whole set of financial institutions, their assets and liabilities, trade and other types of credit and 'the ease or difficulty encountered by spenders in their efforts to raise money for the purpose of spending on goods and services'.[2]

The Radcliffe Committee, in hearing evidence about the operations and activities of financial institutions and whilst recognising the great differences between these, were impressed 'not by these differences but by the fact that the market for credit is a single market'.[3] By this they meant that the same financial institution might supply both short- and longer-term finance and that borrowers were prepared, if one source of finance was curtailed or unavailable, to switch to another. It was thus the fact of highly developed money and capital markets and the way they operated that greatly influenced the Committee in emphasing the need to control 'the liquidity position of the system as a whole'.[4] They were sceptical about the emphasis and importance traditionally attached to control of the money supply.

For the Committee monetary policy in general was not very important. 'We envisage', they wrote, 'the use of monetary measures as not in ordinary times playing other than a subordinate part in guiding the development of the economy'.[5] They felt, however, that it might have a role in times of emergency. By monetary measures they had mainly in mind control of bank advances, capital issues and consumer credit. They rejected from among such measures 'any restriction of "the supply of money"'.[6] They believed that controlling the forms of credit mentioned would have quick effects because they 'are the most important and efficient sources of credit for those wishing to raise additional credit'.[7] They recognised that these controls had disadvantages: control of advances might encourage the development of rival institutions; hire purchase controls had 'severe directional effects which are potentially harmful to economic progress';[8] and quantitative control of capital issues would be almost bound to be arbitrary in its incidence. For reasons such as these they felt that these controls should not be resorted to in ordinary times.

The Radcliffe Committee, in drawing attention to the concept of 'liquidity' and the significance of financial institutions other than the banks for monetary policy, were following in the footsteps of two American economists, J. G. Gurley and E. S. Shaw.[9] But the latter never went as far as the Radcliffe Committee in playing down the importance of the money stock and its control. Gurley and Shaw thought that monetary policy, directed primarily towards affecting the banks, might be less effective because of the

---

[1] *Report*, p. 132, par. 389.
[2] *Ibid.*
[3] *Ibid.*, p. 142, par. 125.
[4] *Ibid.*
[5] *Ibid.*, p. 182, par. 511.
[6] *Ibid.*, p. 187, par. 524
[7] *Ibid.*, par. 525.
[8] *Ibid.*, p. 183, par. 513.
[9] 'Financial Aspects of Economic Development', *American Economic Review,* September 1955; 'Financial Intermediaries and the Saving-Investment Process', *Journal of Finance,* May 1956; 'The Growth of Debt and Money in the United States, 1800-1950: A suggested Interpretation', *Review of Economics and Statistics,* August 1957; and *Money in a Theory of Finance,* Washington, 1960.

lending and borrowing activities of other financial institutions, but they certainly did not dismiss it.[1]

This whole area remains extremely controversial. However, the extreme position of the Radcliffe Committee which suggests that there is no stable or systematic link between money and income is not generally accepted by United States economists and is perhaps becoming less widely held in this country[2] The corollary is, of course, that the money supply does matter in relation to income and economic activity, though this does not imply that income is a constant multiple of the money stock.[3] On the other hand it must not be inferred that the position taken here is discounting the importance of non-bank financial institutions for monetary policy. Their importance can, in fact, be accepted without at the same time understating the significance of the money stock. It is this middle position which is taken in this chapter.

III.7 Finance Houses

A finance house is an institution which specialises in the financing of hire purchase and other instalment credit. There are hundreds of companies involved in this business but the bulk of it is carried on by about twenty of the large firms. Many of them are subsidiaries of the clearing and other banks. Hire purchase debt generally takes the form of a down-payment by the purchaser with the rest of the debt being paid off by instalments over a specified period. The period varies with the type of product and may be as little as six months for some household goods or as much as five years for industrial machinery; the period for cars—the most important type of hire purchase debt—may be up to three years. The finance houses attempt to organise their contracts so that the debt outstanding at any time on the hire purchase transaction is less than the value of the product being acquired; this gives them some security and indicates why they concentrate on financing the purchase of durable or semi-durable goods rather than perishable goods. In practice hire purchase debt is frequently paid-off well in advance of the terminal period. This is important in assessing the liquidity of finance houses' assets.

Deposits are the single most important liability of the finance houses. It is only since the early 1950s that they have come to rely on deposits as a major source of funds for their activities. They were forced in this direction by the recurrent restrictions on bank advances and the restraints imposed on capital issues.[4] Deposits are of two main kinds; fixed term deposits, usually for three or six months, and deposits subject to notice of withdrawal, again normally three to six months. Deposits may, however, be for as long as twelve months. The deposits earn interest which ranges upwards from Bank rate; there is no inflexible link with Bank rate, as in the case of the clearing banks, and the rates paid are substantially in excess of those paid by the latter. The chief depositors are industrial and commercial companies, banks and overseas residents. Current accounts are not unknown amongst the finance houses but do not appear to be a significant part of their business. Banks provide most of the remaining funds to the finance houses by means of discounting bills and by advances. Capital and reserves are also important.

---

[1] It is difficult to do justice to the views of the Radcliffe Committee, as the degree of scepticism they showed towards the money supply varies in different parts of the Report. See, for instance, pp. 132-35, p. 179, pp. 182-83 and p. 187.

[2] The Radcliffe Committee wrote, 'In a highly developed financial system the theoretical difficulties of identifying "the supply of money" cannot lightly be swept aside. Even when they are disregarded, all the haziness of the connection between the supply of money and the level of demand remains: the haziness that lies in the impossibility of limiting the velocity of circulation'. p. 187, par. 523.

[3] The distinction being made in the text is between the *variability* and *instability* of the income velocity of circulation of money, where this is defined as income divided by the money stock. Velocity in this sense may and does vary in response to changes in interest rates and other variables. But this does not make velocity unstable. In principle and, indeed, in fact the variability of velocity can be explained to a substantial degree. Numerous studies of the demand for money both in the United States and this country support this assertion.

[4] See section V of this chapter.

Hire purchase outstanding usually accounts for some 80 per cent of their assets. Not all the hire purchase outstanding is owed directly to the finance houses; part of it arises from the purchase by the latter of debt from retailers and is known as 'block discounts'. Retailers do of course retain some hire purchase debt, but the finance houses own the bulk of it. Their next most important asset is advances and loans. These include loans to garages to finance stocks of vehicles, to property companies and short-term loans to industrial and commercial companies. Very few assets are held in liquid form; the houses rely on their ability to attract additional deposits, on their borrowing powers and on the speedy repayment of their assets.

The finance houses, as already mentioned, have been subjected to severe restrictions in raising funds for their business. But their activities have also been greatly affected by controls over the terms on which they are allowed to trade. The government has from time to time stipulated, as an instrument of economic policy, the minimum down-payments that must be made on different products and the maximum repayment periods.[1] There is evidence that controlling down-payments and repayment periods has, at least, a strong initial impact on hire purchase business and consequently on demand for consumer durables. The total effect on demand is less certain as consumers may transfer, at any rate, some part of their frustrated down-payments and instalments to the purchase of other goods. It is evident that hire-purchase controls are highly discriminatory both as regards products and borrowers. The consumer durable industries, especially the car industry, are seriously affected in organising their production and sales by the frequent changes in the controls. The borrowers most affected are those unable to tap alternative sources of credit. From the point of view of credit control this is, of course, an advantage, though it has the unfortunate implication that it gives the authorities a vested interest in the perpetuation of imperfections in the capital market.

III.8 Building Societies

Building societies are mutual or non-profit making bodies which specialise in the provision of finance for the purchase of both new and second hand houses. There are some six hundred building societies, just about one quarter of the number some seventy years ago, together with a network of branches. They cater for millions of customers both as lenders and borrowers.

Over 90 per cent of the liabilities of building societies are shares and deposits. Both are essentially deposits, so that the term share is something of a misnomer. However, the shareholder is a member of the society whereas the depositor is not, and the latter has a prior right of liquidation over the shareholder. Deposits earn a slightly lower rate of interest than shares. Shares and deposits are subject to notice of withdrawal, though in practice both are paid on demand or on very short notice. The interest rates on shares and deposits are quoted net of income tax which is paid by the societies at an average or composite rate and is less than the standard rate of tax. In May 1968 the interest rates recommended by the Building Societies Association were 4½ per cent on paid-up shares and 4¼ per cent on deposits.

Mortgages usually account for over 80 per cent of the assets of building societies and are predominantly for private house purchase. Most mortgages are for between twenty and thirty years with continuous repayment by instalments. The average life is about ten years, making the assets of building societies much shorter than might appear. The recommended interest rate on mortgages was 7⅝ per cent in May 1968. But this is the gross rate as these interest payments are chargeable against income tax assessments.

All other assets, except such things as premises, are classified as liquid assets by the societies. Both the type of asset and the maturity distribution are regulated by statute. At the end of 1967 the actual liquid assets ratio was 17.9 per cent of total assets; the

---

[1] See, section V below.

ratio itself is not directly under statutory control. Cash holdings are relatively small and seasonally vary substantially.

The building societies dominate the market providing finance for house purchase. The finance they provide is therefore relevant, directly and indirectly, to the activity of the house building industry. The societies cannot for long expand the supply of finance to borrowers unless there is a corresponding net inflow of funds from new shares and deposits; otherwise they would deplete their liquid assets and in time risk upsetting public confidence in their management. The interest rates the societies pay and the relationship they bear to competing rates would appear to be a major determinant of the net inflow of funds to the societies.

If Bank rate is taken as a rough measure of competing rates it is found that by and large the *smaller* the differential between Bank rate and the rates on society liabilities the larger the net inflow of funds, and vice versa. In fact, the societies do not change their rates with every change in Bank rate; they prefer relative stability in their rates. From the point of view of effectiveness of monetary policy this may be rather important. For instance, if Bank rate is raised as part of a restrictive policy measure and the societies do not raise their share and deposit rates they will probably soon have to curtail the supply of advances, which will presumably in time tend to depress house building activity, thereby supporting the generally restrictive measures of the authorities. Thus, given the behaviour of the building societies, the effectiveness of an increase in Bank rate in curtailing credit for house purchase depends crucially on its timing. If however it is desired to insulate house purchase and house building from the effects of generally restrictive economic policy, then the reactions of the building societies are not, on the face of it, so helpful. The question of how this insulation might be achieved and the economic, political and social consequences of attempting to do so, have not received adequate attention.

III.9 Other Financial Institutions

The United Kingdom is particularly rich in the variety and number of its financial institutions. The term 'rich' is used advisedly. For financial institutions that are able to mediate freely between borrowers and lenders help to make more efficient the allocation of scarce resources. 'Improvements in their efficiency and the development of new financial intermediaries are analogous to productivity increases and innovations in industry.[1] However, limitations on space prevent more than a brief mention of some of the remaining major financial institutions.

Post Office Savings and Trustee Savings Banks

The Post Office savings bank and Trustee savings banks offer a range of facilities, many of them similar, to depositors. Both of them accept deposits which earn interest at 2½ per cent per year; the first £15 of interest is free of income tax. Depositors with at least £50 in the 2½ per cent account may also hold deposits in investment type accounts on which higher rates of interest are paid. In 1965 the Trustee savings banks were given power to provide current accounts with chequing facilities and the Post Office is preparing a 'new' system for transmitting payments, based on the continental giros, which take their name from the idea of funds 'gyrating' within the system.

The funds on deposit at 2½ per cent are paid directly to the National Debt Commissioners, an official body with certain responsibilities for the national debt, who invest them in government securities. Both the Post Office and the Trustee savings banks have slightly more freedom in employing the funds obtained through their investment accounts. As well as investing directly in government securities they lend to local authorities. Thus

---

[1] N. J. Gibson, 'Financial Intermediaries and Monetary Policy', Hobart Paper 39, Institute of Economic Affairs, 1967, p. 12.

the Post Office and the savings banks are channels by which funds flow directly to central and local government.

Insurance Companies

There are over five hundred insurance companies engaged in business in the UK. But far the greater part of the business is carried on by those members of the British Insurance Association, some two hundred and sixty in number, which have their head offices in the UK. The discussion below concentrates on these.

Insurance falls into two main categories, life insurance, and a catch all, general insurance, which includes fire, marine, motor and other accident insurance. Life insurance for the most part gives rise to long-term liabilities which the companies must be in a position to meet. This gives them an interest in long-term investments and in assets that may be expected to increase in capital value over the years. General insurance, on the other hand, is carried on much more on a year-to-year basis, ideally with the premiums for the year being sufficient to cover the risks underwritten and to allow for expenses and the accumulation of limited reserves. So the disposition of funds arising from general insurance is largely governed by short-term considerations; assets must be quickly realisable without undue fear of capital loss.

The insurance companies, with total investments at the end of 1966 of £10,600 million, are of great importance in the UK's capital markets. They are large holders of both government and company securities.

Investment Trusts

Investment trusts are limited companies which specialise in the investment of funds provided by their shareholders or borrowed from debenture holders or other lenders. Despite the term 'trust' they do not operate under trust deeds, which specify the terms and conditions governing the management of the investment funds. In addition to investment trusts there are private investment companies and investment holding companies which often perform similar functions. But these are not considered to be investment trusts in the sense used here and are not discussed in this chapter. Attention is concentrated on the group of nearly three hundred investment trusts that currently make returns to the Bank of England.

Investment trusts expand by raising funds from new capital issues and by retaining some of the income and capital profits from previous investments. But once again it is the asset side of the balance sheets that is of chief interest. At the end of 1967 the total market value of assets of investment trusts making returns to the Bank of England were £3,970 million. Nearly all of this was invested in company securities, practically all ordinary shares. Over a third of the company securities were those of overseas companies.

This extremely heavy concentration of investments in ordinary shares is a post-war phenomenon. Before the war investment trusts had substantial holdings of fixed interest securities. But the fear of inflation eroding the real value of fixed interest investments has encouraged the investment trusts to rearrange drastically the distribution of their assets. The size of the investment trusts makes them important operators in the ordinary share market. They also fulfil an important function in helping to finance small companies by holding their unquoted securities. Their freedom to invest overseas has been seriously affected by government restrictions and tax measures.

Unit Trusts

Unit trusts perform a similar function to investment trusts. But unlike the latter they do operate under trust deeds and have trustees, often a bank or insurance company. The unit trusts are authorised by the Board of Trade and are run by managers who are quite distinct from the trustees. Some one hundred and fifty-six unit trusts made returns to the Bank of England at the end of 1967 and the number continues to grow; in 1960 the figure was fifty-one.

Unit trusts do not issue share capital and are not limited companies but they issue units which give the owners the right to participate in the beneficial ownership of the trusts' assets. The units are highly marketable as they can always be bought from or sold to the managers at prices which reflect the market value of the underlying assets. As more units are demanded the managers provide more; for this reason they are sometimes called 'open-end' trusts as opposed to 'closed-end' trusts, such as the investment trusts which do not expand in this way.

Like the investment trusts the assets of the unit trusts are almost entirely company securities, made up of ordinary shares. But in contrast with the investment trusts over 90 per cent of the assets are domestic and less than 10 per cent overseas. At the end of 1967 the total assets of the unit trusts were £790 million.

The Stock Exchange

The stock exchange provides a market for variable price securities, both government and company securities. Without this market where securities may readily be bought and sold the whole business of raising funds through outside sources would tend to be more expensive and less efficient. The London Stock Exchange is by far the most important in the UK and is the one of primary interest here. However, most of the major cities have stock exchanges and currently a movement is afoot to integrate their activities more closely and ultimately to form a single UK stock exchange.

A feature of the stock exchange is the jobbing system. Jobbers are traders in securities; they act as principals, buying and selling on their own account and making their profits on the difference between their buying and selling prices which they generally stand ready to quote for the securities in which they specialise. This function can be extremely important in giving stability to the market which might otherwise be much more volatile and possibly mislead investors.

Brokers generally act as agents for customers, buying and selling on their behalf, usually but not always through jobbers.

Speculation is a term frequently associated with the stock exchange and nearly always carries overtones of abuse and criticism. To a substantial degree this reflects ignorance of the functions of the stock exchange, though this is not to imply that speculation is always necessarily beneficial. However, when it is not the so-called harmful kind, speculation may reflect some other basic restrictions of one kind or another which inhibit the efficient operation of the market. But if the speculator is doing his job, and in the long run he will go out of business if he is not, he will be helping to keep the price of shares in touch with economic realities, damping down the effects of irrelevant rumours and information; he will, in fact, be improving the economics communication system.

Traditionally the terms 'bulls' and 'bears' have been applied to particular types of speculation though they are now used more generally to refer respectively to markets tending to rise and fall in price. But traditionally a 'bull' was someone who bought securities on a rising market hoping he would be able to sell them at a profit before he had to pay for his purchase. The 'bear' sold shares that he had not got, on a falling market, in the hope that he would be able subsequently to buy and deliver them at a lower price.

An idea of the massive scale of stock exchange activities can be obtained from the figures on turnover, that is, sales and purchases. The total turnover, during 1967 was about £36,000 million. Turnover of British government securities was some £28,000 million. Clearly, the stock exchange is of major importance to the financial activities of the authorities.[1]

---

[1] The effects of taxation on the operation of the capital market are touched on below, pp. 68-9.

IV   THE TAXATION SYSTEM

IV.1   Introduction

The Treasury, in its evidence to the Radcliffe Committee, made it clear that at least since 1948 it had relied primarily on fiscal measures 'for the regulation of the pattern and total of effective demand . . . monetary measures being regarded as having only a supporting role'.[1] Thus in the official mind fiscal measures were the dominant policy instrument. The importance the authorities attach to fiscal policy represents a victory for Keynesian over classical ideas.[2] For Keynesians the state, through its taxation and expenditure, can and should influence the level, forms and rate of growth of economic activity. Monetary policy is secondary and by comparison relatively unimportant.

The classical view as implied earlier is in some ways precisely the opposite; monetary policy is of prime importance and fiscal policy is secondary, if of any significance at all.[3] This classical view had previously been stubbornly held by the Treasury between the wars and hence the use of the term 'victory' in referring to the equally stubbornly held Keynesian views of the Treasury since the Second World War. It will be evident that if the analysis and emphasis of this chapter is at all near the truth then there is an unmistakable irony in the official approach to policy over the last forty years. For, at the risk of oversimplification, between the wars the official approach neglected and perhaps misunderstood the role of fiscal policy and since the Second World War, monetary policy.[4]

IV.2   The Size of Government

It is well known that governments in this century have become, in terms of their own activities, far more important in relation to the economic life of the community. Nevertheless, it is by no means straightforward to measure the size of government economic activity relatively to the rest of the economic system. Perhaps the best that can be done is to take a number of different measures.[5]

One of these is the direct claims the government makes on the volume of goods and services available to the community in any time period. In this context 'government' includes central and local government, but excludes such things as the nationalised industries or more generally, public corporations. Table 2.4 (page   ) shows that government expenditure has claimed around 20 per cent of the gross national product for most of the 1950s and 1960s. The figure was over 23 per cent in 1952, declined to around 19 per cent in 1958, and has gradually increased once more to over 23 per cent.

---

[1] *Report*, p. 184, par. 516.
[2] J. M. Keynes, 'The General Theory of Employment, Interest and Money', 1936, and 'How to Pay for the War: A Judicial Plan for the Chancellor of the Exchequer', 1940.
[3] See above, pp. 44-5.
[4] For further discussion, see below, pp. 87-8.
[5] See A. R. Prest, 'Public Finance in Theory and Practice' (3rd edition), *Weidenfeld and Nicolson*, pp. 200-07, for a discussion of some of the issues involved.

TABLE 2.4

Central and Local Government (Including National Insurance Funds) Current and Gross Capital Expenditure on Goods and Services as a Percentage of Gross National Product at Market Prices, 1951-67.

Year	1951	1952	1953	1954	1955	1956	1957	1958	1959
%	22.1	23.3	23.0	20.9	20.0	20.1	19.7	19.3	19.6
Year	1960	1961	1962	1963	1964	1965	1966	1967	
%	19.5	19.7	20.2	20.2	20.4	20.7	21.4	23.2	

Source: NIBB, 1960 and 1967, and Preliminary Estimates of National Income and Balance of Payments 1962 to 1967, Cmnd. 3571.

Note: The figures exclude capital formation by public corporations. Its inclusion in 1967 would have increased the figure from 23 to 28 per cent.

It is arguable that the foregoing understates the 'size' of government. For instance, no account was taken of subsidies, grants and debt interest paid by the government and its net lending. The reason for this is that these are mainly classified as transfer payments. That is, the government raises the necessary funds by taxation and borrowing and transfers them back to the community and overseas. Thus the government does not buy goods and services directly as far as this type of expenditure is concerned. But there is no doubt that these transfers are extremely important and do influence the economic system. When they are included in government expenditure then the previous percentages are greatly increased. Table 2.5 shows that the 1956 percentage is raised to around 34 per cent of gross national product and that over the next ten years the trend has been upwards, with the 1966 figure approaching 39 per cent. Clearly, grants, subsidies, debt interest and net lending have been increasingly important over the last ten years or so as a component of government expenditure.

TABLE 2.5

Central and Local Government Combined Current and Capital Expenditure as a Percentage of Gross National Product at Market Prices, 1956-67.

Year	1956	1957	1958	1959	1960	1961
%	33.8	34.6	34.9	35.2	35.0	36.0
Year	1962	1963	1964	1965	1966	1967
%	36.2	36.0	36.4	37.6	38.6	

Source: NIBB, Table 4.7, 1967.

IV.3 The Budget

The budget is traditionally the annual financial statement which the Chancellor of the Exchequer makes in the House of Commons. The statement includes an account of the revenue and expenditure for the previous financial year and estimates for the year ahead. In the ordinary way there is only one Budget, but in times of crisis a supplementary budget may be introduced to give the chancellor the opportunity to modify his earlier policies by altering taxation and expenditure. Tables 2.6 to 2.8 (pages 64-5) bring together in an aggregated form the main features of the 1968 Budget accounts. The 1968 budget was presented on 19th March, over two weeks earlier than usual because of the precariousness of the economic situation.

TABLE 2.6

Central Government Revenue 1968-69 (estimated)

£ million

Inland revenue

Income tax	4,401	
Surtax	250	
Death duties	346	
Stamps	105	
Profits tax	15	
Corporation tax	1,426	
Capital gains tax	44	
Special charge	70	
Total inland revenue		6,657

Customs and excise

Tobacco	1,045	
Purchase tax	887	
Oil	1,101	
Spirits, beer and wine	723	
Betting and gaming	100	
Other revenue duties	10	
Import duties act, 1958	190	
Temporary charge on imports less export rebates	− 44	
Total customs and excise		4,012
Motor vehicle duties		413
Selective employment tax (gross)		1,393
Total taxation		12,475
Miscellaneous receipts		400
Grand total		12,875

Source: Financial Statement, 1958-69

TABLE 2.7

Central Government Supply Services and Consolidated Fund Standing Services 1968-69 (estimated)

£ million

Supply services

Total defence budget		2,271

Other supply

I	Government and exchequer	181	
II	Commonwealth and foreign	264	
III	Home and justice	231	
IV	Industry, trade and transport	1,993	
V	Agriculture	392	
VI	Local government, housing and social services	4,335	
VII	Education and science	433	
VIII	Museums, galleries and the arts	15	
IX	Public buildings, etc.	265	
X	Smaller public departments	16	
XI	Miscellaneous	118	
Defence purchasing (repayment) services		3	
Total other supply			8,246
Supplementary provision			208
Total supply services			10,825

Consolidated fund standing services

Payment to the National Loans Fund	515	
Northern Ireland—share of reserved taxes, etc.	219	
Other	30	

Total	764
Consolidated fund surplus	1,386
Grand total	12,875

Source: Financial Statement, 1968-69

TABLE 2.8

National Loans Fund 1968-69 (estimated)

£ million

(i) *Payments*

Interest and expenses of national debt		1,475
Loans (net)		
To nationalised industries	921	
other public corporations	146	
local and harbour authorities	505	
private sector	− 7	
within central government	179	
Total		1,744
Grand total		3,219

(ii) *Receipts*

Interest on loans and profits of the Issue Department of the Bank of England	960	
Balance of interest met from the Consolidated fund	515	
Total		1,475
Consolidated fund surplus		1,386
Residual item		358
		3,219

Source: Financial Statement, 1968-69.

The receipts of the Exchequer shown in Table 2.6 fall under five main headings: inland revenue, customs and excise, motor vehicle duties, selective employment tax and miscellaneous receipts. The first two refer to the great revenue-collecting departments of state; the major taxes and duties are discussed extensively below. Motor vehicle duties are collected by the local authorities on behalf of the Exchequer. The selective employment tax is also discussed below. Miscellaneous receipts include interest and dividends, broadcast receiving licences and certain other receipts.

The two main categories of expenditure shown in Table 2.7 are supply services and consolidated fund standing services. The first is voted annually by Parliament. The second is a standing charge against revenue.

The National Loans Fund is a new-comer to the Budget accounts. Broadly speaking it is intended to carry further the separation of current and capital items in the accounts. Most of the domestic lending of the government and all of its borrowing transactions are now to appear in the National Loans Fund. Table 2.8 clearly shows just how important the central government is as a source of capital funds for the nationalised industries and local authorities. The government must raise these funds either through taxation or by borrowing. In these accounts there is a large estimated surplus from the consolidated fund so that the residual item of £358 million is much smaller than it has been recently.

To explain adequately the financing of this residual item would necessitate going far beyond the immediate budget accounts and involve an extensive discussion of the financial transactions of the central government. However, it may be useful to indicate a few of the factors involved. For instance, an increase in the note issue as previously mentioned will help to finance it as will net purchases of government securities by the Post Office and Trustee savings banks. If these sources of funds are insufficient the government may have to borrow from the banking system, probably by issuing Treasury bills. The amount that must be borrowed will actually rise if there is an increase in the gold and foreign currency reserves. This is because the government must make sterling available to the Exchange Equalisation account to enable it to purchase an inflow of gold and foreign currency. Clearly, the budgetary system and monetary and financial system are highly interdependent and hence so are monetary, fiscal and credit policy.

The annual Budget as an instrument of fiscal policy has frequently been criticised because of its inflexibility in the light of changing economic circumstances. This criticism needs to be examined from at least two points of view, taxation and, separately, expenditure.

The major taxes such as income tax and corporation tax are annual taxes and in the ordinary way cannot be varied between Finance Acts.[1] Thus, though it might be thought desirable, because of changed economic conditions, to alter these taxes this cannot be done without all the inconvenience of a supplementary Budget. However, the authorities have more leeway over some other sources of revenue. From the point of view of flexibility one of the most important is the power, granted in the Finance Act 1961, to vary the rates of nearly all customs and excise duties and purchase tax by at most 10 per cent.[2] Thus there are now substantial powers to vary taxes between budgets. This, of course, leaves other problems, such as the timing and scale of tax changes. It is argued below that the authorities have been far from successful in this respect.

Government expenditure may be planned years in advance of its formal inclusion in the budget estimates. The plans can be and are modified, but this again gives rise to problems. Much of the expenditure is on a continuing basis and cannot be easily altered. Moreover, it may be extremely costly to slow down or postpone some kinds of expenditure, particularly investment expenditure. For these kinds of reason variation of government expenditure is not an ideal instrument of fiscal policy.

The Budget accounts, as already indicated, are incomplete in a number of ways. They deal, for example, only peripherally with local government finances and the national insurance funds.[3] Yet both of these 'tax' the community, the first mainly by levying rates and the second through insurance contributions. For the calender year 1967 rates were some £1,440 million and national insurance contributions £1,700 million. Together they amount to the equivalent of over 60 per cent of the taxes on income in the same period.[4] The scale of taxation in the UK may be better appreciated when it is realised that taxes, rates, national insurance and minor other contributions totalled almost £13,000 million in 1967 or over 33% of GNP at market prices.[5]

IV.4 Income Tax and Surtax

Income tax is payable by individuals and, until April 1966, was paid by corporate bodies, when it was replaced by corporation tax on the latter. Surtax is legally an extension of the income tax as applied to individuals; it does not apply to corporate bodies.

In general, income tax is now chargeable on the income of individuals resident in the UK and on income originating there, even though the recipient may be resident elsewhere. If other countries operated their taxation systems similarly this might give rise to the same income being taxed twice. To obviate or ameliorate this the UK has a network of double taxation agreements. If, for instance, a resident of the UK is taxed in another country on income arising there he is allowed to offset this tax against his UK tax liability.

The amount of tax payable depends on the size of assessable income, and on various allowances and reliefs permitted. Income for tax purposes is classified under five schedules, B, C, D, E and F. Formerly, there was also a Schedule A but this was abolished under the 1963 Finance Act. Schedule A had covered amongst other things the net income

---

[1] The Finance Act puts into law the budget proposals, subject to any amendments made by the House of Commons.

[2] Thus if a current rate of duty is 20 per cent it may be varied between 18 and 22 per cent.

[3] National insurance is discussed at length in chapter 5.

[4] Figures from, Preliminary Estimates of National Income and Balance of Payments 1962 to 1967, Cmnd. 3571.

[5] Inclusion of other government income, e.g. rents, would increase this ratio.

imputed to house-ownership. This is no longer subject to tax and various other items under Schedule A, including rents from land and buildings, were moved to Schedule D. Schedule B is of little interest and has also almost disappeared but covers income from woodlands that are not assessed under Schedule D. Schedule C refers to interest payments from some securities of the UK and overseas governments, where the payments take place in the UK. Schedule D covers the profits of trades, businesses and professions and it is under this schedule that short-term capital gains are chargeable, as are other items such as interest on loans and income from overseas. Schedule E refers to income from offices, employments or pensions. Schedule F is a new schedule introduced under the 1965 Finance Act and refers to taxes on dividends distributed by companies.

To arrive at taxable income it is necessary to take account of the allowances and reliefs given. For 1968-69 the earned income allowance—there is no allowance for investment income—is two-ninths of income up to £4,005 and one-ninth of the next £5,940, giving a maximum allowance of £1,550. The allowance for a single person is £220 and for a married couple £340. The allowance for children varies with age; £115 for those under eleven, £140 for those between eleven and less than sixteen and £165 for those over sixteen, except that these will be reduced by £36 for each child for whom family allowance is paid throughout the tax year. In addition, there is old age and small income relief, allowances for a dependent relative, housekeeper, widows with children, blind people, life insurance premiums, superannuation and mortgage interest.

Once taxable income has been determined the first £100 is taxed at 4s 0d in the pound, the next £200 at 6s 0d and the rest at the 'standard rate' of 8s 3d. These rates correspond respectively to marginal rates of tax on earned income, allowing for earned income relief, of 15.5 per cent, 23.3 per cent and 32.1 per cent.

Surtax is chargeable in addition to income tax on incomes in excess of £2,000. However, allowances are also permitted in assessing the amount subject to surtax. On earned income the earned income relief against income tax is deductible for surtax purposes and there is also a special earnings allowance with a maximum of £2,000. A single person can earn about £5,000 before he has to pay surtax. The surtax rates vary from 2s 0d in the £ to 10s 0d. This makes a maximum combined marginal income and surtax rate of 18s 3d in the £, or a rate of 91.25 per cent.

It is evident from the foregoing that one of the main features of income tax and surtax is their progressiveness. This is, of course, by design. It can be traced to notions of ability to pay. It is assumed that those with larger incomes are or should be able to pay proportionately more of them in taxation. In addition, progressive taxation lends itself to income redistribution to the extent that government expenditure benefits the less well-off in the community. Value judgments are implicit throughout the taxation system.

However praiseworthy or otherwise the particular value judgments, it would be a mistake to see them in isolation from other effects of a highly progressive taxation system. For with progressive tax rates the direct reward for extra work diminishes as income increases. It might be expected therefore that the system acts as a disincentive to additional effort. This, however, need not necessarily be true. It is possible to envisage circumstances where people might have fixed ideas about the amount of income after tax that they wanted and be prepared to work harder to achieve it if taxes were increased. But this possibility seems implausible if marginal tax rates become more and more progressive. The empirical evidence on the matter is not conclusive, at least as far as working harder in existing jobs is concerned. But this may reflect the inadequacy of the empirical methods as much as anything else.

Furthermore, it is suggested that there is evidence that steeply progressive taxation is a serious disincentive to movement from one job to another. It is difficult to get a sufficiently large income after tax to compensate for the costs of upheaval and change. If this is correct then the tax system misallocates resources and is a drag on economic efficiency and growth. Following the ability-to-pay principle may be costly in these terms.

There is also no doubt that highly progressive taxation stimulates tax avoidance—the search for loopholes in the law permitting a reduced tax bill. If it is possible to spend less than a pound on advice to save a pound in tax then clearly this is a powerful incentive. The energies and resources of lawyers, accountants and tax experts generally are diverted into socially costly tasks. And on a more fundamental level the benefits of, say, greater equality are bought by an extension of the powers of government and restrictions on individual freedom. Who is to say that greater equality is the greater good?

IV.5 Capital Gains Taxation

There are now two capital gains taxes, the short-term and the long-term tax. The original short-term tax was introduced under the Finance Act 1962 and, with the exception of gains on the disposal of such assets as tangible moveable property and a dwelling house, taxed gains on assets disposed of within six months of purchase as if they were unearned income, except for land where the time period was three years. Losses were permissible as an offset against gains. The 1965 Finance Act modified these provisions. The main change was to extend the time period from six months to twelve months for the operation of the short-term tax, the three year period for land being reduced to twelve months.

The long-term tax was also introduced in the Finance Act 1965. Gains are taxable on disposal of assets, however long the assets have been held. The gains are taxed at a rate of 30 per cent except that an individual with gains which do not exceed £5,000 is taxable at one half his maximum rate of income tax and surtax that would be chargeable if the gains were treated as if they were unearned income. For an individual liable at the standard rate the chargeable rate is therefore 20.6 per cent instead of 30 per cent. For gains over £5,000 the full income and surtax rates become operative unless the 30 per cent rate would lead to a smaller charge. The foregoing applies to individuals, as gains realised by companies are ordinarily chargeable to corporation tax.[1] Special provisions relate to the taxing of unit trusts, investment trusts, superannuation funds and other bodies.

The major justification put forward for the introduction of capital gains taxation is on the grounds of equity. The argument is roughly as follows. An individual may purchase a £100 worth of securities in 1968 and find that in 1969 they are worth £200. If he sells the securities and if there were no capital gains tax he could maintain his capital intact and still have £100 to spend, therefore this £100 is essentially income and should be taxed as such. But is this really equitable with progressive income tax rates? It might be that if the £100 were spread over a number of years a lower tax charge would arise. Does this mean that gains should be averaged over a number of years or would a compromise solution be to charge rates somewhat less than income tax rates? The UK long-term gains tax seems to favour the latter.

In discussing the £100 gain above nothing was said about prices. But if prices have risen by 5 per cent over the period then £105 would be required to maintain real capital intact and the remaining £95 would be worth only some £90 in real terms. Is it legitimate to tax nominal gains as opposed to real gains? The equity argument is by no means as straightforward as it might seem.

Capital gains taxation is, of course, important for other reasons besides those of equity. It may affect investment and saving, the functioning of the capital markets and pose difficult problems of administration. To the extent that the return to investment takes the form of capital gains—especially the return to risky investment—taxing them may discourage such investment. This discouragement may, however, be mitigated to some extent, since the tax is postponable and payable only on realised capital gains. The allowance of losses as an offset to capital gains also works in the same direction. Never-

---

[1] From 1967-68 chargeable gains of individuals are to be exempt from tax if, after deducting allowable losses, they do not exceed £50 for the year.

theless, the effect may well be to depress investment.

The effects on saving are perhaps even more problematical but they may also be adverse, as may the effects on the operation of the capital markets. Since the tax is on realised gains this encourages the retention of the same securities as, of course, the holder has the income on the tax that would otherwise have to be paid if the securities were realised. There is therefore a discouragement to switching between securities which reduces the flexibility of the market and perhaps makes the raising of capital more costly. A possible offset to the reduction in the flexibility of the market is the realisation of capital losses since these are allowable for tax purposes against corresponding capital gains.

The administrative problems are particularly great where problems of valuation arise. This is especially true of changes in the value of assets which do not ordinarily have a market value; an example is unquoted securities. The problems of valuation may become less acute as time proceeds and the community gets accustomed to the tax.[1]

IV.6 Corporation Tax

Corporation Tax was introduced under the Finance Act 1965 and came into full effect from 6th April 1966. Before that the profits of companies were subject to income tax and a profits tax of 15 per cent. Thus corporation tax is a part substitute for these. It is only a part substitute as in addition income tax has to be paid at the standard rate on dividends. To guard against evasion, companies are responsible for deducting tax on dividends and so the shareholder still receives his dividend net of tax as he did under the previous legislation. Special provisions relate to the incidence of corporation tax on unit trusts, investment trusts and insurance companies; provision is also made to permit double taxation relief against overseas taxes.

Corporation tax draws a forceful distinction between the company and the shareholder, taxing each as separate entities and in so doing discriminating between retained and distributed profits—for whereas the former is subject to corporation tax the latter is also subject to taxation on dividends. This distinction or bias is highly relevant to questions of equity, fiscal policy, investment and saving, and the operation of the capital markets.

Perhaps the simplest way to approach the equity argument is to contrast the tax position, if all profits were distributed and taxed as 'personal' income, with the current arrangements. The former would seem to be the more equitable. For the present system favours the retention of profits within the company, tending presumably to increase its value, and hence the value of the shareholder's stake in the company. But this increase in value to the shareholder is not subject to tax until it takes the form of increased dividends or realised capital gains. These may be postponed until far into the future and so are not comparable to taxation of profits as 'personal' income.

A basic argument in favour of the corporation tax is the opportunity it gives the authorities to distinguish between the personal and the company sector for policy purposes, and under the present system the encouragement given to profit retention in the belief that this stimulates investment and economic growth. The authorities may, for instance, wish to curtail consumption expenditure with as little adverse affect as possible on investment expenditure. An increase in income tax, leaving corporation tax unchanged, should tend to have the desired effect and may even encourage smaller dividend distributions, leaving more funds available to companies for investment purposes. The former income tax-profits tax combination did not quite have this flexibility.

The foregoing analysis begs, however, a number of important questions. Amongst

---

[1] This section and the next rely heavily on Prest, *Public Finance in Theory and Practice*, pp. 287-301.

these are the following. Should future consumption be preferred to present consumption, in so far as larger current investment makes possible a larger future income and so consumption? Are the companies with retained profits the ones which should grow? This is not at all self-evident. It means that companies avoid the discipline of having to raise funds in the market and probably favours the larger established company at the expense of the smaller or newer company. Furthermore, greater encouragement of profit retention tends to reduce the flow of funds through the capital market to the detriment of companies dependent on it. The corporation tax also tends to distort the operation of the capital market by encouraging firms to rely more on loan or debenture capital at the expense of ordinary or other forms of share capital, since the interest on the former is allowed as a cost in the calculation of profits and hence tax, whereas this is not true of the latter. It may be argued that the gains from introducing the corporation tax (and the capital gains taxes) outweigh the disadvantages. But there is little evidence to show that the pros and cons were weighed carefully in advance of their introduction.

Clearly, the corporation tax raises many complex issues, the answers to which are far from being self-evident. The issues raised range beyond those of economics and bring in such considerations as the extent and role of government intervention in society. To ignore these considerations is to examine only part of the total problem.

IV.7 Depreciation and other Allowances

In assessing liability to corporation tax allowance is made, broadly speaking, for all the costs incurred by the company, including, as mentioned above, interest on loans and debentures but not dividends paid on shares. Depreciation allowances are also generally permitted on physical assets, but not all physical assets; there are no allowances on such things as retail shops, showrooms and offices. The allowance is at a rate of 4 per cent on the value or written down value of industrial buildings; 15 per cent is the standard rate for industrial machinery but for some it may be as high or, exceptionally, higher than 25 per cent.

In addition to depreciation allowances for wear and tear successive governments have attempted to stimulate investment by various kinds of investment incentive. Three main kinds are or have been operative in the UK; initial allowances, investment allowances and investment grants. Initial allowances, introduced in 1945, are permitted in the first year in addition to the ordinary depreciation allowances. In other words the rate at which depreciation may be written off is accelerated; the total amount of depreciation permitted remains 100 per cent. Investment allowances on the other hand, introduced in 1954 and abolished in January 1966 with the advent of investment grants, did permit more than 100 per cent of the cost of the asset to be written off over its life. Thus if the investment allowance was 20 per cent—it was normally allowed in the year the investment took place—the total allowances would be 120 per cent.

Investment grants are cash grants to manufacturing, construction and extractive industries. The grants vary both regionally and to a limited extent according to the type of asset. The general rate is 20 per cent (for 1967 and 1968 only the rate is raised to 25 per cent) of the cost of *new* plant and machinery; expenditure on commercial vehicles and services do not qualify for grants. In the development areas—most of Scotland and Wales, Merseyside, large areas of northern England and south-western England—the grants are 40 per cent (45 per cent for 1967 and 1968 only) of the cost of new expenditure on plant and machinery. Investment in ships and computers receive special consideration. The grants themselves are not taxable but depreciation allowances are now calculated on the cost of the equipment less the cash grant. Intitial allowances are still granted on those forms of capital expenditure, such as industrial buildings and second-hand machinery which do not qualify for investment grants.

This whole system of allowances and grants gives rise to many complicated issues, only a few of which can be touched on here. The first is whether depreciation allowances should be on an original or replacement cost basis. This question would be of little or no significance if prices were generally stable. In periods of rising prices, it would seem necessary, however, if the community is to preserve its physical stock of capital, that allowances should be made on a replacement cost basis.

But if the problem is approached in a different way the argument is by no means as clear-cut in favour of a replacement cost allowance. Suppose a firm purchases a piece of equipment and thereafter prices rise, including the price of the equipment. Thus the capital value of the old equipment rises, giving a capital gain to the firm. If allowances were permitted on a replacement cost basis the firm is, in fact, receiving untaxed capital gains. Is this equitable in relation to other sections of the community or is it a useful compromise to allow only original costs in calculating depreciation, so that the apparent capital gains are subject to corporation and income tax? The answer is far from obvious.[1]

Initial allowances, investment allowances and, more recently, investment grants should all act as a stimulus to investment. The first two may be regarded as reducing the amount of tax payable, and to that extent make investment more profitable. The third is, of course, a direct subsidy to investment and the benefits do not depend, as they do in the case of the first two, upon the availability of profits out of which to pay taxes. It is not at all self-evident that the subsidy is to be preferred as it may mean that investment takes place in forms of dubious profitability—there is therefore the likelihood of misallocation of resources.

But the main feature of the investment grants is the extent to which they are discriminatory. They make investment in certain places more profitable than in others and some types of investment more profitable than other types. This, of course, is by design and is intended to stimulate investment in the places and in the forms the government desires. It may be questioned if the wishes of the government should be so influential, rather than the interacting decisions of consumers, savers and investors, and if the government has the necessary knowledge and ability to implement its wishes. The evidence to date is not reassuring on this latter point as the government has had great difficulty in estimating the sums required for the payment of investment grants.

Both investment grants and initial allowances are potentially a flexible instrument of fiscal policy in that they can be varied either to encourage or retard investment as economic conditions require. But the emphasis here must be on 'potential flexibility'. For the timing and actual amount of variation in grants and allowances are crucial to their use as fiscal instruments. It may be doubted that government or anyone else has the knowledge to manipulate these instruments successfully. Indeed, as far as the management of the UK economy is concerned, it is argued below that their use has probably been destabilising.[2]

IV.8 Selective Employment Tax

The selective employment tax was introduced in the May 1966 budget and came into effect in September 1966. The tax is paid by all employers in the public and private sectors and from September 1968 is at a rate of 37s 6d a week for men, 18s 9d a week for women and for boys under eighteen, and 12s 0d a week for girls under eighteen. Though all employers pay the tax some of them have it refunded, some in the development areas are in addition paid a premium and some get no refund. Employers in manufacturing industries in the development areas receive a premium of 37s 6d. That is, they pay 37s 6d per man per week, but get a refund of 75s 0d. Outside the development areas employers in manufacturing industries just have the tax refunded and so get no premium. Employers in transport, agriculture, the public service, nationalised industries, extractive

---

[1]   See Prest, *Public Finance in Theory and Practice*, pp. 320-36, for further discussion.
[2]   See Section V below.

industries and charities also have the tax refunded. Finally—apart from hotel employers in certain parts of development areas who do get a refund—employers in the construction and the service industries, including wholesale and retail distribution, banking, insurance, finance and the like, receive no refund. Furthermore, to qualify for refunds more than half the persons employed in an establishment must come in the refund category, i.e., they must be engaged in manufacturing activities, transport, etc.

Two main reasons are given for the introduction of the selective employment tax. The first was the wish to tax services which were supposed to be lightly taxed compared with certain manufactured products which are subject to excise duties and purchase tax.[1] The second was to release labour, broadly from the service industries, for employment in manufacturing industry.

Neither of the two reasons are convincing. For one thing not all manufactured products, or even consumer goods, are subject to excise taxes or purchase tax. Thus in so far as these taxes distort relative prices, and this was a reason for introducing the selective employment tax, there was no distortion to be corrected in the case of these goods. Furthermore, in so far as there is price distortion of some goods, it scarcely follows that the way to correct it is to introduce a further distortion, especially as at its best the new tax could quantitatively only be described as the crudest form of correction, bearing little relationship to the relative weights of taxation on different kinds of product.

The second reason is equally unconvincing. Underlying it is the idea that somehow it is more in the 'national interest'—whatever that means—to employ labour in manufacturing rather than other pursuits. However, if the individual wishes of a community are expressed in the way they spend their incomes, there is evidence to suggest that as those incomes grow a higher proportion of the working population are drawn into the service industries.[2] If fulfilling the wishes of the community in this sense is or reflects the national interest, then the selective employment tax is opposed to it.[3] If on the other hand what the government wants is, by definition, the national interest then the selective employment tax has a place, though few will, or perhaps should be satisfied by this as a definition of the national interest. Finally, the tax has given rise to much litigation to determine what is or is not manufacturing and to the reorganisation of activities so that they become 'manufacturing'. Such reorganisation is never costless and may from a social viewpoint be economically wasteful.

IV.9 Customs and Excise Duties and Purchase Tax

The group of duties and taxes under this heading are generally called 'indirect' taxes since they are not usually collected from the final purchaser but from the manufacturer, trader or wholesaler. The term customs duties refers to duties imposed on imports, whereas excise duties are imposed on domestically produced goods. Purchase tax is levied on both imports and domestically produced goods but does not apply to goods that bear excise duties: it is different from excise duties in that it is charged on broad ranges of goods rather than on a particular good or group of goods. Customs duties may be primarily for revenue raising purposes, being levied on imported goods which are similar to the domestic goods that carry excise duties, or primarily for giving protection to British goods or preference to Commonwealth goods and, more recently, imports from the European Free

---

[1]   Excise duties and purchase tax are discussed on pp. 72-3.

[2]   In so far as an additional reason for taxing services was to release labour for manufacturing industry as a help to exports it may be ill-founded, particularly in the light of the findings of a recent report on invisible exports. See, *Report of the Committee on Invisible Exports,* October 1967. It is noteworthy that the Chancellor, in his March 1968 Budget, announced an inquiry into the effects of the selective employment tax.

[3]   Thus evidence that the selective employment tax is achieving a redeployment of labour may well be economically harmful, though it has already been claimed as a sign of success and an argument for extending the tax. See, *The Times,* March 2 1968.

Trade area.

As may be seen from Table 2.6 the large revenue yielders are tobacco, oil, alcohol and purchase tax. Tobacco and oil together are estimated to yield £2,146 million in 1968-69, or almost 19 per cent of total revenue from taxation, and alcohol and purchase tax a further 13 per cent. Purchase tax is currently charged at four different rates on the wholesale value, but is not chargeable on exports. Such things as clothes, footwear, kitchenware and wallpaper are charged at 12½ per cent; confectionery, ice cream and soft drinks at 20 per cent; cars, gas and electrical appliances and drugs and medicines at 33⅓ per cent; and jewellery, gramophone records, watches, clocks and cameras at 50 per cent.

An outstanding feature about the duties and taxes on tobacco, oil and alcohol is their scale, the large proportion that they represent of the purchasing price. For instance, the duty on a gallon of petrol costing 5s 11d is 3s 11d. Ordinarily it might be expected that something which has the effect of substantially increasing the price of a product would lead to less of it, perhaps much less of it, being bought. By and large this does not seem to have happened with these three products—their demands are said to be inelastic with respect to price. However, some doubts are beginning to be expressed about the buoyancy of the revenue from tobacco, though this may be due to other causes besides the scale of taxation. The, at any rate, apparent inelasticity of demand with respect to price implies that these duties and taxes may have little direct effect on the allocation of resources. But there will be an indirect effect because the funds withdrawn by taxes from consumers will scarcely be spent by the state in the same way as if they had been left in the hands of the former. This reallocation of expenditure is no doubt intended to increase the welfare of the community, immeasurable though that may be.

It is often argued that indirect taxes are to be preferred because they are less of a disincentive to the supply of labour than direct taxes. The chancellor had this in mind in presenting his March 1968 Budget. But it is an extremely difficult issue to be at all certain about and depends on many factors, such as the scale of the duties and taxes to be substituted, say, for a reduction in direct taxes or for foregoing an increase, and the type and the extent of the goods involved. For an individual may well consider not only the direct tax on extra earnings but also the real value of goods and services that can be bought with additional income.

It is also arguable that on equity grounds indirect taxes are regressive in that they fall more heavily on the relatively low income groups. There would seem to be some truth in this as far as tobacco, beer and some purchase taxes are concerned, but possibly to a less extent for petrol, though bus fares are obviously affected by oil duties. On the other hand the relatively less well-off would seem to obtain substantial benefits from government welfare and other services. But if the community opts for extensive government expenditure on welfare services and education it seems unavoidable that one way or another a large proportion of the tax revenue must be raised from the mass of taxpayers. If at the same time the latter are important beneficiaries from government expenditure then they are indirectly paying for perhaps all of or a major part of these benefits. If this is correct then a substantial part of government revenue and expenditure is a process of taking funds from particular individuals and then handing them back either directly or in the form of services that the government thinks they ought to have. This may not be as odd as it seems but it begs some fundamental questions.

IV.10 Death Duties

Estate duty is the only duty now payable on death, except for the application of the capital gains tax. Death counts as a realisation of assets and gains in excess of £5,000 are subject to capital gains tax, but any tax payable is deductible in assessing the value of the estate subject to estate duty. The duty is charged on all property in Great Britain— Northern Ireland has separate provisions—that passes or is deemed to pass on death, irrespective of the domicile of the deceased. Property outside Great Britain is also chargeable if the deceased was domiciled in Great Britain. *Inter vivos* gifts are taxable if made within seven years of death, or one year in the case of charities, and gains arising on the making of *inter vivos* gifts, and indeed gifts generally, which total more than £100 in any year are liable to capital gains tax. Estates of less than £5,000 are exempt from estate duty, those between £5,000 and £6,000 are assessed at 1 per cent of the value of the whole estate and between £8,000 and £10,000 at 4 per cent. The maximum rate is 80 per cent on estates of £1 million and over.

The main reason for estate duty is the belief that gross inequality in the distribution of wealth is undesirable. But experience in Great Britain would suggest that estate duty has not been very effective in reducing the inequality of wealth. However, it may be somewhat more effective in combination with the capital gains tax which in general taxes gains arising on wealth transfers both outside and within the *inter vivos* period. But whatever may be thought about extreme inequality of wealth distribution it is scarcely realistic to imagine a reasonably free society without some and perhaps substantial wealth inequality. This kind of judgment seems to be inseparable from this type of policy issue.

V   POLICY SINCE THE EARLY 1950s

V.1   War and Post-War Background

During the war monetary policy was not relied upon as an active policy instrument. The decision was made to finance the war on the basis of low interest rates and to the extent that this required a substantial growth in the money supply, as it did, the threat of inflation was controlled or, at least curtailed by such measures as physical controls, rationing and taxation. These measures, of course, did not prevent a marked accumulation of financial assets on the part of the public. Table 2.9 shows a selection of these.

Table 2.9

Selected Financial Assets of the Public, 1939 and 1946

Year	Currency		Bank deposits		Post Office deposits		Trustee savings bank deposits		Savings certificates	
	Actual £ m	% of National Income	Actual £ m	% of N.I.	Actual £ m	% of N.I.	Actual £ m	% of N.I.	Actual £ m	% of N.I.
1939	454	9.0	2248	44.6	551	11.0	252	5.0	382	7.6
1946	1332	16.7	5097	63.9	1981	24.8	670	8.4	1604	20.1

Sources: AAS; The British Economy, Key Statistics 1900-1966; Trustee Savings Bank *Year Book.*
Note: Savings certificates are a form of national savings and a liability of the government.

The actual figures are not very meaningful when looked at in isolation, but when expressed as percentages of national income immediately give some indication of what was taking place. In fact, the community was accumulating financial assets at a very rapid rate relatively to its income. This accumulation was by no means voluntary, but was the consequence of a number of factors, including the physical controls and rationing mentioned above preventing the purchase of commodities, and the incentives and propaganda encouraging saving in wartime.

The existence of these assets, together with the losses and depletion of physical assets in wartime, might be expected to affect economic behaviour after the war, and as restrictions began to be removed. For people would presumably say to themselves; 'I have got these assets which earn some interest, but it would be much nicer to have a new car, radio, washing machine, clothes', and so on. In other words, unless the production of these goods was greatly expanded or severe, physical controls and restrictions retained or, perhaps, interest rates allowed to rise to unprecedented levels, there would be strong upward pressure on prices.[1] In practice, the government only gradually relaxed controls; rationing and restrictions persisted into the early 1950s. And even in 1958 the Radcliffe Committee felt that whilst much of the post-war liquidity of the system had been absorbed it still remained more liquid than before the war.

This problem of excess liquidity, implying that the return from holding financial assets is less than might be obtained from holding other kinds of assets, added greatly to the difficulties of monetary and credit policy in the early post-war years and for much of the 1950s. For taken in conjunction with expectations of rising interest rates and prices, which were present for much of this time, there is a powerful incentive to exchange financial assets for real assets. For rising interest rates raise the fear that the nominal price of fixed interest marketable securities will decline and rising prices that their real value will decline. It is therefore extremely unlikely that relatively small increases in interest rates and restriction of the money supply and credit would have much effect on expenditure in these conditions. On the contrary they might even accentuate the problem in so far as the restrictive measures were adjudged inadequate and anticipated to be a prelude to stiffer policies to come. It is thus hardly surprising that the Radcliffe Committee concluded that during the postwar period traditional monetary policy had been relatively ineffective. However, as mentioned previously, the Committee unfortunately went further than this and tended to dismiss monetary policy generally, and manipulation of the money supply in particular, as effective policy instruments.[2]

The growth of the public's holdings of financial assets reflected in part the growth of the national debt. Between 1939 and 1946 whilst the war was being financed it increased from just over £7,000 million to under £24,000 million or from about 1.4 times national income to three times national income. Much of the debt was short-term in the sense that it had a relatively short period of time to go to maturity before it had to be renewed. This presented the authorities with an almost continuous refinancing problem and one which was accentuated by the continued growth of the debt in the early post-war years.

The cost of servicing the debt or its interest cost grew with the debt, giving the authorities the additional problem of raising the necessary revenue and, as a substantial proportion of the debt was foreign held, putting a strain on the balance of payments.[3] Governments and treasuries faced with these problems have clearly a strong vested interest in keeping down the interest cost of the debt. This they attempted to do in these post-war years, though not necessarily for this reason alone.

Despite extensive physical restrictions on both the home market and on imports, the use of foreign exchange controls and heavy taxation, domestic prices increased between 1945 and 1951 by about 40 per cent and the balance of payments remained a persistent problem. The official foreign exchange reserves and the policies pursued were never adequate to allay fears about the stability of the exchange rate of the pound—rightly in the light of events in 1949. It was against this kind of background and renewed pressure on the balance of payments, accentuated by the outbreak of the Korean War, that the 'new' monetary policy was introduced.

V.2 The Early Years: 1951-54

In November 1951 Bank rate was raised to 2½ per cent after being held at 2 per cent for almost twenty years, except for a few weeks at the outbreak of the Second World War. The Treasury bill rate rose from around ½ per cent to about 1 per cent. At the same time

---

[1]   There is no precise way to describe what is an 'unprecendented interest rate'. It may be supposed that a Bank rate of, say 12 per cent would qualify, with companion rates at similar levels.
[2]   See above, pp. 55-7.
[3]   At the end of 1945 overseas sterling holdings were some £3,600 million, between four and five times their pre-war level.

holders of Treasury bills were 'offered', up to a sum of £1,000 million, a longer dated security in exchange, called a serial funding stock and yielding 1¾ per cent interest.[1]

These were not the only monetary and credit policy measures taken about this time.[2] But those mentioned represented a 'new' departure in the sense that the previous commitment to essentially fixed low short-term rates, and, particularly, a fixed Bank rate was abandoned. Monetary and credit policy were to be more flexible in future.

The 'new' monetary policy was introduced with large claims for its ability and power to influence and improve the functioning of the economic system.[3] The previous reliance on physical controls and fiscal policy had fallen into disrepute amongst a wide range of commentators on economic affairs.

In spite of the claims made for monetary policy it was never relied on as the chief means of regulating economic activity, but was almost invariably combined with physical controls and fiscal measures, the whole action being called a 'package deal'. For instance, in late 1951 and early 1952 when interest rates were raised severe import restrictions were also imposed and some, though not major, changes were made in taxation.

The balance of payments improved during 1952 and, at least on the surface, remained satisfactory throughout 1953 and into 1954. The foreign exchange reserves which had fallen markedly between 1950 and 1952 rose substantially, though not by as much as the sterling balances, that is, the sterling holdings, mainly of overseas countries. These holdings could be a threat in the future to the extent that they might be withdrawn in times of crisis. At the same time production and output recovered, probably helped by an expansionary budget in 1953, the removal of some physical controls and a reduction in interest rates.

Thus in this period economic policy seemed to be working relatively well, though prices continued to rise. The Radcliffe Committee, 'looking back with the benefit of hindsight', argued that, 'the authorities went too far in the direction of stimulating demand, and . . . were too slow to change direction'.[4] Be that as it may economic policy at the time seemed to be having a measure of success. But, clearly, this could not be attributed solely to monetary policy. However, for the time being monetary policy was back in favour.

V.3   Monetary Disillusion: 1954-57

In the second half of 1954 the balance of payments on current account was threatening to run into deficit and the authorities felt obliged late in 1954 to permit Treasury bill and other rates to rise. In January 1955 Bank rate was raised, followed by another increase in February, and hire purchase controls were reintroduced. But in the 1955 Budget the Chancellor of the Exchequer 'reduced taxation and planned for a larger overall deficit than in the preceding year', relying, in his own words, on 'the resources of a flexible monetary policy' to counter, if it should arise, an over-rapid expansion of demand and any associated balance of payments difficulties.[5]

Demand, however, continued to expand and the foreign trade balance remained adverse, 'Monetary policy was not operating as rapidly as had been expected'.[6] In July the clearing banks were requested by the Chancellor of the Exchequer to bring about a

---

[1]   The word 'offered' is a euphemism as far as the banks are concerned. The Radcliffe Committee reports (p. 140, par. 406) that 'The banks were in effect instructed to take about £500 million out of the total'.

[2]   The banks issued a warning that requests for advances would be examined very critically and early in 1952 hire purchase controls were introduced, stipulating the minimum down-payment and maximum period for repayment on a range of consumer durable goods.

[3]   See the account in J. C. R. Dow, *The Management of the British Economy, 1945-60,* Cambridge University Press, pp. 66-70.

[4]   *Report*, p. 142, par. 413

[5]   *Ibid* p. 144, par. 418.

[6]   *Economic Survey,* 1956 Cmd. 9728, p. 35, par. 68.

'positive and significant reduction in their advances over the next few months'.[1] They had risen by some £290 million in the first six months, equivalent to an annual growth rate of about 30 per cent. At the same time hire purchase restrictions were made more severe and measures were announced to restrain public investment. But the balance of payments position continued to be unsatisfactory, partly because of an outflow of funds from London, encouraged by rumours that the official margins between which the exchange rate was held might be widened.[2] In October there followed a supplementary Budget which raised both purchase tax on consumer goods and profits tax.

By the beginning of 1956 the balance of payments position had improved but to the authorities internal demand seemed dangerously strong and so additional measures were taken to restrict it. The banks were asked to continue to curtail their advances; Bank rate was again raised, hire purchase restrictions were strengthened, public investment was further reduced and investment allowances were suspended.[3] Despite the request to the banks advances continued to rise until 'the Chancellor of the Exchequer took the un-precedented step of summoning the representatives of the clearing banks and the main banking associations to a meeting on 24th July, in order to ask that "the contrac-tion of credit should be resolutely pursued".'[4]

Demand seemed to be under better control in the second half of 1956 though at the end of the year events were overshadowed by the nationalisation of the Suez canal and the crisis that ensued. Once this had subsided interest rates were permitted to decline, though the banks were still expected to curtail their lending.

Despite the latter, the 1957 Budget was expansionary, containing widespread reductions in taxation. But by the summer of 1957 there was another balance of pay-ments crisis, though the current account had a substantial surplus. In other words the capital account was reflecting the trouble and the foreign exchange reserves fell by almost £200 million between June and September. This fall in reserves is widely attributed to movements of short-term funds out of London and the delaying or hastening of pay-ments as the case might be in anticipation that the German mark was to be revalued.[5] On 19th September Bank rate was raised by 2 per cent to 7 per cent, its highest level since 1921. The banks once more were required to curtail advances and public investment pro-grammes were again reduced.

Clearly, economic policy including monetary policy cannot be judged satisfactory over the three years briefly reviewed. Prices continued to rise, and though the exchange rate was held the balance of payments was a recurring problem, with the foreign exchange reserves being much too small to take care of movements on both current and capital account.[6] Economic growth had continued but rather unevenly and at the relatively low rate of about 2 per cent per year.

There would therefore appear to be grounds for disillusion with economic policy as a whole in terms of its inability to achieve its various goals. Monetary policy was particu-larly suspect. Interest rates had risen to higher and higher levels, yet advances had con-tinued their upward trend, so that the authorities felt forced to insist on their direct curtailment. Clearing bank deposits had actually declined between 1954 and 1956—they increased in 1957 but not quite back to the 1954 level—and yet monetary policy was evidently ineffective.

---

[1]   Quoted in *Radcliffe Report*, p. 144, par. 417.
[2]   The official margins were $2.78-$2.80 to £1.
[3]   See above for a discussion of 'investment allowances', pp. 70-1.
[4]   *Radcliffe Report*, p. 146, par. 422.
[5]   Importers fearing that sterling might be devalued *vis-a-vis* another currency have an incentive to hasten their payments. Exporters have the opposite incentive. This phenomenon is known as 'leads and lags' in payments.
[6]   There is reason to believe that the authorities were not wholeheartedly committed to a fixed exchange rate throughout this period. See the account in Dow, 'The Management of the British Economy 1945-60', pp. 80-90.

V.4   1957-61

It was mentioned above that in late 1957 the balance of payments on capital account was under severe pressure. The current account had continued in surplus and remained strongly so during the first quarter of 1958. Unemployment had for some time been gradually increasing; in 1955 it had averaged 1.2 per cent and in 1958 was to be over 2 per cent. There seemed from this and other evidence to be some basis for encouraging expansion, though prices and wages were still edging upwards.

Bank rate was reduced from 7 to 6 per cent in March 1958 and by the end of the year was down to 4 per cent. In July all restrictions were lifted on bank lending—the first time this had happened since the war—and later in the year hire purchase restrictions were removed. The 1958 budget was mildly expansionary: estimated expenditure increased slightly, initial allowances were raised and some reductions were made in purchase tax and other duties. Later in the year initial allowances were increased again. Both monetary and fiscal policy were expansionary.

The expansionary policy was carried substantially further by the 1959 budget. The standard rate of income tax was reduced by 9d from 8s 6d to 7s 9d; and purchase tax and some customs and excise duties were also reduced. These reductions were estimated to leave the public in 1959-60 with some £300 million over and above what they would otherwise have had at their disposal. In addition to this there was a once for all repayment of £71 million of post-war credits—these had been forced payments made to the government during the Second World War.

Monetary policy continued to be expansionary though there was no reductions in Bank rate in 1959. But the rates on short- and long-term government securities did decline, though only for about the first six months of the year.[1] Treasury bill rates, on the other hand, tended to rise. Between 1958 and 1959 clearing bank deposits increased by about 4½ per cent and their advances by some £600 million, or by about one-quarter. Over the same period their investments fell by about £300 million or 15 per cent. The banks, with their new found freedom, were engaged in a massive rearrangement of their assets towards a more preferred distribution.

Between 1958 and 1959, under the influence of these expansionary measures, output increased by around 4 per cent and unemployment declined. Prices and wages remained relatively stable. But the balance of payments was beginning to show signs of strain. A £350 millions surplus on current account in 1958 dropped to £150 million in 1959 and, in the last quarter of 1959, the current account showed a small deficit. The foreign exchange reserves which had increased by £284 millions in 1958 fell by £119 millions in 1959. However, £58 millions of the latter was accounted for by an increased gold subscription to the I.M.F.

By early 1960 the authorities were showing some concern about the balance of payments. In January Bank rate was raised to 5 per cent and interest rates generally on government securities were tending to rise, though the authorities remained heavy net purchasers of gilt-edged securities, acquiring £274 millions in the first quarter. These purchases must have prevented interest rates from rising as much as they would otherwise have done and thereby slowed down the adjustment process.

Despite the more restrictive monetary policy the Budget made only minor changes in taxation, which were estimated to increase revenue—more than otherwise would occur— by only £22 million in 1960-61, though by substantially more than this in a full year. Meanwhile, government expenditure was planned to grow by some £350 millions over the 1959-60 outturn and the Budget surplus was to be somewhat smaller. Thus the Budget

---

[1]   The authorities were heavy net purchasers of gilt-edged securities during the 4th quarter of 1958 and throughout 1959, acquiring £431 millions. These purchases helped to maintain the prices of government securities or, alternatively, helped to prevent or curtail a rise in interest rates. See E. Victor Morgan, 'Funding Policy and the Gilt-Edged Market', *Lloyds Bank Review,* October 1962, pp. 40-53.

was, in fact, expansionary, though these figures do not show the whole picture.

A few weeks after the April Budget additional measures were taken to reinforce monetary and credit restriction. The first call was made for special deposits and hire purchase controls were reintroduced. A second call for special deposits was made in June and at the same time Bank rate was raised to 6 per cent. Monetary and credit policy were to be restrictionary whilst fiscal policy continued to be expansionary.

The underlying balance of payments position remained disturbing. Imports were increasing rapidly and in the first six months of the year were some 15 per cent greater than in the corresponding period of 1959. The current account deficit was £77 million and the long-term capital account continued to run a deficit, as it had for a number of years. Despite these deficits the foreign currency reserves increased, which may be attributed in part to a marked inflow of funds to London, attracted by the relatively high interest rates.

Whilst the rate of growth of economic activity had slowed down in the first half of 1960 this gave no immediate relief to the balance of payments. The deficits on current account in the second half of the year were actually greater than in the first half. But once again the reserves increased, largely because of a large inflow of funds to London. This persistent inflow of funds, which might just as quickly be withdrawn, worried the authorities and prompted them to lower Bank rate in two moves between October and December from 6 to 5 per cent. The authorities were anxious that these reductions in Bank rate should not weaken credit restriction as they fully appreciated that the current and long-term capital accounts of the balance of payments did not justify it, nor did the behaviour of prices and wages which continued to move upwards.[1] And yet they reduced hire purchase restrictions a month later in January 1961.

The crisis, which had been imminent for so long, finally broke at the end of February 1961 when funds began to leave London in anticipation of the revaluations of the deutschmark and the guilder. The authorities managed to mobilise substantial central bank support for sterling and it survived the immediate foreign exchange crisis. But the pressure on sterling persisted, with reserves continuing to fall even though the balance of payments on current and long-term capital accounts was showing signs of improvement. The crisis reached a new peak in July when the authorities were forced to introduce a battery of restrictive measures. Bank rate was raised from 5 to 7 per cent, a further call was made for special deposits, the 10 per cent surcharge on customs and excise duties and on purchase tax was used for the first time and government estimated expenditure for 1962-63 was to be reduced by some £300 millions.[2] And the chancellor, Selwyn Lloyd, called for 'a pause in the growth of wages, salaries and dividends'[3]—one of the early attempts at an incomes policy in the UK. At the same time the I.M.F. made available, on the request of the UK, funds totalling $2,000 million, $1,500 million immediately and $500 million as a standby credit.

The four years from 1957-61 could not be described as years of achievement for the policy makers. The expansion had barely got under way in 1958 and 1959 when balance of payments problems began to arise and domestic activity had, it seemed, to be slowed down if the exchange rate was to be held. But the balance of payments worsened during 1960 and the whole process culminated in the crisis of July 1961. Throughout the period wages and prices continued their upward movement. Perhaps it can be counted on the credit side that unemployment fell from just over 2 per cent in 1958 and 1959 to a little over 1½ per cent in 1960 and 1961.

---

[1] *BEQB,* March 1961, Vol. 1, No. 2, p. 3.

[2] The April 1961 Budget had been deflationary in the sense that the chancellor had budgeted for a substantially larger surplus than in the previous year. The surplus arose mainly because of the expected buoyancy of the revenue rather than because of increased taxation. Planned expenditure actually rose. But clearly the effects of the Budget were going to be too long delayed to alleviate the current crisis.

[3] *BEQB,* September 1961, Vol. 1, No. 4, p. 5.

The policy instruments which the authorities relied on were almost exclusively monetary, credit and fiscal. If, given a fixed exchange rate, a satisfactory balance of payments is given pride of place amongst the goals to be realised then the authorities seriously over-expanded in 1958, and, perhaps even more so, in 1959. By their activities in the gilt-edged market in late 1959 and early 1960 they slowed down the rise in interest rates which would otherwise have taken place. They pursued essentially contradictory monetary credit and fiscal policies in the first half of 1960, the one restrictionary, the other expansionary. In late 1960 they reduced Bank rate to stem the inflow of funds whilst the underlying balance of payments was seriously in deficit and in January 1961 they relaxed hire purchase restrictions. And the April 1961 Budget should have been much tougher given the flight of foreign funds from London in March. In retrospect economic policy seems to have been seriously at fault.

It may be asked if it is legitimate to give the balance of payments primacy as a goal. The answer would seem to be yes. For in the final analysis the authorities were prepared to sacrifice both growth and employment and other subsidiary goals. Should they have done so is quite a different question and is touched on in the final section of the chapter.

V.5   1961-64

In the second half of 1961 the balance of payments on both current and long-term capital accounts improved, though it would be a mistake to attribute the whole improvement to the July measures. Economic activity had been slowing down for months before these were introduced and from about the last quarter of 1960 the trend of imports had been downwards. Production was tending to decline and unemployment to increase. But despite the latter wages and prices continued to rise rapidly; many wage agreements had been negotiated in advance of the July measures. Nevertheless by October 1961 the authorities felt able to reduce Bank rate from 7 to 6½ per cent and by April 1962, after four further reductions, it was down to 4½ per cent.

The 1962 Budget was essentially a 'standstill' budget; the net changes in taxation were negligible, though many individual changes were made and, as already mentioned, the short-term capital gains tax was introduced. Government expenditure was planned to increase slightly and the budget surplus to remain much the same as for 1961-62.

Industrial production began to recover early in 1962, but unemployment remained relatively high. The authorities felt that the economy needed some additional stimulus. Hire-purchase restrictions were relaxed somewhat in June, the first repayment of special deposits was made, followed by two others before the end of the year. In October the previous requests to the banks and other financial institutions to exercise credit restraint were withdrawn. The Chancellor of the Exchequer announced a further repayment of post-war credits and additional increases in investment in the public sector. In November he announced that in his next Budget he proposed to introduce tax concessions to encourage investment in plant and machinery and industrial building. At the same time he reduced tax on cars from 45 to 25 per cent.

Many of these measures were taken in the light of continued slackness in the economy in the second half of the year. Despite the slackness, imports continued at a high level and the balance of payments remained barely satisfactory. Prices and wages maintained their upward trend. The economy was clearly very delicately balanced. Resources were not fully employed, yet wages and prices were rising, and any expansion of output might be expected to lead to balance of payments difficulties.[1]

The authorities, nevertheless, decided to stimulate the economy further. The top rate of purchase tax was reduced from 45 to 25 per cent and in January 1963 Bank rate was

---

[1]   'Imports may continue to rise as home demand increases', *BEQB*, December 1962, Vol. II, No. 4, p. 242, and, 'there is little sign of a substantial rise in exports', *ibid.*, March 1963, Vol. III, No. 1, p. 4.

lowered from 4½ to 4 per cent. These measures were followed by a highly expansionary budget. Taxation for 1963-64 was reduced by some £269 million, government expenditure was to rise by about 7½ per cent over the previous year, and for the first time for many years a deficit was planned. At the same time there was to be a borrowing requirement of almost £690 million.

Under the cumulative influence of this series of expansionary measures, combined with an increase in exports, activity grew rapidly and unemployment fell. Prices and wages went on rising. For the first half of 1963 the balance of payments on current and long-term capital account remained in surplus, but then ran into deficit. The foreign exchange reserves fell by £53 million during the year.

Early in 1964 the authorities began to fear that the pace of economic activity could not be maintained, mainly because of the weakness of the balance of payments.[1] For some months Treasury bill and other rates had been rising and in February Bank rate was raised from 4 to 5 per cent. The Budget increased taxation by about £100 million, mostly on tobacco and alcohol. Government expenditure was to go up by some £570 million or almost 8½ per cent. A small Budget surplus was planned, together with a large borrowing requirement of £790 million. The increased taxation might do something to check the growth of consumption expenditure, whereas the enlarged expenditure and borrowing requirement were bound to add to total demand. The chancellor was aware that he was taking a gamble, whether justifiably or not remains to be seen.[2]

Production continued to expand, though not as fast as in 1963, and unemployment declined substantially. Wages and prices rose rapidly. The authorities permitted some rise in interest rates, but at the same time kept it in check by purchasing in the first three-quarters of the year some £230 million of gilt-edged securities. Clearing bank deposits and advances grew quickly, at 7.3 per cent and 11.3 per cent respectively, over the twelve months from September 1963.

Meanwhile the balance of payments deficits on both current and long-term capital account grew larger. The figures are shown in Table 2.10 (below). Between the 1st and 3rd quarters of 1964 the combined quarterly deficits increased from £155 million to £250 million. For a time the seriousness of the position did not show up in the foreign exchange reserves as funds continued to flow to London. But this precarious inflow changed to an outflow in the third quarter as sterling holders became aware of the balance of payments situation. Another crisis had almost matured.

TABLE 2.10

Balance of Payments Deficits—Current and Long-Term Capital Transactions

£ million

		June 1963–December 1964				
1963			1964			
						Cumulative
1st qtr	2nd qtr	1st qtr	2nd qtr	3rd qtr	4th qtr	Total
60	83	155	170	250	201	919

Source: ET, September 1967, p. XVIII.

The new Labour government decided to take immediate action and in October announced a temporary surcharge of 15 per cent on most imports, except foods and raw materials, and a tax rebate on exports. These measures were followed by a special Budget in November which increased the tax on petrol by sixpence a gallon; proposed, from April

---

[1] *BEQB,* March 1964, Vol. IV, No. 1, p. 3.

[2] He emphasised in his budget speech that the size of the increase in taxation required was a matter of judgment and that if circumstances altered further remedies might be required. Reported in *BEQB,* June 1964, Vol. IV, No. 2, p. 87

1965, to raise the standard rate of income tax by sixpence, to introduce a long-term capital gains tax and to levy corporation tax on companies instead of income tax and profits tax.

In the words of the Bank of England, 'Opinion abroad . . . was not reassured' by these measures and 'the gilt-edged and equity markets weakened sharply, mainly as a result of the uncertainty engendered by the proposals for a new capital gains tax and the corporation tax, and this weakness added to the difficulties in the foreign exchange markets.[1] When two Thursdays elapsed without any increase in Bank rate—the usual day for changes— 'confidence weakened and there was renewed heavy selling [of sterling] in the market. Sales on Friday were exceptionally large, and, as part of the government's policy to maintain sterling at its present parity, Bank rate was raised on Monday the 23rd November from 5 per cent to 7 per cent.[2] But confidence was still not restored and on the following two days heavy selling of sterling continued. The authorities quickly negotiated credit facilities of $3,000 million.[3] The crisis had passed its peak.

The three years from 1961 to 1964 bring little credit to the policy makers; if anything, they reflect in terms of the culminating crisis a worse performance than over the previous four years. Economic activity was slow to recover after 1961, the balance of payments was almost a continuous problem or threatened to become one and prices and wages continued to rise throughout. The cumulative effects of monetary, credit and fiscal policy in late 1962 and during 1963 were over-expansionary and inconsistent with a satisfactory balance of payments position, price stability and sustainable economic growth. The failure to take adequate measures, during the first ten months of 1964 prior to the election, in face of a mounting balance of payments deficit, which in the third quarter of the year was running at an annual rate of £1,000 million, is one of the most irresponsible episodes in the history of economic policy in the post-war period.[4] The new Labour government also failed to come fully to terms with the extent of the crisis and some of their early measures accentuated the problem.

V.6   1964-68

Though the 1964 currency crisis may have passed its peak with the announcement of the large overseas credit facilities for the support of sterling, it was by no means over. The pound remained under pressure for the next couple of months as funds continued to leave London, and in the fourth quarter of the year the foreign exchange reserves fell by £80 million, 'in spite of the I.M.F. drawing of £357 million and the net receipt of £145 million of other special assistance'.[5]

By the time of the April Budget the balance of payments position had improved some-what, unemployment remained low at 1.6 per cent, prices and wages had gone on rising over the previous six months and production was greater than in late 1964. There were few, if any signs that the November measures were having a depressing effect on the economic system.

The Budget was estimated to increase taxation by £164 million, mostly from higher duties on tobacco, alcohol and motor vehicles. Government expenditure was expected to

---

[1]   *BEQB*, December 1964, Vol. IV, No. 4, p. 256.

[2]   *Ibid.*

[3]   It is extremely informative to contrast the content and emphasis of the Bank of England account of the crisis with that of the Treasury. A brief quotation from the Treasury's account will have to suffice here. 'In the second half of November a large-scale withdrawal of funds from London began to take place. Strong defensive measures were taken: first, Bank rate was raised from 5 to 7 per cent; secondly, massive new credit facilities totalling $3,000 million, were negotiated with Central Banks overseas.' *Economic Report on 1964*, H.M. Treasury, p.4.

[4]   This statement takes for granted that the authorities were serious about maintaining the exchange rate.

[5]   *BEQB*, March 1965, Vol. 5, No. 1, p. 11. The I.M.F. is discussed in chapter 3. The drawing mentioned was under the standby facility previously arranged with the I.M.F.

rise by 10 per cent, with revenue rising rather more, so that the surplus was to be about £100 million greater than in the previous year. On the other hand government borrowing was to rise substantially and to more than absorb the expected surplus. Overall the budget could hardly be called deflationary. The chancellor also announced a tightening up of exchange control to reduce the net outflow of funds on private long-term capital account.

Just after the Budget the Bank of England became very concerned about the growth of advances and the commercial bill holdings of the banks. It called for special deposits, emphasising that the call should be allowed to affect the banks lending activities and should be 'mitigated as little as possible by the sale of investments'.[1] The banks were also told that their lending to the private sector 'should not increase at an annual rate of more than 5 per cent during the twelve months to March 1966.[2] Clearly, by this time the authorities had little confidence in their special deposits instrument which by now had essentially been superseded by direct control of advances.

In June Bank rate was reduced from 7 to 6 per cent and hire purchase restrictions were increased. The reduction in Bank rate seems odd. The authorities, explaining it, emphasised that this was still a very high rate and that it did not imply any relaxation in credit restriction.[3]

But the pressure on sterling was still causing concern even though the reserves had been strengthened by a further drawing in May from the I.M.F. The chancellor announced in July—less than four months after the Budget—new restrictions on public and private expenditure and further controls on foreign investment.

The deficit on current account remained large—over £100 million—in the third quarter but improved dramatically in the final quarter. For the year as a whole the deficit on current and long-term capital account was £342 million compared with £776 million in 1964. The position had improved but cumulative deficits of these magnitudes could not be sustained on the basis of reserves available or potential borrowing powers of the UK government.

During 1965 production grew by about 3 per cent, unemployment remained low around 1.5 per cent and prices and wages continued to move upwards at rapid annual rates—retail prices by almost 5 per cent and average weekly earnings of manual workers by 8 per cent. The money supply grew by some 6.5 per cent, more than twice as fast as output, though this was supposed to have been a period of monetary and credit restraint.[4]

Early in 1966, the Bank of England, still worried about the high level of activity in the economy and the state of the balance of payments, reinforced credit restriction to the private sector by asking the banks not to increase their lending, until further notice, above the levels previously agreed for March 1966. Hire purchase restrictions were also further intensified and £316 million of official holdings of dollar securities were transferred to the reserves. The Budget in May 1966 increased taxation by £386 million, most of it attributable to expected receipts from the introduction of the selective employment tax. But these would only begin to accrue to the Exchequer from September. Government expenditure was estimated to rise by 8.5 per cent and revenue by rather more, yielding a surplus of £1,047 million. But this was to be more than absorbed by lending, leaving a net borrowing requirement of £287 million. Once again this could scarcely be called an overall deflationary budget, though the chancellor said he wanted to ease the pressure of demand. Other Budget measures included further restraints on overseas investment.

---

[1] *BEQB,* June 1965, Vol. 5, No. 2, p. 111.
[2] *Ibid.* Other financial institutions were similarly instructed.
[3] This statement seems contradictory in that it is to be expected that as interest rates decline the demand for credit will increase. The authorities presumably believed that they had so effectively controlled the supply of credit that a reduction in interest rates would not enable demanders of credit to get any more.
[4] The money supply is defined here to be, currency in circulation with the public plus net deposits of UK residents with the banking sector. *FS,* March 1968.

Unemployment remained low, prices and wages went on rising and the balance of payments on current and long-term capital account continued in deficit. Heavy selling of sterling developed in June and worsened in July, perhaps accentuated by the seamen's strike, rising interest rates overseas and measures taken by the United States authorities to strengthen their balance of payments position.

The renewed pressure on sterling stimulated the authorities to take additional measures. Bank rate was raised from 6 to 7 per cent; a further call was made for special deposits; hire purchase restrictions were made still more stringent; a surcharge of 10 per cent was imposed on purchase tax rates and on the duties on alcohol, oil and petrol; surtax rates were increased by 10 per cent for one year and postal charges were raised. 'A six-months standstill on prices and on wages, salaries and other types of income was imposed, to be followed by a further six months of severe restraint'.[1] And increased restrictions were placed on foreign expenditure, including the introduction of the £50 travel allowance for persons. Later in the year the Bank of England, attempting to strengthen the reserves, arranged increased credit facilities with other central banks.

In the second half of 1966 industrial production declined, unemployment increased, wages remained practically stable, the rise in prices slowed down and the balance of payments, after a deficit of £148 million on current and long-term capital account in the third quarter ran a surplus of £136 million in the final quarter—the timing of payments was still probably feeling the effects of the seamen's strike and imports were down in the fourth quarter in anticipation of the lifting of the temporary import charge. For the year as a whole industrial production remained almost static, wages went up by about 3.5 per cent and prices by around 2.5 per cent. The money supply increased by over 6.5 per cent, much the same as in the previous year. The balance of payments had a deficit on current and long-term capital account of £175 million.

At the turn of the year the authorities were optimistic that a surplus would be achieved in the balance of payments in 1967. Funds were returning to London enabling most of the outstanding short-term debt to central banks to be repaid by the end of March. Production was showing signs of picking up after the decline in late 1966, but at a rate that the authorities thought might be sustainable, as with around 2 per cent unemployed there seemed to be some capacity for further expansion.

Bank rate was reduced from 7 to 6½ per cent in January; two further reductions brought it down to 5½ per cent by May. The authorities managed to make substantial sales of government securities as interest rates declined, especially in the early months of the year. The chancellor in the Budget left the volume of taxation essentially unchanged. Estimated expenditure went up by some £1,500 million, about 14 per cent, and revenue by slightly less, leaving an estimated surplus of £637 million. But loans to industry and others were planned at £1,580 million, leaving a net borrowing requirement of £943 million. The impact of this increased volume of government and government financed expenditure could in time only be expansionary and also inflationary, especially if major reliance was placed on the banking system for its financing. It makes little sense to say that the chancellor 'did not propose to take any substantial action to influence demand'.[2] He had already done so.

The optimistic expectations about the balance of payments were not fulfilled. Both the first and second quarters of the year showed deficits on current and long-term capital accounts.[3] In May sterling came under pressure, after poor trade figures for April, and

---

[1]   *Economic Report on 1966,* H.M. Treasury, p. 6.
[2]   *BEQB,* June 1967, Vol. 7, No. 2, p. 121.
[3]   The balancing item in the accounts was positive for both quarters and sufficient to offset the deficits.

before war broke out in the Middle East, putting the pound under additional strain.[1] Interest rates which had previously been falling began to rise just after the reduction of Bank rate to 5½ per cent, a move which now seems most untimely. The authorities gave massive support to the gilt-edged market, purchasing £338 million of securities in the second quarter, most of it presumably in May and June.

Notwithstanding the precarious position of sterling and the balance of payments the authorities decided, as unemployment at over 2 per cent was thought uncomfortably high, to give some stimulus to domestic activity. Hire purchase restrictions were partly relaxed in June and August, increased social security benefits were to be introduced from November, the payment of investment grants was to be speeded up and a new regional employment premium was to be paid in the autumn to manufacturing establishments in the development areas. These measures led to increased sales of sterling.[2]

With interest rates rising abroad and the balance of payments in the third quarter in overall deficit, partly as a consequence of the Middle East crisis and the closure of the Suez canal delaying exports and making imports expensive, the Bank raised Bank rate from 5½ to 6 per cent in October and early in November to 6½ per cent. But these measures were not enough to stem speculation against sterling and the reserves continued to fall even when buttressed with substantial credit from overseas central banks. The authorities came to realise 'that, without severe new measures, there would be another substantial deficit in the balance of payments next year; and the widespread conviction that the measures taken would include devaluation of sterling precipitated a further out-flow of funds.

Devaluation took place on 18th November'.[3]

Additional measures were introduced or announced at the same time. Bank rate was raised to 8 per cent; bank lending to the private sector, except for exporters, was to be held at current levels; hire purchase terms on cars were tightened; *future* defence expend-iture was to be reduced; the corporation tax was to go up from 40 to 42½ per cent in the next Budget and selective employment tax premiums paid to manufacturers outside the development areas were withdrawn. New credits were negotiated with the I.M.F. and overseas central banks to a total of almost $3,000 million and the rest of the Treasury's portfolio of dollar securities—£204 million at the new rate of exchange—was brought into the reserves.

The foreign exchange market soon took the view that the measures taken to curtail the domestic economy were inadequate. The pound again came under pressure in December as funds were withdrawn from London. The whole position was further com-plicated by fears for the gold value of the dollar and the London market experienced very heavy demands for gold.

It need scarcely be said that 1967 was an appalling year for economic policy, though

---

[1]   The strain should not be exaggerated. In particular, much of the Middle Eastern holdings of sterling were transferred to banks abroad, which continued to hold the sterling in London, with no loss to the reserves. See *BEQB*, September 1967, Vol. 7, No. 3, p. 219.

[2]   'Following the announcement of further relaxations in hire purchase restrictions . . . there were fairly heavy sales of sterling.' *ibid.*, December 1967, Vol. 7, No. 4, p. 339.

[3]   *Ibid* p. 336. It was again worth contrasting the description above with that given by the Treasury. 'By late autumn it was plain that the balance of payments was still in serious disequilibrium and likely to remain so in 1968, particularly if the Suez Canal remained closed. In the circumstances, and given the intensity of the speculative pressure which had built up against the pound, drastic corrective action was imperative. With unemployment exceptionally high and the recovery of out-put from the impact of the July 1966 measures barely established, renewed deflation was un-acceptable to the government. Devaluation was therefore decided upon; and on the 18th November a new exchange parity of £1=$2.40 was declared.' *Economic Report on 1967*, H.M. Treasury, p. 7. Few observers would accept that the action was as nice and deliberate as this account suggests. There is evidence that the government on taking office in 1964 had deliberately rejected devalua-tion and were not converted to it until it was forced upon them by the balance of payments position and possibly the inability to continue massive foreign borrowing at the old exchange rate.

it should be added in mitigation that the problems were accentuated by a number of un-predictable factors, the Middle East war, closure of the Suez canal and the Liverpool and London dock strikes. However, the underlying economic situation, in terms of the failure to achieve the various policy goals, had been chronically unsatisfactory for years to the extent—that the problems were familiar and becoming more serious.

In the middle of January 1968 the Prime Minister announced cuts in the growth of public expenditure for 1968-69 and the following year. Slightly later the Chancellor of the Exchequer stated that he was bringing forward the Budget from early April to 19th March. In the intervening two months there was a massive increase in consumers' expend-iture in anticipation of increased taxation in the Budget and the pound felt the effects of intensive speculation in the gold market in the expectation that the official dollar price of gold might be raised. This speculation subsided with the introduction of the dual market system for gold in March 1968.[1]

The 1968 Budget brought the largest increases in taxation of any Budget in the period under study. For the year 1968-69 they totalled £775 million. Income tax rates were unaltered but various changes were made in allowances; customs and excise duties and purchase tax were increased, as were motor vehicle duties and the selective employment tax, and for 1967-68 a special charge was levied on investment incomes in excess of £3,000. Total expenditure was to increase by over £600 million or by 5.6 per cent. Total revenue was expected to rise by £1,698 million or by over 15 per cent, which was calculated to leave a large surplus of £1,386 million. But this is to be more than absorbed by loans, leaving a borrowing requirement of £358 million.

The Budget was generally welcomed as being what the economy needed, in terms of encouraging the release of resources for exports to take advantage of devaluation. It is true that if allowance is made for expected price increases government and government financed demands will increase only slightly in real terms and by less than the anticipated 3 per cent or so growth in output. But is still remains that the Budget has an overall deficit and is to that extent more expansionary, given the level of expenditure, than if the deficit had been covered by taxation. Furthermore, how expansionary hinges critically on the way the government finances the deficit. If it relies heavily on the banking system this will increase the money supply, despite strict control of bank lending to the private sector, and in itself be expansionary. The expansionary stimulus may not matter, depend-ing on how output grows and on the other demands placed on it.

As production has been almost static in the last three years and unemployment at around 2.5 per cent is relatively high there should be scope, in terms of capacity available, for a substantial increase in real output. The demands placed on it by consumers, investors, government and exports are, with perhaps the exception of government, difficult to fore-cast. But it should be remembered that the behaviour of consumers and investors will reflect not only the recent policy actions of the government but expectations about the future. These will be highly coloured by past experience, especially the persistent rise in prices, encouraging purchases now rather than later. Furthermore, behaviour will be affected by accumulated money holdings and other financial assets and liabilities. To the extent that there is an attempt to substitute real assets for financial assets an increase in demand for current goods may be expected. This whole process will be accentuated if the authorities are determined, as seems likely, to bring down interest rates.[2] A prices, incomes and dividends policy may for a time restrain or even prevent increases in *nominal* prices, but it will not prevent the kind of balance sheet substitution described above and the accompanying demands on real resources.[3]

---

[1] This issue is fully discussed in chapter 3.
[2] Bank rate was reduced from 8 to 7½ per cent on 21st March.
[3] The term 'nominal' is used because price fixing by the government at levels below those which would rule in competitive markets will tend to cause a reduction in quality, hence real prices will rise. Output may also be adversly affected.

All these possibilities may not greatly matter provided the balance of payments responds as hoped to devaluation. The response is to a degree unpredictable as exports depend heavily on events in the rest of the world, particularly the level of economic activity. Imports, on the other hand are greatly affected by domestic policy. For what it is worth this writer expects further balance of payments crises, given a serious commitment to such policy goals as a fixed, or at any rate temporarily fixed exchange rate, full employment, rapid economic growth and some more freedom of action, for the individual members of the community in economic matters.[1] But unless there is some international, political, economic or military upheaval the crisis may be postponed to late 1969 or even 1970, especially if devaluation helps to bring a substantial temporary improvement in the balance of payments.

V.7 Policy in Retrospect

In terms of the goals set out in the introduction, and some of which have again just been referred to, economic policy since the early 1950s must be judged a failure. The pound has been devalued, balance of payments crisis have followed each other with almost monotonous regularity, price stability has been the exception rather than the rule and economic growth has been fitful, and low by recent international standards. The only goal achieved more or less consistently has been 'full' or nearly 'full' employment.

It seems highly likely that the simultaneous achievement of these goals over an extended period of time is impossible given the policy instruments at or likely to be at the disposal of the authorities and taking for granted a reasonable degree of economic freedom for the individual as a consumer and producer. It is in no sense fortuitous, given the official economic goals and their extension into such areas as regional policy, that the authorities have found it necessary to interfere more and more with the decisions of individuals. The logic of espousing a large number of goals is the necessity to acquire more instruments or method to realise them.[2]

But even if it is assumed that the number of instruments is theoretically sufficient to realise the goals it does not follow that they will be realised. For the knowledge almost certainly does not yet exist that would enable the instruments to be manipulated in terms of timing and magnitude so as consistently to achieve the goals.[3] Nevertheless, time and time again in the period under review the timing and magnitude of official policy measures were badly astray, accentuating the then current economic problems. In other words a different application of the measures might have more nearly achieved the set of goals.[4]

At the risk of oversimplification and to be rather more specific it seems to the writer that the authorities have fairly consistently failed to appreciate the inflationary significance of large budgetary net borrowing requirements, or alternatively, of overall budgetary deficits. In financing these and at the same time managing the continuously maturing national debt the authorities have favoured short-run stability of interest rates with a consequent neglect of the money supply and the time lags before monetary and fiscal measures show much effect. Related to this was the failure to appreciate the length of the adjustment period required to absorb the accumulation of financial assets during and after the war. The Radcliffe Committee, whilst aware of the extended adjustment period, nevertheless seems to have misread the situation by tending to dismiss the money supply, and in so doing perpetuated the mistakes of policy. However, it does not, of

---

[1] These points are taken up again in the next section.
[2] See, J. Tinbergen, *On the Theory of Economic Policy*, North-Holland Publishing Company, Amsterdam, 1966.
[3] The text implies that theoretically the goals might be achieved *exactly*. This is only to simplify the exposition. At best the goals would only be more or less achievable. That is, there would be a random or stochastic element attached to them.
[4] The phrase 'more nearly achieved' begs the question of what is an optimum choice of goals and especially of how to measure the trade off of a bit more of one goal against a bit less of another. This seems unavoidable and raises again the whole question of judgment.

course, follow that improved fiscal and monetary policies will realise all the economic policy goals the authorities have in mind. Nor, even if an incomes prices and productivity policy is added and additional international liquidity is provided, does it seem likely.[1] Furthermore, the more the former is extended the more individual economic freedom will be diminished.

Society must, and indeed is continually, making judgments, implicit or otherwise, on these matters. The larger the number of specific goals it wishes the state to have or determine on its behalf, then logically it must concede to the state the need for it to have an increasing number of instruments at its disposal. Alternatively, society might decide that the state should pursue on its behalf only a limited number of goals, such as full employment, and be rather less concerned about price stability, fixed exchange rates and the balance of payments; or it might opt for a more or less stable rate of growth of income, giving less attention to the other goals mentioned. But whatever emerges society cannot escape the necessity of choice, either by default or by design.

REFERENCES AND FURTHER READING

Bank of England Quarterly Bulletin.
The British Banking System, Central Office of Information, Reference Pamphlet No. 65, HMSO, 1964.
British Financial Institutions, Central Office of Information, Reference Pamphlet No. 24, HMSO, 1966.
The British System of Taxation, Central Office of Information, Reference Pamphlet No. 10, HMSO, 1965.
Capital Gains Tax, No. 560 (1966), Board of Inland Revenue.
Corporation Tax, No. 570 (1966), Board of Inland Revenue.
J. C. R. Dow, 'The Management of the British Economy, 1945-60', Cambridge University Press, 1964.
Financial Statistics: Notes and Definitions, Central Statistical Office, HMSO,
N. J. Gibson, 'Financial Intermediaries and Monetary Policy', Hobart Paper 39, Institute of Economic Affairs, 1967.
E. Victor Morgan, *Monetary Policy for Stable Growth,* Hobart Paper. 27 (2nd edition), Institute of Economic Affairs, 1966.
W. E. Norton, *An Econometric Study of the United Kingdom Monetary Sector 1955-66,* unpublished Ph.D. thesis, University of Manchester, December 1967.
A. R. Prest, *Public Finance in Theory and Practice* (3rd edition), Weidenfeld and Nicolson, 1967.
Report of the Committee on the Working of the Monetary System (Radcliffe Committee), Cmnd. 827, HMSO, 1959. Principal Memoranda of Evidence (3 Volumes) and Minutes of Evidence, HMSO, 1960.
R. S. Sayers, *Modern Banking* (7th edition), Oxford University Press, 1967.
J. Tinbergen, *On the Theory of Economic Policy,* North-Holland Publishing Company, Amsterdam, 1966.

---

[1]   It should be apparent to the reader of this chapter that to blame the 'gnomes' of Zurich for recurrent balance of payments crises is at best to confuse cause and effect.

3

Foreign trade and the balance of payments

I THE UK BALANCE OF PAYMENTS

I.1 Foreign Trade and the UK Economy

The UK is an 'open' economy, by which is meant that the volume and structure of production and consumption of goods and services is dependent on international trade and division of labour. In the case of the UK this dependence is heavy. To maintain the present population at current standards of living it is necessary to import something like half of our total food requirements and the bulk of industrial raw materials. Broadly speaking, these are exchanged for manufactured goods which constitute the bulk of our exports of goods, though, as we shall see, the pattern of trade also involves the exchange of services, 'invisible' trade, on a massive scale. The monetary values of these and related international transactions are collected together in the Balance of Payments Account which forms an integral part of the general system of National Income Accounts of the country.

The importance of foreign trade and the balance of international payments for the prosperity and growth of the UK can scarcely be doubted by anyone who followed newspaper reports and discussions during the balance of payments crisis of 1964-67, but this crisis was only the latest demonstration of Britain's intimate dependence on foreign trade. In the nineteenth century the main trends in the growth of industrial production and real income have been shown to be closely connected with trends in our foreign trade, and major business fluctuations in the period were the result of a complex interaction of fluctuations in exports and residential building activity. The main cause of the heavy unemployment in the UK in the inter-war period is also undoubtedly to be found in adverse trends in our export trade.

The Second World War created a new set of foreign trade problems for the UK. Wartime destruction of merchant shipping, together with the forced liquidation of profitable overseas investments in the period before Lend-Lease, led to a marked decline in Britain's invisible receipts from abroad. On the payments side it was necessary to pay interest on a greatly increased level of indebtedness arising from the war, and to this was added a big increase in overseas expenditure by the government. In the early post-war years, full employment and reconstruction were possible only as a result of massive economic aid from the USA and Canada. In 1945 and 1946 the Anglo-American and Anglo-Canadian Financial Agreements provided the UK with long-term loans of $3.75 billion and $1.25 billion respectively. These loans were to be repaid in equal instalments over a fifty year period beginning December 1951 with interest at the very low rate of 2%. Further aid from the USA in the form of substantial grants was received under the European Recovery Programme during the years 1948-51. Ironically, it was the Anglo-American Loan Agreement that produced the first of Britain's post-war foreign exchange crises, the 'convertibility crisis' of 1947. This resulted from a premature attempt to make sterling freely convertible into gold or dollars on account of all current transactions. The policy, a requirement of the 1945 Agreement, had to be abandoned after five weeks because of the heavy drain on UK reserves. The second foreign exchange crisis came in 1949. In the course of an economic recovery, based on a huge expansion of exports and stringent control of imports, the country was forced by a speculative crisis to devalue the pound by 30% in September 1949. Since 1949 there have been six further foreign exchange crises, which have had powerful repercussions on general economic policy, culminating in the prolonged disturbance from 1964 to 1967 which led to the second UK post-war devaluation of 14.3% in November, 1967.

Although Britain is often considered to be unusually dependent on foreign trade it is worth noting that our degree of dependence is actually less than that of some of our European competitors in international trade. For member countries of the OECD it is possible to compare the ratios of total exports or imports, inclusive of 'invisible' transactions, to national income on the basis of data which has been adjusted to allow for international comparisons. The UK export ratio for 1965 was 25% or roughly the same as the average of European members of the OECD. It was considerably less than that of some members like the Netherlands (54 per cent), Belgium (44 per cent), Switzerland (35 per cent) and Denmark (35 per cent), about the same as West Germany (23 per cent), and rather higher than Italy (21 per cent) and France (18 per cent).

TABLE 3.1

UK Imports, Exports and National Income for selected years

	1938		1955		1967	
	£ mill.	per cent	£ mill.	per cent	£ mill.	per cent
Imports						
Goods	835	82.3	3386	70.2	5673	69.1
Services	142	14.0	1095	22.7	1941	23.6
Property income net of tax	37	3.7	343	7.1	600	7.3
Total	1014	100.0	4824	100.0	8214	100.0
Exports						
Goods	533	56.0	3073	65.5	5023	63.2
Services	190	20.0	1104	23.5	2025	25.5
Property income net of tax	229	24.0	517	11.0	896	11.3
Total	952	100.0	4694	100.0	7944	100.0
Gross National Product (factor cost) £ mill.	5175		16978		33924	
Total Imports % GNP	19.6		28.4		24.2	
Total Exports % GNP	18.4		27.7		23.4	

Source: NIBB, 1967, *Preliminary Estimates,* 1968. (Cmnd. 3571)

In Table 3.1 the quantitative dependence of the UK on exports and imports is illustrated with figures for selected years, and the broad structure of trade is also shown. Both total exports and total imports currently amount to approximately 24 per cent of the value of GNP at factor cost, the percentage having increased substantially as compared with 1938, though it has fallen since 1955, and still further from the very high levels attained in 1951 when total exports and imports were 32 per cent and 35 per cent respectively of GNP. The high levels in 1951 were caused on the import side mainly by abnormally high import prices following the 1949 devaluation and the Korean War, and on the export side by the success of the post-war export drive. Since 1951 the prices of both exports and imports have tended to rise more slowly than the prices of goods and services in general (import prices having actually declined on trend), whilst the volume

of exports and imports (excluding property income) has grown faster than the volume
of national product, but not sufficiently fast to offset the relative decline in prices. Hence
the decline in the ratio of exports and imports to GNP in current values, though the ratio
in constant prices has tended to increase.

From Table 3.1 we see that the breakdown of total exports and imports into goods,
services, and property income shows only minor changes in structure between 1955 and
1967, but considerable changes as compared with 1938. On the export side the share of
net property income in total receipts from abroad has fallen sharply since 1938, when such
receipts constituted almost one quarter of the total. Even so, more than a third of total
receipts are generated by the export of services and receipt of property income. On the
import side the share of goods has fallen substantially since 1938, whilst payments for
services, including expenditure overseas (excluding transfers) by the government, and
property income, now account for about 31 per cent of total imports.[1] Some explanations
of trends will be given later in Section II.

I.2   The Concept of the Balance of Payments

Before we can proceed to examine the structure and behaviour of the UK balance of payments it is necessary to define this concept more rigorously. The balance of payments is,
in principle, a record of all economic transactions, during a period of time, between
residents of the UK and residents of the rest of the world. By residents of the UK we mean
private individuals living permanently in the UK, the UK central and local authorities, and
all business enterprises etc. located in the UK. The term includes agencies of the UK
government which operate abroad, but excludes any foreign branches or subsidiaries of
UK firms.

The balance of payments is usually set out in terms of values in sterling, though it is
obvious that, in principle, every transaction involves some foreign currency. The necessary
conversion factors are supplied by a set of foreign exchange rates which are determined
by day to day dealings in the foreign exchange market, subject to government interference
via the routine operations of the Bank of England acting as manager of the Exchange
Equalisation Account, which is the legal custodian of UK reserves of gold and foreign
exchange.

The previous statement requires some qualification since the pound sterling like the
US dollar is regarded as a 'key' currency in international trade. This means that foreign
trade may be carried on specifically in terms of these currencies which are internationally
acceptable to a greater or lesser extent. The key currency principle is particularly important in relation to the collection of countries known as the *Sterling Area* or the *scheduled
territories* as listed in official publications.[2] Imports into the UK from these countries
lead to the creation of *Sterling Balances,* i.e., British bank deposits, Treasury bills and
other UK government securities owned by non-residents of the UK. Normally such
balances are temporary, being liquidated either by the purchase of exports from the UK
or by conversion into foreign exchange to settle payments with other countries. Sterling
balances also arise when countries in the overseas sterling area sell goods to non-members
and exchange the foreign currencies so acquired for UK bank deposits, and it is the
custom for members of the sterling area to keep the bulk of their international reserves in

---

[1]   Note that the figures in Table 3.1 exclude private and government transfers. These items are
      included in the current account of the balance of payments because of their recurrent nature but
      it is arguable that they belong more properly to the capital account. Until 1965 private transfers
      were of negligible net importance. Government transfers form a considerable part of current
      government expenditure overseas. In 1967 they accounted for 0.5% of GNP and their inclusion
      in imports in Table 3.1 would raise the figure given by 2.2 per cent.

[2]   Broadly consisting of the Commonwealth except Canada plus South Africa, Eire, Iceland, Jordan,
      Kuwait and some others.

the form of sterling balances.[1] So sterling balances constitute a revolving fund with constant changes in the structure of ownership. Outstanding balances at any time represent short or long-term lending to the UK government, not always voluntary as the unfortunate owners of balances 'blocked' by the exchange control in the early post-war period would testify. Such lending is chiefly at the initiative of central banks or other official bodies, which acquire the sterling balances from their own residents in exchange for local currency and hold them as reserves. Sterling balances also arise when firms etc. in non-sterling countries purchase UK money for use in normal trade and financial operations, and balances are also held by international organisations like the IMF and the International Bank.

Before the war the outstanding total of sterling balances was of the same order of magnitude as the UK official gold reserve, the exact values at the year-end 1939 being £517 million and £545 million respectively. During the war the outstanding total of sterling balances increased enormously to a level of £3567 million at year-end 1945 of which some two-thirds was held by sterling area countries, whilst the gold reserve increased only to £610 million over the same period. The war-time increase in sterling balances occurred because the countries concerned supplied goods and services on credit to the UK government. Naturally, with the ending of hostilities the UK government was under pressure to release these balances for the purchase of essential goods and services since substantial sums were owned by relatively poor countries like India and Egypt. Despite the post-war balance of payments problems of the UK the volume of sterling balances was reduced by end-1949 to £3143 million but the Korean War and its effect on primary product prices caused a subsequent increase in total to £3577 million by the end of 1951. Since 1951 the outstanding total has been steady with some cyclical fluctuations, the average value outstanding (excluding international organisations) being about £3500 million during the period 1951-62 (inclusive). The 1962 year-end total was £3501 million.[2]

From 1963 onwards the series for overseas sterling holdings was discontinued and a new series was published giving external liabilities and claims in sterling, net liabilities on the new basis for year-end 1962 being £3166 million (excluding international organisations). Appendix Table A-8 gives summary data for both series.

I.3   The Structure of the UK Balance of Payments

In official statistical practice the UK balance of payments is divided into three main sections. These are:

(1)   the Current Account
(2)   the Long-term Capital Account
(3)   Monetary Movements.

In general economic analysis items (2) and (3) together are often referred to as the capital account. In addition to the three headings there is a separate item known as the *balancing item*. It represents the sum of errors and omissions in the various headings and has a value such that aggregate payments equal aggregate receipts for the balance of payments as a whole. A positive entry means (a) an unrecorded net export if the capital account is regarded as correct, or (b) an unrecorded net reduction in assets if the current account is regarded as correct. Short-run changes in the item are almost certainly due to unrecorded capital movements but the item cannot be analysed with confidence in the longer run. It is often assumed, however, that the more volatile capital elements in the balancing item

---

[1]   In recent years this custom has been modified as members of the overseas sterling area have added to their own reserves of gold and non-sterling exchange. See A. R. Conan, 'Sterling: The Problem of Policy', *Westminster Bank Review,* November, 1967.

[2]   It is impossible to give here an adequately detailed account of the evolution of the sterling area in the post-war period. For an excellent short summary the reader is referred to Scammell, *International Monetary Policy,* chapter 9.

will cancel out when this is averaged over a number of years. Hence the term 'normal' balancing item, which is assumed to represent, mainly, the unrecorded flows of net exports.

The current account is mainly concerned with items giving rise to income and expenditure flows in the national income account, i.e. exports (credits) and imports (debits) of goods (visible trade) and exports and imports of services (invisible trade). It also includes some items which ought to be classified as capital items, e.g. private transfers such as gifts and migrants' funds and government transfers such as economic grants to Commonwealth and other countries. Thus the true nature of the current account balance is blurred—not seriously in the case of private transfers, but government transfers represent a significant percentage of total government payments.

The two sides of the current account, debits and credits, or payments and receipts, need not balance in principle and rarely do so in practice. If total receipts exceed total payments we speak of a current account surplus, whilst an excess of payments over receipts is a deficit on current account.

An export or import surplus can only arise to the extent that offsetting or accommodating transactions arise in the two sectors of the capital account. This is because, for the balance of payments as a whole, every receipt of foreign exchange must be matched by a corresponding payment, since we are dealing with actual transactions recorded during a past accounting period. The country as a whole may be likened to an individual household or firm which cannot spend more than it receives without liquidating assets, including cash, or going into debt. As a first approximation we could say that the items in the two sectors of the capital account are *induced* by the net outcome in the current account. A deficit in the current account may be financed either by long-term borrowing in the long term capital account or by short term borrowing or liquidation of foreign exchange reserves in the monetary movements account whilst a surplus in the current account implies the net acquisition of foreign assets. But this is too simple a view for any country and certainly for a key-currency country like the UK.

Capital account transactions may originate quite independently of the current account (though they may affect the current account) and such capital items may be termed *autonomous*. As an example, the UK government may decide to make a long-term loan to a Commonwealth government and may do this without knowing precisely what the state of the UK current account will be when the proceeds of the loan are spent or transferred. Or a firm or household in the UK may, with permission of the exchange control, purchase real or long-term financial assets abroad merely as an act of investment and will expect to be supplied with the necessary foreign exchange regardless of the state of the current account at the time of the transaction. In each of these cases it is possible that the autonomous act of lending abroad will alter the level of economic activity abroad and at home and cause the levels of UK exports and imports of goods and services to differ from the levels which would have occurred in the absence of the loans. Thus *autonomous* capital transactions have *induced* effects in the current account.

But what happens if the aggregate of such autonomous long-term transactions fails to be matched by an equivalent surplus of UK exports over imports even allowing for any induced trade flows? Britain is then in the position of an individual who invests in long-term securities to an amount greater than the difference between his income and expenditure. The answer in both cases is that the difference must be made up out of cash balances or by borrowing short-term. We should say that the combined deficit on current and long-term capital account was met by accommodating or induced changes in the monetary movements sector. The sum of the balances on current account and long-term capital account is often referred to as the *basic balance* and this balance is assigned a key role in the assessment of performance. There is much to be said for this approach since it allows for inter-dependence between the current and capital accounts and reduces ambiguity which might be caused by arbitrary allocations of certain items to one account rather than the other.[1]

The upshot of all this is that the various sectors of the balance of payments are related by complex forces and government attempts to influence any sector in isolation may not be successful. If the government tries to reduce the size of the long-term capital outflow in order to increase its gold and foreign exchange reserves it may find that the net effect is a reduced surplus on current account with little change in reserves. We return to this problem in Section III.

TABLE 3.2

UK Summary Balance of Payments, 1963—67 (£ mill.)

	1963	1964	1965	1966	1967
CURRENT ACCOUNT (credits + debits —)					
Visible Trade					
Imports (f.o.b.)(—)	4370	5016	5065	5263	5673
Exports and re-exports (f.o.b.)(+)	4287	4471	4784	5116	5023
Visible balance	— 83	—545	—281	—147	—650
Invisibles					
Government (net)					
Military	—236	—267	—267	—273	—258
Other expenditure	—145	—165	—179	—188	—191
Other invisibles and transfers (net)	+580	+575	+617	+577	+585
Invisible balance	+199	+143	+171	+116	+136
CURRENT BALANCE	+116	—402	—110	—31	—514
LONG-TERM CAPITAL ACCOUNT[1]					
Official investment (net)	—105	—116	—84	—82	—54
Private investment (net)	—50	—258	—148	—20	+28
BALANCE OF LONG-TERM CAPITAL	—155	—374	—232	—102	—26
Balance of current and long-term capital transactions (basic balance)	—39	—776	—342	—133	—540
BALANCING ITEM	—71	+45	+104	—13	+220
MONETARY MOVEMENTS[1]					
Exchange adjustments	—	—	—	—	—101
Miscellaneous capital (net)	—47	—16	+52	—121	+70
Changes in liabilities in non-sterling currencies (net)	—16	+218	—137	—148	+193
Changes in external liabilities in sterling (net)	+115	+48	+70	+135	+288
Changes in account with IMF	+5	+359	+499	—2	—318
Transfer from dollar portfolio to reserves	—	—	—	+316	+204
Changes in gold and convertible currency reserves	+53	+122	—246	—34	—16
BALANCE OF MONETARY MOVEMENTS	+110	+731	+238	+146	+320

[1] Assets: increase—/decrease +. Liabilities: increase +/decrease—.

Source: Preliminary Estimates of National Income and Balance of Payments 1962 to 1967, (Cmnd. 3571).

---

[1] In some discussions the 'normal' (positive) balancing item, estimated at about £50-£60m is included in the basic balance.

An outline picture of the UK balance of payments in recent years is given in Table 3.2 and Summary data for a longer period is given in Appendix Table A-7. The balance of visible trade is usually negative but is normally compensated by a surplus on invisible trade to give an overall surplus on current account; though since 1959 this has been true only in 1961, 1962 and 1963. Government net invisibles, i.e., net expenditure on military and diplomatic services plus transfers of economic aid, etc. are persistently negative but these are more than compensated by other net invisibles which will be shown in more detail later.

The balance of long-term capital is negative in most years, indicating that Britain was increasing her overseas assets. It also tends to be variable in size which is due since 1959 mainly to variations in net private investment. Net private investment is the outcome of substantial flows of investment in both directions by firms (direct investment) in over-seas branches and portfolio investment (the purchase of foreign securities) and 'other' investment which includes substantial direct investment by oil companies. It is the inflow to the UK since 1959 which is the main cause of fluctuations in the net balance. The balance of current and long-term transactions or basic balance shows the overall amount of accommodating finance which has to be provided by monetary movements and the balancing item.

For a detailed description of the constituent items in the monetary movements account the reader must be referred to official sources, e.g. the *Balance of Payments Orange Book* published each year around August. In general the account covers all identifiable changes in short-term assets and liabilities arising from the international transactions of individuals, firms, home and overseas banks and official organisations like the IMF and the Exchange Equalisation Account. The account illustrates the fact that, for a country like the UK, a deficit or surplus on current and long-term capital account is not to be thought of simply as representing a net loss or accretion of reserves of foreign exchange.

As an example of the way in which the balance of payments account is interpreted we may take the crisis year 1964. From Table 3.2 we see first that there was a serious visible deficit of £545m. This was explained mainly by the big increase in the value of imports of goods from 1963 occasioned by the stockbuilding which accompanied the 1963-4 boom. Government expenditure abroad increased in 1964 to £432m whilst other invisibles declined slightly, leaving the net surplus on invisible trade at £143m, a low figure compared with previous years. The deficit on current account was, therefore, abnormally high at £402 million. The long-term capital account showed a negative balance of £374 million, again abnormally high. The basic balance was, therefore, negative at £776 million. Allowing for the positive balancing item of £45 million the sum of £731 million had to be financed in the monetary movements account. Yet the table shows that reserves of gold and convertible currencies actually decreased only by £122 m over the course of the year. The main explanation of the difference is that the UK government was able to borrow its requirements of foreign exchange from the IMF and from a number of central banks overseas. The counterpart of the IMF loans to the UK is shown as an increase in sterling balances owned by the IMF (£359 million). The central bank assistance to the UK took the form partly of an increase in external liabilities in sterling, which was largely offset by a reduction in net sterling liabilities to other countries. Further short-term finance was provided to the extent of £218 million by the part of overseas central bank assistance which was initially granted in the form of foreign exchange deposits and by net borrowing abroad by UK banks. Some £16 million of this short-term finance was absorbed in meeting a net increase in short-term assets under the heading of *miscellaneous* capital movements. Note that in 1965 a deficit on the basis balance, net of the balancing item, was compatible with an increase in the gold reserve as a result of a further substantial drawing by the UK on the IMF, whilst in 1966 and 1967 a decline in the gold reserve was avoided by the sale of dollar securities owned by the UK government and the transfer of the proceeds to the official reserve. The special item in 1967 'Exchange adjustments' is a balancing entry made necessary by the revaluation of official liabilities and assets denominated in gold or foreign exchange, following the devaluation.

I.4   Equilibrium in the Balance of Payments

We have seen that the balance of payments as a whole must necessarily balance because of the way it is constructed. This does not mean that the balance of payments is always in a state of equilibrium. It is necessary, therefore, to consider the meaning of this concept and its importance for economic policy.

The following discussion takes for granted the fact that the UK is a member of the IMF and has, therefore, accepted the obligation to maintain the foreign exchange value of the pound within very narrow limits of a par value, the level of which can only be changed with the consent of the IMF when necessary to correct a 'fundamental disequilibrium' in the balance of payments. If the foreign exchange rate was not 'fixed' in this way but was free to vary under the influence of forces of supply and demand in the foreign exchange market there would be no apparent problem of economic policy in regard to the balance of payments.[1] Any tendency for the level of imports, including purchases of foreign securities, to exceed the level of exports would imply an excess demand for foreign exchange and this would reduce the foreign exchange value of the pound. This would raise the cost of imported goods in sterling and reduce the cost of British exports in terms of foreign exchange and, provided certain conditions were satisfied, the excess demand for imports and foreign exchange would be eliminated by market forces. The necessary conditions relate to the elasticities of demand and supply for imports and exports in the aggregate. Limitations of space preclude a discussion of the merits and demerits of such a system but its main disadvantages are threefold. First, it is argued that constant fluctuations in the foreign exchange rate make it difficult for businessmen to carry on the job of international trade and investment. Secondly, fluctuations in the exchange rate are likely, given present institutional conditions, to accelerate the rate of inflation. Thirdly, a freely fluctuating exchange rate is likely to encourage speculation and this may amplify unnecessarily the extent of the fluctuations, with implications for the first two arguments.[2]

A system of fixed exchange rates necessarily implies that the authorities have access to a buffer stock of reserves of gold or foreign exchange or short-term borrowing facilities[3] so that a temporary excess demand for foreign exchange by its residents can be met. If such a temporary excess demand is quickly reversed by natural forces (i.e. the reversal of a mild inventory boom which first raises and then reduces the demand for imports relative to trend) and the reserves are adequate in size to meet the cumulative excess demand for foreign exchange, no problem exists. If the excess demand for foreign exchange is not quickly reversed, or reserves are inadequate to act as a buffer, a disequilibrium situation exists.

A country can only run a persistent deficit on current account if it has unlimited reserves of gold or foreign exchange to draw upon or if it can borrow persistently from the rest of the world to finance the deficit. No country has unlimited reserves and persistent short-term borrowing would be unwise, even if it were possible, since there is always a danger of cessation or reversal of the short-term capital inflow. In either case the immediate result must be that foreign exchange reserves are liquidated at a rate which may shatter confidence in the country's ability to maintain the external value of its

---

[1]   In the sense of preventing loss of reserves, but the consequences of this automatic balancing of the foreign exchange market might raise awkward problems in other directions so that some short-term stabilisation would be regarded as necessary.

[2]   For a fuller discussion see Scammell. *International Monetary Policy*, pp. 92–9.

[3]   The UK can borrow short-term by raising Bank Rate, and therefore other short-term interest rates, relative to levels in other financial centres. This induces an increase in sterling balances. This mechanism tends to fail, however, if foreigners fear an imminent devaluation.

currency and a speculative foreign exchange crisis results. A persistent deficit matched by a long-term capital inflow is both possible and unobjectionable if the capital inflow is associated with policies to raise productive capacity and to stimulate the flow of exports or reduce dependence on imports. In the absence of such long-term loans, or grants of aid, the balance of payments may be said to be in disequilibrium if the value of imports persistently threatens to exceed the value of exports. A country faced with this situation must then introduce measures of economic policy to restore equilibrium in the balance of payments; indeed, such policy measures will be forced on the country by the threatened exhaustion of exchange reserves.

The previous argument needs to be qualified in a number of ways. For a given value of the exchange rate there will tend to be a positive correlation between the level of expenditure on imports and the level of employment or national income. The precise quantitative relationship may change through time as tastes and relative costs etc. change, but some positive co-variation is highly probable. This means that, if import values exceed export values at a given level of employment and income, a decline in employment and income will tend to restore the balance; indeed such a decline in incomes may arise automatically in certain cases owing to the operation of what is called the foreign trade multiplier process. Excess imports will not normally be eliminated completely by the automatic multiplier process unless the sum of expenditures on domestic investment and government purchase of goods and services falls more rapidly than levels of savings and tax collections, as income falls, but such a result may be contrived by economic policy.[1] The implication is that potential disequilibrium *may* be concealed if the country is operating at substantially less than full employment levels of output, an example of this being the UK situation in the 1920s. A corollary is that disequilibrium exists if an economy cannot pursue a policy of growth at full employment levels of output without being threatened with a persistent import surplus. Disequilibrium may also exist if a potential persistent import surplus is prevented by the imposition of abnormally severe restrictions on international trade; tariffs, import quotas and exchange control. The problem here is the definition of 'abnormal' and this can be settled only by reference to general aims and achievements in the field of international trade policy. Finally, for a relatively advanced and rich country like the UK the idea of equilibrium as a mere balance in the current account is too limited. UK governments have accepted the obligation to provide economic aid in the form of outright grants and long-term concessionary loans to under-developed countries, particularly those in the Commonwealth. There is also the fact that free mobility of capital from the UK to the rest of the sterling area is a traditional policy[2] and aside from the benefits of such lending to the receiving countries, the interest and dividends which result form an important part of our invisible earnings, whilst the capital export itself may benefit UK exports of goods or reduce the cost of imports. The UK government must also repay long-term loans from foreign governments of which the chief are the Anglo-American and Anglo-Canadian loans of 1945-6 which jointly involve an annual capital repayment of some £30m.[3] In addition to all this it is essential that the UK should build up her international reserves to a level adequate to meet a temporary disequilibrium in the balance of payments, allowing for temporary outflows of short-term capital.

---

[1] For a detailed discussion of this macroeconomic theory the reader must consult general texts. Good discussions are to be found in Brooman, *Macroeconomics,* and Kindleberger, *International Economics.* In a full analysis account must be taken of the 'feedback' effect of reduced imports on the level of exports, but this does not alter the conclusion given in the text above.

[2] The voluntary controls announced in the 1966 Budget may well mark the beginning of the end of this policy. See below, section III.

[3] Repayment of principal and interest on these North American loans may be deferred to the end of the century if the UK government considers it necessary. The right may be exercised only seven times and has been used in 1957, 1964 and 1965. Interest is payable at 2% on the sums deferred.

I.5   A Formal Definition of Equilibrium and Disequilibrium

The preceding discussion leads to the following definition. The balance of payments is in long-term equilibrium when the average current account surplus over a period of good and bad years is sufficient to cover (i) the required level of net external investment including debt repayment and grants of aid, and (ii) the required trend increase in foreign exchange reserves, without recourse to less than full employment levels of output and without recourse to trade and payments restrictions inconsistent with accepted international obligations. If these conditions are not satisfied the balance of payment may be said to be in a state of 'fundamental disequilibrium'.

The definition is tautological unless there is an independent specification of target levels of external investment, full employment etc. This is inevitable since such targets must, in principle, be subject to continuous political discussion and re-specification. Notice, also, that disequilibrium is a two-sided concept, a deficit disequilibrium for one country implies a surplus disequilibrium for at least one other country. In practice it is always difficult to get the governments of surplus countries to recognise this obvious truth, though recognition is likely to be rapid if the country switches from a state of persistent surplus to one of deficit.

Although reference is made to 'fundamental disequilibrium' the definition proposed is not taken explicitly from the Articles of Agreement of the IMF which nowhere defines this critically important concept. Some writers have chosen to define 'fundamental disequilibrium', in the IMF context, as a persistent tendency to lose reserves or the acceptance of 'abnormal' policy measures to prevent this. In the case of the UK a persistent tendency to lose reserves is scarcely a relevant criterion since any serious loss of reserves in the post-war period has tended to provoke a speculative foreign exchange crisis which could annihilate the official reserves within a year in the absence of corrective policy measures. The secondary drain in reserves is partly a consequence of the liquidation of sterling balances, to avoid a decline in their foreign exchange value caused by the anticipated devaluation, and partly by the so-called 'leads and lags' effect, whereby foreign payments due to the UK are delayed and payments by UK importers accelerated, to avoid any windfall losses which devaluation would produce. The *Radcliffe Report* (p. 236) estimated that the size of the leads and lags effect could amount to hundreds of millions of pounds and the actual sum involved will inevitably increase as the current level of trade increases.[1]

I.6   The UK Balance of Payments Since 1952—an Assessment

The formal definition of equilibrium will now be used to assess the performance of the UK balance of payments in recent years. We shall argue that the UK balance of payments, whilst never very strong before 1958, degenerated between 1959 and 1967 into a state of fundamental disequilibrium. It remains to be seen whether the 1967 devaluation and related policy measures will remove the disequilibrium.

Table 3.3 presents annual averages for the main items in the balance of payments for the periods 1952-5, 1956-60, 1961-4 and 1965-7. The first three periods cover complete short cycles of activity ending in a boom year with abnormally heavy imports and a serious deficit on current account. For 1965-7 the cycle is incomplete though the period again ends with a serious deficit year.[2]

---

[1]   The leads and lags effect could also apply to payments between the overseas sterling area and non-sterling countries. Since many sterling area countries failed to follow the UK devaluation in 1967 this source of leads and lags should end but could be replaced by new leads and lags between the UK and such sterling area countries.

[2]   The dating of the cyclical periods is arbitrary and it could be argued that the third cyclical period should be dated 1961-5. We have chosen to end it in 1964 since the figures for 1965-7 should reflect the impact of the government's major policy aim of improving the balance of payments position.

TABLE 3.3

UK Balance of Payments, Annual Averages for Selected Periods (£ mill.) and Average Annual Growth Rates of GDP

	1952-5	1956-60	1961-4	1965-7
Visibles net	−260	−95	−221	−359
Invisibles net	+327	+230	+183	+141
(Government)	−99	−210	−376	−452
(Other invisibles)	+426	+440	+559	+593
Current balance	+67	+136	−38	−218
Long-term capital[1] (net)	−160	−187	−140	−120
Basic balance	−93	−51	−178	−338
Balancing item	+69	+90	0	+104
Monetary movements[1]	+24	−39	+178	+235
(Change in gold etc. reserve)[1]	+19	−79	+82	−99
GDP (factor cost) average annual growth rate between selected years[2]	1951-55	1955-60	1960-64	1964-67
	2.9%	2.4%	3.6%	1.6%

[1] Assets: increase −/decrease +. Liabilities: increase +/decrease −.
[2] Calculated from expenditure estimates at constant (1958) prices.

Sources: UK Balance of Payments 1967 *(CSO):* ET, March 1968. Detail may not add to totals because of rounding.

In assessing the figures it is useful to have in mind the targets for achievement which have been set from time to time by the government. In the early post-war years the government was naturally preoccupied with the urgent problem of eliminating current account deficits and Britain's dependence on foreign aid, but by 1953 it was possible to take a longer view. The 1953 *Economic Survey* revealed that 'Over a period of years it is estimated that the annual surplus on current account needed to provide for commitments, and for some increase in gold reserves, might amount to something like £300-350 million' (p. 44). In 1959 the sights had been raised further and according to the *Radcliffe Report* (p. 232) the rough order of achievement for the early 1960s was to be an average current account surplus of £450 million, the increase being mainly in the form of a higher long-term capital outflow.

From Table 3.3 it is evident that the average current account surplus for the first cyclical period 1952-5 was well below the 1953 target level. To some extent this can be explained by revisions of the basic data which have reduced the size of the average surplus by some £60m. The revisions, however, also reduced the net long term capital outflow by a similar amount and left the basic balance more or less unchanged. It is clear from the negative basic balance of £93m. that the UK was not achieving a current account surplus big enough to cover the actual net long-term capital outflow, let alone a higher target level. Allowing for the positive balancing item there was, during this period, a small cumulative worsening of the monetary movements account including a reduction of £76 million in the level of reserves.

The second cyclical period shows a distinct improvement in performance. The current account improved by an annual average of £69m which is explained by a pronounced improvement in the visibles account associated with a favourable movement in the net barter terms of trade.[1] The invisibles account worsened as a result of the substantial increase in the deficit on government account, with other invisibles showing only a small

[1] This is the ratio of export prices to import prices. A rise in this ratio is conventionally described as an 'improvement' or 'favourable' and a fall in the ratio as a 'deterioration'. These terms may be misleading if the change in relative prices reduces or increases the purchasing power of foreign exporters to the UK and thus causes offsetting movements in the volume of UK exports.

increase. The net outflow on long-term capital account increased but by less than the change in the current account so that the basic balance was reduced slightly to a level of −£51m which was easily offset by the favourable balancing item. As a result the monetary movements account showed a cumulative improvement of £195m over the period with gold and convertible currency reserves increased by the substantial total of £395m.

One might say that the balance of payments was in a state of long-term equilibrium during the period 1956-60, despite the failure of the current balance to match the 1953 target since the actual long-term outflow was covered and it was possible to improve the reserve-liability position. But this satisfactory performance was achieved only at the cost of a lower rate of economic growth as compared with the previous cyclical period. The UK unemployment ratio was allowed to increase from 1.2% in 1955 to 2.3 per cent in 1959 though it fell to 1.7 per cent for the boom year of 1960. Between 1955 and 1958 real GDP increased only at the rate of 1.3% per annum and the volume of imports of goods at about the same rate so that, allowing for falling import prices, the value of goods imports (f.o.b.) in 1958 was roughly the same as that for 1955. Resumption of more rapid growth between 1958 and 1960 brought with it an adverse swing in the current account of £605m and showed how precariously based had been the surpluses of 1956 and 1957.

The third cyclical period 1961-64 saw a striking deterioration in the UK balance of payments. The current account worsened by an annual rate of £174m. This occurred partly because of the continued increase in the size of the government deficit, which more than offset the improvement in 'other' invisibles, and partly because of a deterioration in the visibles account, which resulted from accelerated growth of imports caused by the higher average growth rate of GDP. There was some decline in the average net long-term capital outflow, arising mainly from increased investment in the UK by foreigners, but the average basic balance deteriorated by £127m per annum compared with 1956-60. The period saw two severe foreign exchange crises in 1961 and 1964, each involving massive drawings from the IMF and each connected with a complex of deflationary measures including 7 per cent Bank rate. The cumulative adverse balance in the monetary movements account amounted to £712.million of which £328 million was a decline in the level of the reserve of gold and convertible currencies.

Throughout the fourth period, 1965-67, the improvement of the UK balance of payments was a major concern of UK government policy. The policy measures used will be discussed below in Section III but it is clear from Table 3.3 that in spite of a marked decline in the rate of growth of GDP, the actual performance of the balance of payments for 1965-7 was worse than that for 1961-4. It is true that the years 1965 and 1966 showed a progressive improvement on 1964 and that relapse in the current account for 1967 was partly explained by factors outside the UK government's control, e.g. the deceleration of world demand and the closure of the Suez Canal with its adverse effects on the cost of UK imports of oil and shipping services. From Table 3.3 we see that the average balance on current account worsened during 1965-7 by some £180 million as compared with 1961-64, whilst the long-term capital account showed a smaller deficit of £120 million. The average basic balance worsened by £160m compared with 1961-4 or £56 million per annum if calculated net of the large average balancing item. The monetary movements account showed a cumulative adverse balance of £704 million for the three-year period.

As reference to Appendix Table A-7 will show there were also sizeable deficits on monetary movements account for 1959 and 1960. There are grounds for regarding 1958-59 as a genuine turning point in the history of the UK balance of payments and as marking the onset of a state of fundamental disequilibrium.

Throughout the 1950s the UK had been removing the battery of restrictions on free international trade and payments which had served during the war-time and early post-war periods to protect her balance of payments. The trade controls had the effect of reducing the UK propensity to import with particular emphasis on imports from the dollar area so as to conserve current earnings and reserves of dollars. The payments controls were designed to restrict the convertibility of sterling acquired and held by various groups of non-residents for the same reason. In 1958 the pound was made freely convertible into gold or dollars for all non-residents in respect of current transactions and in 1958 and 1959 most of those remaining import controls, which operated as foreign exchange saving rather than as strategic or protective devices, were eliminated. It is true that substantial reductions in import controls had been made in 1953 and 1954 and that preparations for the move to convertibility had been made in 1955 when the Exchange Equalisation Account had been instructed to support the rate for Transferable Account sterling within 1% of the official exchange rate.[1] The main impact of these earlier relaxations had been concealed by the deflationary policy of the period 1955 to 1958. After 1958 the UK was operating under a relatively free trade and payments system (apart from the normal tariff structure which had been reduced somewhat in GATT negotiations) and any expansion of effective demand was bound to inflate the import bill. In fact the joint effect of the relaxations plus the stockbuilding boom of 1959-60 was to expand UK imports by 23 per cent between 1958 and 1960, and imports of manufactures, on which remaining controls before 1958 had been most severe, increased by 56 per cent in the two-year period.

In retrospect it is difficult to understand the optimism of the 1959 target. It seems probable that it had become obsolete long before the change of government in 1964. Official views may have been reflected in the NEDC targets which aimed to convert the 1961 current deficit into a surplus by 1966 of £300m (with a positive balancing item of £100million), which was later revised down to £225m with a balancing item of +£50m. Whether we measure achievement against any of these targets, or merely against the identified long-term capital balance, it seems impossible to evade the conclusion that between 1959 and 1964 the UK balance of payments was in a state of fundamental disequilibrium. The persistence of deficit since 1965, in spite of corrective policy measures, supports the conclusion.

An implication of the persistent weakness of the basic balance in the period 1959-67 is that the monetary movements account for the period shows an adverse balance of £1709 million, an amount roughly equal to 156% of the official reserves of gold and foreign exchange at the end of 1958. Even then the level of UK reserves was far too low for a major importing nation which was also a trading and reserve currency country. If we take the ratio of end-year reserves to imports for the same year the UK ratio for 1958 stood at 30 per cent. This compared with 154 per cent for the USA and 48% for the average of the other main industrial nations.[2] By 1963 the corresponding ratios were 23 per cent for the UK, 91 per cent for the USA and 47% for the other main industrial nations.

---

[1] Transferable (Account) sterling was one of the four types of sterling after the consolidation of the exchange control system in 1954. Other types were: (1) balances held by residents of the sterling area which could be used freely within the area but not outside it; (2) American Account sterling which could be used anywhere and was fully convertible into dollars at the official exchange rate; (3) Security sterling which accrued to non-residents of the sterling area from the sale of assets in the UK and, in principle, could be used only for re-investment in sterling assets. Transferable sterling could be used to make payments to any Transferable Account country or to the sterling area but in practice could be converted into dollars in unofficial free markets at a discount. Such conversions involved a loss of dollars to the UK since residents in the dollar area could make payments to the sterling area by acquiring Transferable sterling, at a discount, and the dollars accrued to the Transferable account countries instead of to the UK. In 1958 the Transferable and American accounts were consolidated. Security sterling remained for some years and was usually sold at a discount because of limitations on its use. In April 1967 it was abolished and non-residents were free to repatriate the proceeds from the sale of sterling securities at the official rate. It was hoped that this concession might encourage overseas investment in sterling securities.
Reserve ratios quoted here are calculated from data given in IFS. The other main industrial nations are the EEC countries and Switzerland, Austria, Denmark, Norway, Sweden, Canada and Japan. Reserves include gold, foreign exchange and the 'reserve position in the IMF', the last item being the amount which can be drawn more or less automatically from the IMF.

The relatively poor reserve-import ratio of the UK and its deterioration over the five-year period is clearly indicated by these figures. In fact the UK ratio was inferior not only to the average of the industrial nations, but also to that of the less developed nations. It may be argued that relative figures prove little about the absolute adequacy of the reserve of the UK and that the rest of the world could profitably have learned from the UK how to economise on international reserves. This argument makes little sense in the light of the numerous foreign exchange crises which the UK has experienced in the post-war period. Even if we allow for the full exercise of drawing rights on the IMF (which, technically, are not available to deal with short-term capital outflows) the UK reserves have been too small to cover both the absorption of temporary deficits on the basic balance and the related speculative flight from sterling. The weakness of the UK reserve position is illustrated by events in the last quarter of 1964. At the end of September the resources immediately available to the UK consisted of first-line reserves of £907million plus an IMF standby credit of $1000 million and a further $1000 million of short-term facilities with US and European Central Banks. In addition the UK could have mobilised, at relatively short notice, the dollar securities held by the Treasury and worth some £500 million, plus (on 1961 precedent) a further drawing on the IMF of some $1400 million. In spite of the fact that the major part of the 1964 basic deficit had already been financed by the end of September these resources proved insufficient to maintain confidence in the external value of sterling. The UK was saved from a crisis devaluation only as a result of the potential support of the massive short-term loan of $3000 million mounted in November by eleven Central Banks and the Bank for International Settlements.

Since May 1965 when the UK made a further drawing on the IMF of $1400 million the UK has been operating substantially on borrowed first-line reserves. In February 1966 and again in November 1967 the first-line reserves were raised by the transfer of the Treasury's dollar portfolio, the total transfer being valued at $1375m. This transfer should be taken into account when comparisons of reserves are made with periods before 1966. Periodic attacks on sterling have been met with the assistance of increased swap arrangements and other short-term assistance from Central Banks, the details of which are unimportant. By the end of December 1967 the total first-line reserve stood at £1123 million (at the new rate of exchange) or some 17% of imports (c.i.f.) for 1967. Of this total some £520m was the result of the dollar portfolio transfer and some £915 million was short- or medium-term borrowing from the IMF and other sources due for repayment at various dates to the end of 1970 at the new rate of exchange.

In Section III we shall discuss the policy implications of the fundamental disequilibrium in the UK balance of payments. In the next section we examine some trends in the constituent items of the current account and discuss the main causes of the decline in UK performance which led to a state of disequilibrium.

II   RECENT TRENDS IN UK FOREIGN TRADE

II.1   Merchandise Exports

We are primarily concerned in this section with trends in exports of manufactures which dominate our export trade.[1] This can be seen in Table 3.4 where the percentage of exports classified as manufactures has risen from 81% in 1955 to 85 per cent in 1967. For the period 1935-38 the share was about 75%. The growing importance of manufactures is partly accounted for by the steady elimination of exports of coal and coke which accounted for 8% of total exports for the period 1935-8, but only about 2% in 1955 and less than 0.5% in 1967. To some extent coal exports have been replaced by exports (but

---

[1]   The classification of manufactures is conventional and includes the SITC groups 5-8 viz. (5) Chemicals, (6) Classified by material, (7) Machinery and Transport Equipment, (8) Miscellaneous manufactures.

not net exports) of petroleum products which increased from 1% (1935-8) to 2.3% in 1967. Since 1955 exports of all non-manufactured goods have grown at one-half the average annual rate of exports of manufactures. Re-exports, which for 1935-8 amounted to 13.5% of exports of home-produced goods have declined greatly in significance in the post-war period. By 1955 they were only 3.9% of home exports and 3.7% in 1967.

TABLE 3.4

Commodity Structure of UK Merchandise Trade 1955 and 1967

SITC group	Description	Imports (c.i.f.) 1955 %	1967 %	Exports (f.o.b.) 1955 %	1967 %
0,1	Food, beverages, tobacco	36.2	27.4	5.8	6.6
2,4	Basic materials	28.5	15.7	3.9	3.0
3	Mineral fuels, etc.	10.4	11.4	4.7	2.6
5,6	Semi-manufactures	19.4	24.9	38.6	34.8
7,8	Finished manufactures	5.2	19.3	42.3	50.1
9	Unclassified	0.3	1.3	4.7	2.9
	Total %	100	100	100	100
	Value £ mill.	3936	6442	2957	5026

Sources: AAS and *ROT.* Exports for 1955 from AAS 1964 have been adjusted to include, in Group 6, the value of exports of precious stones, etc.

The UK Share of Exports of Manufactures

In 1955 the UK share of exports of manufactures from the twelve main exporting nations[1] was 19.8%. By 1967 it had fallen to 11.9%. This persistent decline in the UK share of 'world' exports, so often quoted, was resumed after 1950. Between 1937-8 and 1950 the UK share of 'world' exports of manufactures actually increased against the secular trend—from 21.3% to 25.4% according to one estimate—but changes in the statistical basis make exact comparisons difficult. Britain's relative success between 1945 and 1950 owed much to the successful export drive of the Labour government but this was helped by the post-war sellers' market, which resulted from the general shortage of capacity relative to demand and the impaired productive and exporting abilities of Germany and Japan, whose shares had fallen to less than half their pre-war values.

Between 1950 and 1955 Germany made a rapid recovery in 'world' exports and roughly doubled her share, largely at the expense of the UK. By 1967 she accounted for 19.7% of the 'world' total as compared with 15.5% in 1955. During the same period the Japanese share increased from 5.1% to 9.9%. These gains were achieved mainly at the expense of the UK and, after 1957, also the USA.

Explanations of the Declining Share

Of itself the declining UK share of 'world' trade, or its obverse, the slower growth of UK trade by value and volume, is of no great importance. There is no reason, in a world of nations with different rates of population growth and economic growth per capita, why any one country should invariably match the world growth rate. But taken in conjunction with the definite deterioration in the UK performance on current account the trend becomes significant, and explanatory factors must be sought so that appropriate policy measures may be directed to improve UK performance. It seems that there is no single explanation of the poor performance of the UK. Various factors have operated jointly to

---

[1] These are USA, UK, EEC countries, Sweden, Switzerland, Canada and Japan. In 1965 they accounted for 86% of world exports of manufactures (excluding Russia, China and Eastern Europe).

produce the relative decline in share and these can be considered under three main headings.

Structural Factors

It has been suggested that the growth of UK exports has been retarded because of undue concentration on commodities or markets with a relatively slow rate of growth of demand. The importance of this sort of factor depends on the time period chosen for analysis; before 1955 they may have been quite important but since then their joint importance has been minimal. In 1957 the *Board of Trade Journal*[1] showed that between 1951 and 1955 about one-quarter of Britain's loss of share of exports of manufactures might be explained by the joint area-commodity structure. This meant that if Britain had retained in 1955 the same relative share in exports of each commodity group to each market as in 1951, the differential growth rates of the various commodity-markets would nevertheless have reduced her share by one-quarter of the observed reduction, leaving the remainder to be explained by other factors. In 1965, The *Board of Trade Journal*[2] repeated the analysis, on a slightly different basis, for the period 1954-64. The conclusion reached was that of the total loss of share of 6.46 percentage points between the two years only 0.36 points (5.5%) could be explained by the joint area-commodity pattern. Using the 1957 method of analysis the conclusion reached was that no part of the loss of share could be explained by the area-commodity pattern.

Table 3.5 shows the distribution of UK and 'world' exports, for 1956 and 1966, by main markets and commodity groups, together with trend growth rates over the period. Over the decade the UK has become much less dependent on markets in primary producing countries whose total imports have grown only about half as fast as imports into industrial countries. Exports from the UK to Canada and the non-OECD sterling area are notable for their low growth both absolutely and relative to 'world' exports. The UK has done well relative to others in exports to Japan and the Sino-Soviet bloc but absolute levels of exports are small. In terms of combined size of market and growth rate it is clear that the USA and industrial Europe have been the most important destinations for UK exports.

In the commodity analysis the Table shows that by 1966 the structure of UK exports differed only slightly from that of the main exporters. As compared with 1956 the UK had reduced her dependence on the slow-growing textiles group[3] and had succeeded in maintaining relatively high shares of the rapidly growing machinery group. The UK also increased her share of chemicals which also had an above average growth rate.

Competitive Factors

If the UK relative decline in export performance cannot be explained by an adverse commodity-market structure we must seek explanations elsewhere, and a number of possible quantifiable and non-quantifiable explanations have been proposed. These cover prices, designs, delivery dates, after-sales service, salesmanship, etc.

It is clear that UK prices have risen faster, during the 1950s and 1960s, than those of our chief competitors.[4] Over the 1954-66 period UK prices rose at 2.2% per annum, compared with 1.2% for the main manufacturing countries including the UK, implying that UK prices were rising about 1.2% per annum faster than those of our competitors. This may seem a trivial difference but it can be shown that, if higher relative prices were the *only* cause of the loss of UK share, the actual decline between 1954 and 1966 of 7.6

---

[1]   'Trends in Exports of United Kingdom Compared with other Countries', *BTJ,* 30 March 1957.
[2]   'Trends in UK and World Exports of Manufactures', *BTJ,* 3 December 1965.
[3]   In 1954 the share of textiles in UK exports was as high as 15.1%.
[4]   Indices of prices of exports of manufactures may be found in the statistical tables of the *NIER.*

TABLE 3.5

Exports of Manufactures from UK and Main Manufacturing Countries ('World') by Market and Commodity, 1956-66[1]

	Pattern of exports 1956		Pattern of exports 1966		Growth rates 1956-66 (Values)	
	UK %	'World' %	UK %	'World' %	UK %	'World' %
EXPORTS TO:						
OECD Europe	26.7	34.8	37.3	45.9	8.5	12.2
EFTA excluding UK	8.6	13.7	12.9	14.9	8.8	10.0
UK	–	3.9	–	4.2	–	10.0
EEC	13.4	18.0	18.4	27.1	8.3	13.7
United States	8.1	10.3	12.0	12.9	9.1	11.7
Canada	6.0	9.5	4.3	7.1	1.6	6.1
Japan	0.6	1.1	1.3	1.6	14.6	12.8
Industrial Countries totals[2]	41.4	55.7	54.9	67.5	8.0	11.3
Latin America	4.7	12.7	3.4	6.9	1.4	2.7
Non-OECD Sterling Area[3]	43.2	15.9	29.5	11.7	1.0	5.8
Sino-Soviet Bloc	1.6	2.0	3.7	3.3	14.2	14.6
Other Primary Producers	9.1	13.7	8.5	10.7	4.3	6.5
Primary Producers totals	58.6	44.3	45.1	32.5	2.2	5.8
Totals	100	100	100	100	4.9	9.2
EXPORTS OF:						
Chemicals (5)	9.3	11.3	11.0	12.1	6.6	9.7
Textiles (65)	11.0	9.7	6.1	6.7	−4.9	5.6
Metals and metal manufactures (67, 68, 69 excluding 681)	15.0	19.8	12.1	15.5	2.2	6.3
Machinery, non-electric (71)	18.4	18.2	24.3	20.9	7.7	10.6
Electrical machinery etc. (72)	8.4	6.9	8.1	8.9	5.0	11.8
Transport equipment (73)	19.8	14.8	18.5	15.9	3.4	8.4
Other manufactures (8 and rest of 6)	18.0	19.3	19.8	20.0	6.8	9.6
Total Manufactures (5-8)	100	100	100	100	4.9	8.9

Source: BTJ, 27 October 1967, p.vi. Tables 2, 3, 4. Figures in brackets in commodity analysis refer to the SITC Groups.
   The growth rates in the lower part of the table are as computed by the Board of Trade and are derived by fitting straight lines to the logarithms. Similar growth rates are not available for the upper part of the table because of discontinuities in the data. The growth rates given here are computed from terminal values and for 'world' exports should be used only as a general indication of the trend.

Notes
[1] Main manufacturing countries are listed in footnote 1 of p. 103
[2] OECD countries including Japan
[3] Sterling area excluding UK, Iceland and Ireland. For 1966 Rhodesia is excluded from the sterling area and included in 'Other primary producers'.

percentage points, or an annual *rate* of decline of share of 3.8%, would imply a relative price elasticity of demand[1] of about −5, a figure which is certainly high, but not impossible. An elasticity of −2.5, a more plausible value, would explain about 40% of the UK loss of share in 'world' exports between 1954 and 1966 and the actual values may well be higher.
   The exact quantitative significance of relative price movements for export volumes or values should be measured by econometric techniques, but technical problems make it difficult to get clear and unambiguous answers. Relative price changes often occur in

---

[1] This is an elasticity of UK export volume with respect to the ratio of UK prices to those of the rest of the world. The derivation of the result is too complex to present here; it assumes that the volume of UK exports is a constant proportion of the volume of exports from the rest of the word multiplied by the relative price to the power of $-e$ where e is the relevant elasticity

conjunction with other changes which operate in the same direction on the level of exports, short period and long period reactions to changes in price and other variables may be different, and there are conceptual problems involved in the application of price theory to large aggregates like the volume of exports. A number of the earlier econometric studies suggested that relative price changes might be comparatively unimportant in causing changes in the level of exports. In recent years there has been a tendency to dispute the significance of these earlier results and to play down the so-called 'elasticity pessimism' which they generated. Experience of the effects of tariff changes and devaluations have made it clear that relative prices do matter for export performance in the field of manufactures and one recent econometric study[1] has indicated that longer-run price elasticities of demand may be as high as −3 to −5. The NEDC Report *Export Trends* (p.16) concluded that changes in the UK relative costs and prices had been *an* important factor but not the *only* important factor responsible for our loss of share. It would seem prudent to make the elimination of further increases in relative costs and prices an urgent task of economic policy. Emphasis on costs may well be important since the process of competition may force exporters to limit their relative price increases at the expense of profit margins, with consequent adverse effects on investment, productivity and export promotion.

Export performance is not simply a matter of relative costs and prices. At a general level behaviour in this field may be usefully interpreted in terms of the theory of mono-polistic competition which stresses the importance of non-price factors where products are not homogenous. One might, therefore, expect to find the volume of exports of manufactures to be sensitive to factors like quality and design of products, the time period between orders and deliveries, including the degree to which promised delivery dates are fulfilled in practice, the size and effectiveness of after-sales services, the degree to which manufacturers are prepared to cater for local market conditions and the effect-iveness and scale of their market research, advertising and sales promotion activities. Complaints that UK exporters have been negligent under all these headings have been numerous and seem endemic in the history of UK export performance. Historical studies have revealed the same sort of complaints in the nineteenth century as those which have appeared regularly in the 1950s and early 60s.[2]

Unfortunately, it is not easy to quantify these various factors and test their influence by econometric methods, but expert studies have usually agreed that they carry con-siderable weight. In periods where the UK has lost market shares to important competitors in certain commodity groups, in the absence of significant price differentials, these factors must have been of overriding importance.[3]

Successful export performance depends upon supply conditions as well as demand, and it has been suggested that export opportunities have been lost by the UK because of inflationary pressures which diverted exportable goods to the prosperous home market. Acceptance of this view would lead to the policy conclusion that our export performance would improve if the economy were operated at lower levels of domestic demand and higher levels of unemployment. It is argued that this would also tend to reduce the rate of inflation and improve export demand via the cost-price factor. Opponents of this view have stressed the complementarity of export and home supplies and argue that reducing the level of demand will inhibit investment arid productivity and thus the supply and quality of exportable goods. This is a complex problem which involves unsolved issues of economic theory and policy.

---

[1]   H. B. Juntz and R. R. Rhomberg, 'Prices and Export Performance of Industrial Countries 1953-63', *Staff Papers IMF,* July 1965.

[2]   R. Hoffmann, *Great Britain and the German Trade Rivalry, 1875-1914* (University of Pennsylvania Press), 1933, pp. 21, 80.

[3]   See S. J. Wells, *British Export Performance* (Cambridge) 1964, p. 61.

The problem has been discussed in Chapter 1 and it is unnecessary to repeat the analysis here. The crude factual evidence seems to support the view that, in the short run, export performance is worsened by a high pressure of demand. It is true that the annual rate of increase of exports is highest during the domestic booms, when UK manufacturing production has grown most rapidly. But this is explainable by the fact that the volume of world exports has grown most rapidly during the same boom periods. What is significant is that the rate of decline in the UK share of world exports has been most rapid during the domestic booms.

Other Factors

Some part of our loss of share of trade has been caused by alterations in competitive advantage outside the control of UK exporters. The reduction of trade discrimination in our favour during the 1950s is an example which may have had serious consequences for our exports to the sterling area. The major impact appears to have occurred as a result of the ending of severe import quotas against the USA and Japan which enabled these countries to capture substantial shares of these markets from the UK. This effect may have been reinforced by a small reduction in tariff preference margins enjoyed by the UK in the Commonwealth trading area.

Finally, there is the factor of export finance, the supply of which can be an important influence on the achieved level of exports, where a large and growing proportion of the trade consists of capital goods. In such conditions the exporter may find that the pre-condition for effecting a sale is the provision of a medium or long-term loan to the potential importer. Since the exporter himself will not normally be able to finance more than a fraction of such required loans, he must resort to a financial intermediary and this will only be possible if he can insure the transaction against any commercial, political or exchange risk. The *Radcliffe Report* referred to evidence of exports being lost to UK firms because the Export Credits Guarantee Department, the government department which provides virtually the whole of export insurance in the UK, was not prepared to offer insurance for a long enough period of time, the effective limit being some six to nine years from the date of contract regardless of the life of the capital asset exported. In 1960 it was announced that this limit would be abandoned where the longer term credit was necessary to match that offered by competitors. Further improvements in the provision of insurance and credit were announced in 1961, 1962 and 1965-7, which broaden the coverage, reduce the cost and simplify procedure. Inadequate finance should no longer be a factor hindering the growth of UK exports. However, as the *Radcliffe Report* emphasised, such improvements represent in part an extension of international investment which may raise exports but not immediate receipts of foreign exchange. It is unlikely that recent improvements will do much to deal with the balance of payments problem during the next few years and they contrast oddly with the policy measures to reduce the outflow of capital abroad.

II.2   Merchandise Imports

In many discussions of the recent balance of payments crisis, attention was focussed on the role of excessive imports, especially those of manufactures. Between 1963 and 1964 the value of total imports rose by some 15% and manufactures rose by 27%. Similar high increases were recorded in the periods 1958-60 and 1954-5. But these dramatic increases are inflated by stockbuilding in the booms[1] and exaggerate the trend growth rates of both classes of imports.

In the early post-war period the volume of imports was held down by various controls in order to limit the balance of payments problem. Taking the 1938 volume as 100 the

---

[1]   Cf. Chapter 1.

volume of total imports was still only 95 in 1951[1] and did not exceed the 1938 level until the year 1955, when the index stood at 105 whilst industrial production had increased to some 156% of the 1938 level. By 1951 the volume of exports had increased to 173% of the 1938 level. Despite these disparate trends in merchandise trade volumes, the visible deficit in 1951 was £689m compared with £302m for 1938. The large relative increase in export volume was offset by a substantial deterioration in the net barter terms of trade which by 1951 had worsened by 28% from the 1938 value. Import average values in 1951 were some 4.4 times their 1938 level compared with some 3.2 times for exports and a doubling of all prices entering into GDP. The net result was a ratio of imports (f.o.b.) to GDP in current values of 27.1% for 1951, the highest level in the post-war period. Since 1951 the ratio has fallen, with minor cyclical fluctuations, to 16.9% for 1967 as import prices fell absolutely on trend until 1962 and relatively to prices of final output until 1967. In 1938 the ratio of imports to GDP was 16.8%.

TABLE 3.6

UK Imports, Exports and GDP, Average Annual Growth Rate (%) for Selected Periods 1952-67

	1952-5 to 1956-60	1956-60 to 1961-4	1961-4 to 1965-7	1952-5 to 1965-7
Exports (inc. re-exports)				
f.o.b. value	4.9	3.9	5.2	4.6
Imports f.o.b. value	3.5	4.4	5.8	4.5
GDP current prices	6.5	5.9	6.0	6.1
Export volume	3.2	2.9	3.5	3.2
Import volume	4.3	4.6	4.4	4.5
GDP 1958 prices (expenditures)	2.5	3.1	3.0	2.9
Imports manufactures value	7.7	10.2	11.3	9.6
Imports manufactures volume	8.9	9.7	8.6	9.1
Imports non-manufactures value	2.0	1.6	2.6	2.0

Source: NIBB and *ROT* for basic series since 1954 with extensions back to 1952 from *Key Statistics* and AAS.

The stockbuilding cycle is so evident in series for imports that the estimation of growth rates is an arbitrary business. The growth rates given in Table 3.6 are average annual rates between cyclical periods and may be reasonably representative of the trends. There are several features worthy of comment. Firstly, in terms of *volume* imports have grown more rapidly than exports and GDP. Secondly, in terms of *values* imports grew less rapidly than exports or GDP. The difference between volume and value growth rates of exports and imports is accounted for by the improvement in the terms of trade at about 1.6% per annum over the full period. The consequence of a reversal of this trend, without compensating developments elsewhere, would be really serious for the UK balance of payments. Equally serious would be an increase in the achieved rate of growth of GDP without measures to check the inevitable acceleration of imports that would result. Thirdly, the very high trend rate of growth of imports of manufactures is evident, whether one works in volumes or values, with the implication that the value and volume growth rate of other imports was extremely low. It is clear from Table 3.6 that the deterioration in the visible trade account after 1960 is accounted for by an acceleration of import demand and by a deceleration of export growth for the period 1961-4, and that the acceleration of imports is largely explained by the rapid and accelerating growth of imports of manufactures. It seems a reasonable inference from this that in so far as UK imports have been 'excessive'

---

[1]   Most of the index numbers used in this paragraph were taken from the series published in *The British Economy: Key Statistics 1900-1966* (London and Cambridge Economic Service).

Foreign trade and the balance of payments

in level and growth, it has been the manufactured component of imports which is to blame and on which policy measures should be directed, in so far as this is possible.

The rapid growth of imported manufactures has resulted in substantial changes in the commodity and area structure of UK imports since the early 1950s. Tables 3.4 and 3.7 show the percentage analysis for 1955 and 1967. The share of manufactures increased by a factor of 1.8 over the period whilst that of finished manufactures increased to 3.7 times the 1955 level. Compensating falls occurred in food etc. and basic materials. Changes in statistical classification rule out exact comparisons with pre-war levels but compared with the 1935-8 average the shares of manufactures and fuels have roughly doubled with compensating falls in other categories. Present proportions therefore represent a genuine structural change and not recovery from an abnormal post-war position. From Table 3.7 we see that industrial regions have increased their share of UK imports as the share of manufactures in total imports has increased. Almost one-half of UK imports in 1967 came from EEC, EFTA and the USA and some 62% of these imports were manufactures. As primary products have declined in share, so the sterling area has declined in importance as a source of imports. On the export side the change in the area structure has been broadly similar, with increases in the shares of EEC and EFTA and a decline in the sterling area share. The share of exports to the USA has increased substantially since 1955.

TABLE 3.7

Area Structure of UK Merchandise Trade 1955 and 1967

Region or Country	Imports (c.i.f.) 1955 %	1967 %	Exports (f.o.b.) 1955 %	1967 %
Sterling Area	39.4	27.4	47.0	30.4
North America	19.5	19.7	11.8	16.5
USA	(10.7)	(12.6)	(7.0)	(12.2)
Latin America	6.1	4.5	3.8	3.3
Western Europe	25.7	36.4	28.1	38.0
EEC	(12.6)	(19.6)	(14.0)	(19.2)
EFTA	(11.4)	(14.6)	(11.7)	(15.1)
Soviet Union and E. Europe	2.7	3.9	1.2	3.3
Rest of World	6.6	8.1	8.1	8.5
Total	100.0	100.0	100.0	100.0
Value £ mill.	3936	6442	2957	5026

Source: ROT, BTJ. November 18, 1966. Some figures for 1955 supplied by Board of Trade. Rhodesia is included in Sterling Area for 1955 and in Rest of World for 1967. In 1965 Rhodesia accounted for 0.5% of UK imports and 0.7% of UK exports.

Causes of the Rising Share of Manufactures

The UK is not alone in taking a rising share of imports in the form of manufactured goods. In recent years this has been a trend in most industrial and trading nations. Figures given in the NEDC report *Imported Manufactures* show that between 1957 and 1963 the share of manufactures (excluding non-ferrous metals) in total imports increased as follows: Germany 20.6% to 38.3%, France 22.4% to 43.3%, Italy 23.5% to 44.0%, USA 27.8% to 40.7%. Substantial increases also occurred in the Netherlands, Belgium and Sweden. On the same basis the UK share increased from 16.1% to 27.7%. The UK share looks low in comparison. These increasing shares are natural given the recent trend of increasing inter-trade between industrial nations, which is associated with the progressive removal of barriers to trade in manufactured goods and the development of regional free trade areas like the EEC and EFTA. Unlike the UK most of the countries have been able to increase their imports of manufactures without incurring any persistent balance of payments problem. In the case of the UK the rapid growth of imported manufactures and the loss of share of exports suggest that an overall lack of competitiveness in manufacturing production is reinforcing the effects of greater international specialisation and exchange. One might therefore expect to find the reasons for higher imports of manufactures similar to the reasons put forward to explain our loss of share of exports and this is indeed the case.

According to the NEDC Report 'there is no single dominant reason to account for rising imports that applies over the whole range of manufactures'. *Prices* and *costs* were found[1] to be a major factor in a wide range of semi-manufactures and finished consumer goods, the foreign prices being lower for a variety of reasons including economies of scale, lower labour costs, reductions in tariffs for EFTA countries and price-cutting resulting from excess capacity abroad in the case of steel products. Relative prices were not considered important in the field of machinery where the main factor appeared to be superior *technical performance* and *design* or the absence of any effective British substitute. British deficiencies in *market research* and *marketing* generally were found to be important in the case of machinery and some consumer goods. *Shortage of capacity* has been a factor encouraging imports in the boom periods and it is suggested that there may be a 'ratchet effect' here which tends to raise the trend growth rate;[2] foreign suppliers capture markets in the boom and are not completely displaced subsequently when pressure is reduced in the UK home market. A final factor is the tendency for international companies to rationalise production of different products in different countries, which obviously leads to a greater degree of interchange, and should be compensated on the export side as long as the UK continues to attract a normal share of foreign enterprise. There seems to be some tendency for such companies to be less parochial than UK firms when it comes to the purchase of capital equipment; the so-called 'invisible tariff' of national preference does not apply.

II.3   Invisible Trade

The importance of invisible trade for the balance of payments of the UK is illustrated by Tables 3.1 and 3.3. In 1938 invisible receipts accounted for 44% of total export receipts and invisible payments were 18% of total payments. By 1967 the proportions had altered to 37% for receipts and 31% for payments. Whilst the interconnection, through income-expenditure flows, between visibles and invisibles must not be forgotten, Table 3.3 shows that *proximately* the existence of a surplus on current account between 1952 and 1960 was dependent on a net surplus on invisible account and that the average deficit from 1961 onwards would have been much worse without the surplus on net invisibles. Despite the importance of invisible trade, this section of the UK foreign accounts has been comparatively neglected in professional studies of the UK balance of payments. It is well known that estimates of invisible receipts and payments are less accurately known than the corresponding figures for visible trade, and they exist exclusively in terms of current values, volume or average value series for the aggregate components being either non-existent or unpublished.[3] Until recently no attempt had been made to organise and analyse statistics of world trade in invisibles in the way that this has been done for visible

---

[1]   It should be noted that the findings of the *Report* were based not on econometric techniques but on evidence collected from various Economic Development Committees. Much of the evidence appears to reflect the views of trade and industrial users of imported commodities and should not be regarded as final.

[2]   See F. Brechling and J. N. Wolfe, 'The End of Stop-Go', *LBR,* January 1965.

[3]   NIBB does give constant price estimates and 'price' (strictly average value) indexes for the aggregate of exports and imports of goods and services, but it is not easy to separate the sectors.

trade. As a result of two recent pioneering studies[1] the veil of ignorance has been partially removed, but further basic research is needed if our understanding is to progress beyond the descriptive level.

From Table 3.3 we have seen that the average annual surplus on invisibles declined from £327m for 1952-5 to £183m for 1961-4 and £141m for 1965-7 and that this adverse trend reflects a rapid increase in the average deficit on the government sector of this account. Excluding the government sector, all other invisibles, net, showed an average surplus of £426m for 1952-5 and £440m for 1956-60 and this increased to £559m for the period 1961-4 and £593m for 1965-7. Table 3.8 shows annual averages for debits, credits and the net balance by main sub-divisions for each of the cyclical periods since 1951.

TABLE 3.8

UK Trade in Invisibles, Annual Averages for Cyclical Periods

		1952-5 £m	1956-60 £m	1961-4 £m	1965-7 £m
Debits	Government	233	278	418	494
	Shipping	481	635	692	770
	Civil aviation	39	60	101	152
	Travel	99	156	228	290
	Other services	182	218	268	351
	Interests, profits, etc.	287	380	444	574
	Private transfers	69	104	124	179
	Total debits (−)	1390	1830	2275	2810
Credits	Government	134	69	42	42
	Shipping	538	632	663	799
	Civil aviation	39	68	124	176
	Travel	93	139	184	219
	Other services	327	420	529	633
	Interest, profits, etc.	513	635	799	955
	Private transfers	73	98	116	128
	Total credits (+)	1717	2061	2458	2951
Net	Government	−99	−209	−376	−452
	Shipping	+57	−3	−29	+29
	Civil aviation	0	+8	+23	+23
	Travel	−6	−17	−44	−71
	Other services	+145	+202	+261	+282
	Interest, profits, etc.	+226	+256	+355	+381
	Private transfers	+4	−6	−8	−51
	Total invisibles *net*	+327	+230	+183	+141
	Total less Government	+426	+440	+559	+593

Source: UK Balance of Payments. Preliminary Estimates for 1968. Detail may not add to totals because of rounding.

From Table 3.8 we see that the average net deficit on government account just about doubled in successive periods to 1961-4 after which the rate of increase was checked. Between 1952-5 and 1956-60 the deterioration in the net balance owed more to a decline in defence aid (credits) from the USA than to increases in government expenditure. Subsequently the main cause of the increased deficit was rising expenditure. For the period 1961-4 some 59% of the average debit was accounted for by military expenditures, about 9% by administrative and diplomatic expenditures and the remaining 32% by

---

[1]   E. Devons, 'World Trade in Invisibles', *LBR*, April 1961, and British National Export Council, *Britain's Invisible Earnings: The Report of the Committee on Invisible Exports*, London 1967.

transfers of economic aid, subscriptions to international organisations and a small amount of military aid. These proportions altered slightly for 1965-7 to 54%, 10% and 36% respectively. The bulk of net government expenditures is incurred in the overseas sterling area, the proportions being 68% for 1961-4 and 62% for 1965-6.

The biggest contributor to the net surplus on invisibles in the item *interest, profits and dividends* which is the difference between considerable flows in each direction. On the credit side the major part (some 95%) of the income flow represents the return on private UK investment abroad which cumulated to some £4,500 mill. over the period 1952-67. On the debit side the rapid growth is explained by two factors, the general increase in interest rates over the full period and the rapid increase in the level of private investment in the UK after 1959. Between 1952-5 and 1965-7 the average annual growth rate of debit items, at 5.7%, has exceeded the growth rate of credit items, at 5.1%. Continuance of recent government policy aimed at reducing the private capital outflow whilst encouraging an inflow therefore threatens to check the future growth rate of the favourable net balance of this sector of invisible trade.

The other main contributor to the net surplus is *other services* which covers such items as receipts and payments for education, films, royalties, commissions and banking services (excluding interest payments). Over the full period 1952-5 to 1965-7 both debits and credits have grown at about the same annual rate of 5.4%, but there was a sharp increase in the growth of debit items from 1961-4 to 1965-7 which, if maintained, will retard the previously rapid growth of the net balance for this sector.

Payments for *civil aviation* services show a very rapid growth rate on each side of the account with a small net surplus which has been remarkably stable since 1961. In respect of *shipping* services there are heavy payments on each side of the account but the net flow is small in relation to the levels of debits and credits. The deterioration in the net balance on this account during the 1950s and early 1960s appears to have been checked and reversed during the period 1965-7. According to the BNEC Report several factors may explain the worsening of the UK net balance on shipping services in the period before 1965. These are: (1) the relative decline in the UK share of world tonnage; (2) the decline in the proportion of cargoes carried to and from the UK in British ships; (3) the disproportionate tonnages involved in the transport of imports and exports, given that shipping costs reflect volume rather than value of cargoes and that the proportion of import cargoes carried in UK ships has declined faster than that of export cargoes.[1] The improvement in the net balance after 1964 may possibly be explained by the relative stability of the import volume of foodstuffs and basic materials in conjunction with factors (2) and (3). Factors (2) and (3) imply a decline in UK comparative cost advantage in the provision of shipping services but this is not necessarily explained by rising relative costs. The UK has to contend with unfair competition in shipping from nations determined to maintain their own shipping industry, by discriminatory practices or subsidies, for military reasons or national prestige. Similar considerations limit the operation of comparative advantage in civil aviation and make prediction of trends difficult for both industries.

The two remaining sectors in the invisible account are *travel* and *private transfers,* both with rising adverse balances. Travel items show a high growth rate on each side of the account with debits growing at 8.9% and credits at 7.0% over the period 1952-5 to 1965-7. Private transfers have shown a negligible net balance until 1964. In the last few years the flow of debits has risen substantially. A major factor here has been the growing volume of funds transferred by UK emigrants.

Excluding the government sector, trend growth rates in UK invisible trade have been similar to those in merchandise trade since 1956. Between 1956-60 and 1965-7 private invisible credits grew at an annual average rate of 4.8% compared with 4.5% for exports and re-exports of goods. Invisible imports grew at 5.2% over the same period compared

---

[1] See BNEC Report, pp. 123-34. Their fourth factor, the decline of the re-export trade, seems more relevant to the longer-run trend.

with 5.1% for goods imports. Between 1961-4 and 1965-7 all these growth rates increased somewhat with the balance favouring merchandise trade. Invisible credits grew at 5.4% compared with 5.2% for goods, whilst invisible debits grew at 6.5% compared with 5.8% for goods. Given the size of the net surplus on invisibles it would take many years before the surplus was eroded significantly, if such rates were maintained, but the existence of substantial excess growth rates of debits over credits in the two main net surplus sectors gives cause for concern.

We conclude the present Section with a brief examination of the Kennedy Round of trade negotiations. These negotiations, which were conducted under the General Agreement on Tariffs and Trade (GATT), were completed in 1967 and the results are bound to influence the trends in UK trade in manufactures in the next few years.

II.4   GATT and the Kennedy Round

Although it is often classed with other post-war international organisations, such as the IMF and the IBRD, the GATT is not strictly an organisation but an international agreement between member governments which commits them to a code of behaviour in matters of tariffs and trade policies. It was originally intended as a provisional agreement, pending the entry into force of the proposed International Trade Organisation, but, with the failure of the ITO to materialise, the provisional agreement became the reality and GATT has grown in strength and influence over the last two decades and has an impressive record of achievement, particularly in the field of negotiated tariff reductions.

The basic aim of GATT was to secure a progressive reduction in the extent of barriers to international trade by inter-government negotiation and agreement. In so far as the complete abolition of barriers to trade is impossible, it was intended that residual barriers should take the form of tariffs rather than of import quotas or other restrictions, since tariffs were regarded, rightly or wrongly, as less arbitrary in their operation and less likely to reduce international trade and welfare. Great emphasis is laid in the Agreement on the principle of non-discrimination. Each party to the Agreement is entitled to claim 'most-favoured-nation' (mfn) treatment. This means that any tariff concession made by any party to any other party is immediately generalised, since no member may be treated less favourably than the most-favoured member.[1] The principle of equal treatment is supposed to apply also to non-tariff barriers to trade, but in such cases the principle is easier to state than to apply. The Articles of GATT set out comprehensive rules of commercial policy to which parties are committed. The force of these rules is weakened by a number of loopholes and escape clauses in the Agreement but these are mitigated by a further principle underlying the Agreement. This is that disputes between members on matters of tariffs or commercial policy have to be settled by consultation and negotiation rather than by retaliation. The implementation of this principle is assisted by the existence of a permanent Secretariat to the GATT, located in Switzerland, and, since 1953, of an informal court to hear and report on disputes.

The major achievement of GATT has been a series of six tariff conferences terminating in the Kennedy Round, in which, through multilateral negotiations, very substantial reductions in tariff barriers have been secured, all of which are generalised for all parties through the mfn principle. Progress in the reduction or elimination of other trade barriers has been less spectacular. The major failure of GATT has been its virtual confinement to trade in manufactured goods. For trade in agricultural products the Agreement has been largely inoperative. This failure in agricultural trade has given rise to misgivings on the part of less developed countries who are parties to the Agreement and to complaints that

---

[1]   Exceptions to this rule had to be allowed to deal with existing preferential tariff arrangements, such as the Commonwealth Preference System, but it was intended that such preferences should be reduced gradually through negotiation. The basic principle of non-discrimination has recently come under heavy attack and it is probable that GATT policy will have to be revised. See H. G. Johnson, *The World Economy at the Crossroads,* Chap. 3.

GATT is a 'rich man's club'. It seems likely that continuing pressure will be exerted through UNCTAD[1] for a reshaping of GATT's principles in directions more favourable to this group of countries.

Negotiations under the Kennedy Round proved to be very lengthy, extending from May 1964 to 30 June 1967. Completion of the negotiations was assisted by the pending expiration of powers to cut tariffs given to the President of the USA under the Trade Expansion Act of 1962. In previous tariff conferences procedure had been for individual countries to bargain for tariff reductions on particular products with parties most concerned with such trade, the resulting reductions being generalised under the mfn clause. For the Kennedy Round it was felt that greater progress would be made through tariff reductions across the board, with minimal lists of exceptions. The USA was authorised to halve all tariff duties as of July 1962, with only ten exceptions, subject to reciprocity, and to abolish completely all duties not exceeding 5%. With this sort of setting hopes were high of spectacular achievements from the negotiations. In the event sights had to be set somewhat lower, but the results were still highly significant.[2] According to the Director-General of GATT the main industrial countries made tariff reductions on imports valued at $26 billion in 1964. Over two-thirds of these reductions were of 50% or more, whilst a further fifth were between 20% and 50%.[3] For the UK tariff cuts averaged some 38% on all industrial goods originating outside the Commonwealth Preference Area and EFTA. In terms of actual trade volumes the major beneficiaries from the UK cuts were the EEC countries, the USA and Japan, with average tariff reductions of 37%, 40% and 34% respectively. On the export side the major gains to the UK will acrue from tariff cuts by the same set of countries. For the EEC the weighted average tariff reduction on dutiable industrial imports from the UK was some 36%, with corresponding figures for the USA and Japan of 41% and 35%. In contrast to the results for industrial tariffs, progress in the Kennedy Round on agricultural tariffs and non-tariff barriers to trade was relatively small.

It is difficult to quantify the results of tariff reductions on the scale of the Kennedy Round and the averages quoted can only be a rough guide to the significance of what was achieved. It seems to be generally agreed that, in terms of size and trade coverage the tariff cuts of the Kennedy Round were vastly more important than those achieved in any previous set of negotiations and that, for a wide range of industrial products, tariffs will cease to be of major importance as a barrier to trade. Reductions of this magnitude could not be applied instantaneously, so the cuts will take effect in stages over a five-year period. For the UK and most nations involved the timetable calls for a two-fifths cut on 1 July 1968, with the remainder in equal instalments on 1 January 1970, 1971 and 1972. The USA chose to operate the reductions in five equal stages ending on 1 January 1972. Countries may advance the timetable if they wish and may effect all the reductions in a single stage for products of interest to under-developed countries. The UK indicated a willingness to follow this practice if other industrial nations would reciprocate.[4]

The effects of the Kennedy Round should be to create additional flows of UK exports and imports of manufactures, as the cuts take place over the next few years, as compared

---

1   The first UN Conference on Trade and Development was held in 1964 and was attended by some 120 nations. Proceedings of the Conference were published in *UNCTAD–Final Act with Related Documents* (Cmnd. 2417). The Conference is supposed to reconvene every three years whilst continuous activity will be maintained by a Secretariat under the Director-General, Dr Prebisch, and a Trade and Development Board meeting twice yearly. The second session of the Conference took place in New Delhi in February-March 1968 without substantial results.

2   A summary of results as affecting the UK is available in *The Kennedy Round of Trade Negotiations,* (Cmnd. 3347).

3   E. Wyndham White, 'Order in International Trade Relations', *National Provincial Bank Review,* Nov. 1967, p. 5. This article gives a useful summary and appraisal of GATT.

4   At the time of writing, proposals were being made to modify the timetable to ease the problem of correcting the USA balance of payments deficit.

with levels which would otherwise have been attained. The net effect on the UK balance of trade is unlikely to be of any great significance, but this does not mean that the cuts are pointless since the welfare effects depend on the absolute increase in trade on both sides of the account whereas the balance of payments effect depends on the difference between these magnitudes. It has been argued that the UK stands to gain in net exports since the value of exports subject to tariff cuts will normally be greater than the value of imports likewise affected. But the UK may lose on the export side in so far as tariff cuts by EFTA and Commonwealth countries reduce the margin of preference enjoyed by UK exports in those markets. The actual changes will, in any case, depend on a number of unpredictable factors including the reactions of domestic producers to the prospect of increased foreign competition and the extent to which the possible gains in overseas markets are not frustrated by inelasticities of supply in the export goods industries. In the case of the EEC countries the tariff reductions on UK exports will eventually help to minimise the degree of discrimination against imports from the UK which will have reached its full extent with the final tariff adjustments which were due to take place in mid-1968. Assuming that the Kennedy Round results are implemented in full and that the outbreak of protectionist revival in the USA, with its dangers of retaliation, is suppressed, the consequence of continued exclusion of the UK from the EEC should not be severe.[1] The common external tariff on non-agricultural products should be of the order of 8% on average, which is about 50% less than the comparable figures for the UK and the USA, and cannot be regarded as a serious barrier to trade.

III   ECONOMIC POLICY AND THE BALANCE OF PAYMENTS

III.1   Introduction

Two years ago, in the first edition of this book, we took the view that the UK required an improvement in the average basic balance, over the next five years, of some £500m per annum and that the most appropriate policy measure to achieve this would be a devaluation of the pound. The belated acceptance by the government of the logic of devaluation, whether by intellectual conversion or by force of circumstances, and their acceptance of a similar target for improvement in the balance of payments make possible a less polemical discussion of policy on this occasion. The major necessary condition for a return to equilibrium has been taken and the problem of policy is now one of implementing successfully the supporting measures which are required to make the devaluation effective. It will require several years of careful management before we can say that the UK balance of payments problem has been solved and the potential fruits of devaluation may be lost at any stage by internal mismanagement, even if we are not beset by further external hazards beyond the government's control.

The proposed improvement in the balance of payments has not been precisely defined. At the time of devaluation, government statements referred to 'an improvement of, at least, £500m' leaving it unclear whether the improvement was to be in the current account or basic balance and whether the base level was to be 1967 or some average of years. In his 1968 Budget speech the Chancellor seemed to have raised the target to an actual basic surplus of the order of £500m. Even if this optimistic target could be achieved for the period 1969-71 it would allow no more than the repayment of the debts due by 1970 (the sterling value of which has been raised by devaluation) and the reconstitution of that part of the first line reserve which represents the transfer of the Treasury dollar portfolio. The true first line reserve would be little better in absolute size than it was in 1963 and, allowing for the growth of trade, would be worse as a proportion of imports. No

---

[1]   They will probably be much less severe than the effects of entry into the EEC, since even the most convinced advocates of entry concede that this would produce a serious short-term balance of payments problem for the UK. The alleged longer term benefits from entry are largely unproven.

allowance is made here for repayment of the short-term assistance from central banks provided during the devaluation crisis and subsequently.[1] The precise amount used has not been disclosed but must have run into hundreds of millions of pounds. In June 1968 the IMF standby was activated and used to reconstitute part of the central bank facilities, thus converting the amounts repaid into medium-term debt due for repayment by 1971. It is possible that some help might come from an increase in sterling balances, but the longer term prospect of this is doubtful after devaluation. It seems probable that the IMF repayment due by 1970 will need to be matched by reborrowing for a further period and that the UK will be highly dependent on short-term inter-central bank facilities (or some longer-term substitut for years to come. On the credit side a large reserve may be less necessary if the pound does not seem overvalued, though experience shows that a run on the pound is not impossible even if the balance of payment is basically sound. In the longer run one must allow for the beneficial effects of devaluation to erode in the absence of measures to correct the trend of declining UK competitiveness in international trade.

III.2 Policy Measures 1964-67

Before the devaluation of 18 November 1967, there was little in the way of non-temporary policy measures which had any substantial impact on the longer-term improvement in the balance of payments. This was inevitable given the hostile rejection of devaluation by both major political parties and the virtual prohibition of resort to drastic commercial policies or exchange control by our obligations under GATT and the IMF. As long as devaluation was an unmentionable word in official circles the UK was operating under a gold bullion standard and balance of payments policy had to be circumscribed by that fact, apart from judicious tinkering. The gold standard remedy for a disequilibrium is outright deflation of effective demand, output and the money stock which leads, in theory, to a fall in home prices relative to those abroad, with consequential equilibrating changes in trade flows. The sterling crises of 1951, 1955 and 1961 were followed by deflationary measures strong enough to cause an increase in levels of unemployment and the facts indicate that such policies were effective in reversing the current account deficits until growth of demand was resumed. Such *absolute* deflation could, perhaps, be justified as a measure to deal with a temporary crisis caused by an inflationary boom leading to over-full employment. Given the downward rigidity of wages and prices in the UK economy the role of such policy in the correction of fundamental disequilibrium is obviously limited, unless the government is prepared to accept a trend increase in the percentage of unemployed resources.

The policy aim of recent governments therefore became a variant of the gold standard discipline, viz, *relative* deflation. The idea was that the growth of the UK price level should be restrained by various measures to a rate below that experienced by our competitors so that relative prices and trade flows could follow the gold standard rules. The relative deflation was to be achieved by a variety of policies including the control of the growth of demand and the money supply, an effective incomes policy and measures to promote the growth of efficiency and productivity which would also satisfy the other major policy aim, a higher rate of economic growth. The effectiveness of such an overall policy requires not only that the domestic measures succeed but also that foreign governments co-operate by failing to restrain their own inflations. The major limitation of the policy is its inevitable slowness; a 3% relative deflation needs to be maintained for five

---

[1] At the time of devaluation the UK received new facilities of $1500m from the main central banks plus an IMF standby of $1400m. These facilities were additional to the existing swap agreement with the USA (see below, III.9) and other swap arrangements with central banks and the Bank for International Settlements ($1000m) which are related to fluctuations in sterling balances. Further assistance of, at least, $1000m was provided at the Washington gold-crisis meeting in March 1968.

years to have the same impact as a 16% devaluation. If foreign export prices grow more slowly than 3% per annum—or decline—then some absolute fall in UK prices is necessary.

For the UK the disequilibrium was too severe and the reserve-liability position too weak for such a policy to succeed. The reduction in the current account deficit from 1964 to 1966 was achieved mainly by the retardation of the annual rate of growth of real GDP to 2.1% compared with the 3.6% per annum growth between 1960 and 1964. The further improvement in the current account to mid-1967 was helped by a further dose of deflationary measures in July 1966 and the introduction of the statutory wage and price stand-still. Unemployment grew rapidly and for four quarters the average value index for UK exports of manufactures was held constant at 118% of the 1958 level. If this rigorous control of incomes, prices and demand could have been maintained for several years it might have made some impact on the balance of payments problem (though it would not have solved it), but the maintenance of such a policy for such a period would have been politically impossible. In the event it could not be held for more than a year. There is little doubt that the growing unpopularity of the government's policies, which was given practical demonstration in the election results in the first half of 1967, led to mild re-flationary measures in June to August of that year designed to sustain the new 3% growth target which had been announced in the 1967 Budget Speech. The relatively mild impetus to imports in conjunction with other adverse trends in the balance of payments in the second half of the year led to renewed doubts about the government's ability to maintain the sterling parity and, inevitably, to the fourth stage of the 1964-7 crisis and the final acceptance by the government that devaluation was unavoidable.

The other policy measures adopted during the period may be dealt with briefly. In October 1964 the government imposed a temporary import surcharge (i.e. tariff) of 15% on most manufactures and semi-manufactures. This was reduced to 10% in April 1965 and finally abandoned in November 1966. The surcharge was a technical violation of GATT and the EFTA agreement, though each of these agreements permits other kinds of negotiated import restrictions to meet temporary disequilibrium in the balance of pay-ments. The surcharge was unlikely to contribute to the longer-run solution of the balance of payments problem, its purpose being as an emergency device to restrain the growth of imports that contributed so much to the 1964 deficit. Its effectiveness was obscured by other cyclical factors but estimates suggest that it may have reduced the level of imports, over the full period, by some £150-£350m below the level that otherwise would have obtained.

In October 1964 the government also introduced a system of rebates of indirect taxes for exporters which was estimated to be worth, on average, about 2% of the value of sales. This system of export subsidies was consistent with the rules of GATT, but the impact could only be slight. Withdrawal of the rebate was announced when the pound was devalued, though it had been intended as a permanent device. Judging by the reaction of exporters to the withdrawal the rebate was more important than its low percentage value might have indicated. The export rebate was later reinforced by improvements in the system of export finance and insurance, by measures to improve information services to exporters and to increase the degree of export promotion through overseas trade fairs, collective market research, etc. It was suggested that the Selective Employment Tax[1] introduced in the 1966 Budget would operate as a disguised export subsidy by virtue of the refund, with premiums, to manufacturers. The argument was doubtful in view of the smallness of the net subsidy after tax and the possible increase in the cost of services consumed by manufacturers. Any small favourable effect on visible exports had to be balanced against the adverse effects of the tax on substantial sectors of invisible exports. The refund of the SET premium to manufacturing industry in non-development areas was also withdrawn when the pound was devalued.

---

[1]   See Chapter 2

A major long-term policy measure of this period was concerned with government expenditure overseas. We have already seen in Section II that the deterioration in the current account after 1960 could be attributed arithmetically, though not necessarily causally, to the growth of this expenditure. In the National Plan of 1965, and other policy statements, the government expressed its intention to reverse this trend and bring about an absolute reduction in overseas capital and current expenditure (including aid) by 1970. The rate of increase of current net expenditure was, in fact, substantially reduced after 1965 so as to convert an average annual growth rate of 14.0% for 1956-60 to 1961-64 60 into one of 5.4% for 1961-4 to 1965-7. From 1966 to 1967 the level of overseas current expenditure actually declined by £12m. The revision of defence policy of January 1968 and the proposed acceleration of the UK military withdrawal from the Far East suggest that we may be dealing here with a genuine change in trend, though it remains to be seen whether the government can resist the clamour for increased aid to under-developed countries and whether unforeseen events may not force a reversal of the planned reduction in overseas military expenditures. Even a drastic change of trend of this nature could make little impact on the UK balance of payments problem in the short period and the longer run impact is uncertain. The prospective demand for UK exports is bound to be affected adversely since a considerable part of economic aid has been 'tied' to UK exports and there is probably a substantial feedback on exports from military expenditures. In the longer run the ending of the UK military presence in the Far East is likely to reduce the strength of trading links between the UK and that region.

III.3 Devaluation

Devaluation of the pound by 14.3% was announced on 18 November 1967, after seven months in which the prospects for the balance of payments had worsened dramatically and the spot rate for sterling against the dollar had declined from par in April to its effective lower limit. The final days before the announcement saw the development of a full scale foreign exchange crisis, with massive intervention in the foreign exchange market by the authorities, against a background of rumours that the government was seeking international loans of various sizes, some of which were supposed to be conditional on devaluation of the pound. At the time of the 1967 Budget the Chancellor, Mr Callaghan, was still predicting a substantial improvement in the balance of payments with a prospective surplus for 1967 and a 'substantial' surplus for 1968. By early November it was clear that 1967 would show a massive deficit on current account and that this would continue into 1968 in the absence of remedial measures.

The main causes of this progressive deterioration during 1967 were the poor performance of exports after the first quarter as world exports of manufactures declined under the influence of recessions in Germany and the USA, the failure of imports to decline following the anticipated rise in the first quarter after the removal of the import surcharge, the effects of the Arab-Israeli war and the closure of the Suez Canal which added some £20m per month to the UK import bill and, later, the effects of the dock strikes in London and Liverpool which affected the flow of exports more than the flow of imports. To a great extent these adverse factors were of a temporary nature but this did not prevent them for influencing opinion in the foreign exchange market, where the initial decline in the spot rate for sterling in May 1967 had followed the UK decision to re-open negotiations for entry into the Common Market. Given the long-term weakness of the balance of payments, such a move was bound to revive discussion of devaluation and the easing of the prices and incomes policy after June 1967 led to further doubts regarding the government's ability to maintain the parity of sterling.

Whether the government was converted intellectually to the belief that devaluation was the appropriate policy, or had to accept devaluation as a result of *force majeure,* in the absence of a medium-term international credit, is a question best left to future historians. Contemporary accounts of behind-the-scenes activity differ. What is clear is that the size of the devaluation was discussed in advance with the major countries affected and seems to have been set at the upper limit of what was possible without provoking retaliation. The government was criticised for delaying the final decision to devalue and for delaying the announcement once the Cabinet had taken that decision. The delays were alleged to have involved a considerable loss to the reserves. The counter-argument of the government was that some cost to the reserves was justified as the price of consultation which precluded retaliatory exchange rate changes on the part of our main competitors in international trade.

The Mechanism of Devaluation

Devaluation is a logical method of producing rapid changes in relative prices at home and abroad, so that expenditure-switching by residents and non-residents will increase a country's net receipts of foreign exchange on current account. Under the IMF system an approved devaluation is effected by reducing the par value, in gold, of the pound sterling. If other member countries leave their par values unchanged, or reduce them by less than the UK reduction, the immediate effect is to raise the existing prices of UK imports and exports of goods and services in terms of sterling.[1] On the import side the higher sterling price will operate to reduce the demand for imports by reducing the total market demand and by making profitable an extension or original production of import substitutes. On the export side producers may reduce their prices in foreign exchange whilst retaining a higher price in sterling, so that additional quantities may be sold abroad and the needed extra resources may be profitably diverted from the home market. Both these effects will raise the level of demand for domestic resources so that, unless devaluation occurs when a country has unemployed resources, which may be absorbed into production, it is essential that it should be supported by measures to reduce the level of domestic demand. Otherwise the resources needed to meet the new demand for exports and import substitutes will not be available, and the devaluation may achieve nothing more than the creation or aggravation of an inflationary situation.

If devaluation is to succeed there must be a net saving of foreign exchange on imports and/or a net increase in earnings of foreign exchange from exports. The outcome will be determined by a complex of supply and demand elasticities in the relevant markets and these will have different values depending on the time period allowed for adjustment. The price effects of devaluation may be obscured by income effects if devaluation leads to changes in the level of total output. In the following discussion such effects are excluded since we assume a background of full employment. The precise nature of the elasticity conditions required for a successful devaluation is a complex issue and reference should be made to general texts for a full discussion. There seems to be little reason to doubt that the UK devaluation is easily capable of producing an improvement in the current account of the required order of magnitude, *provided* that the necessary supporting policy measures are effected. On the import side devaluation is almost certain to save foreign exchange since at worst the volume of imports and their prices in foreign exchange are unchanged. Opponents of devaluation, who argue that the bulk of UK imports consist of food and raw materials for which the demand is inelastic, ignore the fact that the elasticities concerned in the problem are elasticities of *excess* demand and supply. Thus the volume of imports may decline even if final demand is totally inelastic, provided that domestic production of import substitutes may be extended or created as post-devaluation prices increase in sterling. The growing importance of imports of semi-finished and finished manufactures for which production of import substitutes is relatively easy, and demand

---

[1] The 14.3% devaluation of the pound refers to the reduction in the value of the pound in terms of gold (or any foreign currency with an unchanged gold value). As a matter of arithmetic, the value of gold (or foreign currency) in terms of sterling is raised by 16.7% so that this becomes the percentage increase in the sterling price of imports and exports, assuming that foreign currency prices remain unchanged.

elasticity relatively high, adds to the presumption that foreign exchange will be saved on the import side. On the export side there is a gain in foreign exchange if the elasticity of demand exceeds −1 and this seems a safe assumption. Most commentators now seem prepared to accept a medium-term value of around −2 and the actual value may well prove to be higher.

The following estimates give some idea of the possible order of magnitude of the improvement in the UK current account as a result of devaluation. Although we are conceptually concerned with an improvement in terms of foreign exchange, the estimates will be given in terms of current sterling values since it is in this form that the target improvement in the balance of payments has been stated.

According to estimates produced by the National Institute of Economic and Social Research, the overall elasticity of demand for imports should be of the order of −0.7 and import prices, in sterling, may be expected to rise by about 13.5% when the full primary effects of devaluation are complete. This calculation appears to allow for some reduction in import prices in foreign currency for non-devaluing countries, where British demand is an important determinant of the world market price.[1] Taking imports of goods for 1967 at the round figure of £5600m the implied volume reduction in UK imports would be 9.5% (13.5% × 0.7) so that the value of imports in sterling would actually *rise* by about £150m. (The value of imports would fall in terms of foreign exchange since both volume and foreign prices would decline.) This calculation assumes that the import demand schedule is unchanged as a result of devaluation and that this will be contrived by government policy. The effect of devaluation on exports is complicated by the policy changes which accompanied devaluation. The impact effect of devaluation would have raised the sterling receipts from UK exports to non-devaluing countries by 16.7% which could be viewed as an export subsidy to be deployed *either* in reducing prices in foreign currency *or* in raising profit margins to finance export promotion and non-price competition. From the 16.7% it is necessary to deduct an allowance of about 2.5% for the ending of the export rebate and the SET premium refund and, also, an allowance for higher export costs resulting from increased import prices and increased indirect taxes in the 1968 Budget, which might be assessed, optimistically, at around 3.5%. Thus the supply price of exports has to be raised by about 6% and this reduces the maximum scope for price reductions in foreign currency to non-devaluing countries to about 9%,[2] less any part of the devaluation subsidy which is used to raise profit margins. Taking exports for 1967 as £5000m and assuming that non-devaluing countries account for five-sixths of total exports and that increases in profit margins have roughly the same effect as price reductions, the increase in the sterling value of exports to non-devaluing countries comes out at about £1050m for an elasticity of −2. The higher cost of exports to devaluing countries might reduce this figure by about £50m leaving the net increase in exports at around £1000m.[3] The net gain over 1967 on merchandise trade would be of the order of £850m. No account is taken of the import content of the extra exports (and import substitutes) since this is assumed to be counter-balanced by the import content of the reduced domestic expenditure arising from the supporting policies.

In addition there is likely to be some improvement in the invisibles account. Little is known of the sensitivity of items in this account to price changes, but travel, transport services and other services are expected to show a net improvement in terms of foreign exchange, as compared with the pre-devaluation levels. The balance on interest and dividends should improve since the bulk of receipts are due in foreign exchange, whose sterling value will increase, whilst the bulk of payments are due in sterling and these will

[1]   See NIER, November 1967
[2]   Strictly 9.2%, i.e. (16.7 − 6.0) ÷ 116.7 and expressed as a percentage.
[3]   The increase is calculated by raising £4167m first by 6%, the increase in costs, and then by 18%, the volume increase due to the price reductions in foreign currency. For the devaluing countries the assumed elasticity of demand leads to a 12% volume decrease.

have a lower value in foreign exchange, though such gains may be lost temporarily as long as short-term interest rates have to be held at abnormally high levels. The overall effect of devaluation on net government overseas expenditure is unpredictable. If economic aid is held to its sterling value the cost in foreign exchange will fall but this may well be offset by increases in the foreign exchange cost of other government expenditure. Overall gains of the order of £100-£150m for the invisibles account have been predicted but these predictions are bound to be subject to a wide margin of error. The overall improvement in the current account could be of the order of £950-£1000m over 1967. Given the actual deficit for 1967 of £514m this would not produce the required surplus of £500 m on the basic balance, but something like half the 1967 deficit can be ignored as due to temporary factors. On this basis a current account surplus of £700-£750m should be possible when the full effects of devaluation have accrued (subject to normal growth of exports and imports) and this should allow for a net long-term capital outflow of about £200m whilst meeting the target surplus for the basic balance. The gains on current account are bound to be reduced, to some extent, by the policy measures taken by the USA to reduce its overseas expenditure on current account during 1968 and 1969 but may be potentially higher than those indicated above if the elasticity of demand for exports proves to be higher than -2.

Policy Measures to Support Devaluation

It cannot be emphasised too much that the potential gains to the balance of payments from devaluation will not be realised unless the government takes measures to release resources from domestic use to make room for the expansion of exports and import substitutes. The extent to which this point has been stressed in discussions in Parliament and the press is a welcome sign that the full implications of devaluation, as a policy, are now much better understood. The principle is clear, but exact computation of the required cuts in domestic expenditure is made difficult in practice since it is not easy to predict the size and phasing of the potential demand on resources. Although unemployment was relatively high at the time of devaluation the margin of excess capacity was too small to dispense with resource-releasing policies. A further complication arises from the fact that full employment output will increase over time as a result of the background increase in productivity whilst substantial claims on additional output will result from uncompleted multiplier effects and from the expected growth of demand arising from government expenditure, real investment and induced consumption.

The volume of resources to be released will need to exceed the required improvement in the current account balance to the extent that devaluation worsens the terms of trade and this outcome must be assumed for a devaluation by the UK. This point may need some explanation. If we consider the national income (Y) as being the sum of expenditures by consumers (C) plus domestic investment (I) plus government current expenditures (G) plus exports (X) minus imports (M), we may rearrange the national income identity in the following form:

$$X - M = Y - (C + I + G).$$

The balance of payments is equal to the difference between national income and domestic expenditures. For a given level of national income (assuming full employment) it might seem that an increase in the balance $(X - M)$ of, say, £500m need only imply a reduction in domestic expenditures of the same amount. This is true as long as we work in terms of current prices and assume a fixed money value for national income. But implications for *real* resources can be seen only if the identity is interpreted in terms of constant prices. If the net barter terms of trade worsen the volume difference between exports and imports will be greater than the value difference and the volume reduction in domestic expenditure must be increased accordingly.

Some part of the required release of resources will occur naturally in certain conditions.

The increase in import prices will raise the level of costs and prices of goods produced and consumed. If consumers and investors are constrained by a fixed total of money incomes their real expenditures will fall and part of the fall will release domestic resources. This effect will be weakened if expenditures are maintained in real terms by reductions in the propensity to save or the dishoarding of idle money balances or if money incomes are allowed to rise as a result of the inflationary effects of devaluation. Even if aggregate monetary expenditures do not increase it is possible for expenditure on import substitutes to rise but if the demand for imports is inelastic, as we have assumed, then aggregate spending on imports will rise and less is available for spending on *all* domestically produced goods including import substitutes. In general the impact of resource releasing policies will have to be concentrated on current expenditures by consumers and the government, since it is undesirable that real investment should fall and thus inhibit the growth of capacity.

Consumers' expenditures will be reduced by higher import prices and by the massive tax increases announced in the 1968 Budget. Reductions in proposed government expenditures of some £400m were announced with devaluation and further reductions of £300m for the fiscal year 1968-9 and £416m for 1969-70 were announced in January 1968 after an agonising reappraisal of public expenditures and commitments. Further savings are due to take effect in future years as the planned reductions in external defence commitments take effect. It is impossible to assess the adequacy of the proposed economies since this depends on unknown technical factors and uncertain future developments in the UK and world economies. The fact that government economies merely reduce the rate of increase of government spending is not important, since potential output will be increasing, provided that the cuts are genuine and are not invalidated later by changes in policy financed by supplementary estimates. The government cuts include both reductions in expenditures on resources and reductions in transfer payments and the resource-releasing potential of the latter is uncertain but probably small. The Budget tax increases include taxes on capital and the aggregate reduction in expenditures will be considerably less than the increased tax yield. Apart from uncertainties arising from the growth of world demand and the rate at which devaluation affects trade flows, it would require a sophisticated consumption function and an input-output table for the whole economy to judge the total effects. Above all the extent to which consumers release resources will be determined by the government's success in the control of inflation and the growth of effective demand. In general terms all that can be said is that the whole approach to the problem of making devaluation effective compares favourably, so far, with that following the 1949 devaluation when a massive increase in the defence programme, following the Korean War, interfered seriously with the needed growth of capacity for investment and exports.

Prices and Incomes Policy

A major potential threat to the success of devaluation lies in the possible acceleration of the wage-price spiral. It is natural for organised labour to demand higher wages because of the higher prices of imported consumer goods and import substitutes. If such increases are allowed, but are offset by a reduction in profit margins, there is no secondary increase in prices but merely a redistribution of incomes. The squeezing of profit margins is likely to reduce the supply of funds for the finance of investment and also to damage entrepreneurial incentives and, for this reason, will be resisted. If profit margins are not squeezed prices will rise following the wage increases, this will generate further wage demands and further price increases, etc., etc. The ultimate increase in the level of costs and prices as a result of this inflationary process depends on the proportion of factor incomes which are allowed to increase in this way. If all production costs consisted of wage payments and payments for imported materials and money wage rates had to rise in proportion to the rise in final costs it can be shown that a given percentage increase in the cost of imports would ultimately raise the general level of costs by the same percentage. If the higher levels of wages and costs were financed by the activation of idle balances or by creation of new money, the level of real effective demand would be maintained and there would be no reduction in the volume of demand for imports. Export supply schedules would also shift upwards as a result of cost increases so as to neutralise the benefits of devaluation. In practice it is unlikely that things would go as far as this, since some incomes would be squeezed in real terms, and, in any case, the process would take time to reach its limit. Nor would it imply a complete loss of benefits from devaluation, as it sometimes suggested, since the real value of overseas obligations in sterling would be reduced. These arguments provide cold comfort and it is clear that these induced inflationary effects of devaluation should be minimised.

This is a serious challenge for government policy and it is unlikely that the aim will be achieved on the basis of a purely voluntary prices and incomes policy. It is important to see that the problem is not peculiar to devaluation since any policy designed to improve the balance of payments must reduce the domestic consumption of resources.[1] On balance the difficulties are likely to be less severe than those which would have resulted from a prolonged attempt at relative deflation. At the time of writing the government was preparing for the new stage of prices and incomes policy which would follow the expiration, in August 1968, of its existing powers under the 1966 and 1967 Acts, and intentions were revealed in the White Paper published in April 1968.[2] The details of these proposals are discussed in Chapters 4 and 5 of this book and need not be repeated here. An important feature of the proposals is that wage increases will not be approved to offset increases in the cost of living caused by the price effects of devaluation or tax increases arising from supporting policies. In the short run to 1969 the policy will probably succeed but the real test will be its successful implementation over a period of years subsequent to 1969 so that the necessary cumulative payments surplus can be achieved. Trade unions and businessmen would do well to reflect that, if devaluation fails, the only feasible alternative policy will be a return to absolute deflation. The real choice is between moderate restraint of incomes for the whole population and the harsh impact of increased unemployment for the few.

Devaluation and Sterling Balances

If opinion were sampled among professional economists we should probably find a majority view that devaluation came several years too late. Government resistance to devaluation was undoubtedly influenced by the view that it was an 'immoral' policy. This 'moral' objection to devaluation rested on two major grounds, the effects on trade and the effects on owners of sterling balances. The first line of attack argued that devaluation was an 'unfair' method of gaining a competitive advantage in trade which would provoke hostility and retaliation and a chaos of competitive devaluations. So far, at least, events have vindicated the counter-arguments of those who disputed this forecast.

The second line of attack on devaluation was that it would be a breach of faith with owners of sterling balances since it depreciated the value of such balances in terms of foreign exchange. This is a complex issue which cannot be discussed adequately in a short space.[3] Holders of sterling are well aware of the IMF rules, which permit devaluation in cases of fundamental disequilibrium, and on the whole they hold sterling because it suits them and not out of motives of charity towards the UK. The interest received on such

---

[1]   Some policies would reduce the needed shift of resources to the extent that they did not involve a worsening of the net barter terms of trade, e.g. massive resort to protection through tariffs or import quotas. Such policies are precluded by international obligations and would, in any case, invite retaliation.

[2]   *Productivity, Prices and Incomes in 1968 and 1969* (Cmd. 3590).

[3]   For an excellent pre-devaluation discussion see F. Hirsch, *The Pound Sterling, A Polemic,* (Gollancz, 1965) pp. 84-7.

balances provides a sizeable compensation against the risk of devaluation when compared with the alternative of holding gold and the excess of interest rates in the UK over rates abroad compensates for the risk of holding sterling rather than foreign currencies. The losses taken by the Bank of England on forward contracts outstanding at the time of devaluation can be viewed as actual compensation for those who hedged in this market. Even so, substantial holdings of official balances may have suffered a reduction in foreign exchange value as a result of devaluation and it has been suggested that this and related factors may induce a liquidation of some official sterling balances, whilst more pessimistic observers foresee the disintegration of the whole sterling area system. Normally one might expect a recently devalued major currency to be the safest repository for funds but there are too many uncertainties in the present situation for confident application of this precept.

The interaction between the UK sterling balance problem and the problem of the basic balance led to suggestions that the UK should get rid of the 'burden' of acting as a reserve currency country. Proposals were made that those balances which constituted reserves should be 'taken over' by, say, the IMF and replaced by a longer term debt to the Fund. Balances held for purely commercial reasons are excluded from such proposals. Such a transfer would require changes in the organisation of the IMF.

It is doubtful if this transfer, even if acceptable to holders of balances and to the Fund, would provide much relief for the UK. It is true that we should be saved from the problems involved in a liquidation of official balances in the present unhealthy reserve-liability position and that a greater proportion of official reserves would be freed for meeting temporary deficits in the basic balance. Also there would be less need to aim for an increase in the official reserve. But these advantages would be illusory if the new debt to the IMF were not a perpetual obligation. The sum involved would be of the order of £2500m and repayment over, say, a 20-year period would mean a required extra surplus on current account of £125m per annum. The virtue of the sterling balances to the UK is that they represent a form of borrowing, which, in the aggregate, and in the long-run, may never need to be repaid. The short-term benefits to the UK would be doubtful since the balances proposed for transfer are the least susceptible to speculative or precautionary movements and the remaining balances could still present a substantial short-term threat to the official reserves. Since the UK could scarcely avoid a gold guarantee on balances transferred to the Fund, a better policy would be to offer such a guarantee on official balances, leaving unofficial balances to seek cover, as required, in the forward exchange market. In return for the guarantee it might be possible to negotiate a lower interest charge on such balances and the future level of the exchange rate would be free to be determined on commercial grounds without constraints arising from considerations of prestige and morality.

III.4 Policy Measures and the Capital Account

The government may seek to correct a deficit on the basic balance of payments either by measures to improve the current account or by measures to reduce the net long-term capital outflow or by a combination of the two policies. A number of measures were taken in 1965 and 1966 to reduce UK private long-term investment abroad and to convert a net outflow into a net inflow. The 1965 Budget introduced more stringent controls over direct investment outside the sterling area. Such investment would have to show substantial short-term and continuing benefits to the balance of payments (in the form of associated exports and flows of invisible receipts from dividends and profits) if exchange were to be made available at the official rate. Investment would still be allowed, however, if financed out of foreign borrowing or from investment currency, purchased at a premium, though measures were also introduced to reduce the potential supply of funds under the latter heading. In July 1965 it was announced that *no* official foreign exchange would be provided 'for the time being' for such direct investment. Measures to reduce portfolio investment outside the sterling area were introduced in April and July 1965 by way of stricter exchange control. Investment currency represents balances accruing to sterling area residents from the sale of non-sterling assets. Prior to the new measures, such balances could be reinvested abroad and general exchange control on capital movements ensured that such balances could be sold at a premium in relation to the official exchange rate. The new measures effectively produced a partial repatriation of such foreign assets, first by requiring that certain assets which previously would have added to the overall stock of investment currency must be sold in the official exchange market at the official rate and secondly, by requiring that 25% of proceeds of any sales of foreign assets must be surrendered for sterling at the official rate. Thus enforced repatriation was combined with an element of taxation. The April 1965 measures were estimated to reduce the net outflow by some £100m a year and the July 1965 measures were to produce a further and possibly temporary reduction of some £45m. In addition to these measures various changes in the basis of company taxation, including the new corporation tax, were expected to operate eventually to reduce investment abroad and increase foreign investment in the UK, but the full impact of these measures was not expected for a number of years. In the 1966 Budget the policy was extended by the introduction of 'voluntary' controls on investment in four developed sterling area countries (Australia, New Zealand, S. Africa and Ireland).

These measures to control the capital account gave rise to considerable controversy and it is possible that a reversal of the policy might result if devaluation generates a larger than expected autonomous surplus on current account. Since such an outcome is by no means assured, it may be worth while to discuss the problem of control in some detail.

The argument for control, as stated by the government in the 1965 National Plan, was that 'the extent of the capital outflow has not been commensurate with what the United Kingdom can afford, and a change in policy towards overseas investment . . . was essential. Much of the benefit of overseas investment accrues to the recipient countries, and the return from overseas investment is on average considerably less, from the point of view of the national economy, than the return on home investment . . . The benefits of overseas investment to the balance of payments—in the form of interest and dividend income, and of increased exports of goods and services—are of course recognised, but in many cases these benefits accrue only over a longer period. And in a time of acute strain on the balance of payments short-term considerations must be given weight' [p. 71]. These arguments call for critical discussion on a number of points. We begin with the concept of 'what we can afford' in the way of foreign investment. To suppose that this is determined by the actual surplus on current account would be erroneous, because of the causal linkage between the capital and current accounts. Any foreign investment may involve repercussions on levels of exports and imports, in so far as it affects the level of activity at home and abroad, and this is particularly likely in the case of direct overseas investment. It is a mistake, therefore, to assume that the balance on current account will be invariant against a change in the level of capital exports. If exports of goods decline by substantially the same amount as the reduction in capital exports what becomes of the concept of 'what we can afford'? It may be objected that such an outcome is improbable and that the basic balance will show *some* improvement when direct investment is reduced, even if the size of the improvement is uncertain. In this case the previous level of direct investment will have been partly financed, under a fixed exchange rate system, by drafts on UK reserves or by an increase in short-term liabilities abroad, so that the foreign invest- ment will have involved a change of assets. But such an exchange of assets is not essential since a devaluation of the pound can increase the autonomous surplus on current account so as to finance the desired level of foreign investment without any worsening of the UK reserve-liability position. There may be good reasons for avoiding devaluation simply to maintain a level of foreign investment without loss to reserves but to argue that we cannot *afford* foreign investment because it would involve devaluation, without reference to the real costs and benefits of such a policy, is essentially question-begging and reduces to a straightforward defence of the existing exchange rate.

What then are the real costs and benefits of foreign investment? Suppose first that there is a complete linkage between the capital and current accounts so that, say, an extra £100m of foreign investment leads automatically to an increase in net exports of the same magnitude, provided that the additional net exports can be made available. In this case there is clearly no risk of loss of reserves, nor is it necessary to adjust the exchange rate. If we are working in the context of a fully-employed economy the real cost of the foreign investment is an opportunity cost, the cost of the foregone domestic consumption or investment which has to be reduced by market processes and/or by government intervention in order to free resources for the additional flow of net exports. To simplify the discussion we assume that monetary-fiscal policy is used to ensure that the whole impact falls on domestic investment. The problem then reduces to one of comparison of the alternative yields of home and foreign investment. If the linkage between capital and current accounts is incomplete the analysis becomes more complicated and the real costs of overseas investment are more difficult to estimate. An extra £100m of foreign investment will induce an extra flow of net exports of less than this amount. We again assume a devaluation sufficient to raise the increase in net exports to £100m. Under conditions of full employment the extra flow of net exports induced by devaluation must involve a reduction in domestic expenditure, but, in this case, the opportunity cost of £100m of foreign investment may be greater than £100m of home investment if devaluation results in a worsening of the net barter terms of trade. The *volume* of net exports may need to increase by more than the increase in *value,* and the extra volume must be released from domestic use. The extra cost of foreign investment will be greater the smaller the linkage between the capital and current accounts and the greater the deterioration in the terms of trade for a given percentage devaluation.[1] Assuming zero linkage and that a 1% devaluation will increase the flow of net exports by 2% of the existing level of exports, whilst worsening the terms of trade by ½%,[2] the opportunity cost of an extra £100m of foreign investment would be of the order of £125m. The extra £25m would reduce to zero as the degree of linkage increased to unity.

The actual size of the degree of linkage between capital and current accounts is unknown and can only be estimated with difficulty and subject to a wide margin of error. Considerable interest was aroused by the conclusions of the *Reddaway Report* which was commissioned by the CBI to investigate such problems.[3] The Report estimated that an extra £100 invested in the overseas subsidiaries of British firms engaged in mining and manufacturing would raise the level of UK exports by only £9 as compared with the level obtaining in the absence of the investment. This degree of linkage was much lower than previous discussions had assumed. The estimate has to be used with caution since it reflects the average experience of a sample of firms in a range of industries over the period 1955-64. It was derived, not on the basis of econometric study, but through discussions with representatives of the firms involved and the margin of error is probably large. Apart from such considerations there are several reasons for believing that the Reddaway Report under-estimates the feedback from investment to exports.

First, the £100 of investment relates to the increase in the overseas assets of the UK subsidiaries, not all of which need be financed from the UK. For mining and manufacturing, over the period 1956-65, the average UK 'stake' was some 75% of the total of net

---

[1]   It is theoretically possible for the terms of trade to improve as a result of devaluation but this outcome is unlikely for a country like the UK.

[2]   These percentages are rough estimates based on the sort of values assumed for elasticities of supply and demand in informed discussions of the devaluation.

[3]   W. B. Reddaway and others, *Effects of UK Direct Investment Overseas: An Interim Report,* Cambridge, 1967.

operating assets.[1] Secondly, the relationship is valid only if the theoretical model under-lying the Report is valid and this assumes *inter alia* that an act of overseas investment proceeds regardless of whether it is financed by the UK or not. For reasons too complex to discuss here, the effect of the various assumptions of the model is to eliminate multi-plier effects on trade flows and thus the feedback from investment to UK net exports. Thirdly, the relationship is based on a period when it may be argued that UK exporters were trading with an overvalued exchange rate so that the competitiveness of UK exports was reduced. After the 1967 devaluation the pound should no longer be over-valued and the degree of feedback from overseas investment to exports should increase. The opportunity cost of £100m of foreign investment will still exceed £100m of fore-gone home investment, but allowing for the size of the UK 'stake', a reduction of £100m of home investment should enable the build-up of more than £100m of net operating assets overseas.

We now consider the relative benefits of home versus foreign investment. The extra flow of foreign investment will raise productivity abroad and part of this additional out-put will accrue to the UK in the form of interest and profits. The reduction in home investment will reduce the level of national output as compared with the level it might otherwise have attained. Will the yield to the UK from foreign investment be less than that from home investment as argued in the National Plan?

It is true that much of the benefit from overseas investment goes abroad, if only because profits accrue net of overseas taxes, but this is also true of foreign investment in the UK. Since UK net investment abroad has been the difference between substantial opposite flows, any attempt to prune the UK outflow runs the risk of retaliation and any net loss to the UK (but not necessarily to the world) involved in allowing a free flow of investment will be a very small percentage of GNP, of which some part is a beneficial transfer to countries with a lower income *per capita*. It is not easy to quantify the dif-ference in marginal returns from home and foreign investment, though some data is available on average returns. The *Reddaway Report* has estimated that the average rate of profit (net of overseas taxes) over the period 1956-64 was 8.5% for mining and manu-facturing subsidiaries (or 12.3% if capital appreciation is included) and 13% for oil companies. These figures cover a large sample of companies and relate profits to the UK 'stake' in the net operating assets of overseas companies at book values. For mining and manufacturing there were wide variations in rates of return around the average in respect of different industries and different countries.

Although the average rate of return to the UK on overseas direct investment may be lower than that on home investment in manufacturing (about 14-15% before tax), the important difference is that overseas investment yields a return explicitly in foreign exchange, whereas home investment does not *necessarily* do so and is unlikely to do so on average. Before 1965-7 the rate of growth of invisible receipts on account of interest divi-dends and profits was higher than that of merchandise exports by value. Since the benefits of direct overseas investment are not restricted to the receipt of interest and profits one is forced to conclude that the case for a *permanent* reduction in the outflow of such investment from the UK is decidedly weak.[2] A further point is that it is not necessary, in practice to choose between the alternatives of foreign and home investment. The extra resources for foreign investment can be drawn from those released by reduced domestic consumption It is far from obvious why the government should give free rein to the consumer's

---

[1] *Interim Report,* Table IV.3, p. 40.
[2] From the standpoint of the individual company it may well be the case that home and overseas investment are complementary and not competitive. The UK company may benefit from economies of scale of various types and from an interchange of technical knowledge. See Reddaway, *op. cit.,* p. 131, and J. H. Dunning, 'Further Thought on Foreign Investment', *Moorgate and Wall Street,* Autumn 1966.

propensity to import, whilst restricting the propensity of firms to import titles to real assets which bring in a return in foreign exchange.

Is there a case for temporary restrictions on foreign investment? Our argument so far has assumed the willingness of the government to devalue so that foreign investment need not involve a drain on reserves. A reserve currency country like the UK might well reject a trivial devaluation designed purely to enable an increased flow of foreign investment even if the theoretical case for the policy were judged to be sound. But this was not the case in 1965 and 1966 when a major devaluation was required and even the total elimination of foreign investment would not have saved the situation. In this sort of situation temporary controls on direct investment will only serve to postpone the day of reckoning and the ultimate crisis will probably be more severe than it need have been. Temporary control of portfolio investment may be justified in such circumstances to prevent what may amount to a flight from the currency but this leaves the underlying cause of the flight untreated. A case for temporary control might exist if a high level of foreign investment was causing an undue loss of reserves at a time when the balance of payments could not be regarded as being in fundamental disequilibrium. Given the volatility of international capital flows some periodic loss of reserves is inevitable and the ideal remedy is a sufficiently large volume of international reserves to act as a buffer. If this is not the case it would be preferable for the country to borrow abroad short-term as long as this could be done at a rate of interest less than the yield on outward investment. If short-term borrowing abroad is impossible there might be a case for restricting the outflow of portfolio investment rather than of direct investment, since the rate of return is appreciably lower on the former and interruptions to the latter flow will probably involve long-term damage to the operations of UK firms abroad and to the flow of exports.

Since foreign investment is a two-way process the extent to which permanent control of the outflow is required will depend on the size of the desired outflow relative to the inflow. Undue preoccupation with events in 1964 has tended to obscure the fact that the average annual rate of net private foreign investment had fallen substantially during the period 1961-4 as compared with 1956-60. It is true that between 1961 and 1964 the balance of private investment abroad swung from an inflow of £113m to an outflow of £258m. But capital movements are bound to be volatile and it was incorrect to regard this swing as evidence of a longer-term trend. Table 3.9 shows annual averages for the main headings in the long-term capital account for the various cyclical periods. It is not the case that private investment abroad by the UK had been growing at an excessive rate before 1964. In fact, the averages for 1956-60 and 1961-4 show only a slight upward trend and reference to annual data in Appendix Table A-7 will show that the annual total had been relatively stable at about £300m since 1957, the exceptions being 1962 when the total dropped to £242m and 1964 when it increased to over £400m. Government long-term investment (net) has increased substantially, on average, until 1961-4, but the annual growth rate of combined government and private investment abroad was about 3.6% between 1956-60 and 1961-4, which would have presented no problems given a satisfactory current account balance and normal growth of trade. The inadequacy of the current account during 1961-4 was obscured by a large increase in the flow of long-term capital to the UK from abroad, and it was the combination of a relatively low inflow and a relatively high outflow that produced the large net outflow in 1964. The rate of increase of foreign investment in the UK has been very high since 1952-3. Between 1958 and 1965 some 82% of the direct component of this investment was from North America, mainly from the USA. American investment overseas is undertaken for a variety of reasons including the advantage of lower production costs, the opportunities provided by high growth industries abroad and the opportunities provided by the development of a large integrated market in Europe. Before 1963 much of the US investment in the UK must have been influenced by the expectation that the UK would provide a base for operations inside the Common Market. It is impossible to predict the future trend of such investment in the UK. It would probably increase given a revival of serious negotiations for UK entry into the EEC, but it remains to be seen what will develop in this direction. The other main controlling factor will be the state of the balance of payments of the USA, where restraint of private investment abroad has been used in an attempt to reduce the persistent outflow of gold in recent years. The intensification of this control, announced by President Johnson on 1 January 1968, could reduce the inflow of direct investment to the UK for 1968 by some £50m if the controls are fully implemented.

TABLE 3.9

UK Long-term Capital Account, Annual Averages for Selected Periods (£ million)

	1952-5	1956-60	1961-4	1965-7
Government (net)	−40	−56	−93	−73
Private investment abroad	−180	−298	−322	−337
Direct	n.a.	n.a.	−233	−281
Portfolio	n.a.	n.a.	+11	+62
Other	n.a.	n.a.	−100	−118
Private investment in UK	+60	+167	+275	+290
Direct	n.a.	n.a.	+172	+190
Portfolio	n.a.	n.a.	+41	−28
Other	n.a.	n.a.	+62	+128
Private investment (net)	−120	−131	−47	−47
Balance of long-term capital	−160	−187	−140	−120

n.a. : not available
Assets: increase −/decrease +. Liabilities: increase +/decrease −.
Source: UK Balance of Payments, 1967, *ET,* March 1968.

It is evident, from Table 3.9, that the UK controls did not reduce the average flow of private investment abroad during the period 1965-7. Average levels of direct and other investment increased as compared with 1961-4 but these increases were offset by a substantial increase in net disinvestment in the portfolio category. Private investment in the UK showed little change on average between the same periods, an increase in the inflow of direct and other investment being offset by a switch in the direction of portfolio investment. The small reduction in the net balance on long-term capital account was entirely explained by the decline in net government loans.

It seems most unlikely that devaluation will not be successful enough to remove the average basic deficit for 1961-7 after allowing for some reduction in the inflow of private investment. Whether it will provide the extra surplus in the current account to allow repayment of debts and more freedom of external investment, remains to be seen. If not the government will be under pressure to maintain permanent control on the flow of private investment abroad, since a further devaluation will be out of the question in the near future, except as part of a general revision of foreign exchange rates. If permanent control cannot be avoided it is desirable that the impact should be on portfolio investment rather than on direct investment. It may be necessary to consider the repatriation of a substantial proportion of outstanding portfolio investment abroad, which according to Bank of England estimates was valued at £3,200m, at market prices, at the end of 1966.[1] Such a repatriation would have to be gradual so as to avoid embarrassment to the foreign countries concerned, and the possibility of retaliation. Selective measures of this type are objectionable but may represent a last resort measure for the necessary improvement of the UK reserve-liability position.

---

[1] *BEQB,* September 1967, p. 266.

III.5 The Need for Additional Policy Measures?

What happens if the outcome of devaluation is unsatisfactory? Are there any additional policy measures that the UK government could and should take to meet this situation? There are two reasons which justify this somewhat pessimistic line of enquiry. Firstly, the government may mismanage the supporting policies so that devaluation proves ineffective. Secondly, the next few years may see a reduction in the growth of world demand for exports of manufactures, while UK imports may grow more rapidly than was expected, whether or not a higher growth of real GNP materialises.

Between 1963 and 1966 the growth of exports of manufactures from the main industrial nations was exceptionally high at 13.2% per annum. From 1966 to 1967 the growth rate fell to 6.9% and the level of exports was more or less constant throughout the calendar year. It is true that the 1966-7 rate was much the same as the mean growth rate between 1960 and 1963 but at the beginning of 1968 it was thought that the growth of real income in the main industrial countries might fall to a rate well below the rate achieved between 1960 and 1966 and this would inevitably reduce the growth of demand for exports. There were also fears that the ratio of world trade to production might decline as a result of attempts by the USA to correct the disequilibrium in the American balance of payments. If this could be achieved by exchange rate changes there need be no fall in the ratio of trade to production. The reluctance of the US government to devalue the dollar has forced it to resort to policies of the type used by the UK in the pre-devaluation period, such as restrictions on overseas investment and curbs on tourist expenditures and proposals for an import surcharge and export levy have been made. In Congress there has been an apparent revival of protectionist sentiment and demands for the imposition of import quotas. The danger of such policies is that they may lead to retaliation and the breakdown of the system of international co-operation on trade and payments that has been built up during the post-war years.

It is doubtful if there are any further policies, short of absolute deflation, that the UK could adopt if the target improvement in the balance of payments fails to be achieved. The UK could probably invoke Article XII of GATT to justify the temporary imposition of import quotas, provided these were non-discriminatory, but the administrative machinery for the policy has long been disbanded and the cost of recreating this machinery for a short period could be disproportionately heavy. Any permanent return to import quotas would be a clear violation of GATT. Import quotas have the disadvantage that they apply only to merchandise trade, usually manufactures, and they reduce the efficiency of world production by introducing distortions in the pattern of international specialisation. It is true that invisible imports can be restrained by the reimposition of effective exchange control, but this policy falls foul of UK commitments as a member of the IMF. Having agreed to accept the obligations of Article 8 of the IMF Agreement with effect from February 1961 the UK must make foreign exchange freely available for current international transactions, though IMF rules allow control of capital movements.[1] It is unlikely that the Fund would be willing to release the UK from this commitment, though minor infringements, such as the restrictions on travel expenditures outside the sterling area, are tolerated.

Apart from the international objections to such policies they would be futile substitutes for devaluation if the latter failed because of the failure to implement supporting policies. If imports are restrained by quotas and exchange control it is still necessary for the government to reduce effective demand so as to release resources for domestic production and the inflationary implications of the policies need to be inhibited. It is naive to suppose that, in general, domestic substitutes can be produced at the same cost as the

---

[1] Exchange control is still applied nominally to current payments outside the sterling area but is either a formality within generous limits or, outside these limits, is designed to ensure that exchange is genuinely needed for current payments and is not a disguised capital movement.

excluded foreign goods. If the government cannot take the necessary measures to support devaluation it cannot take them anyway. A similar objection applies to any other policy measure designed to switch demand from imports to domestic production and from domestic consumption to exports.

We are left with the conclusion that there is no real alternative to devaluation short of absolute deflation. If the government has the political courage to deflate absolutely there is no reason why it should not do this to make devaluation effective and the severity of the 1968 Budget suggests that this will be done. There is probably enough margin in the potential effects of devaluation on trade flows to absorb the negative effects of the necessary balance of payments adjustment by the USA and to allow for some degree of failure of the incomes policy. We must hope that the international environment will not impose any additional burden on the UK balance of payments. The future growth of world trade will be influenced favourably or unfavourably by developments in the international monetary system and our final comments are directed to this problem.

III.6 Reform of the International Monetary System

The last few years have seen extensive discussion of the need to improve the international monetary system and to raise world reserves. Numerous plans have been suggested to accomplish these ends, but progress towards a solution acceptable to the main interested parties has been slow. Although there has been a steady decline in the ratio of world reserves to world trade throughout the post-war period, there is no general agreement that reserves are inadequate in total, nor is there any objective test by which this question could be decided. Between 1950 and 1967 the ratio of world official reserves of gold and foreign exchange to world imports of goods declined from about 80% to about 33%, the latter figure being well below equivalent ratios in the depressed 1930s, and less than the ratio for 1928. In 1967, however, there were conditional reserves available in the form of IMF drawing rights to the value of $21 billion or 10% of world imports. Since October 1962 the IMF resources have had the potential support of the General Arrangements to Borrow by which it can mobilise up to $6 billion of reserves from the Group of Ten countries (EEC, UK, USA, Sweden and Japan) so as to reduce the possible need to invoke the 'scarce currency' provisions of Article 7 of the IMF Agreement. Apart from this there has been the development of *ad hoc* measures of inter-central bank co-operation such as the *swap* arrangements between the USA and other countries, whereby each agrees to lend balances to the other for a specified time or to accumulate balances of the other's currency to an agreed limit for a given time period.

The UK has benefited greatly during the last few years from this sort of agreement, the size of which has been increased periodically. From a modest level of S50m in 1962 the UK-USA swap facility increased to $750m in November 1964 and to $2000m in March 1968. The overall total of swap facilities between the USA and other central banks was increased from $700m in 1962 to $9,355m in March 1968. Other examples are the Basle credits of 1961 when several European central banks agreed to hold excess balances of sterling up to £300m for three months and the very large short-term credits extended by central banks to the UK in the November 1964 crisis and at the time of devaluation.

It has been said that the *ad hoc* measures are themselves proof of the need for more formal and more permanent measures to raise reserves. Certainly there is agreement that present trends in world trade and liquidity, if continued, could lead to a dangerous pressure on reserves. There has also been concern about the dependence of present world reserves on foreign exchange in the form of dollar and sterling balances, in view of the weakness of both currencies and the persistent loss of gold by the USA. The fact that pressure on world reserves has coincided with problems of balance of payments adjustment for the two main currencies has complicated reform and made for delay. From the standpoint of the IMF system the remedy for the two problems was simple. The pound and the dollar should have been devalued sufficiently relatively to the other main currencies to solve the adjustment problem, whilst all currencies should have been devalued in terms of gold to an extent which would ensure an adequate value and growth rate of the stock of world monetary gold. This solution came near to achievement in March 1968 when speculative buying of gold in Europe threatened such a drain on US gold stocks that their ability to maintain the gold price at $35 per oz. was in doubt. The crisis was halted by the adoption of a two-tier gold price with the central banks committed to transact between themselves at $35 per oz. whilst the price for gold for industrial use and private hoarding was to be determined by market forces. The problem of insulating the two markets from each other made this a short-term expedient and it may well be that the official gold price will have been raised by the time this book is published. At the time of writing it was hoped that the new system would operate long enough to allow the introduction of the proposed scheme for IMF Special Drawing Rights (SDRs) which would make it possible to reduce progressively the need for gold as a means of international settlement.

Under the proposed scheme, which may be modified before becoming effective, the IMF will create quantities of a new reserve asset, SDRs, which will be allocated to members in proportion to their IMF quotas. Member countries will be required to accept drawing rights from other members in exchange for convertible currency up to a limit of twice their allocation. The incentive to accept a transfer of SDRs will be provided by the fact that they will be gold guaranteed and will carry an interest payment. It is expected that deficit countries will use part of their allocation of SDRs in conjunction with existing reserves when making international settlements and will reverse these transactions when they move into surplus. As a method of raising world reserves the SDR scheme is superior to a rise in the gold price since it avoids the waste of resources involved in the mining and storage of monetary gold and the alleged political undesirability of a subsidy to South Africa and Russia. Also the reserve increase will not be allocated on the arbitrary basis of existing gold stocks and the size of the increase can be controlled by the IMF, whereas an increase in the gold price would have to be substantial enough to convince speculators that no further increase was likely for a number of years.[1] The fact that SDRs are to be used in conjunction with gold and will carry a gold guarantee indicates that it will be many years before international reserves can be created exclusively by book entries in an international central bank. For the foreseeable future the new reserve asset will be an ingenious means of stretching the stock of monetary gold.

Final discussions on the proposed scheme took place at a ministerial meeting of the Group of Ten in Stockholm in March 1968. Agreement was then reached that the executive directors of the Fund should prepare a final draft of the necessary amendments to the IMF Agreement. This would be submitted for approval to the Governors of the Fund and, if accepted by the necessary majority, will have to be ratified by the various member countries of the Fund. It is doubtful, therefore, if the scheme will be ready for activation before 1969. Even then it is a contingency scheme and though the Managing Director of the Fund can propose its activation, such a proposal would be pointless unless it was clear that it would be welcomed by a majority of participating members.

The introduction of SDRs may provide a long-term solution to the problem of adequate growth of world reserves but it will not solve the other main problem of the international monetary system, at the time of writing, the correction of the balance of payments deficit of the USA. The practical solution to this problem has been indicated above, but this is inoperable as long as the gold value of the dollar remains a sacred cow to the monetary authorities of the USA. If the other main industrial nations do not wish

[1]   Counter-arguments exist to most of the objections to raising the gold price. For fuller discussion see Harrod, *Reforming the World's Money*, London 1965, and Cassell, *Gold or Credit?*, London 1965.

to see the currency value of gold increased the appropriate remedy is an upward revaluation of those currencies in terms of the dollar. Failing this remedy, the USA will have to persist with policies appropriate to a gold bullion standard. It may be that gold speculators will force the issue and compel the slaughter of the sacred cow. In this case the machinery of the IMF will be needed to ensure the establishment of a system of exchange rates compatible with general international equilibrium. There is no economic reason why such a technical readjustment of parities should lead to a period of chaos in the international trading and monetary system. It will do so only if the monetary authorities of the leading industrial nations take leave of their senses.

REFERENCES AND FURTHER READING

Brooman, F. S., *Macroeconomics,* Allen & Unwin, 1962 and 1967.
Kindleberger, C. P., *International Economics,* Irwin, 1963.
Johnson, H. G., *The World Economy at the Crossroads,* Oxford, 1965.
McMahon, C., *Sterling in the Sixties,* Oxford, 1964.
Reddaway, W. B., *Effects of UK Direct Investment Overseas: An Interim Report,*
    Cambridge, 1967.
Scammell, W. M., *International Monetary Policy,* Macmillan, 1964.
Wells, S. J., *British Export Performance,* Cambridge, 1964.
Worswick, G. D. N., and Ady, P. H., *The British Economy in the 1950s,* Oxford, 1962.

Official Publications

Bank of England Quarterly Bulletin
Board of Trade Journal (weekly)
Economic Trends (Regular analyses of balance of payments in March, June, September
    and December issues)
IMF Annual Report
NEDC Reports, especially *Exports Trends* (1963) and *Imported Manufactures* (1965)
Report of Committee on the Working of the Monetary System, (Radcliffe Report)
    (Cmnd. 827), (1959)
Report on Overseas Trade (Board of Trade, monthly trade statistics)
UK Balance of Payments Orange Book (CSO, annually)

4

Industry and commerce

I   THE ORGANISATION AND STRUCTURE OF INDUSTRIES

I.1   The Concept of an Industry: the Standard Industrial Classification

An industry or trade is simply a convenient classification of economic activity. For various purposes we might wish to group activities which are linked by a common market, process, technology, factor of production, area served, location of production, and so on. Such classifications would not automatically coincide and there is no single definition or classification of industries which is best for all purposes. That most commonly used and on which nearly all UK official statistics are based is the government's Standard Industrial Classification.

Under the SIC the outputs of establishments[1] are distinguished primarily on the basis of the physical and technical properties of their principal products (i.e. those accounting for the largest proportion of their total output). Establishments are grouped into twenty four Orders, which cover broad groups of industrial activity and which are subdivided into Minimum List Headings and in some cases even finer subdivisions.

With the help of the SIC we can define more precisely the scope of 'industry and commerce'. Industry is normally understood to include manufacturing; construction; and the public utilities, gas, water and electricity (Orders III-XVI inclusive, XVII and XVIII), which are sometimes referred to as 'secondary activities', together with the 'primary' sector—agriculture, forestry and fishing; and mining and quarrying (Orders I and II). Commerce is often thought of as the provision of services required in the distribution and exchange of goods between the points of production and final use. This would cover only transport and communications; wholesale and retail distribution; and insurance, banking and finance (Orders XIX, XX and XXI respectively). However, a somewhat wider coverage of industry and commerce may be adopted, to include also miscellaneous services (Order XXIII) and a part of professional and scientific services (Order XXIV).

The availability of SIC based data permits much investigation and analysis which would not otherwise be possible. But there is need for some caution and due regard for the method of compilation. For instance, there is inevitably some arbitrariness in determining product similarities; physical and technical resemblances among products cannot be measured precisely. Secondly, the whole of an establishment's output is classified in the industry of its principal product: since the subsidiary activities of these establishments may be diverse the classification does not provide us with homogenous groups and, what is more, some part of the total output, employment, etc. shown for any group will properly belong elsewhere. Moreover, quite apart from shortcomings of this nature, SIC data may be of limited usefulness for some purposes. Thus, use of data based on a production-oriented classification such as the SIC could be mis-leading as evidence of the existence of monopoly or oligopoly, for these are essentially *market* rather than industry phenomena.

I.2   The Size Structure of Industries and Trades

An idea of the proportion of aggregate output originating in each industry and trade may readily be gained from a table like 4.1 (page 136). This shows the share of total national

---

[1]   I.e. 'factories' or 'plants' or, officially, '. . . the whole of the premises under the same ownership or management at a particular address (e.g. a factory or mine) rather than 'firms' or 'enterprises', which are units of ownership and control.

output[1] originating in thirteen individual sectors in 1950, 1958 and 1966. The engineering industries and distribution are clearly the largest individual groups and transport, other manufacturing and construction the three next largest. In 1966 all the remainder fell within a range of 2.4 per cent to 4.3 per cent of GDP, agriculture being the largest. However, when making statements such as these it is important to remember the basis on which industrial classifications are drawn up and the fact that, for instance, the engineering and allied industries group is composed of a very large number of quite disparate subtrades.

Changes in the contribution of each industry to total GDP are clearly the result of their differing rates of growth of output. The industrial pattern of output growth 1950-67 is charted and to some extent explained in section 1.3 of this chapter. Here we simply record the structural effects.

Significant changes between 1950 and 1966 in the size ranking of the thirteen individual sectors in Table 4.1 have occurred in only two cases, mining and quarrying (which fell from eighth to thirteenth position) and chemical and allied industries (which rose from eleventh, equal with insurance banking and finance, to joint seventh). In other cases movements have not been of more than one place in either direction. Similarly, since 1950 there have been only minor changes in the proportion of GDP originating in the main broad sectors of the economy. Thus manufacturing now accounts for only slightly more than the one-third it contributed then, the main increase having occurred since 1958. Similarly, at some 52.6 per cent of GDP in 1966 the share of industry as a whole was only 2.7 percentage points larger than in 1950. Lease change of all occurred in commerce, which on the narrower of the two definitions suggested earlier maintained an exactly unchanged share of 22.9 per cent over the whole period. Accordingly, it is in the remaining sector, miscellaneous services, public administration and defence, etc. that one finds the decline offsetting the enlarged share of industrial production.

Rapid alteration in the shares of output originating in these broad sectors of the economy is not to be expected. Over the very long term, as economies develop from relatively primitive states, there appears to be a general tendency for the bulk of economic activity to shift from the primary to the secondary and tertiary sectors. Some consistency with this trend may be seen in Table 4.1 insofar as there has been growth of secondary activities at the expense of primary ones (tertiary activities, however, retaining much the same share). But in a country like the UK, which has already developed to a fairly high level, drastic changes are not to be expected over a period of only fifteen years. At the same time it should be remembered that a 1 per cent shift in resources between sectors will be large in absolute terms—say, approximately, £1,000 million worth of assets or 250,000 workers.

The industrial distribution of capital, output and employment is obviously interrelated, but because of differing capital/labour, capital/output and output/man ratios the relative sizes of industries will not be the same in each case. Thus, for instance, in 1958 chemical and allied industries accounted for some 16 per cent of total capital employed in manufacturing and construction (excluding textiles) but 6 per cent of manpower and 9 per cent of output. In the same way the rate of growth of an industry need not be the same or similar in all three dimensions and may even be contrary. Thus in agriculture total employment has fallen, although both output and the value of capital stock have increased. The industrial distribution of employment is discussed in chapter 5, and shown in tabular form in Table 4.2 (page 137). Some idea of the allocation of capital stock between industries is given in Table 4.3 (page 138). Even the most cursory inspection of these will show that while it may be perfectly valid and indeed most appropriate for some purposes to measure the relative size of growth of industries in terms of employment or capital rather than output, the measures are in no sense substitutes for each other.

---

[1]   GDP by industrial origin represents the value added in production by each industry [= total sales *less* the value of goods and services currently used up in production (inputs from other industries and imports)]. It is perhaps the nearest approximation in value terms to the concept of work actually done by an industry.

TABLE 4.1

UK GDP by Industrial Origin 1950, 1958 and 1966

(at 1958 prices)

£million

	1950 £m	1950 per cent	1958 £m	1958 per cent	1966 £m	1966 per cent
Agriculture, forestry and fishing	768	4.5	873	4.3	1,117	4.3
Mining and quarrying	720	4.2	713	3.5	620	2.4
Manufacturing:						
Food, drink and tobacco	659	3.8	804	4.0	997	3.8
Chemical and allied industries	438	2.5	636	3.2	1,049	4.0
Metal manufacture	553	3.2	636	3.2	795	3.1
Engineering and allied industries	2,174	12.6	2,898	14.4	3,941	15.1
Textiles, leather, clothing	955	5.5	860	4.3	1,032	4.0
Other manufacturing	959	5.6	1,169	5.8	1,672	6.4
Total manufacturing	5,742	33.3	7,003	34.9	9,524	36.6
Construction	1,016	5.9	1,181	5.9	1,642	6.3
Gas, electricity and water	351	2.0	524	2.6	791	3.0
Transport and communications	1,423	8.3	1,599	8.0	2,111	8.1
Distributive trades	2,076	12.1	2,442	12.2	3,078	11.8
Insurance, banking and finance	432	2.5	540	2.7	783	3.0
GDP[1]	17,213	(100.0)	20,085	(100.0)	26,050	(100.0)

Source: Derived from NIBB data.
Note: [1] Includes other services, public administration and defence, and ownership of dwellings.

TABLE 4.2

Distribution of UK Total Working Population by Industry 1950, 1958 and 1966

Thousands

	1950	per cent	1958	per cent	1966	per cent
Agriculture, forestry and fishing	1,262	5.6	1,090	4.6	478	1.9
Mining and quarrying	856	3.8	858	3.6	580	2.3
Manufacturing:						
Food, drink, tobacco	841	3.7	954	4.0	841	3.3
Chemical and allied industries	473	2.1	538	2.3	528	2.1
Metal manufacture	542	2.4	562	2.4	619	2.4
Engineering and allied industries	3,522	15.6	4,105	17.3	4,008	15.7
Textiles, leather, clothing	1,902	8.4	1,671	7.1	1,422	5.6
Other manufacturing	1,436	6.3	1,517	6.4	1,638	6.4
Total manufacturing	8,716	38.7	9,347	39.5	9,055	35.5
Construction	1,468	6.5	1,528	6.5	1,725	6.8
Gas, electricity and water	360	1.6	382	1.6	431	1.7
Transport and communications	1,812	8.0	1,789	7.6	1,629	6.4
Distributive trades	2,360	10.5	3,000	12.7	3,035	11.9
Services	4,040	17.9	4,335	18.3	5,468	21.4
Total in civil employment	22,539	(100.0)	23,663	(100.0)	25,538	(100.0)

Source: AAS.

Tables such as 4.1, 4.2 and 4.3 together give us a good idea of the size structure of industries in the UK, but tell us nothing about the functional relationships between them. Three sorts of interdependence between industries may conveniently be distinguished. First, interdependence will arise in final product markets (i.e. sale of goods to final consumers, for investment and export) in so far as one industry's products are to some degree substitutes for or complements to the others. Secondly, interdependence will arise from competition between industries in factor markets. But thirdly, structural interrelationships will also arise from the inter-industry flow of intermediate products. These are the output of one industry and raw material input of another and demand for them is derived from the final product demand of the purchasing industry. This last type of interrelationship is important when we are considering the *ultimate* effect of some initial development in final product or factor markets on the outputs of different industries and hence on their relative sizes. For instance, a change in the pattern of final demand, whether an autonomous change in taste, an income effect, or the result of advertising campaigns, may obviously affect the final outputs of two or more industries (unless it so happens that the products concerned fall within what has been defined as a single industry). Hence there will be an immediate, direct effect on their sizes and the overall pattern of production. But there will also be secondary effects on the industries producing intermediate products used by those whose final output has changed. In turn, these will set up a further round of indirect effects, and so on, so that a chain reaction of disturbances is set off. The final structural changes resulting from the original change in the pattern of demand will depend on the whole of this process, not just the immediate effects on final output.

I.3   The Growth of Output by Industry 1952-67

Index numbers of real output in thirteen major industrial and commercial sectors of the economy are shown in Table 4.4. This shows that over the period the growth rates for individual industries have differed widely from the overall average of 2.8 per cent per annum. The chemical and allied industries and the public utilities have both achieved more than double this rate and 'other manufacturing', insurance banking and finance, construction

TABLE 4.3

UK Gross Capital Stock at 1958 Prices, New, by Industry 1951, 1953 and 1966

£ thousand million

	1951	per cent	1958	per cent	1966	per cent
Agriculture[1]	0.5	0.7	0.6	0.7	0.8	0.7
Mining and quarrying	1.0	1.4	1.3	1.6	1.5	1.4
Manufacturing, excluding textiles:						
Food, drink, tobacco	1.5	2.2	1.9	2.3	2.7	2.5
Chemical and allied industries	1.7	2.4	2.7	3.3	4.0	3.7
Iron and steel	1.4	2.0	1.9	2.3	2.7	2.5
Other metals, engineering and allied industries	5.4	7.8	7.0	8.4	9.2	8.5
Bricks, pottery, glass, cement	0.4	0.6	0.6	0.7	0.9	0.8
Timber, furniture, etc.	0.2	0.3	0.3	0.4	0.4	0.4
Paper, printing and publishing	1.1	1.6	1.3	1.6	1.7	1.6
Leather, clothing, other manufacturing	0.9	1.3	0.9	1.1	1.3	1.2
Total manufacturing (excluding textiles)	12.6	18.1	16.6	20.0	22.9	19.4
Construction	0.4	0.6	0.7	0.8	1.3	1.2
Gas, electricity, water	5.6	8.1	7.2	8.7	10.6	9.8
Transport and communications[2]	10.6	15.3	11.5	13.9	12.4	11.5
Distribution and other services[3]	5.6	8.1	7.0	8.4	11.8	11.0
Other industries[4]	4.8	6.9	4.6	5.5	4.5	4.2
Total gross capital stock[5]	69.5	(100.0)	82.9	(100.0)	107.7	(100.0)

Source: NIBB

Notes:

[1] Plant and machinery only

[2] Railways; road passenger transport (exluding taxis and private hire cars); shipping; harbours, docks and canals; air transport; postal, telephone and radio communications. Excludes roads.

[3] Distributive trades; insurance, banking and finance; professional and scientific services; miscellaneous services; road haulage; taxis and private hire cars; miscellaneous transport services and storage.

[4] Textiles, hospitals and universities, private schools, agricultural buildings and vehicles.

[5] Includes private and public dwellings, roads and other public social services.

and the engineering group have all grown at a rate well above the average. Two sectors with markedly below-average growth are metal manufacturing and textiles, leather and clothing. But in both cases the figure shown for the average annual increase is slightly misleading. For metal manufacturing this is because output was apparently above trend in 1952 and below it in 1967 so that the real growth trend is understated. In textiles, etc. output was at a low level in both terminal years, but it would be an exaggeration to speak of any growth trend up to the early 1960s, the main advances having been made since then. Only in mining and quarrying was there an actual decline over the period as a whole, and this was despite a maintained level of output up to 1956.

For a fuller and more satisfactory explanation of the causes underlying a particular industry's growth rate detailed study and econometric techniques are required. Here we attempt only to illustrate some of the more significant and obvious factors determining the observed growth in some industries contained in Table 4.4 (page 140).

The effect of rising incomes on the composition of final demand has apparently been an important determinant of the rate of growth of individual industries in a number of cases. For instance, this factor probably explains the comparatively slow growth trend in food, drink and tobacco (although from 1958 to the mid-1960s there was rising real expenditure on some types of drink, notably spirits) and, within the food group, a shift away from basic foods towards more sophisticated and high protein products. This has meant fairly rapid growth in some markets (like processed meat, fruit and vegetables) but virtual stagnation in others (like milled grain, bread, flour, sugar and confectionery). But undoubtedly the most striking manifestation of rising incomes has been the extension of car ownership both at home and abroad: the number of private cars currently licensed in Great Britain rose from 2.8 million in 1953 to 10.3 million in 1967. One result has, of course, been rapid growth in the vehicles sector of the engineering and allied industries at some 4.0 per cent per annum from 1952-67, compared with 3.5 per cent for engineering as a whole. However, other factors have also been important. Protection of the home market by import controls was an important contributory factor to an especially high rate of growth between 1952 and 1960 (6.5 per cent per annum) and the longer term growth trend, as well as short term output levels, may well have been affected by alterations in purchase tax (in particular a large reduction in 1962) and hire purchase regulations.

Apart from vehicle production, the other sector most affected by the increase in private motoring has been transport, especially on the passenger side. The growth of transport services alone is understated in Table 4.4 since the output series there includes some other activities but takes no account of private motoring and, as table 4.5 (page 141) shows, this is the major explanation of the very rapid increase in passenger mileages travelled, at a rate of 4.4 per cent per annum from 1953-66. The full impact of private motoring on the public road and rail services cannot be measured. Certainly the whole of the *actual* declines shown in Table 4.5 can fairly safely be attributed to this cause, but how much public passenger traffic might have risen had there been no dramatic increase in private motoring is unknown. Public services were first to feel the effects of rising car ownership, with an especially rapid fall in the mid 1950s and a further sharp reduction between 1964 and 1966. It is mostly stage services that have been affected, as there has been some increase in contract work. On the railways, passenger traffic rose slowly to a plateau in the late 1950s, but fell off rapidly thereafter. Despite very rapid growth (a more than threefold rise since 1958) inland air traffic is still of only slight importance except on certain particular routes.

In a number of instances technical developments have been a major factor helping to determine an industry's growth rate. In chemicals, for instance, extensive product innovation and modification has led to the substitution of new chemical products for other existing ones and this has been a major factor, though not the only one, making chemicals and allied industries the fastest growing group in all manufacturing. One of the most striking examples of this is synthetic resins where physical quantities produced rose more than sixfold between 1950 and 1967. Again, far-reaching technical developments (along with new weapons systems, development of the G.P.O. telecommunications network and railway modernisation—themselves part cause, part effect of the technical progressiveness shown) have made a major contribution to very rapid expansion in the electronics section of the electrical engineering industries—one of the fastest growing individual industries in the economy. A third instance of very rapid growth based on technical development is provided by man-made fibres. Since 1958 output of synthetic materials (by weight) has more than doubled, and this expansion has helped the recovery of output of the textiles group as a whole after 1958 (Table 4.4). (Some growth has also occurred since 1958 in the hosiery and knitwear trades, but in other parts of the group there has been continued stagnation and decline, notably in cotton textiles, where output of yarn and cloth fell by 26 per cent and 22 per cent respectively between 1958 and 1966).

Among industries adversely affected by the introduction of new products have been leather (owing largely to the substitution of synthetic for natural materials in the footwear industry) and, a more important case, steel. Iron and steel dominates UK metal manufacturing, but growth since 1952 has been relatively slow at 1.8 per cent per annum. However, the displacement of steel by other materials, like plastics, only partly explains this relatively slow growth. In addition there have been other technical developments making for econ-

TABLE 4.4

UK Index Numbers of Output at Constant Factor Cost 1952-67 (1958 = 100)

	1952	1953	1954	1955	1956	1957	1958	1959	1960	1961	1962	1963	1964	1965	1966	1967	Average cumulative increase, per cent per annum 1952-67.
Agriculture, forestry and fishing	92	94	96	95	100	102	100	104	111	111	115	120	126	129	128	132	2.4
Mining and quarrying	105	105	106	105	105	104	100	97	94	93	95	95	95	92	87	85	−1.2
Manufacturing:																	
Food, drink and tobacco	87	90	91	94	96	98	100	104	107	110	112	115	118	121	124	124	2.4
Chemical and allied industries	69	78	87	92	96	100	100	111	123	125	129	139	152	159	165	171	6.3
Metal manufacturing	95	93	99	107	109	110	100	104	121	114	108	113	128	134	125	118	1.5
Engineering and allied industries	80	83	89	98	96	99	100	105	113	114	115	119	128	133	136	134	3.5
Textiles, leather and clothing	93	108	110	109	108	108	100	107	113	111	109	112	119	121	120	116	1.5
Other manufacturing	78	85	95	101	98	100	100	108	118	119	120	125	139	142	143	145	4.2
Total manufacturing	83	88	94	100	99	101	100	106	115	115	115	120	130	134	136	134	3.2
Construction	86	92	95	96	101	101	100	106	111	120	121	121	135	138	139	145	3.6
Gas, electricity, water	74	77	84	88	92	96	100	103	110	116	125	133	137	145	151	156	5.6
Transport and communications	94	96	97	99	101	101	100	104	110	112	113	117	124	129	132	134	2.4
Distributive trades	81	86	91	95	96	98	100	106	110	113	113	117	121	124	126	128	3.1
Insurance, banking and finance	81	84	89	92	92	96	100	110	116	120	122	128	137	140	145	148[1]	4.1
Professional and scientific services	83	85	88	90	94	97	100	103	105	110	114	116	119	124	128	131[1]	3.1
Miscellaneous services	92	94	95	97	97	98	100	103	108	111	112	116	125	126	127	130[1]	2.3
GDP[2]	87.0	90.5	94.3	97.5	98.4	100.0	100	104.5	110.1	112.1	113.5	117.3	124.4	127.7	129.7	131.0	2.8

Source: NIBB

Notes: 1 Estimated
　　　　2 Includes public administration and defence, and ownership of dwellings.

TABLE 4.5

Estimated UK Inland Passenger Mileage 1953-66[1]

Thousand million passenger miles

	1953 per cent	1959 per cent	1966 per cent	Percentage change 1953-1966
Air	0.2 (0.2)	0.4 (0.3)	1.1 (0.5)	+450
Rail	24.1 (20.6)	25.5 (16.8)	21.5 (10.5)	−10.8
Road:				
Public service vehicles	50.7 (43.3)	44.1 (29.0)	36.3 (17.8)	−28.1
Private transport	42.1 (35.9)	82.1 (54.0)	145.1 (71.2)	+244.7
TOTAL	117.1 (100)	152.1 (100)	204.0 (100)	+74.2

Source: AAS
Note:[1] Percentage figures in brackets show respective contributions to the total in any one year.

omies in the quantities of steel consumed by user industries while a further important factor has been the decline of a substantial proportion of the steel using sector of the economy, notably coal, railways, shipbuilding and defence, though there have been some offsetting increases elsewhere, such as in vehicle production.

The way in which *process,* as distinct from *product* innovation influences as industry's growth is via its effect on supply price. Changes in relative prices, from whatever source, have undoubtedly been important determinants of industry growth rates in many cases. The relative decline of chemical prices, for instance, has been an important factor reinforcing the substitution of chemical products for others and hence in contributing to the growth of that sector: in 1966 the price index of output of the chemical and allied industries stood only around 8¾ per cent above its level in 1952, compared with a rise for all manufacturing industry of some 32 per cent. Chemicals represents an unusually clear-cut instance of the effects of relative price movements, for in many cases the precise effects are peculiarly difficult to distinguish. For instance, we have seen that much of the development in passenger transport services may ultimately be attributed to rising real incomes and car ownership. How far these developments may also have been due to changes in the relative prices of different types of transport is less clear. In the first place, it is difficult to determine how large a part is played by the costs of travel by different modes in consumers' car purchase decisions. Secondly, while it is true that both rail and bus fares have risen very much faster over the period than have private motoring costs (with the main increases in rail and bus coming when traffic falls were greatest) it is not entirely clear how far these have been the result rather than the cause of reduced traffic.

The problem of distinguishing the effects of relative price movements is also encountered, in a somewhat different form, when considering the relative rates of growth of the four energy producing industries—coal, gas, electricity and petroleum. Between 1952 and 1966 UK fuel consumption increased much less rapidly than GDP, growth in one being around 28 per cent compared with approximately 49 per cent for the other.[1] Over the period the direct use of coal fell markedly in both absolute and percentage terms, while there were

---

[1] Although the difference between these two figures is perhaps surprising at first sight, too close a degree of correspondence is not to be expected. An 'energy coefficient' (i.e. percentage growth of fuel consumption per 1 per cent growth of GDP) of less than one may be expected in industrial fuel consumption (around 60 per cent of total consumption) as a result of technical economies in fuel use and also of structural changes in the economy if, for instance, faster growing industries are not intensive fuel users. Domestic consumption is presumably a function of the price of fuel (as a whole) and of household incomes. Their precise effects are not immediately clear but, for whatever reason, consumers' expenditure on fuel and light has in fact grown more or less in line with total personal consumption expenditure, and hence slightly more slowly than GDP.

quite dramatic increases for both oil and electricity (Table 4.6).[1] Quantities of gas consumed fell slightly up to 1961, recovered sharply in 1963-64 to the 1950 level, and continued to rise in 1965 and 1966, the turn-round in the industry's fortunes being due to the use of cheaper imported natural gas supplies and reformed refinery gas.[2]

TABLE 4.6

UK Fuel Consumption 1952-66[1]

Million tons of coal or coal equivalent, direct use

	1952 per cent	1958 percent	1966 per cent	Per cent change 1952-66
Coal	114.8 (49.7)	99.2 (40.1)	61.6 (20.8)	−46.4
Electricity	38.0 (16.5)	53.8 (21.7)	91.8 (30.9)	+141.8
Oil	24.8 (10.7)	41.5 (16.8)	90.9 (30.6)	+266.7
Gas	20.0 (8.7)	19.1 (7.7)	22.7 (7.7)	+13.5
Total Fuel[2]	230.8 (100)	247.5 (100)	296.9 (100)	+27.8

Source: AAS.
Notes:
[1] Percentage figures in brackets show respective contributions to the total in any one year.
[2] Includes coke, breeze and other solid fuels, liquid fuel derived from coal and methane used at collieries.

One factor underlying these trends which is probably *not* connected with relative price changes for different types of fuel has been structural change in the economy as, for instance, in the decline in rail and growth of road transport. A more important factor, however, has been the replacement of coal by other fuels in many uses, e.g. the transfer to electricity in the iron and steel industry; to diesel fuel and electricity in rail transport; to oil in power generation (until curbed by government action to protect the coal industry); and to oil, electricity and gas in industrial and domestic space heating. And it is very difficult to estimate precisely the relative importance of the parts played in this substitution by changes in relative fuel costs and by developments affecting the technical efficiency of different fuels for various purposes; for the effects of the latter are felt only through changes in equipment costs and it is not easy to distinguish these from changes in relative fuel costs. Actual changes in relative fuel prices have been extensive. In particular, oil prices fell by some 14 per cent in 1958 with the emergence of a world oil surplus and, despite the imposition of a 2d per gallon duty on fuel oil in 1961 (equivalent to a 23s per ton subsidy on coal, and subsequently raised to 2.2d per gallon), fuel oil prices have risen

[1] The effects of the fuel consumption trends shown in Table 4.6 on the output trends of the energy producing industries shown in Table 4.4 may not be immediately obvious. The very rapid increase in petroleum is concealed within, and contributes to the high rate of growth of chemical and allied industries. The growth rate of the public utilities as a whole understates that of electricity at least up to 1964, since gas was virtually stagnant. In mining and quarrying (in which coal represents over nine-tenths of output) the overall decline in output has been much smaller than the fall in direct consumption of coal and up to 1954 output was in fact rising. The main reason for this is that although electricity competes with coal in *direct* fuel consumption, the industry is itself a very large coal consumer. Thus the decline in direct coal consumption has been to some extent offset by rising sales to the electricity industry, whose share in total coal sales has risen over the period from less than 20 per cent to some 39.4 per cent.
[2] The effects of North Sea natural gas had not at this stage been felt. The cost of imported and refinery gas, at around 7d to 8d per therm, compared with a cost of 1s 1d for gas produced by the traditional carbonisation process. After much dispute, the likely cost per therm of North Sea gas appears as if it will be around 2½d per therm.

much less markedly than coal since the mid 1950s. Thus there is a strong *prima facie* case for thinking that relative price changes have been important in the substitution of oil for coal. On the other hand, electricity consumption has also increased very rapidly despite price increases relatively to some substitutes, and here technical factors would seem predominant, given the difficulty in replacing electricity for lighting purposes and in many domestic and industrial power uses and given also its convenience for supplementary domestic heating.

Relative price movements of a particular kind—changes in relative supply prices of overseas and UK suppliers—have been an important determinant of the growth or decline of some industries. Thus, foreign competition from low cost countries, especially Japan, eastern Europe, Italy and Portugal, has been a major factor underlying the output performance of textiles, leather and clothing. The main burden appears to have fallen on textiles, especially cotton and low-priced woollen goods, although footwear has also been affected. Production for export (some 25 per cent of total output for the group as a whole in the early 1950s) was affected first, and home sales as well in later years. Again, lack of competitiveness in world markets in a situation of surplus world shipbuilding capacity may be held largely responsible for the decline of shipbuilding and the closely related marine engineering industry, which were once major UK industries, but now form a minor and declining proportion of engineering output. In an expanding world market competition from Japanese and Swedish yards in particular has resulted in total UK shipbuilding output in 1967 standing at a level some 13 per cent below that of 1950, despite growth at around 3¾ per cent per annum up to 1956. In the case of both cotton textiles and shipbuilding the falls in output experienced have resulted in government action to assist the industries (which is considered in section III.6 of this chapter).

For a complete or partial explanation of production trends in some industries we need look no further than the output performance of important user industries. The decline of a substantial steel using sector—defence, railways, shipbuilding and coal—as a factor in the slow growth of steel production has already been mentioned. To this might be added other examples—fast growth of vehicles and some other engineering industries and hence of demand for chemicals and rubber products (included in 'other manufacturing'); rapidly rising electricity consumption (at some 7½-8 per cent per annum) and hence production of generating switching and transmission gear for the national grid), and of insulated wire and cables; and modest growth or decline in a number of mechanical engineering industries supplying specialised plant and equipment to industries where neither prospects nor the level of investment have been high, e.g. textiles. One important example to be included under this heading is inland freight transport. For here not only the overall growth of traffic but also changes in the mode of transport used can to a large extent be traced to production trends of particular industries or commodities.

Growth total inland freight traffic between 1952 and 1966 has been relatively slow at some 2.2 per cent per annum (Table 4.7, page 144) compared with both passenger transport (4.4 per cent per annum) and industrial production (3.5 per cent). Much of the explanation for this comparatively modest rate of growth apparently lies in the decline in coal and coke production and slow growth (and a reduction of traffic movements per ton produced) in the steel industry, two heavy transport users. These two factors are also important in accounting for the declining share of rail which, being particularly suited to long-haul, large bulk work, has always been heavily dependent on carrying coal and coke and crude materials. The more flexible road haulage industry is less heavily committed to particular industries or commodities but at the same time has been more fortunate in that some sectors which *are* heavy road transport users (e.g. building and construction) have been growing rapidly. Coastal shipping, like rail, is heavily dependent on long-haul, bulk loads, but in this case a decline in coal and coke carrying has been offset by increased oil

F

Industry and commerce

shipments. Oil is also the explanation of the recent increase in transport by pipeline which, however, as yet accounts for a very small fraction of the total.

Government action is the final major factor influencing industry growth rates which we shall consider. Output levels and growth rates in many industries are affected, sometime unintentionally, by taxation, hire purchase controls, tariffs, etc. In addition there are a number of cases where government action or involvement is especially noteworthy.

TABLE 4.7

UK Inland Freight Transport 1952-66[1]

Thousand million ton/miles

	1952 per cent	1959 per cent	1966 per cent	Per cent increase 1952-66
Road	18.8 (37.2)	28.1 (50.6)	41.5 (61.2)	+120.8
Rail	22.4 (44.4)	17.7 (31.6)	14.8 (21.8)	−33.9
Coastal shipping	9.0 (17.8)	9.5 (17.2)	10.6 (15.6)	+17.8
Inland waterways	0.2 (0.4)	0.2 (0.4)	0.1 (0.1)	−50
Pipelines	0.1 (0.2)	0.1 (0.2)	0.9 (1.3)	+800
Total	50.5 (100)	55.6 (100)	67.9 (100)	+34.1

Source: AAS.
Note:
[1]   Percentage figures in brackets show respective contributions to the total in any one year.

One such is building and construction. Work commissioned in this industry represents mainly private and public investment expenditure, and the effects of government action are felt in two main ways. One is the direct impact of central and local authority decisions on investment in housing and other construction projects. The other is that the level of private investment is very sensitive to monetary and fiscal measures.

Investment in housing and other building and construction (at constant prices) rose very rapidly between 1952 and 1967 at some 5.9 per cent per annum. This is considerably more than the rate of growth shown for the construction group in Table 4.4, the difference arising mainly because of less rapid expansion in the repairs and maintenance section than for new work. Over the period considerable changes occurred in the balance between housing and other building and construction work. There have also been some rather abrupt changes in trend in the various sectors. Together these factors help explain the course of expansion in construction shown in Table 4.4.

In 1952 and 1953 construction activity was at a high level because of public spending on housing to deal with the postwar housing problem. Up till then government controls and shortages of materials held almost all private development in check at artificially low levels. Between 1953 and 1958 there was then a very rapid expansion of private house-building and other private building and works. But over the same period public investment on housing fell by half and this was only partly offset by a moderate increase in public spending on other building and works (schools, hospitals, road works, and other civil engineering projects). With these mixed trends in investment expenditure, growth of output of construction was slow from 1953-58, rising only 1.7 per cent per annum. After 1958 private investment in both housing and other work continued to expand rapidly up to 1961. Both were checked in the recession years of 1962 and 1963 but recovered strongly in 1964. In the next two years private housing investment fell by over 11 per cent while other private building investment oscillated. In the public sector there was some recovery of public housebuilding in the late 1950s, with the intensification of slum clearance and urban renewal, and in the early and mid 1960s this growth gained momentum, partly no doubt as a result of political changes. Public non-housing investment continued to expand between 1958 and 1966, at some 7 per cent per annum (5.8 per cent per annum from 1952-58).

The net effect of all these developments was a much faster rate of growth in construction after 1958 than in the earlier period (at some 4.2 per cent per annum), but with virtual stagnation in the 1962-63 recession and in 1966, and very rapid growth in the other years, especially 1964. Over the period 1952-66 as a whole total private investment in building and construction rose by no less than + 268 per cent, the main increase occurring by 1961. Public investment, on the other hand, rose by very much less overall (+ 56 per cent) though starting from a much higher level and with the chief increase coming after 1963. In 1966 the public and private shares of total investments in building and construction were roughly 60 per cent and 40 per cent respectively.

A second industry extensively and continuously affected by direct government policy is agriculture. Through the agricultural support programme the government is able to influence unit costs of home production and also determine the effective prices received by UK producers for many products. The explicit policy objective is to determine the level of home output and equate this with 'such part of the nation's food and other agricultural produce as in the national interest it is desirable to produce in the UK'.[1] Because such a policy exists, the growth of agricultural output shown in Table 4.4[2] and the trends in labour and capital employed and in productivity (Tables 4.2, 4.3 and A-10) can be explained almost exclusively by reference to deliberate government decisions (although the developments actually occurring have apparently not always been as intended).

Current UK agricultural support is based on two main types of assistance to farmers. First, direct grants and subsidies are paid for specific purposes, as for example subsidies for the use of fertilisers, lime and calves and grants for farm improvements, small farmers, ploughing, etc. Second, farmers receive 'deficiency payments' on most major products if the ruling market price is lower than a guaranteed price set by the government. For certain products there are other special arrangements: thus in the case of milk, market prices are fixed; under the Horticulture Acts of 1960 and 1964 horticultural produce is protected by grants and by tariff; and there are arrangements for coordinating the marketing and production of some products, e.g. milk, eggs, sugar-beet and potatoes. Grants, subsidies and guaranteed prices are reviewed every year in the light of production trends, market requirements, world developments, the cost to the Exchequer, farm incomes and efficiency, trading relations with other countries (especially the Commonwealth) and the national economic situation. The revisions are published around March every year, in the *Annual Review*.

Incidentally to ensuring a 'proper' level of home output it is claimed that the policy simultaneously permits certain other policy requirements to be met. In an industry particularly subject to fluctuating supplies and hence marketing conditions, forward planning is facilitated and farmers are given some measure of security of income in that if market prices are unexpectedly depressed the deficiency payments arrangement ensures that the burden falls on the Exchequer.[3] Secondly, consumers are held to benefit from food prices being kept at lower world levels, although the full cost of producing at home is paid through taxation (as a result of which income may be effectively redistributed within the community). Thirdly, since part of the assistance is in the form of grants, these can be directed towards specific improvements in the efficiency of the industry. Finally, by using the present system rather than alternative systems of protection the UK has been

---

[1] Agriculture Act, 1947.

[2] As forestry and fishing are comparatively small, figures for agriculture, forestry and fishing may be taken as broadly representative of trends in agriculture alone.

[3] However, long-term stability would still not be very great if grants and guaranteed prices changed drastically from year to year. Since 1957 there has been some limitation on the extent to which the government can vary guaranteed prices from year to year, but a certain longer-term uncertainty still remains.

able until recently to maintain free entry for foreign produce, especially that from Commonwealth sources (although at the same time opportunities of foreign suppliers must necessarily be reduced by the competition they meet from subsidised UK produce).

On the debit side, one major weakness of the scheme up to around 1963 was that it was 'open ended' and the liability of the Exchequer was unlimited. Guaranteed prices for each product would be set with a desired quantity in mind, but this could be exceeded and deficiency payments were payable whatever the level of output actually produced. Secondly, since the entry of foreign produce into the UK was in the main unrestricted, Exchequer liability was vulnerable to fluctuations in world supply which could depress market prices in the UK and hence enlarge the deficiencies to be made good in any one year. Since 1963 measures have been taken to remedy the situation in two ways. First, standard quantities have been introduced for most products and if these are exceeded producers' average unit returns are reduced.[1] In addition, minimum import prices or quota arrangements have been introduced through the negotiation of bilateral agreements with overseas suppliers.[2] As a result, the rise in total cost of agricultural support does appear to have been checked; from around £200 million in the mid-1950s, the annual cost rose to a peak of £343 million in 1961-62, and a good deal of this increase was apparently unintentional. Since then the figure has fallen back to an average of around £250 million per annum for the years 1964-65 to 1967-68.[3] Thus it can no longer justifiably be said that UK agricultural support involves the government writing a blank cheque for farmers. On the other hand, one of the incidental benefits claimed for the UK policy—namely, in giving security of farm income and facilitating forward planning—no longer applies with as much force as before the change. Moreover, other criticisms of the policy remain.

One is that much of the support is given to efficient and inefficient farmers alike. More fundamentally, the whole basis for maintaining an artificially high level of domestic output can be questioned. In a situation where agriculture receives government support not only in the UK but in most other countries as well, it is difficult to estimate how far UK output differs from its 'natural' size and pattern. But given the level of many guaranteed prices in relation to world levels, the size of direct grants and subsidies and the recent need for import controls, it is clear that if other countries were to continue supporting their own agriculture the level of output would be much less in the UK without government support. To determine how far, if at all, it is in the national interest to devote more resources to agricultural production than would otherwise be the case it is necessary to estimate the benefits precisely.

A common justification is on strategic grounds—a contingency provison against a possible future war or similar emergency. Secondly, enlarging home production is often defended on grounds of import saving; that extra part of total food supplies now produced at home would otherwise have had to be imported.[4] But the *full* effect of agricultural support on the balance of payments is not simply the crude figure of imports 'saved' (even after allowing for the cost of extra imports of feed, fertiliser, etc.). Account must be taken of exports which might have resulted from the use of the same resources elsewhere, net of imports required in these alternative uses. Allowances must also be made for the fact that larger UK food imports might have increased the capacity of overseas food suppliers to buy British exports, and for any difference in terms of trade caused by the smaller scale of UK agriculture.

A third main justification of agricultural support might be that without it there would be a loss of social amenities. In the long run the peculiar charm of the British countryside

---

[1] This was not an entirely new departure. Standard quantities or similar arrangements already existed for sugar-beet, milk, potatoes, eggs and pig meat.
[2] See 1964 *Annual Review.*
[3] Figures include grants, price guarantees, administrative cost, and grant to the Northern Ireland Exchequer of about £10million per annum.
[4] See, e.g. National Plan p. 131.

and the social and cultural value of rural life would be lost. In the short run the operation of scaling down agriculture might, depending on what other measures were taken: (e.g. to promote industry in agricultural areas), result in a waste of existing social overhead capital in some areas and exacerbate problems of congestion and short-term housing and education needs, etc. in towns and cities.

balance of payments is concerned, previous investigations have produced some agreement that further expansion of domestic production would be unlikely to make a positive contribution;[1] opinion is divided as to whether reduction or removal of agricultural support would have a favourable or unfavourable effect, although there is some limited agreement that the effects would probably be only marginal in either direction.[2] Even greater uncertainty persists over the precise value of the supposed strategic and amenity benefits to the community. It is scarcely possible to say whether or not the UK's ability to produce around one half of its food requirements constitutes a rational preparation for any future conflict, given the nature of modern warfare, let alone to measure the precise value of the protection offered, if any. Similarly, it is open to question whether the gains from alternative uses of the countryside for building and recreation would in the long run outweigh or be outweighed by the supposed loss of amenities involved in scaling down agriculture. As for the short run costs and benefits, their relative importance cannot be assessed for two reasons; first, because of the uncertainty over long run benefits against the (suitably discounted) value of which short run costs must be set and, second, because of the variety of possible accompanying measures which might be taken.

What can be said, however, is that it is doubtful whether the kind of appraisal required has ever been officially undertaken. Certainly, if proper evaluation has been undertaken it has never been made explicit. After the period of postwar shortages it was decided that in the national interest the desirable level of home output was 60 per cent higher than in 1938-39, and this was achieved by 1958. More recently the basis for policy has been taken as maintaining the existing shares of home and imported produce (in 1964) and, (currently) a policy of selective expansion, conditional on the maintenance of recent improvements in productivity, to meet the 'major part' of an estimated £200 million increase in food demand between 1966 and 1970 by home production.[3] But whether at the different times these targets have really represented the 'proper balance' between home and over-seas production is not clear, nor has there been any official clarification of how a precise meaning can be given to this frequently used term.

Government policies concerning two further groups of industries, those supplying energy and transport services, have some features in common. In both cases a substantial proportion of supply is nationalised; both are areas over where the divergence between social and private costs is potentially large; neither has until recently been the subject of a coherent overall policy; but in both cases there has recently been some attempt to evolve more comprehensive plans.

The price and investment policies of the nationalised coal, gas and electricity indus-tries apart, past government fuel policy has consisted largely in measures to protect the coal industry from competition from oil.[4] These have included the imposition of a tax on fuel oil (originally 2d a gallon, equivalent to a 23s per ton coal subsidy, and currently 2.2d per gallon); restrictions on the choice of primary fuel for power stations and on

---

1   See J. M. Slater and D. R. Colman 'Agriculture's Contribution to the Balance of Payments', *District Bank Review*, September 1966, and references therein.

2   The studies referred to were all written prior to the 1967 devaluation. At the time of writing no study had been published of the effect of devaluation on agriculture's contribution to the balance of payments.

3   *National Plan*, page 135. See also 1967 and 1968 *Annual Reviews*. The rate of growth of output implied is broadly in line with that of the recent past. If achieved it entails an increase in the proportion of food consumed which is produced at home.

4   In the past coal and oil have been the major primary fuel sources in the UK from which other direct use fuels, notably electricity and gas, are derived.

Industry and commerce

direct fuel use in public buildings; and a virtual ban on all coal imports.[1] Whether the costs of this policy in the mid-1960s (in the form of higher fuel charges to consumers) were more than offset by compensating benefits is open to question and this alone would have merited a full-scale review of fuel policy. In the event, however, it was the emergence of two new, potentially cheap and indigenous primary fuels—nuclear electricity and natural gas—which prompted reappraisal.

The broad objectives of current fuel policy were set out in a White Paper in 1965.[2] The explicit objective now is to supply energy as cheaply as possible to fuel users, subject to considerations of security, adequacy of supplies and, in a more general way, optimal use of resources in the economy. Regard is also to be had to improvements in technology, direct effects on other industries and to manpower and social implications. A second White Paper set out conclusions on the desirable balance and likely future trends of primary fuel use.[3] Published just before devaluation this may now be subject to some modifications but changes are unlikely to be major. Table 4.8 shows that most rapid growth in both percentage and absolute terms is to come from natural gas.

TABLE 4.8

Trends in Primary Fuel Use[1] 1957-1975

Million tons coal equivalent

	1957	1966	1975 (Estimated)	Percentage change 1957-66	1966-75
Coal	212.9	174.7	120[2]	−18	−31
Oil	36.7	111.7	145	+205	+30
Nuclear and hydro-electricity	1.7	10.2	35	+500	+243
Natural gas	−	1.1	50	−	+4450
Total	251.3	297.7	350	+18.6	+17.6

Source: Fuel Policy, Cmnd 3438, 1967
Notes:
[1] The main assumptions underlying the 1975 forecast are that North Sea gas reserves would give 4,000 m.c.f.d. and the price of gas would be such that it could be sold; that there would be no conversion of coal-fired power stations to oil; that the second nuclear power programme would be fulfilled; that oil tax would be 2d per gallon; that no coal would be imported; and that GDP would grow at 3 per cent per annum.
[2] Includes 2 million tons exported.

Revolution of the gas industry, however, will not transform the energy market, since gas will account for only 15 per cent of total supplies in the mid-1970s. Nevertheless this still means that gas, with the other new indigenous fuel, nuclear and hydro-electricity, will take over the rapid growth previously shown by oil. On present plans oil use will expand more or less in line with total fuel use, its share stabilising at around 41 per cent. The share of coal will fall from 59 per cent currently to around one-third in 1975.

Immediate policy changes are minimal. In the short term quite heavy protection of coal is to continue alongside the policy of coal modernisation and concentration of production in more efficient pits. Decisions on fuel use in new power stations up to 1973 have already been taken, and conversions from coal to other fuels are not envisaged except in special circumstances, at least up to 1970. The second nuclear programme 1970-75 will continue as planned and there is to be rapid exploitation of natural gas finds. Ultimately however, protection of coal will disappear or be much reduced. In particular there will be

[1] A temporary slowdown in the rate of pit closures was also made in late 1967 as a short term expedient to moderate unemployment in early 1968.
[2] *Fuel Policy,* Cmnd 2798, HMSO, 1965.
[3] *Fuel Policy,* Cmnd 3438, HMSO, 1967.

free choice of fuel for power stations (the only expanding sector of coal demand), although in sanctioning proposals the minister may take into account 'wider economic consider-ations'. The position regarding coal imports and oil taxation beyond 1975 is not clear.

The 1967 White Paper claims that the proposed policy and projected fuel trends meet the general objectives of fuel policy in the following ways. Deliberate holding back on nuclear power and natural gas and continued long-term support of coal would have been technically retrogressive and impeded access to cheap fuel supplies. However short term moderation of the decline of coal, especially up to 1970 is justified on both balance of payments and social and manpower grounds, the contraction that would otherwise occur being 'unmanageable'. Continued discrimination against oil is also defended on external payment grounds, and increased emphasis on indigenous primary sources is held to enhance security of UK fuel supplies. Adequacy of resources is held to be important only in the case of gas, but rapid exploitation (and hence rapid depletion of a given stock) is, paradox-ically, claimed to be desirable on grounds of the stimulus this will have for further explora-tion and discoveries. Direct effects on other industries are held to be important only in the case of the transport industry (on account of further reductions in coal and coke carrying) and not to necessitate policy modifications.

Of course the forecasts on which the policy is based and, hence, the policy itself are subject to considerable error. In part this is inevitable but, as the White Paper freely admits, it is partly because the techniques of estimation and prediction used were not always the best available. At times, too, there has been resort to assumption when more precise estimates might have been made. One example of this concerns future relative price movements for different fuels. Another is the relationship between rapid exploita-tion of natural gas and the rate of discovery; the assumptions made here were apparently based mainly on past experience in the Netherlands and the crucial question of the price paid to operators is not discussed. The greatest weakness in framing policy, however, has undoubtedly and perhaps inevitably been the assessment of the costs and benefits of alternative policy combinations, and determination of the relative weights to be given to different, conflicting objectives and to short-run as against long-run considerations. Even after allowance is made for the serious difficulties and many imponderables involved there has, perhaps, been undue reliance on qualitative, political and managerial judgment. For instance, in assessing the social consequences of the decline in coal the Coal Board was apparently asked what rate of reduction in employment was 'manageable'. A more satisfactory approach might have been to attempt independently to quantify both the costs to the Coal Board and the social costs to the community of various rates of decline in order to set these against the (discounted) long-term benefits of policies contemplated.

On the whole, however, the 1967 White Paper contained much that was admirable. Relatively speaking it was thorough, and there was clear awareness of the main economic and social problems involved and of the need to balance out short and longer term considerations. It was presented, moreover, as the first phase of a continuing review, in the course of which the use of more sophisticated quantitative methods is envisaged. At the very least it is a step towards a more conscious discharge of a responsibility and authority which has for some time been exercised in a piecemeal, haphazard fashion. It is precisely the sort of appraisal long overdue for e.g. agriculture.

As well as owning a substantial proportion of total transport facilities and determining the criteria on which they operate the government also influence the cost of private trans-port through the licensing system, and taxes on fuel and vehicles. In addition, it is respon-sible for undertaking and financing road building and the provision of the other services ancillary to road use. But up to the present there has been little evidence of the govern-ment using its powers to provide a coherent transport policy. For instance, the extensive road building programme has been carried out independently of railway modernisation; in deciding on rail closures the government has largely failed to consider the full effects on road congestion, and it has made no attempt to ensure that the wider obligations of, for example, the nationalised rail undertakings are adequtely allowed for. In the absence of a coherent policy there is considerable doubt whether the pattern of transport services provided reflects the true costs of their provision to the community. This applies equally to both freight and passenger traffic, but consideration of the latter only will serve to illustrate the general nature of the problem.

Rail passenger fares are set on a standard passenger-mile charge (though somewhat less rigidly now than in the past) despite wide variations in the cost of providing individual facilities, e.g. between well-loaded express journeys and local, stopping services, especially in remote areas. The same is generally true for public road undertakings. Hence in both cases when passengers choose between alternative journeys and modes of transport they do so on the basis of a uniform contribution per mile to the total cost of all the operations of the undertaking, rather than on the opportunity cost of providing the particular service used. Moreover, when the alternatives include private motoring there are further complications. The total payments made by road users for the use of roads (in the form of fuel and licence duties and purchase tax on vehicles) bear no close relationship to the total costs incurred by the road authorities in providing the road system. More important from an economic viewpoint, the payments made by individual road users bear no relation at all to the opportunity costs they incur in using the road system. This is even more so when the social cost element is taken into account. Here perhaps the largest omission at present is that vehicles using crowded city centres do not pay directly for the congestion costs they impose on others. The amounts involved may be large. Thus the Smeed Committee found that the congestion costs incurred by a car or similar vehicle in central London rose from 4d per mile at 20 m.p.h. to 2s per mile at 12 m.p.h. and no less than 6s per mile at 8 m.p.h. (a not unrealistic speed for rush-hour periods).[1] The various effects are difficult to identify, but almost certainly road users in congested areas are paying substantially less than the opportunity costs they incur; users in uncongested areas, the reverse.

The full ramifications of the transport problem go much further than this,[2] but enough has been said to indicate that extensive reappraisal of government policy is required. The solution advocated for both passenger and freight is for the price of each service to equal the opportunity cost of its provision. Assuming that difficulties of practical application could be overcome, there is no doubt that this would result in considerable changes in the present composition of transport services. On the passenger side it would mean significant price reductions on well-loaded express rail journeys, and in consequence considerable alteration in the pattern of long distance travel. On the other hand, many local stopping services would disappear, unless giving rise to substantial social benefits. The effects on commuter traffic are less easy to foresee; but there would clearly be substantial increases in the cost of private motoring in urban areas and this might be expected to cause a shift to both rail and public road services, and as such effect a significant reduction in the level of traffic congestion in urban areas, particularly during rush-hour periods.

Without a rational pricing policy for the use of road and rail facilities it is difficult to determine the appropriate investment projects in the transport field—whether to build more long distance motorways; or improve other existing roads; or which part of the railway system really merits modernisation. The need for a more rational government policy has been widely recognised for some time. Most recent developments in policy affecting transport are contained in two sources, the 1967 White Paper setting out price and invest-

---

[1] *Road Pricing, The Economic and Technical Possibilities,* HMSO, 1964.
[2] See K. Gwilliam, *Transport and Public Policy,* Allen and Unwin, London 1964; C. D. Foster, *The Transport Problem,* Blackie, London, 1963; and C. Sharp. *The Problem of Transport,* Pergamon, London, 1965.

ment criteria for the nationalised industries[1] and the massive 1967 Transport Bill.[2]

If capable of application in this area the principles in the White Paper might tend to result in pricing and investment policies in transport undertakings which reflected the true cost of the services provided.[3] This in turn would make for an 'integrated' transport system in the sense of transport requirements being met by a pattern of services involving minimum real cost to the community. To secure an integrated transport system in some sense was the basic intention behind the Transport Bill. However neither the Bill itself nor the four White Papers which preceded it[4] attempted to spell out the detailed implications for transport operations of the general pricing and investment criteria and give the more specific guidance needed to make them practically applicable. This is a serious ommission on two counts. First, transport is an area where because of the frequency of joint products it is often very difficult to find the true costs of providing individual services and where, accordingly, modifications or alternatives to the general pricing principles recommended by the Nationalised Industries' White Paper are recognised as necessary. Secondly, transport is also an area where 'wider social and economic considerations' loom large and Cmnd 3437 is far from explicit as to precisely how these considerations should be treated. That they may, if improperly handled, lead to shortcomings in policy is evidenced in the Transport Bill. Appropriately, provision is made for grants to be given for unremunerative railway services which are desired on wider economic and social grounds; but grants might also be justified for remunerative lines on similar grounds, and make for lower fares or better services, and there is no provision for grants in such cases.[5] Again, it seems that at one point it is assumed that lorries and private cars do create congestion in large cities while buses do not.[6] In both cases the associated policy measures are unlikely to be conducive to the emergence of an optimal pattern of transport services.

The Transport Bill did originally include some specific provisions which could be seen as tending to make prices in road haulage correspond more closely to the costs at present being imposed. First, an additional annual charge of between £50 and £190 was proposed for haulage vehicles to reflect the fact that the roads they use have to be constructed to higher standards or be maintained more frequently. Secondly a mileage impost of from 1s to £5 was proposed for abnormal loads to reflect, albeit approximately, the congestion costs, etc. imposed on the public. Both provisions proved contentious, however, and were subsequently dropped.[7]

But at no stage did the Bill rely entirely on the price mechanism and consumer choice to produce an integrated transport system. Some element of administrative direction of traffic may be discerned in two areas. One is the provision for 'special authorisations' needed for journeys by vehicles over sixteen tons, normally over one hundred miles or more. Still contained in the Bill at the time of writing, though the object of vigorous objections, this may prevent some consignments travelling by road where the user would prefer this but it can be shown that rail or rail/road can provide a satisfactory alternative. Secondly, parking restrictions in conurbations may effectively direct some commuters to travel by rail. Furthermore, much of the Bill is concerned with organisational changes as a means of assisting integration, especially between road and rail. On the freight side there is provision for a National Freight Corporation and Freight Integration Council.

---

[1] *Nationalised Industries: A Review of Economic & Financial Objectives, Cmnd 3437, HMSO, Nov. 1967.*
[2] *See N. Lee 'A Review of the Transport Bill', DBR, March 1968.*
[3] See p. 158.
[4] *Railway Policy*, Cmnd 3439, HMSO,1967;*The Transport of Freight*, Cmnd 3470, HMSO, 1967; *Public Transport and Traffic*, Cmnd 3481, HMSO, 1967; and *British Waterways; Recreation and Amenity*, Cmnd 3401, HMSO, 1967.
[5] N. Lee, 'A Review of the Transport Bill'.
[6] *Ibid.*
[7] However the duty on heavy commercial vehicles was increased in the 1968 Budget.

For passenger traffic the main concern is with problems arising in major conurbations, and four Passenger Transport Authorities have initially been set up (and the London Transport Board has been transferred to the GLC to make, effectively, a fifth). *Inter alia,* these authorities will take over municipal bus undertakings, supervise fares and services, and negotiate with the British Railways Board over the provision of local rail services.

Other provisions of the Bill are to establish a National Bus Company for England and Wales, and a Scottish Transport Group; to create a new carrier licensing system; to make certain financial provisions concerning British Rail, in particular reducing its capital debt substantially[1]; and to provide for grants to the new Passenger Transport Authorities in respect of fuel duty, unremunerative rail services (to be passed on to British Rail), major improvements to track and facilities, and reequipment of bus fleets. Apart from the original two imposts on road hauliers, the Bill makes no provision for direct road pricing as recommended by the Smeed Committee. Rather, following a recent report,[2] road use in cities is to continue for the time being to be controlled via parking restrictions and charges, and the Bill contains some provisions extending powers in this area.

II   THE ORGANISATION OF PLANTS AND FIRMS

II.1   The Size Structure of Plants and Firms in Manufacturing: Concentration

Detailed information on the size distribution of plants and firms is readily available only for manufacturing industry. Table 4.9 (page 153) shows that the great majority of plants (establishments) are quite small.[3] Around three quarters employed less than 100 workers in 1958, average plant size was only 137, and the numbers of plants in the higher size ranges fell off very rapidly, especially beyond the 500 employee level. The small scale of production in British manufacturing becomes much more striking if we add in the 32,640 establishments with up to ten employees for which less detailed information is available. The proportion of plants with under 100 workers now becomes 84 per cent and the average size of plant falls to 88. The high proportion of small plants is repeated in each of the broad industry groups shown in Table 4.9. Such high proportions must mean that small scale production is economically viable in most of the individual industries within each group, or at any rate in those industries which account for the bulk of group employment. It is worth noting that there may often be small scale production opportunities in many individual industries which are commonly thought to consist solely of large units—e.g. soap, chemicals, steel: the (misleading) reputation for large scale which these industries may have often arises from their being associated with the names of very large *firms.* On the other hand there are some industries where small units are few and average plant size is large e.g. oil refining and aircraft; the average number employed per plant in aircraft in 1958 was 798.

Although small plants are numerically predominant the bulk of activity in manufacturing is undertaken by large units. Thus the one quarter of all plants which had more than 100 workers in 1958 was responsible for as much as 81.5 per cent of total employment in manufacturing and the 1.2 per cent of largest plants (with 1500 or more workers each) accounted for no less than 27.4 per cent. Once more a somewhat similar picture is reflected in the main industry groups shown in Table 4.9, the contribution of very large plants being especially large in engineering where the top 3.1 per cent of largest plants were responsible for almost one half of total employment. In the main this is due to the inclusion in the group of the aircraft, motor vehicles and shipbuilding industries. A similar general picture emerges if we calculate the share of large and small plants in total output rather than employment. In fact when this is done the predominance of large

---

[1]   See also p. 161.
[2]   *Better Use of Town Roads,* HMSO, 1967.
[3]   Excludes those employing ten or less workers.

TABLE 4.9

Size Distribution of Establishments by Industry Group and Proportion of Industry Employment by Size of Establishment in Manufacturing. 1958

A = number of plants (excluding establishments with 1-10 employees).
B = number of plants in size range as per cent of industry total (in brackets).
C = percentage of total industry employment in plants in given size range.

Size of establishment (number employed)	Food, drink, tobacco			Chemicals and allied industries			Metal industries[1]			Engineering and allied			Textiles, clothing, footwear[2]			Other manufacturing[3]			All manufacturing[4]		
	A	B	C	A	B	C	A	B	C	A	B	C	A	B	C	A	B	C	A	B	C
11– 99	4,520	(74.7)	18.8	1,603	(67.3)	13.0	5,570	(75.8)	18.4	8,051	(69.2)	10.2	9,011	(71.0)	23.6	9,817	(81.4)	27.4	40,537	(74.2)	18.5
100– 499	1,199	(20.8)	36.4	604	(25.4)	30.8	1,272	(17.4)	24.8[5]	3,254	(27.7)	44.8				2,241	(18.6)	72.6	11,446	(20.9)	32.3
500– 999	143	(2.6)	13.9	91	(3.8)	14.6	273	(3.7)	14.7[6]				3,680	(29.0)	76.4				1,532	(2.8)	13.9
1000–1499	54	(0.9)	9.4	35	(1.5)	9.7	231	(3.1)	42.1[7]										486	(0.9)	7.9
1500+	56	(1.0)	21.6	47	(2.0)	31.8				357	(3.1)	44.9							642	(1.2)	27.4
Total number of establishments	5,754			2,380			7,346			11,662			12,691			12,058			54,740		
Total employment	701,000			437,000			1,003,400			2,609,400			1,323,800			1,130,000			7,512,000		
Mean size of establishments (average no. employed)	122			183			137			222			105			94			137		

Source: Census of Production 1958 and A. Armstrong and A. Silberston, 'Size of Plant, Size of Enterprise and Concentration in British Manufacturing Industry 1935-1958,' JRSS Series A. 1965.

Notes:
1 Metal manufacturing and metal goods n.e.s.
2 Excludes leather
3 Bricks pottery and glass; timber and furniture; paper printing and publishing and rubber only.
4 All census trades.
5 100-399.
6 400-749.
7 750+.

units tends to be even more marked, since they are usually more capital intensive than smaller units and hence contribute more to total output than to employment: thus plants with over 1500 workers contributed some 31.7 per cent to gross output of manufacturing in 1958 compared with 27.4 per cent to employment.

TABLE 4.10

Size Distribution of Enterprises and Proportion of Employment by Size of Enterprise in Manufacturing, 1958.

(excluding enterprises with 1-24 employees)

Size of enterprise (number employed)	No. of enterprises (per cent)	Percentage of total employment in manufacturing
25– 99	14,257 (60.8)	10.5
100– 499	7,240 (30.8)	21.4
500– 1,999	1,481 (6.3)	19.5
2,000– 9,999	395 (1.7)	22.3
10,000–49,999	66 (0.3)	18.6
50,000+	8 (neg)[1]	7.7

Source: Census of Production, 1958.
Note: [1] The actual figure was 0.034

Similar data relating to the size distribution of firms (enterprises) rather than plants is not available for industry groups, although it will be found in the 1958 Census of Production for individual industries. Table 4.10 shows the summary for manufacturing as a whole. Again, the majority of firms employed less than 100 workers but were responsible for only a small proportion of total employment (10.5 per cent) while the 2 per cent of firms employing over 2,000 were responsible for some 48.6 per cent of employment and the minute fraction with over 50,000 workers for as much as 7.7 per cent.

A recent study[1] shows that over the period 1935-58 there has been a steady increase in the proportion of total employment in larger plants and a steady decline in the percentage accounted for by small plants both overall and in most industry groups.[2] Plants with over 1,500 workers accounted for only 15.2 per cent of total employment in 1935 compared with their 27.4 per cent in 1958; firms under 100 had 64.6 per cent and 50.8 per cent respectively. The total number of plants increased in nearly all groups between 1935 and 1951, but subsequently fell in all but three groups up to 1958. Numbers of largest plants increased in most groups over the whole period. The trend towards larger plants was paralleled by a tendency to larger firms, those with over 10,000 employees accounting for 14 per cent of total employment in 1935 and 25 per cent in 1958. Though the number of plants per enterprise remains low (most enterprises being single plant firms) there has been some increase from 1.38 plants per firm in 1954 to 1.43 in 1958.

The Census of Production gives concentration ratios (i.e. the share of total output held

---

[1]   A. Armstrong and A. Silberston 'Size of Plant, Size of Enterprise and Concentration in British Manufacturing Industry 1935-1958', JRSS, Ser. A, 1965. See also, e.g. P. Sargant Florence, *Investment Location and Size of Plant,* Cambridge University Press (NIESR), 1948; *Logic of British and American Industry* Routledge and Kegan Paul, London, 1953, and *Post-war Investment Location and Size of Plant,* Cambridge University Press (NIESR), 1962; H. Leak and A. Maizels, 'The Structure of British Industry', JRSS, Ser. A, 1945; R. Evely and I. M. D. Little, *Concentration in British Industry,* Cambridge University Press (NIESR), 1960; W. G. Shepherd 'Changes in British Industrial Concentration 1951-58', OEP, March 1966; K. D. George, 'Changes in British Industrial Concentration 1951-58'. JIE, July 1967.

[2]   In general these were defined more narrowly than in Table 4.9.

by a small number of the largest firms) for most industries. In 1958 there were 71 manufacturing industries where three firms had less than 30 per cent of gross output but the
remaining 48 industries with ratios of more than 30 per cent accounted for 45 per cent
of gross manufacturing output.[1] An earlier study found that in 41 of 200 industries for
which accurate comparison was possible concentration increased between 1935 and 1941
in 27 trades and fell in only 14.[2] Between 1951 and 1958 there was apparently a somewhat
similar tendency, concentration increasing in 36 of 63 industries, and falling in 16, with
two showing no change and nine undetermined.[3] However, concentration data such as
these and changes in them are to be interpreted with caution for at least two reasons. First,
as mentioned earlier, they relate to industries rather than markets. Secondly, no concentration ratio of the census type can divide industries into homogenous and meaningful
categories; the size distribution of firms or plants both within and outside, in this case,
the group of top three largest firms may be equally as significant as the size of share of
this group in total output or employment.[4]

II.2   The Incidence of Different Types of Firm:[5] Business Objectives in Large Companies

The great majority of UK firms are unincorporated businesses, either sole trading concerns
(where ownership and control resides in a single individual) or partnerships (where there
is some pooling of resources and sharing of responsibilities). The main limitations on such
forms of organisation are their restricted access to sources of borrowed finance and their
unsuitability to large-scale delegation and decentralisation of authority (on account of
the personal liability of the owners). Accordingly, the areas most conducive to non-
incorporated organisations are those where capital requirements are low and where the
minimum optimum scale of production and marketing necessary to compete effectively
is not high.

   While the possibility of efficient operation on a small scale is virtually necessary to
the existence of non-incorporated businesses it is not a sufficient explanation of their
large numbers. For there is no lower size limit to joint stock companies and the private
company permits the retention of effective control by an individual, family or small
group while conferring certain advantages. These include the limitation of personal
liability and easier access to borrowed capital and to litigation. Moreover there were,
until recently, few disadvantages: up to 1965 incorporation made little difference to the
tax liability of the firm, the expense of incorporation was slight and, up to 1967, the
extra paperwork and loss of privacy over trading matters was also slight since the
majority of private companies could gain exemption from the usual obligations of
companies to file annual details of profits, assets, etc. with the registrar of companies for
public inspection. It is probably true that the number of companies has been fewer in
the past than it would be if the owners of small firms acted rationally, with full
information and with due allowance for risk. However two recent developments have
operated to make the existing structure of types of firm more appropriate and, indeed,
have caused some previously incorporated businesses to change their status. First, the
introduction of corporation tax created a tax advantage for non-incorporation in some
cases.[6] Where a small business is incorporated the company and its shareholders now

---

[1]   A. Armstrong and A. Silbertson, *op. cit.*
[2]   R. Evely and I. M. D. Little, *op. cit.*
[3]   A. Armstrong and A. Silbertson, *op. cit.*
[4]   See, e.g. J. S. Bain, *Industrial Organisation,* Wiley, New York, 1959, chapter 4.
[5]   For a more detailed description of different types of firm see, e.g. P. Sargant Florence, *The Logic
      of British and American Industry,* Routledge & Kegan Paul (revised ed.), London, 1961; R. S.
      Edwards and H. Townsend, *Business Enterprise,* Macmillan, London, 1961; or A. J. Beacham and
      L. J. Williams, *Economics of Industrial Organisation* (4th ed.), Pitman, London, 1961.
[6]   See A. R. Prest, 'The Corporation Tax', DBR, September 1965, and the *Economist,* 19th June
      1965, pp. 1419-20.

pay 42½ per cent corporation tax on ordinary income, 42½ per cent on capital gains and income tax plus surtax on distributed profits: unincorporated the firm would pay income tax plus surtax on all ordinary income plus a maximum 30 per cent on capital gains. In some circumstances, e.g. if the owners are in the lower surtax range and there is a high ratio of capital gains to ordinary income, non-incorporation could be more profitable. Secondly, the 1967 Companies Act *inter alia* abolished the exempt private company and at the same time made more onerous the provisions for disclosure of trading information now applying to all companies. This now includes details of profit or loss and turnover by principal activities; exports; salaries of directors if over £10,000 per annum (including any share in profits); political contributions and financial interests in other firms.[1]

Although outnumbered by unincorporated concerns, joint stock companies (public and private) probably account for the major part of all economic activity. One estimate shows that the proportion of total taxable trading income accruing to companies in 1951 was some 55 per cent of the total for all firms.[2] The predominance of companies was much more marked in manufacturing (their share of total income ranging from 65 per cent to 100 per cent depending on the industry taken) in sea transport (97 per cent wholesale distribution (80 per cent) and in sport and entertainments (75 per cent). On the other hand sole trading concerns and partnerships took the predominant share in agriculture (96 per cent), professional services (97 per cent), other services (78 per cent), building (62 per cent), retail distribution (61 per cent) and road passenger transport 56 per cent).

In very large joint stock companies decision making and control is typically exercised by managers while it is the shareholders who own the company.[3] This observed divorce of ownership and control is important when we make theoretical assumptions in economics about the goals which firms seek. Shareholders' interests might reasonably be equated with a maximum return on their investment, that return being some combination of interest received and capital gain. Were equity shareholders in effective control of policy, the traditional assumption that firms seek to maximise profits (either in the short or the long run) might seem reasonable. Where top management exercises the kind of discretion over policy currently observed, such an assumption becomes much less plausible. Although most directors hold shares, their holdings are generally small and the major part of their income is in the form of a salary. Of course firms must achieve a certain level of profit to survive (i.e. to satisfy existing and potential shareholders), and stock option plans, profit sharing schemes of all kinds, profits-linked bonuses, etc. all serve to make profitability important to management. But it may be doubted whether the effect of these is sufficient to ensure profit maximisation in the traditional sense of orthodox economic theory.

If managers are free to determine policy *and* objectives in accordance with their own utility functions, specification of what business objectives are must take into account other possible sources of managerial utility, e.g. sales, growth, 'norms of professional competence', security, and so on.

A number of alternatives to the traditional profit-maximising assumption have now been put forward. Two of the better know are sales maximisation, subject to a profit

---

[1] Other major provisions of the Act gave extra protection to the public against the failure of insurance companies and ended some exemptions previously enjoyed by banks, discount houses and insurance companies. Provision for fuller disclosure of information was not so much to give added protection to shareholders as to make the capital market more efficient in steering capital towards more efficient firms. This represented a new departure in Company Law.

[2] P. Sargant Florence, *Ownership, Control and Success of Large Companies,* Sweet & Maxwell, London, 1961.

[3] See *ibid.*

[4] Reconsideration of the profit maximising assumption may also be appropriate in the case of the sole trader; for it is not axiomatic that the only possible source of entrepreneurial utility is profit.

constraint,[1] and growth maximisation, subject to a stock market valuation constraint.[2] Like profit maximisation, these are really examples of specific managerial utility functions. In addition, one writer has put forward what is claimed to be a more general model of managerial utility, in which the objective function incorporates salary, the number and quality of subordinates, control over discretionary investment and the type and amount of managerial perquisites in excess of those genuinely required for efficient operation of the firm.[3]

All of these reformulations of traditional theory feature firms' goals which are in the form of well-defined maximising imperatives and imply optimising behaviour on the part of firms. Some observers of business behaviour have called for more radical revisions, stressing that firms are organisations and, as such, will exhibit both a number of goals and continuing goal conflict.[4] In practice, too, firms will have limited access to information and lack both the basic data and computational skill necessary for optimising decisions. In any case organisational factors would preclude the possibility of achieving optimal results, even if desired unless we can envisage firms as Weberian 'ideal bureaucracies' with hierarchically arrayed, functionally linked offices and governed by institutional roles in such a way that the whole unit is perfectly mobilised to the attainment of an overall institutional goal.[5] In place of the more usual omniscient rationality models they propose alternatives where firms have limited information and where there may be a number of different goals in the form of aspiration levels—say a fixed sum of profits or a target rate of return on capital which firms attempt to 'satisfice'. The firm's goals will be imperfectly rationalised, may conflict and will be attended to sequentially rather than simultaneously. Both the target levels to be attained and the particular goals sought will change over time.

As a description of the observed behaviour of firms the latter approach appears to have greater contact with reality than more usual theoretical approaches. There is, however, some disagreement over the question of what kinds of theoretical assumptions are most appropriate in understanding and predicting firms' behaviour and the allocation of resources between markets.[6] Regrettably the testing of alternative approaches has not kept pace with the construction of alternative models and we are faced at present with the necessity of choosing between what are little more than a number of rival, untested hypotheses. This choice is a matter of more than purely academic interest. For instance, at various points later in this chapter we shall see how different interpretations of firms' goals and behaviour may lead to different conclusions on matters of government policy at the microeconomic level.

III . GOVERNMENT AND INDUSTRY

III.1 Introduction

Since industries and trades are by definition classifications into which the economic system may be disaggregated, any government action affecting the economy (which in practice would include nearly all government action of any kind) must touch industry and trade at some point. We have already encountered several instances of the effects

1   W. J. Baumol 'On the Theory of Oligopoly' *Economica,* August 1958, and *Business Behaviour Value and Growth,* MacMillan, London, 1959.
2   Robin Morris, *The Economic Theory of Managerial Capitalism,* MacMillan, London, 1964.
3   O. E. Williamson, *The Economics of Discretionary Behaviour: Managerial Objectives in the Theory of the Firm,* Prentice Hall, New York, 1964.
4   See H. A. Simon, 'Decision Making in Economics' AER, June 1959, and R. M. Cyert and J. G. March, *A Behavioural Theory of the Firm,* Prentice Hall, New York, 1963.
5   For a discussion of the concept of the firm in theories of business behaviour see J. W. McGuire, *Theories of Business Behaviour,* Prentice Hall, New York, 1964, chapter 2.
6   See R. G. Lipsey, *An Introduction to Positive Economics* (2nd ed.), Weidenfeld and Nicolson, London, 1966, pp. 397-400, and J. McGuire, *Theories of Business Behaviour,* chapter 1.

of government measures when discussing the recent growth of output by industry. In the present section we shall consider one instance of the micro-implications of an aspect of macroeconomic policy, prices control, but we shall be mainly concerned with state intervention at the micro-level.

The overall objective of policy at this level is, presumably, to secure an allocation and utilisation of economic resources which is optimal in the sense of promoting maximum social welfare, subject to any necessary constraints arising from macro policy. There are a number of reasons why this objective is unlikely to be achieved in the absence of state intervention. For instance, the state of information in markets and industries may frequently be poor and prevent a 'proper' choice being made between alternative products by buyers or between techniques and production possibilities by firms. Secondly, factors of production are rarely highly mobile between firms, industries and regions so that in place of the smooth, rapid adjustments encountered in simple theoretical models, we observe in practice only halting and incomplete adjustments. Thirdly, competition is neither self propagating nor self perpetuating; monopolistic tendencies may emerge and persist. Or, fourthly, firms may not seek an objective or take decisions in a way which leads them to be cost-minimisers; and this may imply non-optimality if the loss to consumers of the output foregone is greater than the gain to producers in pursuing their current behaviour.

Even in the absence of market imperfections of this sort competition would not necessarily produce an ideal result. Where, for instance, an industry gives rise to net external diseconomies of production the size of output which is determined by market forces on the basis of the private costs and returns of the firms concerned will be larger than is consistent with the ideal for the community at large. Or, for instance, the return to the community on firms' R & D expenditure (in the form of more rapid economic growth etc.) may be larger than the return to the firms themselves who, individually, might gain little competitive advantage (and hence receive a low return on funds invested) if the gains of technical advance were quickly diffused. Or, to take another example, a firm's choice of location might be optimal with respect to the costs incurred by itself, but not optimal when account is taken of the effect on the distribution of population and the provision of social overhead capital (schools, hospitals, etc.) and on the incidence of congestion.

Factors such as these create a *prima facie* case for state intervention at the micro-level. But any intervention involves costs and it is also necessary that these should be more than offset by the benefits which accrue.

One rather drastic *form* which intervention may take is state ownership and control. It may be the most appropriate form of action in certain circumstances on purely economic grounds, although the public ownership issue is, of course, heavily overlaid with social and political considerations. Sidestepping the issue of when, if ever, public ownership is inevitable or appropriate it is sufficient for our present purposes to consider what issues of policy arise where it exists. It is to this task which we now turn.

III.2 Public Ownership and Control

We have public enterprise when there is an undertaking which is publicly owned and directed by a branch of the government or a body specially set up for the purpose by the government. It is worth noting the immense size of the activities involved. First, our definition would clearly include public administration (all central and local government activities), defence and public health and education services (say, 11 per cent of GDP 1967). Secondly, there is the large group of nationalised industries—the Post Office, the coal, gas and electricity industries, the two British airlines and air-ports authority, the railways and other nationalised sections of transport (London Transport, the Docks Board, British Waterways, the Transport Holding Company) and, since 1967, the steel industry. Together these industries account for approximately 11 per cent of GDP, bringing the total of all public enterprise to some 22 per cent. Annual investment by the nationalised industries is around £1.7 billion per annum and equivalent to that of all private manufacturing combined. *Total* public fixed capital formation in 1967 amounted to some 47 per cent of the overall total for the economy compared with around 33 per cent in 1938.

It is the nationalised industries part of public enterprise with which we shall be principally concerned in the present discussion. For the most part the other sections provide services for which either no direct charge or only a token one is made to those who use them. Clearly this means that there is no pricing problem to consider but, more important, it also means that economic analysis of the activities concerned is extremely difficult. Discussion of some of the social and economic problems arising in or relevant to a number of the public undertakings concerned will be found in chapter 5.

For an optimal allocation of resources as between any one public enterprise undertaking and the remainder of the economy, output should be expanded until the social utility created at the margin just balances the social opportunity cost imposed. If the money costs actually incurred by the undertaking accurately represent the real cost of production to the community (the social satisfaction foregone by the sacrifice of possible alternative products) and if the undertaking's unit receipts also represent the social value of its own product, this output level is easily determined. Assuming that, over the relevant range of outputs, price (average revenue) is constant or falling and the cost of marginal units is rising, it is that output at which average revenue equals marginal cost. For if the price paid exceeded marginal cost then, clearly, economic welfare could be increased by shifting some resources into the public undertaking and *vice versa*. Thus, in a simple commonsense way we can derive the marginal cost rule for public enterprise pricing.

When applied to the real world, however, the rule may lose a good deal of its validity and there are also considerable problems of practical implementation.[1] Firstly, because of market imperfections elsewhere in the system (including e.g. the exercise of monopoly power and the fact that not all firms may seek to maximise profits) and because of divergences between private and social costs and benefits and other factors, the prices paid by a public undertaking for its inputs will not necessarily tell us the true cost of the community of diverting them from other uses. For similar and additional reasons the price paid in the market may not accurately reflect the social utility created by producing the public enterprise good.

Secondly, where use is made of factors which are fixed in the short run (and in practice the ratio of fixed to variable costs is frequently high in public undertakings), marginal cost pricing will not automatically ensure that total costs are covered by revenue. For marginal and average costs will differ (except at the one output level at which average costs are at a minimum) so that even with price (average revenue) equal to marginal cost in equilibrium there may be either a deficit (where marginal cost is less than average cost) or a surplus (where marginal cost exceeds average cost). There is disagreement between some economists over the acceptability of these surpluses or deficits. Some would argue that they should be tolerated on the grounds that the only permissible pricing criterion is the marginal cost rule, if optimal resource allocation is the objective, and that to make consumers cover total outlays will prevent the optimum being reached. Others contend that if e.g. a deficit is tolerated there must necessarily be some subsidisation of current consumers of the goods by the community at large and this might mean

---

[1] For a fuller discussion of the complex issues involved see E. H. Phelps–Brown and J. Wiseman, *A Course in Applied Economics,* Pitman, London, 1964.; I. M. D. Little, *A Critique of Welfare Economics* (2nd ed.), Oxford University Press, 1960, chapter 11; W. J. Baumol, *Economic Theory and Operations Analysis* (2nd ed.), Prentice Hall, 1965, chapter 16; A. R. Prest and R. Turvey, 'Cost Benefit Analysis: A Survey', E. J., Dec. 1965; and *Minutes of Evidence of Sub-Committee A, Ministerial Control of the Nationalised Industries.* H of C 440-XIII, 26th July, 1967.

that income was effectively being transferred from poorer to richer people.

Where it is decided that some contribution to the cost of fixed factors, or 'overheads' should be made, economists generally prefer a price consisting of two parts (like the two-part telephone and electricity charges) or more complex, multi-part tariffs, one or more of which represents the contribution to fixed costs, the other covering the variable cost of supplying the units actually consumed.

Thirdly, practical difficulties may be encountered in identifying marginal costs in some cases. Where, for instance, there are some factors of production which are not infinitely divisible (i.e. available only in units large relative to a unit of output) 'marginal cost' is arbitrary in that it depends on the size of the unit of output considered and its position in the scale of possible output levels. A common example is where the marginal cost of carrying one more passenger on a not-fully-loaded train is approximately zero, but the marginal cost of carrying an extra somewhat larger group, or of one extra passenger when the train is packed to capacity, may be very high if extra carriages or another train must be put on. Moreover, the marginal cost of the extra factors required may well exceed that of the factors actually used. No one could advocate a pricing policy which took no account of such problems; fortunately they can sometimes be overcome if we are prepared to take as marginal costs the average cost of supplying the unit over which a decision is to be taken, e.g. the marginal train or coal mine. Another important area in which problems are likely to be encountered is the separate costing of goods or services which are the joint products of some factor or factors. Here, unfortunately, there is at present no satisfactory solution.

It should be noted that the general principle of social opportunity cost pricing for public enterprise is not in dispute; disagreement arises and difficulties are encountered only in the practical application of the principle. The issues involved are vital. Unless a 'proper' pricing policy can be arrived at, it is difficult to determine what investment should be undertaken by public enterprise. It is true that cost-benefits analysis, e.g. for roads, may be *possible,* but if correct pricing procedures can be employed the matter is much more straightforward. The connection between pricing and investment should be clear enough. The commissioning of new buildings, plant and machinery by public undertakings is simply the mechanism by which the allocation of resources we have been discussing is accomplished. Given the state of demand and the technical possibilities, it is the setting of price which determines the amount of capacity which will be required and the commercial return on projects undertaken. Thus for an optimal investment policy when prices may be accepted as a true guide, it remains only to identify those projects on which the return is adequate. Frequently, though not invariably, the requirement is that the rate of return in the public sector should be the same as for an 'equivalent' project in the private sector.

Pursuit of a correct approach to pricing and investment policy is necessary for optimal performance of the nationalised industries but is not of itself enough to ensure an optimum in all respects. Resources may be optimally *allocated* as between any public undertaking and the rest of the economy on the basis of the real costs imposed, but in no sense may this be regarded wholly satisfactory if the costs imposed by any public undertaking (or elsewhere) are higher than they need to be because of administrative or technical inefficiency—i.e. if the resources are inefficiently *utilised.* Thus equally important as the price and investment policies of public undertakings is the question of their internal efficiency, e.g. in obtaining the maximum output technically possible from a given stock of resources, in selecting an optimal factor input combination given relative factor prices, and in securing technical advance.

Let us now consider some of the policies relating to the nationalised industries since the war. The original nationalisation Acts laid down a minimum financial requirement that revenue should be not less than sufficient to meet outgoings properly chargeable to revenue account, taking one year with another.[1] In addition, the industries were explicitly required to operate an efficient system of supply and there was also some confirmation in the statutes that they should serve the national interest in some wider, social sense. Subsequently, in 1961, the financial requirements placed upon the industries were tightened considerably. The previously indefinite periods over which financial performance was to be measured were replaced by precise five-year ones; outgoings to be set against revenue were extended to include provision for depreciation at full replacement (rather than historic) cost, a contribution towards future capital development and a reserve for contingencies; and, most important, specific financial targets were introduced, usually expressed as a rate of return on assets employed.[2] The targets varied between industries and in setting them some notional allowance was made for, *inter alia,* non-commercial operations undertaken by way of social services.

Many criticisms may be made of public policy for the nationalised industries both before and after 1961, of which three may be considered of particular importance. First, there was no explicit statement of an economically 'correct' pricing policy. In practice a variety of rule of thumb techniques were used, many open to serious criticism.[3] Moreover, partly because prices were subject to ministerial interference on political grounds, they tended to be too low (a factor which may well have contributed to the very rapid expansion of public sector investment, especially during the 1950s). In so far as a proper distribution of resources was at all an aim for the industries (rather than e.g. mere solvency or a desired degree of self-financing) this was attempted after 1961 by setting financial targets to ensure that public assets secured a similar return (after due allowances) to equivalent ones in the private sector. But many would argue that without recourse to appropriate pricing rules, attainment of the desired result by this means is highly unlikely.

Secondly, whereas there were a number of cases where nationalised industries undertook what were apparently in the nature of social services, there is good reason to believe that this was not properly allowed for. Although some notional allowance may have been made after 1961 in adjusting financial targets, there was little attempt to identify and measure directly the cost of unprofitable services required on social grounds. As a result there must have been much cross subsidisation of unprofitable by commercially sound operations,[4] with a consequent distortion of supply as between the industries and their competitors. Adjustment of financial targets or the intermittent and haphazard transfer of some cost to the taxpayer[5] represented only very crude methods of preventing such a distortion. The existence of some other factors tending to favour the nationalised industries (notably their access to finance at rates reflecting government borrowing power

---

[1] Surpluses of nationalised industries are not exactly comparable with profits in the private sector. Since interest, depreciation, redemption of capital and provision of reserves are chargeable against revenue some items are excluded which would be met from profits in the private sector.

[2] *The Financial and Economic Obligations of the Nationalised Industries,* Cmnd. 1337, HMSO, April 1961.

[3] As, for instance, in the transport sector, see p. 150.

[4] In the absence of a pricing policy related to the costs of providing individual goods and services, there must also have been much cross subsidisation even where no 'social service' issue arose. Indeed, in such circumstances it becomes very difficult to tell which goods and services were truly commercially viable.

[5] As when some £400million of accumulated deficit of British Railways was written off in 1962. A further £800million was at the same time transferred into 'suspense account', carrying neither fixed interest nor fixed repayment obligations. Effectively, the railways were thereby relieved of exactly three-quarters of a total accumulated £1,600million deficit. *Reorganisation of the Nationalised Transport Undertakings,* Cmnd. 1248, HMSO, 1960.

rather than their own)[1] may have had some offsetting effect, but only in an equally hap-hazard way, and would have served to complicate and perhaps distort the situation even further.

Thirdly, a criticism of the nationalised industries themselves was that management was inefficient. Some observers would attribute this, at least in part, to the basic weaknesses of policy already considered. Lack of clear financial incentives and yardsticks, especially before 1961; ministerial interference at many points; failure to distinguish commercially sound and other operations, with the government accepting responsibility for the latter; low prices, leading to low morale, low salaries and inability to attract able managers: there is at least a *prima facie* case that policies in force were inimical to efficient running of the industries. Neither the original Acts nor the 1961 White Paper gave much guidance as to how the 'efficient operation' demanded was to be achieved.

Current policy on financial and economic criteria is outlined in a recent White Paper.[2] Prices are, where possible and subject to some exceptions, to be set equal to marginal cost. Usually this will be long run marginal cost ('the cost of supplying on continuing basis [which] . . . naturally includes provision for the replacement of fixed assets . . . together with a satisfactory rate of return on capital employed') but where there is excess capacity or demand prices should be lowered 'if necessary to the level where the escapable costs of particular services are just covered' (short-run marginal cost). Total accounting costs have still to be covered by revenues,[3] and two- or multi-part tariffs or unit prices proportional to marginal costs are recommended for the apportionment of fixed charges etc. among consumers.

The need to distinguish social costs and social obligations carefully from strictly commercial operations appears to have been recognised, and the government explicitly accepts responsibility for the former. Non-commercial services may in future receive a specific subsidy or in certain circumstances cross-subsidisation may be used;[4] and in investment appraisal wider social costs and benefits may be considered.

The importance of pricing policy for investment is acknowledged and the use is advocated of the discounted cash flow technique of investment appraisal (DCF) which is now fairly well established as the best available, not least because it takes account of the timing of the investment returns.[5] Guidance is also given on the proper treatment of risk and a test discount rate of 8 per cent is laid down to be used in project appraisal. For some projects it is recognised that social cost/benefit analysis will be a more appropriate guide to investment priorities.

There is a general exhortation to internal efficiency, and the point is made that the government's policies for increased productivity apply to the public no less than to the private sector. Some specific items are mentioned in connection with the industries' internal efficiency, including the efficient use of qualified and skilled manpower; and the need for labour saving, for flexibility on both sides of the industries towards manning practices, and for the abandonment of restrictive practices. In addition, the heavy em-

---

1   In some cases, notably electricity and more recently gas supply, the difference between present capital charges and the terms on which capital would be available from the market may not be very great, since the borrowing strength of these growth industries in their own right would be considerable. However, the arrangements involved a substantial element of subsidy in other cases, notably coal and rail. Other examples of specifically favourable treatment would include e.g. protection of the coal industry by import controls and the tax on fuel oil (see p. 147).

2   *Nationalised Industries: A Review of Economic and Financial Objectives,* Cmnd. 3437, HMSO, Nov. 1967.

3   However, since subsidies may be made for some services and since 'the application of wider economic and social factors may involve overall losses' for some industries this so-called 'starting point' of the policy takes on a rather special meaning.

4   In general, however, cross-subsidisation is to be avoided.

5   See, e.g., W. J. Baumol, *Economic Theory and Operation Analysis* (chapter 19) and *Investment Appraisal,* NEDC, HMSO, 1967.

phasis on correct investment appraisal may, of course, be regarded as specific guidance
on an important aspect of efficiency.

Financial targets are to be retained, but largely as an instrument for ensuring managerial
efficiency. The combination of appropriate pricing and investment rules (which incorporate
a 'financial target' for new investment) are in themselves a sufficient guide for policy, and
if these are applied, the financial outturn of the public undertaking, expressed as a rate of
return on assets, follows automatically. The value in calculating this outturn and setting it
up as a target is claimed to be that this then shows the management what is expected of
it and provides a measure of actual performance, to be compared with expected performance.
Clearly the financial objectives have now taken on a different character; rather than the
starting point of operating criteria they now become a derived instrument of management
control.

The White Paper makes a significant shift in the principles underlying policy for the
nationalised industries. It explicitly recognises the connection between investment and
pricing policy, the need to relate price to true cost to arrive at an optimal allocation of
resources, and that the costs taken must be 'true' in the sense, *inter alia*, of being at the
minimum attainable level. Further, there is much more explicit recognition than previously
of the importance of the divergence between the industries' commercial interests and
wider social considerations and promise of a much clearer allocation and acceptance of
responsibilities in this area.[1] Guidance on the correct method of evaluating investments
is, perhaps unusually clear and specific.

It has been suggested, however, that there is room for disagreement over the policies
advocated. Moreover, the White Paper is silent or evasive over many of the practical
problems likely to arise. For instance, the practical problems of measuring marginal costs
for individual outputs are frequently acknowledged, but little guidance is given on their
solution and the White Paper leaves rather vague what is to be done when this is impossible.
Again, there is little discussion or indication of precisely how price and investment
decisions will in fact be based on the real social opportunity costs imposed rather than the
more arbitrary, but much more readily obtained market estimates. To be sure, there is
much exhortation to apply 'correct' procedures and much emphasis on the need for
consistency. But much remains to be determined concerning the detailed application in
individual industries of the general principles advocated and, for instance, the way 'wider
social considerations' are to be treated. In one case where the White Paper is specific—in
setting the 8 per cent test discount rate for investment projects—the reasons underlying
the choice made are not made entirely clear. The rate chosen is stated to be the equivalent,
after allowances for different tax situations, etc. to the marginal 15-16 per cent rate
looked for by private enterprise for equivalent, low-risk investment. How this 15-16 per
cent rate has been arrived at—whether it is an average over firms, over time or over
projects—is not explained. More fundamentally whether it is a correct, socially desirable
cut-off rate and whether the public sector will always take its cue from private enterprise, right or wrong, is not made clear.

In conclusion, two further points may be made. First, there is some reason to believe
that in the past the nationalised industries have been made more directly responsive to
general government policy than has industry generally. It is difficult to say to what
extent, but pressure has probably been greater for them to observe price and wage
restraint and, perhaps, to avoid placing large overseas orders at times of balance of payments crisis. Certainly from time to time they have been obliged to hold back on some
projects and purchases during periods of restriction on public sector spending, e.g. in

---

[1] A potentially significant omission, however, is that there is no indication of what sanction, if any,
will be used if industries fail to meet their financial targets; thus it is not clear how far the government will be willing in practice to subsidise supposedly commercial operations as well as non-
commercial ones.

1966 and 1967. However necessary or desirable this may be for the attainment of other ends of government policy there is some risk that disproportionate pressures on the competitive positions of the public and private sectors may have adverse effects on resource allocation. The possibility of this happening in the future is by no means precluded by the recent policy changes: on the contrary, the White Paper specifically reserves for the government the right to rephase and retime investment, etc. in the light of 'national economic considerations'.

Secondly, there is the question of who will take responsibility for the various decisions and functions involved. The White Paper is quite definite here. As in the past, the government does not intend 'to interfere in the day-to-day management of the industries' although there may be continuous contacts between Whitehall and the industries. Also in line with previous policy, it is the government who will bring to bear wider economic and social considerations in formulating general policy for the industries. The chief innovation is that the government explicitly assumes responsibility where industries are required to act against their commercial interests. The job of the industries is, in the light of the White Paper's instructions on pricing, investment and efficiency, 'to provide goods and services which consumers want and are willing to pay for at prices which reflect their own costs as accurately as possible, and keep these costs at the lowest levels consistent with providing satisfactory conditions of employment and earning a proper return to capital'. Where, however, cost-benefit investment analysis is required, this will be performed in government departments. A second major innovation is the involvement of the NBPI. Largely, it appears, to underline the fact that price and incomes policy applies to both private and public sectors, all major price increases will automatically be referred to the Board. The NBPI is not intended to exercise discretion over financial obligations nor to determine overall policy. Its role will be to examine 'the underlying justification for price increases, their timing, and the extent to which costs could be reduced by increased efficiency'. In the course of this it will look, *inter alia,* at forecasting and decision making techniques.

How satisfactory this division of responsibilities will turn out to be remains to be seen. The arrangements proposed raise a number of questions. Is, for instance, the job that remains for management in the industries—with very limited control over policy and an apparently shrinking responsibility for investment appraisal—sufficient to attrack managers of high quality and to maintain the high morale necessary for efficient operation? Will the NBPI be prevented from *commenting* on financial objectives and general policy? If so, and unless the NBPI can discover new ways to cut costs undiscovered by both the management of the industries and by government departments (who also 'will continue to devise performance indicators for the industries') will the NBPI not become simply a rubber stamp? Might subjecting the industries to two sets of efficiency auditors be further inimical to their independence, initiative and efficiency—or is there always room for another opinion? If the NBPI (with, possibly, the aid of independent consultants) better or less well qualified and well-placed to undertake efficiency audits? Finally, what guarantee is there that different government departments will apply a consistent approach to cost-benefit analysis: might not a central unit for all the industries be more likely to avoid misallocation of resources arising from different evaluations of costs and benefits involved? Clearly the question of how nationalised industries should be run involves questions for the future of who should run them.

III.3 Price Control

Unlike wage increases price changes have not been linked to any 'norm' of acceptability in recent prices and incomes policy.[1] Rather, prices criteria have been set out, defining

---

[1]   See also chapter 1 and chapter 5.

those circumstances in which both price increases and price decreases are appropriate.[1]
In the first, 'voluntary' phase of policy (from April 1965 to July 1966) price rises were
held appropriate where unit costs of output had increased either because of labour cost
increases consistent with the incomes criteria[2] or as result of higher raw material or
capital costs, provided cost reductions in other directions could not reasonably be
expected nor the return sought on capital invested reasonably reduced.[3] Alternatively, a
price increase would be justified if a firm had been unable to secure capital necessary for
expansion 'after every effort had been made to reduce costs' and achieve sufficiently
attractive profits by that means. Price reductions were called for where productivity
increases were above average for industry as a whole; where net unit costs were failing;
and where profits were based on 'excessive market power'.[4] Broadly similar but somewhat more stringent criteria applied in the second, 'compulsory' period, of 'standstill' and
'severe restraint' (July 1966 to August 1967) and there was a reversion more or less to the
original criteria in the third phase (after August 1967). Criteria for the period 1968-69
are much the same, the main difference throughout all phases of the policy, so far as
price criteria are concerned, being the size of labour cost increases 'consistent with the
criteria for incomes'. Price control has been intended throughout to apply equally to the
public and private sectors. Inclusion of the public sector was emphasised in October 1967
when it was announced that all major nationalised industry price rises would in future be
referred automatically to the NBPI. Subsequently, the responsibility of the NBPI in
relation to the nationalised industries has been specified more closely.[5]

The main object in price control policy is clearly to help contain cost inflation. But
although the policy is primarily of macroeconomic significance, there are some important
implications at the micro-level.

One possible adverse micro-effect is that price control may bear more heavily on some
firms and industries than others. The number of cases which the NBPI can handle is
clearly limited. Unless the threat of investigation, coupled with appeals for good behaviour,
is itself sufficient to bring about general restraint this could mean that, either in place of
or in addition to a general slowdown in the rate of increase in the general price level, the
policy might bring about changes in relative prices. This would discriminate against certain
firms and industries and distort the allocation of resources between different uses.
Secondly, firms might seek some 'cost reductions in other directions' which were socially
undesirable. For instance, inability to make price increases might give rise to deteriora-
tions in product quality, service, etc. some (but not necessarily all) of which might be
unacceptable; or R & D expenditure might be cut, especially on projects with low
prospects of immediate commercial returns. However, much would depend on expectations about the duration and strictness of price control and on long run prospects in each
individual case. Thirdly, a price control policy might interfere with the adjustment of
prices and hence demand to changes in the relative real costs of production of different
commodities. Given the criteria laid down for the NBPI and the flexibility they imply

---

[1] See *Prices and Incomes Policy,* Cmnd. 2639; HMSO, April 1965; *Prices and Incomes Acts,* 1966
    and 1967; and *Productivity, Prices and Incomes Policy in 1968 and 1969,* Cmnd. 3590, April
    1968.
[2] I.e., if a price rise was needed in order to pay wage increases up to the norm ($3\frac{1}{2}$ per cent in the
    first phase and nil after August 1967) because productivity increases in the firms in question fell
    short of the hoped-for $3\frac{1}{2}$ per cent overall average.
[3] The policy was not intended to squeeze normal profits. Indeed there has been explicit recognition
    of the need for 'adequate' profits and the fact that higher than average profits may be expected by
    more efficient firms.
[4] Up to April 1967 no case concerning a possible price fall had been referred to the NBPI but its
    enquiries concerning prices in soap and detergents did involve considerations of market power. In
    a statement accompanying the 1968 White Paper it was announced that the Monopolies Commission
    would be brought in to work with the NBPI in cases where prices and growth of company profits
[5] and dividends are *prima facie* based on excessive market power.
    See above, p. 164.

this ought to be avoidable in cases referred to the NBPI[1] —and the same is true of the socially undesirable methods of cost reduction mentioned earlier. But where no price increase is sought and the matter does not come before the NBPI, there is some possibility of undesirable actions being taken by firms in both cases. Fourthly, it is conceivable that in some cases firms might seek to evade price control by introduction of new products or by product changes. Such changes might be spurious and they could reduce efficiency by shortening production runs and increasing costs in other ways.

On the credit side, however, the policy could have beneficial longer term effects. If the ability to pass on cost increases automatically is reduced, firms may be induced not only to resist cost increases but also to seek out and apply cost-reducing measures, e.g. by greater efficiency in production methods: again, however, much would depend on expectations about the duration and strictness of policy and long run prospects. The expected scope for such improvements is greater if we believe that firms adopt satisficing rather than maximising criteria, have limited knowledge and do not undertake continuous search activity than if we conceive of firms as omniscient profit maximisers. In the first case the existence of price control might itself prompt search activity and firms would not necessarily already be at cost-minimising positions, given existing techniques: if all firms were thought to be profit maximising firms in equilibrium, on the other hand, increased efficiency would only be possible as result of technical developments and the added stimulus of price control would be of no consequence.

In its reports on prices and profits the NBPI has taken some pains to make specific proposals on how longer-term productivity might be increased to avoid future price increases.[2] For instance, in brewing it urged the use of operations research techniques to determine optimal locations for distribution depots and the abandonment of costing conventions which made proper appraisal of the performance of retailing units difficult; the gas industry was recommended to make better estimates of future demand and avoid the use of current, inappropriate methods for determining likely returns on investment; and the coal industry was enjoined to take a more realistic account of the future competitiveness of its product. Proposals have also been made urging the adjustment of working and manning practices to new techniques and changes in payment systems and structures, found by the NBPI to be an impediment to more effective use of men and capital assets.

In more general ways, too, the NBPI has sought to modify and improve firms' behaviour, urging greater attention to costs and less preoccupation with the growth of output for its own sake;[3] emphasising to firms that they themselves are often partly responsible for cost increases they regard as beyond their control (e.g. labour costs); and attempting to break down conventions such as the practice of putting up prices on the assumption that cost inflation will continue at the same rate as in recent years. It may never be possible to estimate precisely what productivity gain the NBPI is able to engineer by such means. There is good reason to suppose that some positive benefit will result; it is to be hoped that this is more than enough to compensate for any undesirable effects of the sort indicated earlier.

III.4 Regional Policy and the Location of Industry

Persistent interregional differences in the level of income per head, the rate of growth of output, net emigration rates and, especially, unemployment have created the need for a specific regional policy.[4] Throughout, the unemployment disparities have received greatest attention in policy and their elimination has been desired for its own sake. But there have

---

[1] Price increases are specifically provided for where there are *unavoidable* cost increases.
[2] For useful summaries see NBPI *General Report*, Cmnd 3087, HMSO, 1966 and NBPI, *Second General Report,* Cmnd 3394, HMSO, 1967
[3] Thereby, possibly, calling for a change in basic objectives.
[4] For further details see chapter 5.

been important changes in attendant circumstances since the policy was first initiated. Originally (in 1934) action was taken as part of a policy for national full employment. Currently the context is rather that of attaining a high level of national output and avoiding inflationary pressure. At present, it is argued, the existence of surplus resources, especially labour, in some areas represents a loss of potential output in a situation of manpower shortage in other parts.[1] Moreover, as momentum gathers in the economy inflationary pressure is quickly encountered in the low unemployment areas and this requires restraints to be imposed while spare capacity still exists elsewhere. Elimination of the existing regional imbalance, it is claimed, could permit the economy to be run closer to full capacity for a given degree of inflationary pressure and the process of absorbing the currently unutilised resources would permit more rapid growth than was otherwise possible, at least for a time. It is to be noted that the increased capacity for growth would probably be only temporary; but there would be a continuing benefit in so far, even if the long-run attainable rate of growth were not increased, the once-for-all improvement would mean that future growth took place from a higher base.

Both currently and in the past, the policy chosen in practice has sought almost exclusively to increase demand for labour in the less prosperous regions by inducing firms to relocate or set up there. It is to be noted that an alternative policy, which sought to promote emigration of the population from the depressed regions, might serve the same purpose of bringing currently unutilised resources into use. It does not automatically follow that the present policy of 'work to the workers' will necessarily produce the largest gain in output; it will not do so if, for instance, relocation of industry leads to losses in efficiency, and in appraising current measures and possible alternatives or in determining future policy there is need for appeal to the evidence. Of course, even if 'balanced growth' between the regions is not preferable on these grounds it might still be advocated on social grounds (e.g. because it avoids domestic upheaval, the loss of community life and culture, because of the social effects of over-crowding, etc.)[2] or it might be selected for purely political motives.

The general basis of government policy, under the *Distribution of Industry Acts* since 1945 and the *Local Employment Acts* since 1960 (and with modifications in various budgets) has been to designate areas or districts with high unemployment rates for special treatment designed to attract firms to them. Neither the designated areas nor the financial inducements to firms have remained the same throughout. Currently the latter include government provision of factory units for sale or lease to firms at attractive rates and loans or grants which are conditional on the creation of sufficient employment (at a capital cost not exceeding certain limits, albeit flexible ones). Both types of assistance have been in existence for many years. Firms in development areas also benefit relatively under the system of cash grants for investment which at present cover 45 per cent of the cost of industrial plant and machinery in the areas, compared with 25 per cent elsewhere,[3] and which were introduced in January 1966 to replace the previous tax allowances on investment (which had also operated in favour of the development areas). Finally, since

---

[1]   The loss may not be so great as is often thought. On the basis of an estimate in the *National Plan* (p. 37), the manpower gain from reducing regional unemployment and increasing activity rates in the depressed regions would give an increase in the total labour force of nearly 2 per cent. Total output would not necessarily rise by the same proportion, however, firstly because this depends also on the quantity of capital employed and secondly because a high proportion of the increase in numbers would be women, whose contribution to total output is, rightly or wrongly, below the average.

[2]   Arguments that migration will result in a waste of social overhead capital, etc. (see below, p. 170) are not strictly relevant here. If capital is 'wasted' the implication is that some resources must be devoted to its replacement; the method of bringing into utilisation one kind of wasted resource requires a waste of some others. If this happens it is indeed a criticism of the policy, but the cost involved will already have been reflected in the size of the gain in output which can be obtained.

[3]   At end-1968 these grants will revert to their intended 'normal' levels of 40 per cent and 20 per cent respectively.

September 1967 manufacturers in development areas have received a regional employment premium of 30s per week for each man employed full-time and lower amounts in
respect of women, young persons and part-time workers. Further, the withdrawal at the
time of devaluation of the extra amount paid to manufacturers in addition to their
refund of the S.E.T. did not apply in development areas; this conferred a further relative
cost advantage of 7s 6d a week in the case of adult male employees.

Apart from these now quite substantial positive inducements to firms to move into
development areas a second strand of regional policy since the war has operated via
control on factory development elsewhere through the issue of Industrial Development
Certificates.[1] These have always been readily available in development areas and up to the
late 1950s were fairly easily obtained elsewhere. Since then, however, control has been
applied strictly in the midlands and the south-east. Office development in these areas has
also come under control more recently, beginning with London (in 1964).

One criticism of current policy centres on the most recent alterations in the financial
incentives offered.[2] As a result of changes made and the regional employment premium
in particular (which alone is estimated to double the amount of financial aid given) a much
smaller proportion of the total assistance offered is now tied closely to the creation of
new jobs. Much may now be paid to firms already situated in development areas who do
nothing to increase employment. If this does happen the cost to the government of each
new job created must inevitably rise to an 'unnecessarily' high level. Secondly, replacement of tax allowances by cash grants means that assistance may now be paid to the
inefficient as well as the efficient, since their receipt does not depend on profits being
earned, as did the benefits through tax allowances. Thus present policy may result in
subsidies being paid to firms who contribute nothing to its success and in addition may
help unemployment only by propping up ailing firms.

These arguments carry some force. However, a profit maximising firm, with reasonably
full information and already situated in a development area would presumably now find
it profitable to expand output and employment and seek to do so,[3] and even satisficing
firms with only limited perception would tend to do so in so far as aspiration levels
adjust to what is obtainable and if there is sufficient publicity surrounding the new
measures. Moreover, the new measures may have some positive merits in so far as they
may be more conspicuous and more easily understood by firms; if benefits can more
readily be calculated; and if benefits are more certain (not depending on future profitability, and with a larger proportion of them not depending on satisfying the requirements on new jobs creation). Such attributes may become very important when account
is taken of the way location decisions are taken in practice.

A more fundamental criticism concerns the whole basis of present policy. It asserts
that firms, if left alone, will locate at minimum-cost locations and that any interference
will result in a serious loss of efficiency. This implies higher real costs of production and
a reduction in attainable real output[4] and the implication is that this real cost would
outweigh any other benefits which accrue.

The argument makes two assumptions: first that firms locate optimally on the basis
of costs at different locations and secondly that location significantly affects unit costs.
On the latter point there is some evidence that at least a substantial proportion of
manufacturing is 'footloose', i.e. not critically affected by costs at different locations. One
study estimated that over 70 per cent of employment and net output in manufacturing is

---

[1] The government has also sponsored a certain amount of social rehabilitation, site clearance, etc.
     in the regions.
[2] For a full discussion see T. Wilson 'Finance for Regional Industrial Development', *Three Banks
     Review,* September 1967.
[3] Introduction of a subsidy on employment may also help to offset any previous tendency for
     policy to favour capital-intensive schemes (in so far as subsidies on buildings, plant and machinery
     already exist and would otherwise lower the *relative* cost of capital).
[4] See e.g. A. C. Hobson 'The Great Industrial Belt', *E.J.,* September 1951.

accounted for by trades which are widely scattered; since they have existed profitably in the past while widely dispersed it is perhaps unlikely that redistribution would result in a serious loss of potential output.[1] Another writer suggests that some two-thirds of manufacturing is probably 'footloose' with respect to transport costs, which are obviously important in this context and have always received much attention in location theory.[2] Other evidence is somewhat mixed, however, and perhaps the most that can fairly be said is that while there is insufficient information for a firm conclusion to be drawn, there is little as yet to suggest that a really serious efficiency loss will inevitably result from relocation of at least a fair proportion of manufacturing industry.

As a result, the general criticism advanced above loses some weight; a serious loss of efficiency need not be inevitable. But of course there may still be substantial efficiency losses in individual cases and this suggests that positive financial inducements may be preferable as instruments of policy rather than negative prohibitions (e.g. IDC's). For under the former 'footloose' industries will presumably select themselves and hence the real costs of achieving a given reduction in regional unemployment will automatically be minimised. On the other hand prohibitions on development elsewhere may do harm. For if rigidly applied they may effectively prevent some investment and expansion taking place at all (in non-footloose trades); and a flexible (i.e. non-uniform) application of the policy may give rise to criticisms of unfairness. However this conclusion is only a preliminary one, which may need to be modified in the light of firms' behaviour in taking location decisions.

There is some reason to believe that location decisions are taken in a manner much as is predicted by recent developments in the thoery of the firm.[3] Typically firms do not seek an optimum location but rather an adequate site which satisfies certain minimum requirements (including some which reflect the personal and social desires of the decision makers) and choice is usually made between a very limited number of alternatives— perhaps no more than two or three. If we add to these observations the fact that search will tend to be problem-oriented, and at first narrow, broadening only if no acceptable solution is found; that only simple calculations will tend to be used in decision making; that expected returns may well be calculated on a pre-tax basis only;[4] and that uncertainty will be heavily discounted (or firms will tend to be uncertainty avoiders), a very different picture emerges from the continuous search, optimising behaviour predicted by traditional theory. And these behavioural differences are clearly important in formulating and appraising location policy.

First, the fact that firms would not necessarily select their minimum cost locations if left alone does not of itself mean that the argument that interference necessarily results in an efficiency loss can be dismissed. For the sites selected might be *lower* cost locations than ones to which government policy directs firms, although not optimal ones. On the other hand they might be higher cost locations so that once cost minimising assumptions are abandoned, it becomes impossible to predict whether (assuming that location significantly affects costs) interference will on balance lead to an efficiency gain or loss. Secondly, if location decisions are taken in the manner described, it may be that financial incentives alone will not succeed, or will work only sluggishly. Although higher profits are made attainable in development areas, the response (especially from existing firms) may well be slight if adequate profits can still be earned elsewhere. Thus for an effective policy controls on development outside the special areas, such as IDC's, may be inescapable despite what has earlier been said about their desirability. The use of IDC's or similar controls as an

1　R. J. Nicholson 'The Regional Location of Industry', *E.J.*, 1956.
2　L. Needleman 'What Are We to do About the Regional Problem?' *LBR*, Jan. 1965; see also W. F. Luttrell, *Factory Location and Industrial Movement*, N.I.E.S.R., London, 1962, Vol. 1.
3　An interesting case study of decision making involving choice of a new site will be found in R. M. Cyert and J. G. March, *A Behavioural Theory of the Firm*, Prentice-Hall, New York, 1963, pp. 54-60. See also Luttrell, *Factory Location and Industrial Movement.*
4　See N.E.D.C. *Investment Appraisal* H.M.S.O. 1965.

instrument of policy might also be justified on the grounds that this will prompt wider search activity than would otherwise occur; it could even be that the IDC's perform an important role in bringing to the notice of firms the financial assistance available in development areas. Thirdly, to the extent that expected returns are calculated on a pre-tax basis only, any attempt to operate policy via tax allowances is clearly hazardous and this would be an additional defence of the recent change from the system tax allowances to cash grants. Finally, it is clear that the simplicity and conspicuousness of the incentives offered are much more important to the success of policy if decisions are made in the manner described rather than in that expected of omniscient profit maximisers. Thus it may be that the disadvantages of the most recently introduced incentives should be regarded as just part of the inescapable costs of a policy which really works.

Whether government regional policy has worked up to 1967 is questionable. Up until then there had certainly been very little long-run tendency for regional unemployment rates to come more in line with the UK average and this was, after all, the principal objective.[1] Of course, in the absence of government policy the divergence might have actually widened and in any case there may be still other factors at work, so that observed movements in regional unemployment rates will not serve as accurate indicators of the effectiveness of policy. Yet they do unequivocally indicate that despite government policy there now remains a regional problem of little less severity than at any time in the post war period.

Since mid-1967, as has been shown, there has been a massive extension of existing policy, doubling the financial incentives offered, and there have also been some changes in the nature of the incentives offered which may make for greater success. Whether this will be sufficient to achieve the desired outcome it is not yet possible to say. It is pertinent to enquire, however, whether some resort to the alternative policy, of stimulating labour mobility, might not have been more appropriate and whether, or in what circumstances this policy may be needed even now.[2]

Solution of the regional problem by migration is frequently rejected out of hand on emotional or political grounds or by reference to social costs which are neither identified nor is any attempt at measurement made. Of course there may well be real difficulties and real social and economic costs involved. There clearly are obstacles to the geographical mobility of labour to be overcome. However, this is true also of the mobility of capital, there is no reason to suppose the difficulties need be insuperable, and in any case the extent to which migration already occurs is larger than commonly supposed. It is true, too, that migration of populations might involve some waste of social overhead capital (schools, hospitals, etc.) and some private capital (notably housing); that an unbalanced population and workforce might be left in some regions as the fittest and ablest were first to migrate; and that there might also be intangible losses from the break up of community life and culture. But much would depend on the nature and extent of the migration which took place; marginal population movements in relation to the immediate local environment might not have serious consequences (and could be all that was required), whereas to break up whole local communities might be a very different matter. Similarly, whether migration intensified congestion problems in the midlands and the south-east would depend on the precise pattern of population movements; migration from old industrial centres to expanding towns outside the major conurbations in the prosperous regions might even reduce congestion.

It is very unlikely that a thorough comparison of the costs and benefits of migration and of existing policy would indicate that present policy should be scrapped. But it is quite likely that increased encouragement of migration might be shown to be desirable as

---

[1] See also chapter 5.
[2] For a statement of the case for greater emphasis on migration see, e.g., H. W. Richardson and E. G. West, 'Must We Always Take Work to the Workers?' *L.B.R.*, Jan. 1964. For details of the limited encouragement of migration in current policy, see chapter 5.

an adjunct or an alternative in some circumstances and the two policies need not be mutually exclusive. In all probability migration would be more acceptable in securing a once-for-all levelling up of regional unemployment rates, rather than as a continuous process; for even marginal migration levels, if continuous, would ultimately result in the depopulation and dereliction of large communities, the social costs of which might prove to be overwhelming. However at present any analysis must proceed largely by guesswork, and the need for some systematic appraisal of alternative policies is clear.

As a postscript to the present discussion mention may be made of the complex of regional planning machinery set up between late 1964 and early 1966. Two types of body were created. Regional Councils, consisted of around two dozen members drawn from industry, local government and universities, were to advise on broad strategy and assist in the formulation and implementation of regional plans. They were to work in close collaboration with a parallel system of Regional Boards, composed of senior civil servants representing in each region the various ministries concerned. Authority and responsibility for planning, however, remained with ministers and local authorities. At one time it appeared as if the approach to regional policy would become much wider, shifting from the narrow objective of eliminating interregional unemployment differences to a much wider one of ensuring that the best use of the whole of *every* region's resources should be made in the context of planned or expected national developments. In the event, and for reasons going well beyond the bounds of regional policy this did not happen. While there have been a number of useful studies and reports and a good deal of research is being undertaken, creation of the new machinery does not appear to have significantly altered government regional policy as yet.

III.5 Control of Monopolies, Mergers and Restrictive Practices

Laws regulating competition in the UK now have four principal targets—dominant firm monopolies, mergers, restrictive trade practices and resale price maintenance (RPM). Underlying all the legislation is a basic presumption in favour of competition[1] although precisely what is meant by 'competition' (which could mean the perfect competition model, or the condition that price equals marginal cost, or a 'competitive' market structure, or merely some sort of rivalry between firms) and exactly how competition promotes the public interest is not stated. But all four targets of the control policy may preclude or constrain competition in one or other of these senses and thus, given the underlying presumption, at least merit investigation. The relevant legislation does not spell out the precise ways in which the public interest may be harmed; it does, however, recognise that the situation or business practice concerned may not be undesirable in all respects or in all circumstances. The basic presumption in favour of competition is, therefore, a qualified one.

The need to allow for the possible advantages of monopoly and monopolistic practices as well as their disadvantages is a problem which has to be faced by any government legislating in this field. The advantages of large firms through economies of scale are well known and it may well be that in some cases the size of markets allows for only one firm of minimum optimum scale, or a small group of firms whose behaviour is mutually

---

[1] The attitude adopted in monopoly and merger *investigations* is, theoretically, uncommitted or neutral, but there is still some preference for 'competition' in the legislation in that performance in non-concentrated markets (as defined by law) is not reviewed at all. The existence of government policies seeking to make good the deficiencies of unaided competition (e.g. through the Industrial Reorganisation Corporation (I.R.C.), the Industrial Expansion Bill, finance of R and D, and in individual industries like agriculture, shipbuilding, aircraft and textiles) indicates acceptance by the government that 'competition' may not automatically achieve all that is desired: but this lies outside the area of legislation considered in the present discussion.

accommodating.[1] Again, a degree of monopoly security and profit may be conducive to long-run efficiency via opportunities for forward planning, technical advances and so on.[2] But monopoly power may also result in a misallocation of resources and super-normal profits and even if opportunities for good performance are large the incentive to pare costs and seek technical advances may be correspondingly small in the absence of competititve pressure. Similarly, restrictive practices between firms may be regarded as potentially conducive to either long run efficiency or 'exploitation', while mergers may either lead to a desirable rationalisation of firms and industries into more economic units or represent attempted monopolisation. As mentioned above, the nature of this problem is reflected in the relevant UK legislation. The existence of monopolies and mergers is not made illegal *per se* but rather the results of the merger or the actions of the monopolist are put to the test of the public interest. Since 1956 there has, however, been a general presumption that restrictive trade practices are contrary to the public interest; but escape clauses are provided, again relation to the *effects* of the practices. Moreover, imposing compulsory registration and a general ban subject to exceptions may be seen as a necessary device to facilitate detection of restrictive practices, whose existence is less obvious than that of monopolies and mergers. Since 1964 RPM has also been presumed contrary to the public interest, but also with escape clauses.

Another problem arising in monopoly policy is that where competition does not prevail in every other market, removal of an individual monopoly or monopolistic practice cannot be relied upon to increase welfare (as a result of the ensuing change in resource allocation) and may indeed reduce it. In practice this second problem has not apparently concerned legislators; if taxed with it they might presumably claim that resource *allocation* is not the only consideration and, possibly, that any short-term deterioration must be tolerated as the price of securing the long term aim of eliminating or controlling *all* monopolies.

It was not until 1948 that the first step was taken to control monopoly etc. in the UK, very late in the course of industrial development compared with some countries. The 1948 *Monopolies and Restrictive Practices Act* defined a monopoly situation as where one-third of the supply of goods is controlled by a single firm or group of linked firms. Apart from monopolies created by Act of Parliament such situations were to be investigated at the request of the Board of Trade by a Monopolies Commission. This is an independent administrative tribunal, initially of ten members. Its powers are of enquiry and recommendation only, and it is required to decide whether, considering 'all matters that appear to be relevant' the monopoly is contrary to the public interest. This the 1948 Act defined as 'among other things . . . the production treatment and distribution by the most efficient and economical means of goods of such types and qualities in such volume and at such prices as will best suit the requirements of home and overseas markets'. Elaborating this the Act specifically mentioned organisation to secure progressive increases in efficiency; the encouragement of new enterprise; the 'fullest and best' distribution of men, materials and industrial capacity; technical improvements; the expansion of existing markets and the opening up of new markets. Hearings are private, and majority and minority findings and views can be given in the report. Responsibility for implementing recommendations remain with the Board of Trade which, however, is not bound to accept the findings of the Commission.

In 1953 the Commission's size was increased from ten to twenty-five members and its

---

[1] This, however, is not of itself a sufficient defence of private monopoly or oligopoly, since it ignores other possible deleterious effects. The argument is perhaps of most relevance when applying remedies to monopoly,situations; where there are large economies of scale, public supervision of prices (or even public ownership) may be called for as fragmentation of the monopoly could result in serious efficiency losses.

[2] See Joseph Schumpeter, *Capitalism Socialism and Democracy,* Allen and Unwin, London, 1943; J. K. Galbraith, *American Capitalism,* Hamish Hamilton, London, 1956, chapter 7; J. Jewkes, D. Sawyer and R. Stillerman, *The Sources of Invention,* Macmillan, 1962 and C. F. Carter and B. R. Williams, *Industry and Technical Progress,* Oxford 1957, chapter II.

operations were speeded up by sitting in divisions. In 1956, however, when its responsibilities for restrictive practices were transferred to the newly created Restrictive Practices
Court it returned to its original size and arrangements. Then in 1965, the *Monopolies and
Mergers Act* restored the size and organisation of the Commission, with minor modifications, to what they had been between 1953 and 1956. The 1965 Act also provided for
control of mergers: previously, while monopolies were subject to control, mergers which
would result in a one-third market share were not liable as such. Since the 1965 Act such
mergers, whether actual or intended, or those involving assets exceeding £5million in
value have been liable to be referred by the Board of Trade to the (enlarged) Monopolies
Commission. In addition, special treatment was provided for newspaper mergers, presumably
on account of the political as well as economic implications. The 1965 Act also reinforced
and extended the powers of the Board of Trade, specifically including the publication of
price lists, the regulation of prices, outright prohibition of (or the imposing of conditions
on) acquisitions and the power to dissolve existing monopolies. A further provision was
to extend the legislation to cover the supply of services as well as goods, and monopoly
situations incompatible with UK international obligations.[1]

From 1948 to 1956 restrictive practices were dealt with by the Monopolies Commission, but the basis of the present law is contained in the 1956 *Restrictive Practices Act.*
This defined restrictive practices as agreements under which two or more persons accept
restrictions relating to the price of goods, conditions of supply, quantities or descriptions,
processes, or areas and persons supplied. As with monopolies, there were specific exceptions, for example, those relating to wages and employment, or authorised by statute.
Agreements falling within the scope of the Act were made registrable with the Registrar of
Restrictive Practices who brings them before the Restrictive Practices Court. This has the
status of a High Court and consists of five judges and ten other members appointed for
their knowledge and experience of industry, commerce or public affairs. Agreements are
presumed contrary to the public interest and the onus is on the parties to prove the
reverse by seeking exemption under one or more of seven escape clauses. Valid grounds
for exemption may be found if it can be shown that the restriction gives protection from
injury to the public or benefits to consumers; is necessary to counteract measures taken
by others to prevent competition or to counterbalance a monopoly or monopsony;
avoids local unemployment; promotes exports; or is required to maintain some other
restriction which the Court has found to be not contrary to the public interest. If a case
is made out on one or other of these grounds the Court must be further satisfied that
on balance benefits to the public outweigh detriments. Otherwise, the agreement is
declared void, and continued operation constitutes contempt of court.

In 1956 RPM was excluded from the scope of the Restrictive Practices Act, although
collective, as distinct from individual enforcement was proscribed (i.e. agreements between
a number of suppliers to withhold goods from a retailer who had cut prices on the goods
of one of them). In the late 1950s RPM was voluntarily abandoned in some trades,
especially food (where, significantly, developments in supermarkets etc. have been most
pronounced) but it remained common in most consumer durable trades.[2]

Then in 1964 the 1956 decision was reversed with the passing of the *Resale Prices Act,*
which created a general presumption in law that RPM was contrary to the public interest.
In form the 1964 Act is very like the 1956 *Restrictive Practices Act,* with a general

---

[1] The 1965 Act also provided that some agreements between firms not registrable under the 1956
Restrictive Practices Act and agreements relating solely to exports might be referred to the
Monopolies Commission. The Commission may also be required to make general reports on
classes of agreement, a provision originally made in the 1948 Act but withdrawn in 1956.

[2] See B. S. Yamey, *Resale Price Maintenance and Shoppers Choice,* Hobart Paper 1, London, 1960;
P. W. S. Andrews and F. A. Friday, *Fair Trade,* Macmillan, London, 1960; J. F. Pickering, *Resale
Price Maintenance in Practice,* Allen and Unwin, London, 1966; and B. S. Yamey, *Resale Price
Maintenance,* Weidenfeld and Nicholson, London, 1966.

prohibition subject to a general exception in the case of 'loss leader' selling, and specific exceptions under five possible escape clauses. These provide for continuation of RPM where the parties can prove that abandonment would result in a loss of quality, a substantial reduction in the numbers of shops, long run price increases, a danger to health, or the removal of necessary services. Procedure also closely follows the 1956 pattern, with provision for registration and review by the Restricitve Practices Court; with the onus of proof on the parties; and with a similar overall 'balancing out' of benefits and disadvantages.

Anti-monopoly policy has apparently not made a major impact on the dominant firm problem.[1] In the first place only a small (though recently growing) number of cases has been dealt with. Up to 1956 this was largely because the Monopolies Commission was preoccupied with restrictive practice investigations. However only slow progress was made after 1956 up to the early 1960s, when this was not so. Since then there has been some acceleration.[2] Secondly, the reports themselves have been of varying quality. Some have aroused controversy and adverse comment from outsiders while several have contained minority dissent within them.

Where the Commission has found some competition to exist, it has usually looked favourably upon the firm concerned and not enquired deeply into its performance. But the Commission has not always given due weight to some forms of competition, e.g. from abroad (partly because of the impossibility of getting information from the firms concerned) and from close substitutes (sometimes because the goods in question were not specifically mentioned in the reference). Moreover unless the underlying presumption is accepted that competition promotes the public interest (especially where competition means merely rivalry between firms) the procedure is in any case suspect. The Commission has not generally enjoyed much success in assessing the performance of firms in the industries concerned—admittedly a very difficult task—whether some degree of competition exists or not. One criticism here is that the Commission has not exhibited much initiative in seeking relevant statistical and other information, but rather had tended to pass judgement on the basis of material put before it by the firms investigated.[3] What has appeared most certain to prompt an adverse finding by the Commission has been evidence of e.g. secrecy in takeovers by a dominant firm, or the use of fighting companies to preclude new entry etc., i.e. behaviour which could be taken as evidence of an intention to monopolise. Whether instances of this may have coloured the Commission's review of other aspects of a dominant firm's behaviour and performance is difficult to tell; a factor making judgement difficult is that the reasons underlying the Commission's findings on a particular point are not always stated.

Given the shortcomings of the Commission's reports it is open to question how far failure by the Board of Trade or the government to accept and implement recommendations can justifiably be criticised. But it is certainly true that only a small proportion of recommendations have been acted upon and that strong corrective measures have not been taken. Thus, for instance, advice that Imperial Tobacco should be required to divest itself of its 42½ per cent share in Gallaher's, and recommendations for public supervision of prices in the matches and industrial and medical gases cases were not accepted. Rather the Board of Trade has preferred to seek a solution through informal, voluntary assurances of good behaviour from the firms concerned. Thus in the fertilisers case, Fisons and I.C.I. agreed not to use their position to make unreasonable profits; Imperial promised not to interfere with the management of Gallahers; the Wall Paper Manufacturers gave assurances in respect of interests already acquired in other manufacturers and agreed to confer with the Board of Trade were any of its competitors to dispose of their businesses. There may

[1]   For a detailed review of the work of the Monopolies Commission up to the mid-1960s see
       C. K. Rowley, *The British Monopolies Commission,* Allen and Unwin, London, 1966.
[2]   See *Annual Reports of the Board of Trade on Monopolies and Mergers,* for details of references
       made, reports submitted and published, and short summaries of findings.
[3]   Rowley, *The British Monopolies Commission.*

be cogent reasons for seeking the cooperation of firms rather than imposing a solution by force, and had the Monopolies Commission's recommendations shown extremist tendencies more moderate action than that suggested might have been expected. But one result of the lack of strong recommendations backed up by effective action has been to undermine the psychological impact the legislation might have had as a deterrent to monopolistic tendencies generally.

Between the 1965 Monopolies and Mergers Act and 1967 only nine mergers have been referred to the Monopolies Commission for consideration, though around 170 cases have been screened by the BOT but not referred. In only two instances has the Monopolies Commission found the proposed merger contrary to the public interest. Of necessity the investigations have been much less protracted than dominant firm enquiries.[1] A problem inherent in proposed merger investigations is that while it is reasonably easy to foresee what degree of monopoly (in a static, structural sense) may result in the short term, any assessment of long run effects and of future behaviour and performance is inevitably much more speculative. We have seen that in dominant firm enquiries the Monopolies Commission has been guilty of shortcomings in interpreting behaviour and assessing performance which has already occurred; in merger enquiries the Commission has, to discharge its responsibility satisfactorily, to predict what behaviour will emerge before it can evaluate it. It is interesting that in merger control as in dominant firm policy there has already been some reliance on assurances given by the firms concerned as a protection of the public interest (e.g. when B.M.C. gave undertakings not to use its proposed ownership of the car body firm, Pressed Steel, to put its own competitors, e.g. Rootes and the then independent Jaguar, at a disadvantage).

There is no evidence of any substantial fall in merger activity since 1965—indeed merger activity has intensified[2] in part, perhaps, encouraged by other strands of government policy, notably the IRC and general exhortations to rationalisation. But this, of course, was not the aim of merger policy as in the 1965 Act; rather it was simply to make investigation possible where the public interest might be at stake. Without access to (secret) information of the preliminary screening procedures applied by the BOT it is difficult to assess how adequately this has been achieved.

In terms of cases dealt with, restrictive practice legislation has been very much more successful than monopoly and merger control. Since 1956 the register has accumulated about 2,500 cases, mainly price agreements. How many agreements previously in force were abandoned without ever reaching the register is unknown, but of those on the register over two-thirds have been dealt with, the majority by termination, others by variation of the offending clauses. This does not mean that the Court has actually decided each case. Many have been terminated on the results of 'key' cases as the parties saw the chance of success was slight, and others have been terminated by the 'effluxion of time' and have not been renewed. But the figures probably overstate the success of the policy greatly.[3]

Where cases have come before the court the appropriateness of subsequent abandonment or continuation of the agreement may be questioned on two counts. Firstly there has been a good deal of criticism of both the escape clauses provided in the 1956 Act and the thinking which underlies them. Secondly there has also been much adverse comment on the quality of the Court's decisions; some contain illogicalities and unresolved inconsistencies, while a general tendency to over-reliance on the opinions of the parties

---

[1]   A time limit of six months (or nine in exceptional cases) was set by the 1965 Act.

[2]   The total asset value of large quoted companies (with over £5million assets) acquired by other quoted companies was £291million in 1966 and £242million in 1965, cp. an average of £171 million for 1961-64.

[3]   See C. Brock, *The Control of Restrictive Practices Since 1956,* McGraw-Hill, New York, 1966; R. B. Stevens and B. S. Yamey, *The Restrictive Practices Court,* Weidenfeld and Nicholson, London, 1965. Symposia on restrictive practices will be found in *E.J.,* September 1960, and *O.E.P.* November 1965.

G

and too little independent judgment by the Court has been observed. Some writers have suggested that the nature of the judgment to be made, in particular the balancing of advantages and disadvantages to the public interest and of the interests of different groups etc., is entirely unsuited to a court of law.

A further question relevant to the success of restrictive practice control centres on the likely effects where price agreements and the like have disappeared. The general assumption of the Court has been that removal of a restriction will result in more 'competition' with consequent benefits to the public (generally assumed to be in the form of lower prices) and this attitude may be traced directly to the general presumption in favour of competition underlying the act. In fact the likely effects are difficult to judge. Abandonment of formal, overt price fixing may have led to an increase in informal, secret arrangements in some cases. In others, where restrictive practices merely formalises the kind of behaviour which would in any case occur (e.g. in concentrated, oligopolistic markets), removal of an agreement might very well not affect behaviour even though no collusion of any sort took place. Firm evidence on the consequences of abandonment of agreements is scanty. In his earlier reports the Registrar has acknowledged that in some cases abandonment has in fact not led to marked price falls at least in the short run, and in others where this has happened it has apparently been due to other factors, e.g. a change in the level of demand, or entry of a new competitor, which might themselves have terminated the agreement.[1] But in his most recent report a more optimistic general view is taken.[2] One independent study found *inter alia* that in over half of 146 cases studied, registrable agreements have been replaced by 'information agreements'.[3] These need not be registered if no restriction is accepted, but the exchange of information (usually including price information) may still lead to mutually accommodating behaviour similar to that under restrictive agreements which are registrable under the 1965 Act.[4]

Exclusion of (some) information agreements is one loophole in existing restrictive practice legislation. Another is 'bilateral agreements' where, by a series of agreements between individual firms and, say, a trade association, an effective restrictive practice is achieved through none of the individual agreements are registrable (since only one party accepts restrictions). The Act can also be circumvented by agreements which produce the same effects as one condemned by the court, but are in a legal sense technically different, or by a series of (different) short term agreements which can be maintained until judgment is given. The existence of such loopholes is clearly a shortcoming of the legislation.

Between 1964 and the time of writing there has been only one case where RPM was defended before the Restrictive Practices Court, as a result of which RPM in the confectionery trades was prohibited. Substantial lists have been published from time to time prohibiting RPM in trades which had initially sought exemption but not subsequently attempted to defend the practice, and RPM has also been abandoned voluntarily in many areas without exemption being sought. Altogether, RPM is rapidly ceasing to be a common practice in the UK and manufacturers are in general now able to specify only recommended prices. Price competition between retailers has emerged in respect of some goods (e.g. some consumer durables like electrical goods and in wines and spirits) but as yet there is no weight of evidence of it becoming widespread. Nor is there yet evidence of significant new developments in retailing methods which some argue have been held back in the past by RPM though these may be still to come.

To conclude the present discussion some general points may be made about UK laws seeking to promote competition. The 1965 Monopolies and Mergers Act remedied many

---

[1] Registrar of Restrictive Trading Agreements, *Report for The Period 1st July 1961 to 30th June 1963,* Cmnd. 2246, HMSO, Jan. 1964, paras. 12-17.
[2] Cmnd 3188 HMSO, 1967, chapter 1. See also Cmnd 1603, HMSO, paras. 7-9.
[3] J. B. Heath, 'Restrictive Practices and After', *MS,* May 1961.
[4] A recent judgment has brought some information agreements within the scope of the legislation, if the Court can infer a tracit agreement to observe the prices notified. This would not necessarily be possible in all cases where such an agreement did in fact exist.

shortcomings of the monopoly control aspect, especially by the inclusion of services and mergers and by strengthening the powers of implementation of the Board of Trade. There still remain, however, basic shortcomings related to the limited areas covered; to the inherent difficulties of appraising the performance of firms and industries in the way the Monopolies Commission is asked to do; and to problems of applying satisfactory remedies. On the restrictive practices side the basic problem has changed in some ways since the basic legislation of 1956 and the legislation has not kept pace.[1] In 1956 there was a mass of quite overt price fixing which was thought potentially damaging to the public interest and at which the 1956 Act was aimed. This has now largely been dealt with, at least nominally, and new problems have come to the fore, such as making the policy more comprehensive and dealing with the questions of evasion and enforcement. Further legislation has been promised for some time[2] and may now be not long delayed. *Inter alia* it will almost certainly include action to plug the loopholes in the 1956 Act mentioned earlier and will probably introduce penalties for non-registration of agree-ments.[3] This would undoubtedly result in a somewhat better job being done than at present, along the present lines. However, there is some reason to think that there is need for a more fundamental review of current monopoly and restrictive practice policy and its effects. More precisely, thought might be given to what, if anything, is gained when formal restrictive agreements are abandoned and the whole question of the underlying attitude towards 'competition'; to the desirability of review of restrictive practices by a court of law; and, in particular to the question of whether rivalry between a few large firms can be relied upon to promote the public interest. Interestingly, oligopolistic behaviour is not, as such, a target of the UK legislation, being included only if one firm has more than a one-third market share or if there is some formal agreement between the firms concerned.[4]

The need for a more basic review of current policy is made more conspicuous by the existence of other strands of government policy which seek to make good some deficiencies of competition (via the IRC; in agriculture, textiles, aircraft, shipbuilding; general exhortations to rationalisation etc.). The coexistence of policies which aim to promote competition in some ways or circumstances and restrain or supplement it in others is not necessarily undesirable. But if such policies are applied by different arms of government in an uncoordinated fashion inconsistencies and anomalies clearly may arise. At the time of writing an enquiry is being conducted into possible inconsistencies between the IRC and the Monopolies Commission over mergers and a White Paper is expected ultimately to emerge. There would seem to be a case for some more broadly-based review, to consider the possible integration of existing policies which seek either to

---

1   See the Registrar's latest report, Cmnd 3188.
2   The need was first officially recognised in a (conservative) White Paper *Monopolies Mergers and Restrictive Practices,* Cmnd 2299, HMSO, 1964. The main principles were subsequently endorsed by the Labour government and some points were dealt with in the 1965 Monopoly and Mergers Act. Further restrictive practice legislation has been promised on several occasions since.
3   A new Restrictive Practices Bill is before Parliament as this book goes to press. Its main provisions would (1) exempt from registration agreements which are deemed by the Board of Trade to be in the national interest or which are intended to hold down prices (2) make registrable (a) restrictive agreements relating to standards of dimension, design or quality (previously exempt) and (b) informa-tion agreements which concern the same subject matter as other registrable agreements (3) impose a time limit for the registration of agreements and penalties for non-registration (making parties to the agreement liable to Court action by persons affected and also empowering the Restrictive Practices Court to make restraining orders) and (4) introduce an eighth 'gateway', that the restriction does not directly or indirectly restrict or discourage competition to any material degree (which is presumably intended primarily as a defence of information agreements).
4   The inevitable arbitrariness of the UK 'one-third' rule at the margin may be shown by a simple example; an industry where one firm has 34 per cent of the market and three others have 22 per cent each would fall within the UK legal definition of monopoly whereas an industry where four firms have 25 per cent each would not, although behaviour within the two industries might be very similar.

promotion or restrain competition and also of those seeking to improve industrial efficiency in other ways.

III.6 The Government and Industrial Efficiency

Few strands of government policy fail to touch on industrial efficiency at some point and public concern to promote efficiency is of long standing. However, since the mid-1960s there has been increased emphasis on policies which directly seek to improve efficiency or productivity as part of the effort to secure more rapid economic growth. The measures considered in the present discussion centre on three interrelated themes—structural re-organisation, technical advance and planning at the micro-level. Most are comparatively recent.

Shortcomings in performance of industries with outdated structures (in practice usually those with large numbers of small units) were emphasised at various points in the *National Plan.* Current policy for structural reorganisation includes measures affecting individual industries and also more general approaches applying, potentially, to all industries. Three industries which have received individual attention are textiles, aircraft and shipbuilding.

The *1959 Cotton Industry Act* sought to promote reorganisation in cotton textiles in its changed circumstances following the impact of foreign competition. It provided compensation for the elimination of excess capacity and grants towards reequipment and modernisation. As a result much idle capacity was eliminated but only limited modern-isation took place and the industry was not, in the event, rendered internationally competitive. In the mid-1960s some temporary protection from foreign competition was introduced in the form of quota agreements limiting imports from India, Hong Kong and Pakistan—a step not wholly consistent with the earlier principle of attempting to render the industry internationally viable. Devaluation did not greatly improve matters, because of the industry's dependence on imported raw materials from countries which did not devalue along with Britain and its rivalry in product markets with countries which did, notably Hong Kong. Much uncertainty still surrounds the industry's future and future government policy affecting it after the quotas expire in 1970.

Following the Geddes Report in 1966,[1] the *1967 Shipbuilding Industry Act* established the Shipbuilding Industry Board (SIB) to promote the massive reorganisation programme recommended. This involves greater specialisation between shipbuilding and marine engineering and in the construction of different types of ship. The Board's function is to encourage the merger of existing companies into four or five groups; to administer a total of £37.5 million in grants and loans for regrouping and reorganisation of resources;[2] and to control the extension of £200 million credit at cheap rates to UK shipowners (its provision being conditional on reorganisation for greater efficiency being carried out or planned at the yard where orders are placed).[3] The hope is that when government assist-ance and the SIB disappear in 1970 the industry will have overcome its difficulties, which were seen by the Geddes report as arising from its organisation and traditions, and that the industry may be able to secure and retain a considerable share of a growing world market. At the time of writing there has been some progress towards the desired mergers and a number of large orders have recently been gained. The industry's prospects were affected favourably by devaluation, which was estimated to result in a likely 7-8

---

[1] *Shipbuilding Industry Committee 1965-66 Report,* Cmnd. 2937, HMSO, 1966.
[2] Cf a maximum £67.7million recommended in the Geddes Report.
[3] Previously a scheme offering £75million at 4½ per cent per annum had been offered to UK ship-owners in 1963 and a similar scheme for foreign shipowners was introduced in 1965. Work in hand and on order responded favourably but, with intense international competition, prices were so low that many firms continued to experience financial difficulties.

per cent cut in UK ship prices abroad.

At the end of the 1950s the government used its powers as the aircraft industry's dominant customer to effect a structural reorganisation in the face of a technical environment demanding larger production units, international competition (especially from the United States) and changes in government requirements. It was announced that contracts would not be placed outside five main groups into which the industry was to be reorganised. The ensuing reorganisation simplified the company structure of the industry but apparently did not greatly increase its efficiency or profitability. Subsequently the need for further action and the question of the possible strategic importance of home aircraft production led to the setting up of the Plowden Committee of Inquiry. Reporting in 1965,[1] its recommendations were that the industry should be made to contract to a size compatible with future demand and that there should be concentration on projects where development costs were not disproportionate to market prospects: where this was not so, government requirements should be met by purchases from the United States. The need for collaboration with Europe and for an export drive was emphasised, and further rationalisation of the industry was recommended, by a merger of the two airframe groups (BAC and Hawker Siddeley) with state participation of the new concern. At the time of writing the main implications of the report have been accepted by the government but no concrete proposals concerning the recommended merger have emerged.

Government action over textiles, shipbuilding and aircraft has been designed to rationalise and reequip industries and make them viable in changed circumstances without permanent assistance, rather than to prop them up at an artificially high size level. Such action (which may be seen as attempts to speed up the kind of adaption which would eventually occur as a result of normal market forces) does not raise the same issue of permanent reallocation and a possible 'waste' of resources as, for instance, arises in the case of agriculture. Here commitment of resources is only temporary, and the return on their use (i.e. the greater efficiency created earlier than would otherwise be the case) may well be as high or higher than in alternative employments. If this is accepted there is no reason why action should be confined to particular industries. Establishment of the IRC and, to some extent, the Industrial Expansion Bill, may be seen as provisions for general extension of the kind of policy applied in the three cases just considered.

The IRC was set up in 1966 to seek out opportunities for rationalisation in private industry and initiate and finance mergers which might not otherwise occur.[2] With an initial capital of £150million it was empowered to advance both loan and equity capital and also to hold physical assets for sale or lease. Particular attention was to be given to cases where there were prospects for stimulating exports and technical advance, for it was claimed that it is here that many production units are at present too small and the pace of adjustment through market forces is too slow. The IRC does not have compulsory purchasing powers nor is it intended to support non-viable schemes and so prop up ailing firms and industries. Further, there is no intention that it should acquire a permanent stake in the new enterprises it creates, but rather withdraw once the benefits of rationalisation are assured and re-use its capital elsewhere. Mergers promoted by the IRC are not subject to review under the 1965 Monopolies and Mergers Act but if monopoly situations are created these might subsequently be investigated.

In the first year of its existence concrete results of the IRC's work were few[3]. Recently, however, it has been associated with some spectacular mergers (e.g. Leyland–BMC and GEC–AEI) although the real extent of its initiating and catalytic role is difficult for outsiders to judge. To what extent the IRC will also concern itself with the problem held to lie in the existence in some industries of large numbers of very small units has yet to be seen.

---

[1]   *Report of The Committee of Inquiry into the Aircraft Industry,* Cmnd. 2853, HMSO, 1965.
[2]   See *IRC White Paper,* Cmnd. 2889, HMSO, 1966; and *IRC Act,* 1966.
[3]   See IRC *First Report and Accounts,* H. of C. 252, 1968.

The Industrial Expansion Bill, introduced in early 1968, is not intended solely to
promote structural reorganisation, but one objective is to extend and amplify the work of
IRC and rationalisation schemes are included among those industrial investment schemes
or projects for which government financial support may be given. The Bill provides for a
maximum £150million assistance for schemes which would improve efficiency; create,
expand or sustain productive capacity; or promote and support technical improvements
where these would benefit the economy of the UK or any area of it and where these
developments would not otherwise take place. Support given may take any form (including loans, grants, government purchase of goods or shares or, by agreement, state purchase
of undertakings or parts of them) and the initiative may come from one of several government departments.[1] Where general schemes are involved, covering whole industries or
parts of them, there is provision for the establishment of industry boards, to make recommendations to the sponsoring authority and undertake any administrative tasks delegated
to it.[2] The Bill has aroused some controversy, especially over the provision for state
acquisition of companies and shareholdings and the Bill's alleged discriminatory nature.
Neither principle is in fact new, however; the state has in the past acquired individual
companies or taken holdings in them (e.g. Fairfield's shipyard, Beagle Aircraft and
British Petroleum) and the Bill is no more discriminatory than e.g. the IRC, assistance to
the three industries discussed above, or protective tariffs on some home products. Indeed,
the Bill quite clearly represents provisions to enable a general extension of types of
action previously taken on an *ad hoc* basis with a minimum of administrative and
political delay.

Much of the government's concern to secure structural reorganisation derives from its
desire to stimulate technical progress. This is also one specified aim of the Industrial
Expansion Bill, whether or not structural change is involved. Many other strands of public
policy have some indirect bearing on technical progress e.g. education and manpower
policy, monopoly and restrictive practices control, etc. More directly, the government is
the principal source of funds for R and D work in the UK. In 1964-65 just over 2½ per
cent of GDP was spent on R and D, and of the £771 million total £421 million or 55 per
cent came from government sources (not counting £27 million spent by public corporations) compared with £285 million spent by the whole of private industry. On the
other hand, private industry was the largest sector carrying out work (to the value of
£468 million because nearly half the total cost of work done there was met from government funds.[3] These funds were not provided to finance firms' own projects, but in the
main represented government purchases of R and D on defence projects. Hence the
benefit to private industry would not have been as great as if, for instance, the government had provided grants of the same value. Nevertheless, a substantial overspill of new
developments into the firms' other operations does occur, especially in such fields as
aircraft, electronics, metallurgy, engines and machine tools. Apart from its purchases of
R and D from private industry, the government also sponsors work specifically on
behalf of industry in its own research establishments, while basic and background
research in government departments and universities may also yield longer term benefits.
In addition, direct aid is given in the form of grants to cooperative research associations
in various industries. Of these there were over fifty in 1961, receiving one quarter of their

---

[1]   Ministries of Technology, Power, Transport, Public Buildings and Works, Agriculture, the Board of
      Trade or a Secretary of State.
[2]   The Bill also contains special provisions for certain industrial projects and undertakings and
      increases from £25million to £50million the government loan limit to The National Research
      Development Corporation. (Established in 1949 the NRDC is a government body intended to
      finance development of inventions made in government laboratories and universities and by
      private individuals where this is in the public interest.) The shipbuilding industry is specifically
      excluded up to the time when the SIB is wound up.
[3]   A.A.S.

total income from the government. However, the total value of work done by them is very small in relation to that undertaken in private industry as a whole. It is very difficult to estimate the exact proportion of total R and D work undertaken which benefits industry and is financed by the government: but it would clearly be significant by any reckoning.

Since 1964, and partly as result of the establishment then of a new Ministry of Technology, some further direct measures have been taken to promote technical advance. The concentration of responsibility for R and D within the government is said to have resulted in steps being taken to coordinate purchases of government departments (especially of computers and machine tools) and to ensure maximum industrial exploitation of R and D projects initially undertaken for defence purposes.[1] Outside the government's own sphere, positive action has been mainly in the field of machine tools and electronics (including computers and telecommunications) which are seen as key industries in the process of technical change. Measures affecting computers include financial assistance for development projects and university research, and the establishment of an advisory unit on the use and procurement of computers both in government circles and elsewhere. Action on machine tools has been in the form of R and D contracts, the purchase of pre-production models of new machines for performance testing by government departments, and a government repurchase scheme at guaranteed prices for manufacturers who have invested in numerically controlled machine tools but been dissatisfied with their performance.

The action taken on machine tools arose mainly from an action programme proposed by the Economic Development Committee for the industry. Since 1964 twenty such EDC's have been set up to provide more continuous cooperation on an industry-by-industry basis than had previously existed. The need for such machinery had arisen from moves towards more comprehensive government planning at the national level. The existing EDC's cover perhaps two-thirds of industry (by employment). Like the NEDC they are composed of representatives of government, trade unions and management and their original task was twofold. One function was to serve as a source of information on the performance, prospects and plans of individual industries in the formulation of national plans. The other task of the EDC's was to report on progress towards achievement of plan targets and to take action on matters likely to prevent their attainment. The *National Plan* outlined a number of specific areas where action might be taken by the EDC's, including import saving and various measures to promote exports; standardisation of production; rationalisation for greater efficiency; and industrial cooperation by the exchange of information.[2] Subsequent abandonment of the Plan's growth targets did not by any means render less necessary or desirable fulfilment of this second function.

A very wide range of activities has subsequently been undertaken by the EDC's. Several make regular demand and supply forecasts. Many have sought to probe into factors affecting export performance, sales opportunities in particular markets and import trends. Other topics which have been variously covered include manpower problems, standardisation, stockholding procedures, factors affecting investment, R and D, and the effects of decimalisation, taxation and devaluation. The EDC's also appear to perform a useful function in disseminating information within their industries through their newsletters and reports. There is also some exchange of information between industries and in some cases formal arrangements for cooperation (e.g. between the chemical and engineering industry EDC's to avoid problems in the supply of chemical plant) thus making for some coordination of activities over and above that which is possible through the market. Of course, it might be argued that the activities of the EDC's are precisely the sorts of things which individual firms and their trade associations would tend to do in their own interest and perhaps

---

[1] *National Plan*, pp. 49-50.
[2] *National Plan*, p. 46.

already do. In terms of subject matter there is, indeed, an overlap. But it has been suggested earlier that firms (and organisations of firms) will not necessarily undertake all actions which might seem consistent with their own interests let alone with those of the community at large. Even though there may be some overlap between the activities of the EDC's and of firms and trade associations it is, perhaps, unlikely that the real resources committed to the operations of the EDC's would be better employed elsewhere.

REFERENCES AND FURTHER READING

E. H. Phelps Brown and J. Wiseman, *A Course in Applied Economics* (2nd ed.), Pitman, 1964.

J. H. Dunning and C. J. Thomas, *British Industry: Change and Development in the Twentieth Century,* Hutchinson, 1961.

P. Sargant Florence, *The Logic of British and American Industry* (2nd ed.), Routledge and Kegan Paul, 1961.

P. Sargant Florence, *Ownership, Control and Success of Large Companies,* Sweet and Maxwell, 1961.

J. W. McGuire, *Theories of Business Behaviour,*Prentice Hall, 1964.

K. J. Cohen and R. M.Cyert, *Theory of the Firm: Resource Allocation in a Market Economy,* Prentice Hall, 1965.

W. A. Robson, *Nationalised Industry and Public Ownership,* Allen and Unwin, 1962.

M. Shanks (ed.), *Lessons of Public Enterprise,* Cape, 1964.

A. H. Hanson (ed.), *Nationalisation: A Book of Readings,* Allen and Unwin, 1963.

C. K. Rowley, *The British Monopolies Commission,* Allen and Unwin, 1966.

C. Brock, *The Control of Restrictive Practices Since 1956,* McGraw-Hill, 1966.

R. B. Stevens and B. S. Yamey, *The Restrictive Practices Court: A Study of the Judicial Process and Economic Policy,* Weidenfeld and Nicolson, London, 1965.

C. F. Carter and B. R. Williams, *Industry and Technical Progress,* Oxford University Press, 1957.

K. M. Gwilliam, *Transport and Public Policy,* Allen and Unwin, 1964.

G. D. N. Worswick and P. H. Ady, *The British Economy in the 1950s,* Oxford University Press, 1962.

5

Social problems

I RELATIVE WEALTH AND POVERTY

I.1 The Unequal Distribution of Income[1]

The unequal distribution of income before and after direct taxes for 1965 may be found in Table 5.1. From this table, the following income pyramid has been calculated: 95.8% of tax units[2] received less than £2000 per annum or 73.65% of total income; but after direct taxes, their share increased to 86.27%. 2.9% of tax units received between £2000 and £3000 per year or 6.3% before and 6.44% after income tax. The remaining 1.3% of tax units received over £3000 per year or 20.05% of total income before income tax and 17.29% afterwards.

TABLE 5.1

Distribution of Personal Income UK 1965.

Range of Income before tax		Number of incomes Thousands	Income before tax £ millions	Income Tax and surtax at current rates £ millions	Income after tax £ millions
£	£				
50–	250	3006	616	–	616
250–	300	1586	438	–	438
300–	400	2417	856	11	845
400–	500	2279	1037	35	1002
500–	600	1901	1045	48	997
600–	700	1829	1188	73	1115
700–	800	1832	1374	92	1282
800–	1000	3815	3427	262	3165
1000–	1500	5957	7123	699	6424
1500–	2000	1821	3059	456	2603
2000–	3000	702	1735	354	1381
3000–	5000	286	1083	304	779
5000–10000		132	893	338	555
10000–20000		30	409	230	179
20000 and over		7	226	178	48
Total		27600	27509	3080	21429
Income not included			5337		
Total personal income			29846		

Source: NIBB, 1967, Table 26, p. 33.

Redistribution of incomes takes place through the system of public expenditure, including social security, and taxation. The Central Statistical Office, in *Economic Trends,* estimated the incidence of taxes and social benefits on families of different

---

[1] Capital is distributed far more unequally than incomes, but this problem is not discussed here.
[2] Married couples are treated as single units for tax purposes.

sizes for 1957 and 1959,[1] 1961 and 1962,[2] and 1963 and 1964.[3] The estimates are based on the detailed information obtained from the Ministry of Labour's *Family Expenditure Survey*. The taxes and benefits included in the estimates may be classified as follows: (1) Direct benefits: (a) cash benefits: family allowances, national insurance benefits (i.e. pensions, sickness, unemployment, industrial injury, maternity benefits etc., death grants), non-contributory old age pensions, national assistance grants, war pensions, service grants and allowances; (b) benefits in kind: state education (including school health services) scholarship and education grants, school meals, milk and other 'welfare' foods, national health services. (2) Indirect benefits: housing subsidies. (3) Indirect taxes on final consumer goods and services: local rates on dwellings, customs and excise duties on beer, wine and spirits, tobacco, oil, entertainment, betting, etc., purchase tax, motor vehicle and driving licences, stamp duties. (4) Indirect taxes on intermediate products: rates on business premises, business vehicle licences, duties on oil used by businesses, stamp duties paid by business, import duties on raw materials and other goods and services purchased by industry.

The total of taxes and benefits combined led to very substantial increases in incomes in the lower income ranges and substantial reductions in the higher income ranges. Within each income range the combined effect of all the taxes and benefits enumerated favoured the larger families. Direct taxes and benefits were very favourable to families in the lower income ranges and, within each income range, were more favourable to larger than to smaller families. All indirect taxes combined, when expressed as a proportion of income, did not vary much as between families in different income ranges; the proportion declined slightly as income increased, so that indirect taxes as a whole are mildly regressive. Within each income range, indirect taxes showed a slight tendency to decline as the size of family increased. Indirect benefits, i.e. housing subsidies, were generally small but relatively more important in the lower income ranges and are thus progressive.

All benefits in cash combined to form a much larger proportion of income at the lower than at the higher income levels and are very progressive. The incidence of benefits in kind on families at different incomes level was also progressive and the incidence as between families of different size within each income range was very favourable to larger families.

Income tax and surtax payments absorb a larger proportion of higher than of lower incomes and are progressive; they are less progressive with respect to income, but more favourable to the larger families at given income levels than direct benefits in cash. National insurance contributions absorb a smaller proportion of higher than of lower incomes and are regressive; they form only a small proportion of the income of one- and two-person families in the lowest incomes ranges because these families include a larger number of retired persons. Local rates and duties on tobacco absorb a smaller proportion of income at the higher than at the lower income levels and are clearly regressive. The more or less neutral effect of taxes on alcoholic drink as a whole masks two opposite effects: taxes on beer are mildly regressive and taxes on wines and spirits are mildly progressive. Purchase tax and taxes on oil appear to be slightly progressive, while taxes on intermediate products are regressive. Within each income range, local rates and taxes on drink generally have less effect, proportionately, on larger than on smaller families; the proportions paid in other indirect taxes show little variation as between families of different size.

Whether or not the distribution of income in the UK is estimated as becoming more

---

[1]   ET, November 1962.
[2]   ET, November 1964.
[3]   ET, August 1966. See also J. L. Nicholson, 'Redistribution of Income in the United Kingdom in 1959, 1957, and 1953' in Colin Clark and G. Stuvel, editors, *Income Redistribution and the Statistical Foundations of Economic Policy,* Bowes and Bowes, Cambridge 1964. Data for 1965-6 are analysed in *ET*, February 1968.

or less egalitarian depends to no small extent on the way we compute income.[1] A common means of measuring the inequality of a distribution of income is to express the area between the diagonal and the curve in the Lorenz diagram as a proportion of the area of half the box. The percentages of income and income units are plotted cumulatively along the axes OX and XY, the dotted line representing a typical situation. The measure of inequality is $(A/A+B).100$. If all units had identical incomes then the line would follow the $45°$ line and the proportion be 0%, i.e. perfect equality.

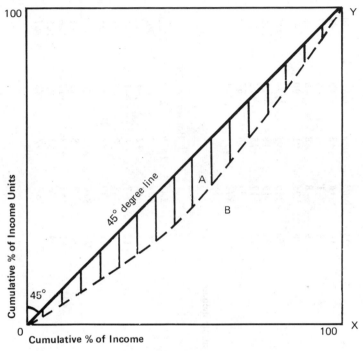

Figure 5.1   The Lorenz Diagram

In the case of one unit holding all income the cumulative distribution line would follow the perimeter of the box (OXY) and the proportion be 100%, i.e. perfect inequality. Thus inequality can be measured as rising from 0% to 100%. A line, for example, to the right of the dotted one would represent greater inequality, i.e. a greater proportion of

---

[1]   Every five years since 1949 and annually since 1962 the Inland Revenue has conducted a survey of the distribution of taxable income which covers approximately 70% of Total Personal Income. The surveys are on a financial year basis and the income recipient is defined as a tax unit, i.e. one unit equals a married or single person. Surveys are published in the Inland Revenue Reports, e.g.

for 1949-50	Report,	No.	94
1954-5	"	"	99
1959-60	"	"	105
1962-3	"	"	107
1963-4	"	"	108
1964-5	"	"	109
1965-6	"	"	110

In each survey there is a considerable preamble on scope and definitions.

TABLE 5.2

Vertical and horizontal redistribution of income UK 1964

A Taxes paid and benefits received by households of two adults and two children

	Range of original income (£ p.a.)					
	560–	815–	990–	1195–	1450–	1750–2565
Average original income £ p.a. (= 100%)	725	905	1089	1304	1574	2044
Cash benefits received (%)	+6	+4	+3	+2	+2	+1
Income tax paid (%)	−1	−1	−4	−6	−7	−11
National Insurance contributions paid (%)	−9	−8	−8	−6	−5	−4
Personal post-tax income (%)	96	95	91	90	90	86
Personal post-tax income (£ p.a.)	696	860	991	1174	1417	1758
Indirect taxes paid (%)	−22	−19	−18	−15	−16	−15
Benefits received in kind (%)	+22	+17	+15	+12	+12	+12
Post-redistribution income (%)	96	93	88	87	86	83
Post-redistribution income (£ p.a.)	696	842	958	1134	1354	1697

B Taxes paid and benefits received by selected household types in the income range £815-990 p.a.

	Household type					
	1A	2A	2A, 1C	2A, 2C	2A, 3C	2A, 4C
Average original income £ p.a. (= 100%)	900	904	912	905	907	905
Cash benefits received (%)	+1	+5	+2	+4	+7	+10
Income tax paid (%)	−12	−7	−5	−1	−1	–
National Insurance contributions paid (%)	−8	−8	−8	−8	−88	−9
Personal post-tax income (%)	81	90	89	95	98	101
Personal post-tax income (£ p.a.)	729	814	812	860	889	914
Indirect taxes paid (%)	−18	−19	−18	−19	−18	−19
Benefits received in kind (%)	+1	+5	+12	+17	+26	+37
Post redistribution income (%)	64	76	83	93	106	119
Post redistribution income (£ p.a.)	576	687	757	842	961	1077

Source: ET No. 154, August 1966.

Notes to Table 5.2: Household Types
  1 A—number of adults.
     C—number of children.
  2 The units are households as defined by the Family Expenditure Survey.
  3 Original income refers to income before the receipt of any transfer income
     e.g. pensions, family allowances.
  4 The benefits in kind include the national health services, state education, school
     health services, school meals, milk and welfare foods and housing subsidies. The
     allocation of benefits in kind is inevitably based on rather crude assumptions, and
     the results should be interpreted with caution.

TABLE 5.3

Gini Concentration Ratios for Inland Revenue distribution of income, UK selected years

1949	35.31
1954	33.89
1959	33.66
1963	32.24

These results are for the Inland Revenue distributions adjusted to a calendar year basis.

Source: T. Stark, 'A Survey of the Distribution of Income in the UK since World War II', unpublished
       Ph.D. thesis, Manchester University Library.

income being held by the top income groups. This measure is known as the Gini Concentration Ratio.[1] Table 5.3 reproduces the Gini concentration ratios for the Inland
Revenue distributions.

There is a clear trend towards greater equality. However, this may be a misleading
result. First, the Inland Revenue excludes all incomes below the effective exemption
limit[2] and several types of non-taxable incomes above these limits. Secondly, the income
unit concept can hide basic changes in the social structure of incomes. For example, an
increase in the proportion of married persons, particularly where the wife also earns, can
lead to a movement of incomes into higher income ranges without there being any
necessary increase in per capita income. Furthermore, there is the whole problem of the
number of dependents, especially children, in each income unit.

The first criticism can be partially overcome by an analysis of the CSO distributions of
income, published in the National Income and Expenditure books, which extend Inland
Revenue surveys to include most State benefit and National Insurance incomes, e.g.
national assistance, unemployment, maternity, sickness grants, educational scholarships
and some incomes in kind.[3] The overall coverage for these distributions is approximately
85% of Total Personal Income. Table 5.4 indicates that the C.S.O. distributions do not
point to any general trend towards greater inequality.

Both the first and second problems (the income unit definition) can be overcome by
readjusting the CSO distributions to a per capita basis.[4] This is achieved by linking up the
total numbers of units and the total numbers of persons and the family size classification
of units. This latter information is provided for most income units in the Inland Revenue

---

[1] It is the simplest, but by no means a wholly satisfactory measure of income inequality. See a
     forthcoming paper by S. A. Moore and T. Stark, 'A Theoretical and Statistical Appraisal of the
     Measures of Income Distribution—A Case Study on the UK'.
[2] The effective exemption limits for 1949, 1954, 1959 and 1963 were £135, £155, £180 and £275
     respectively.
[3] The definitions are outlined in *NIBB*, 1965, p. 97.
[4] See A. R. Prest and T. Stark, 'Some Aspects of Income Distribution in the UK since World War II',
     MS, September 1967.

TABLE 5.4

Gini Concentration Ratios for CSO distribution of income, UK selected years

1949	38.72
1954	39.26
1959	39.25
1963	38.67

Source: T. Stark, ibid.

surveys. In undertaking this adjustment attention must be paid to the extensive double-counting of persons in the CSO distributions. For instance new marriages cause double-counting in the year in which they take place as the wife is counted twice, first as a single person and second as part of a married unit. Similar phenomena occur with respect to divorces and deaths of husbands. Further double-counting occurs on account of the family classification tables. Some persons included in these tables are also represented as separate income units in their own right, e.g. dependent relatives. The inequality indices for the per capita distributions are given in Table 5.5 The interesting feature here, of course, is the reversal of the Inland Revenue trends. There is now a definite trend to greater inequality on a per capita basis.

TABLE 5.5

Gini Concentration Ratios for per capita distribution of income, UK selected years

1949[+]	33.72
1954	34.45
1959	35.62
1963	35.78

[+] Only half of the double-countings were eliminated in this year. However the overall effect on the Gini ratio would not be sufficient to change the rankings of the four years.

Source: T. Stark, ibid.

These results illustrate the importance of clearly defining the scope of data before drawing general conclusions. There are also further problems not touched on here, concerning the definition and measurement of inequality.[1] Dr Stark and Mr Gough maintain there is no marked trend in the decrease in numbers of poor persons which, of course, is another means of judging the extent of income inequality.[2]

I.2   Class Differences and Educational Opportunities of Children

With the passage of the 1944 Education Act, some social commentators envisaged a dramatic change in our social structure, a trend towards a meritocracy in which all children, regardless of their economic or social background, could compete equally in an educational system and rise in occupations according to their relative abilities alone. The brightest children from working class families, it was believed, would have the same opportunity as the brightest children from professional or managerial families to enter universities; and economic classes in the future would be based on relative intelligence. These idealists failed to realise that considerable differences in income produce differences in family and social environment, neighbourhood schools, motivation and goals, and that these factors tend to reduce considerably the opportunities of children from poor families. In fact, children of higher professional people are thirty-three times more likely to

[1] E.g. if the data are transformed to an equivalent adult basis, there is then some movement towards greater equality over the period. *Ibid* p. 227.
[2] See I. Gough and T. Stark, 'Low Incomes in the UK 1954, 1959 and 1963', MS, June 1968.

enter a university degree course than children of semi- or unskilled workers. Only one per cent of university students are born of unskilled parents.[1] And the 1944 Education Act has not altered the relative percentages of economic classes entering universities. For example, Table 5.6 attempts to look at the changing composition of undergraduates from 1928 to 1961. Table 5.6A shows that there has been virtually no change in the percentage of undergraduates from working-class homes; and 5.6B shows that the percentage of university entrants from each class has changed in a similar manner. However, since the size of the manual working class is declining relative to other classes, there has been some improvement in their position.

TABLE 5.6

Social Origins of Students, Great Britain

A   Percentage of Undergraduates from Working-Class Homes

	1928-47 (average)	1955	1961
Manual Workers	23	25	25
Non-Manual Workers	77	75	75

B   Percentage of Boys in each Class entering university

	1928-47 (average)	1961
Manual Workers' sons	1.4	2.6
Non-Manual Workers' sons	8.9	16.8
All Boys	3.7	5.8
Non-Manual Workers' sons ÷ *Manual Workers' sons*	(6.4)	(6.5)

Sources: J. Floud in *Social Mobility in Britain* (ed. D. V. Glass), Routledge, London, 1957. R. K. Kelsall, *Applications for Admission to Universities,* Routledge, London, 1957. *Higher Education,* Appendix II(B), *Cmnd. 2154*–II-I, 1963.

Table 5.7 looks at the highest educational level achieved by a cohort of children born in 1940-41 in Great Britain. The survey was conducted in early 1962 when the children were 21 years old.

TABLE 5.7

Education of Children born in 1940-1. Great Britain

Highest Educational Course (%)		Higher Profes- sional	Managerial & other Professional	Clerical	Skilled Manual	Semi- & Unskilled	All
			Percentages Parents' Occupation				
Higher Education	Full-time:						
	Degree	33	11	6	2	1	4
	Other	12	8	4	2	1	3
Higher Education	Part-time	7	6	3	3	2	4
'A' level/SLC		16	7	7	2	1	3
Other post-school & 'O' level		25	48	51	42	30	40
None of above		7	20	29	49	65	47
Total		100	100	100	100	100	100

Source: Higher Education, Appendix I, *Cmnd. 2154*–I, 1963.

It may be thought that poor people are innately less intelligent than rich people, and that through natural heredity the offspring of the poor are innately less intelligent than the offspring of the rich. It may then be argued that the differences in academic achievement found in Table 5.7 are due to the differences in innate ability of the children of

---

[1]   *Report of Committee on Higher Education,* Cmnd. 2154, HMSO, 1963.

diverse economic groups and not primarily to differences in opportunity. However, the evidence of the Robbins and Newsom Reports clearly points to the incorrectness of such conclusions. The Robbins Report says:

'The evidence presented so far may be summarised as follows. The proportion of middle-class children who reach degree level courses is eight times as high as the proportion from working class homes, and even in grammar schools it is twice as high. As has been shown, the difference in grammar schools is not chiefly due to lower intelligence, but rather to early leaving. However, it is not only in these schools that the wastage of ability is higher among manual working class children. There is much evidence to show that, both before the age of 11 and in later years, the influence of environment is such that the differences in measured ability between social classes progressively widen as children grow up'.[1]

TABLE 5.8

Secondary Modern Schools   Characteristics by Areas

Characteristics	All Secondary Modern Schools	Problem Areas	Slums
1 Teacher turnover: % male teachers holding the same post over last 3 yrs.	65	55	34
2 % with adequate playing fields	30	13	–
3 % with gym facilities	50	25	–
4 % spending at least half time on practical subjects	21	–	10
5 % with seriously inadequate buildings	40	–	79

Source: Half Our Future, Newsom Report, HMSO 1963.

Table 5.8 shows that even where the form of education, e.g. Secondary Modern schools, is the same in slums as in other areas, the facilities are not equal. The secondary education of children of the poor who live in slum areas is hampered by a far greater percentage of seriously inadequate buildings and of teacher turnover than in non-slum areas. Thus, poverty tends to promote the social conditions which help to breed more poverty.

I.3   Social Security [2]

The United Kingdom's comprehensive system of social security attempts to reduce financial hardship in many circumstances. The National Insurance scheme provides, in return for weekly flat-rate contributions, weekly flat-rate cash benefits during sickness, unemployment, widowhood, and on retirement from regular work. Contributors are insurable in any one of three classes: Class I, employed persons; Class II, self-employed persons; and Class III, non-employed persons. All three classes pay the weekly flat-rate contribution, but the rate of contribution differs for each class, and an additional contribution for people in Class I is paid by the employer. The total amount of this weekly flat-rate contribution includes, in addition to a contribution to the National Insurance scheme, a contribution to the National Health Service. For those in Class I, it also includes a contribution to the Industrial Injuries scheme. The employer's part of the Class I contribution also includes the Selective Employment Tax[3] and a contribution to

---

[1]   Report of Committee on Higher Education, *Higher Education*, Appendix I, p. 46, para. 12,
[2]   *Cmnd. 2154*–I, 1963.
       This section is abridged from *Everybody's Guide to Social Security*, HMSO, Nov. 1967 and
       amended with subsequent changes in contributions and benefits.
[3]   See Chapter 2.

the Redundancy Payments Scheme.[1] In addition to flat-rate contributions, persons in Class I, aged 18 or over, are liable to pay a graduated contribution in any week in which their gross pay exceeds £9; graduated contributions vary with size of pay between £9 and £30. Employers can contract employees out of part of the graduated section of the National Insurance scheme if they satisfy the Registrar of Non-participating Employments that the employment is covered by an adequate occupational pension scheme; but then Class I flat-rate contributions are higher than for those who have not contracted out. (See Table 5.9.)

The benefits from National Insurance depend on a person's insurance class. The standard weekly flat-rate sickness benefit for a Class I or Class II man or an unmarried women over 18 years of age[2] is £4 10s. with increases of £2 16s. for an adult dependent, £1 5s. for the first dependent child, 17s. each for the second and third and 12s. for each further child (in addition to family allowances). For an insured married woman over 18 years of age, the flat-rate weekly sickness benefit is £3 2s; but she may be paid the £4 10s. rate if she is maintaining an invalid husband or is living apart from her husband and receiving less than £1 8s. a week from him towards her maintenance. Once a Class I or Class II contributor has paid 156 flat-rate contributions, he can get flat-rate sickness benefits for an unlimited period. Until the 156 contributions have been paid, the sickness benefits are not paid for more than 312 days.

TABLE 5.9

National Insurance Contributions, 1968

Class I			Paid by Employee		Paid by Employer		Total	
			s.	d.	s.	d.	s.	d.
Not Contracted		Men	16	8	41	6	58	2
Out		Women	14	1	26	6	40	7
	Paid at a weekly rate of £6 or less	Men	11	5	46	9	58	2
		Women	9	5	31	2	40	7
Contracted		Men	19	1	43	11	63	0
Out		Women	15	7	28	0	43	7
	Paid at a weekly rate of £6 or less	Men	12	8	50	4	63	0
		Women	10	2	32	5	43	7
Class II		Men					22	2
		Women					18	4
Class III		Men					17	7
		Women					13	10

Notes: (1) Contributions are flat-rate only.
(2) Contributions differ for people under eighteen years of age.
(3) Employers' contributions include SET and redundancy payments.

The rates of flat-rate unemployment benefit, including increases for dependents, are the same as for sickness benefit, and the conditions are also the same except that normally only Class I flat-rate contributions and credits count for unemployment benefits. Flat-rate unemployment benefit is normally payable for up to 312 days in any period of interruption of employment and after the first three days. Unemployment benefit is paid only while the contributor is unemployed and not receiving wages and while he is capable of work and is available for further employment.

Earnings-related supplements are payable to people over the age of 18 and under the minimum pension age who are entitled to flat-rate sickness or unemployment benefit.

The standard weekly rate of the flat-rate retirement pension for those who retire at the

---

[1] See below, p. 192.
[2] There are different benefit rates for people under 18 years of age.

minimum pension age (65 for a man and 60 for a woman) is £4 10s. A man's pension can be increased if he has a dependent wife who is not qualified for a pension or if he has any dependent children. For a married woman whose entitlement depends on her husband's insurance the rate is £2 16s. By staying at work after the age of 65 and up to 70 years for a man and after the age of 60 and up to 65 for a woman increments to the retirement pension may be earned; for every nine flat-rate contributions actually paid between these ages, the retirement pension is increased by 1s. a week. Over the age of 70 for a man and 65 for a woman, the pension can be paid whether the pensioner has retired or not. The contribution conditions for a retirement pension are that the person must have paid at least 156 flat-rate contributions and have been credited with an average of 50 flat-rate contributions a year; if the yearly average is below 50, but at least 13, a reduced rate is paid. An additional graduated pension is paid depending on the number of 'units' earned since the graduated scheme began in April 1961; each £7 10s. for a man and each £9 for a woman paid in graduated contributions—not counting employers' contributions—earns a unit, and each unit counts for 6d. a week addition to pension.

Supplementary benefits are available for those people who are not in full time employment and whose weekly income is below a certain level. Supplementary benefits are of two kinds: supplementary pensions are for old-age pensioners, and supplementary allowances are for those 16 or over, but under pension age, whose income is below the level laid down in the Social Security Act. To calculate weekly income under the Act, different sorts of income are treated differently. Family allowances, pensions and most other national insurance benefits, and maintenance payments are counted as full weekly income. The first 40s. of a man's part-time earnings and the first 40s. of his wife's earnings are disregarded, but a man's and his wife's resources are counted together in working out weekly income. Capital of less than £325 and the interest therefrom is ignored, but if capital amounts to £325 or more, this is not so. In addition to an allowance or pension, supplementary benefits also include sums for reasonable rent and rates and in some cases exceptional expenses (for example, through serious illness).

Family allowances are cash payments to families with more than one child. The allowance is 15s a week where there are two children, with a further 17s. a week for each additional child. There are no contribution conditions for family allowances. The cost is met entirely from taxation.

Industrial Injuries Scheme

The Industrial Injuries Scheme provides insurance against being unable to work, or being disabled, or losing life, because of an accident at work or one of the prescribed industrial diseases. Entitlement to benefit does not depend on the number of contributions paid. The weekly rate of injury benefit for a person aged 18 or over is £7 5s. a week with increases for dependents. There are special rates for those between 17 and 18 years of age, for those under 17 and for children under school-leaving age. Benefit is payable during incapacity for work which falls within the period of 26 weeks from the date of the accident or development of the disease, but not usually for the first three days.

When a person's injury benefit stops and if he still has any disablement, he may receive a disablement benefit. The size of this pension depends on the extent of the disablement and varies from £7 12s. a week for 100% disablement to £1 10s. a week for 20% disablement with lower rates for people under 18. The pension can be increased under certain conditions.

Redundancy Payments

The Redundancy Act 1965 requires employers to give employees advance notice of the termination of employment contracts[1] and requires employers to make lump-sum compensation payments to employees who are dismissed because of redundancy and, in certain circumstances, to employees who have been laid off or kept on short-time for a substantial period. The amount of payment is related to the employee's pay, age and length of service with the employer. The Act established a Redundancy Fund, financed by employer's contributions of 5d. for men and 2d. for women and collected with the flat-rate National Insurance contribution. Employers who make lump-sum compensation payments may claim a rebate of part of the cost (ranging from two-thirds to over three-quarters from the Fund). The employee does not have to pay tax on his redundancy pay, and such payments do not affect his entitlement to unemployment benefit.

I.4   Regional Differences in Wealth and Poverty

The various regions in the UK[2] may be separated into rich and poor regions in accordance with the criteria found in Tables 5.10, 5.11 and 5.12. If our criterion is the average weekly earnings of adult male manual workers employed in manufacturing industries in October 1966, then the three poorest regions are Northern Ireland, Yorkshire and Humberside, and the South-West with 84.8, 93.8 and 95.3% respectively of the UK average; the South-East, Wales and the East and South are the richest with 105.1, 103.5 and 103.0% respectively. However, if our criterion is average hourly earnings for the same workers, then the richest regions are Wales, Midlands and the South-East with 106.0, 104.0 and 103.5% respectively of the UK average; and the poorest are Northern Ireland, Yorkshire and Humberside, and the North-West with 86.4, 91.8 and 95.5% respectively. On the other hand, if our criterion is average weekly household income from 1964 to 1966 then the picture changes again. Northern Ireland is consistently the poorest region, then the North followed by Wales. Note that Wales has fallen from the richest region in terms of average hourly earnings to the third poorest in terms of average household income. The wealthiest regions remain the South-East, the West and East Midlands followed by Yorkshire and the Humberside which was among the poorest in terms of average earnings.

To understand the large shifts in ranking of Wales and the Yorkshire and Humberside Regions, their activity rates must be examined. The activity rate is the number of employees in an age-sex group, expressed as a percentage of that age-sex group in a region's population. While the average UK activity rate was 76.0% for males and 40.4% for females in 1966, in Wales the figures were 67.7% and 30.5%. While the Welsh male activity rate was lower than the UK average, its female activity rate was lower than all the other regions, including Northern Ireland. The number of persons per household, their sex distribution and the numbers retired per household were approximately the same as the UK average; but the numbers of persons working per household were among the lowest in the UK. Therefore, those men who are employed in Wales are paid relatively well, but average household income is low because of high unemployment generally and because few women work for pay.

On the other hand, average male earnings are low in Yorkshire and Humberside, but the male activity rate of 78.3% is higher than the UK average and the female rate 39.3% is only a little below the UK average. Further the average size of households is 2.96 people compared with the UK average of 3.02; while the average number of persons working per household is 1.34, only a little lower than the UK average of 1.36 persons. Therefore, average household income is considerably higher in Yorkshire and Humberside than in Wales because a far higher proportion of the population is employed in the former region.

Generally, the relatively less prosperous regions are characterised in various degrees by higher unemployment rates, lower activity rates, outward migration, and an industrial

---

[1] The statutory minimum length of notices is laid down in the Contracts of Employment Act, 1963.
[2] See also chapter 4 for further discussion of the regional problem.

structure suffering from contraction. In Scotland, population is dense around the Glasgow-Edinburgh areas, but is sparse elsewhere. Except for Belfast, there is not conurbation in Northern Ireland. In Wales and the Northern Region densities per acre, outside the conurbations, are lower than in any other regions except Scotland and Northern Ireland. The low density of these regions may be related to income. In Scotland and the North average incomes per head are far below the national average and are still lower in Northern Ireland. However, the low income per head may be due to the larger size of families in these regions than in others. The low density of these regions is partly due to outward migration to secure higher incomes or simply to secure jobs.

The population tends to move from low to higher income areas, from areas of job scarcity to areas where there are many vacancies. London has more than three times the population of any other conurbation. In the past twenty years the South-East and the Midlands have been the regions of high demand for labour, low unemployment levels, high activity rates, rapid employment growth, net inward migration and considerable pressure on space. However, the density of the conurbations in these regions has created serious traffic and housing problems.

To provide employment in the poorer areas and to reduce congestion in the conurbations the government has designated various areas for development. The Industrial Development Act 1966, which replaced the Local Employment Acts of 1960 and 1963, abolished development districts and instead created certain development areas. Although it is still too early to assess the impact of the new Act on employment, attempts have been made to assess the former Acts. By refraining from issuing industrial development certificates for the construction of all proposed factory building of 5,000 square feet or more in the congested areas and by a generous system of loans and grants, the Board of Trade hoped to attract new industries into the development districts to provide employment (see Chapter 4). Thus in the main the government's policy has been to move the job to the worker rather than the worker to the job.

Studies[1] have indicated the following: firstly, between 1960 and 1966, the rate of unemployment in the development districts fluctuated upwards and downwards in tune with the national unemployment rate indicating that the same factors that effected employment nationally also effected employment in these districts. However, the development districts tended to have persistently high and above national average unemployment rates. Therefore, part of the unemployment in these districts may be reduced by national monetary and fiscal policies, but part is due to structural factors. Development districts have been heavily dependent on industrial activities in which employment has been declining, e.g. coal mining, shipbuilding, fishing, quarrying, forestry etc. Secondly, when statistical adjustments had been made to account for changes in areas covered by development districts and to eliminate the cyclical fluctuations in employment, there was no noticeable reduction in unemployment in the development districts between 1960 and 1966. Thirdly, the rate of growth of population in these districts remained considerably below the growth rate in the major conurbations. Therefore, the policy of bringing jobs to workers in sparse, poor districts and of reducing congestion in the conurbations has not been very successful in the past.

The Ministry of Labour has a number of schemes to increase labour mobility, i.e. to move workers to the jobs. The Resettlement Transfer Scheme benefits unemployed workers who have no early prospect of obtaining suitable and regular work near their

---

[1] Lawrence C. Hunter, 'Employment and Unemployment in Great Britain: Some Regional Consider-ations', *MS*, Jan. 1963; L. C. Hunter, 'Unemployment in a Full Employment Society'. *Scottish Journal of Political Economy*, Vol. 10, 1964. William H. Miernyk, 'Experience under the British Local Employment Acts of 1960 and 1963' *ILRR*, October 1966; A. P. Thirlwall, 'The Impact of British Local Employment Acts of 1960 and 1963', *ILRR*, July 1967; A. P. Thirlwall, 'The Local Employment Acts', *Yorkshire Bulletin*, May 1966; A. P. Thirlwall, 'Regional Unemployment as a Cyclical Phenomenon', *Scottish Journal of Political Economy*, June 1966.

homes and have found approved employment in an area where there are reasonable prospects of resettlement and where suitable unemployed people are not already in the area and available to take that job. The Key Workers' Scheme benefits skilled workers who are required by their employers to move to a project set up in a development district, provided the Ministry is satisfied that they are needed to train local workers for the project. The Nuclear Labour Force Scheme helps unemployed workers recruited in areas of high unemployment who are temporarily transferred to the parent factory of their new employer for training before starting their permanent jobs in the new establishment. The Ministry helps with grants for household removals, fares, a settling-in-grant, lodging allowance and incidental expenses. Aid towards legal and other costs are given under the schemes to workers who are buying and selling their own homes. However, the number of workers who receive these benefits is relatively small. Therefore, in spite of the excellence of the schemes, whether because of little publicity or because of the small funds available, or because of limits on who may benefit from the schemes, they have had very little impact on the labour market.

TABLE 5.10

Earnings and Hours in Manufacturing Industry, Adult Male Manual Workers, October 1966.

	Weekly Earnings		Hours Worked		Hourly Earnings	
	Average	% of UK Ave.	Average	% of UK Ave.	Average	% of UK Ave.
	s. d.					
UK	415 6	100.0	45.0	100.0	110.8	100.0
London and South-East	436 8	105.1	45.7	101.6	114.7	103.5
East and South	428 2	103.0	45.0	100.0	114.2	103.1
South West	396 1	95.3	44.9	99.8	105.9	95.6
Midlands	420 4	101.2	43.8	97.3	115.2	104.0
Yorks. and Humber	389 11	93.8	46.0	102.2	101.7	91.8
North-West	405 7	97.6	46.0	102.2	105.8	95.5
North	408 5	98.3	45.0	100.0	108.9	98.3
Scotland	403 6	97.1	45.7	101.6	106.0	95.7
Wales	430 0	103.5	43.9	97.6	117.5	106.0
Northern Ireland	352 6	84.8	44.2	98.2	95.7	86.4

Source: Abstract of Regional Statistics, 1967

TABLE 5.11

Household Income and Number of Persons per Household, by Region, 1964-66[1]

	Average Number of Persons per Household					Average Weekly Household Income (shillings)
	All persons	Males	Females	Persons Working	Persons Retired	
UK	3.02	1.45	1.56	1.36	0.17	503.38
North	3.09	1.49	1.60	1.22	0.15	422.33
Yorks. and Humber	2.96	1.42	1.54	1.34	0.17	482.47
North West	3.04	1.49	1.55	1.40	0.21	478.88
East Midlands	3.10	1.53	1.56	1.43	0.14	497.59
West Midlands	3.08	1.49	1.58	1.53	0.14	548.60
East Anglia	2.98	1.48	1.50	1.34	0.18	468.46
South East	2.89	1.38	1.51	1.34	0.18	564.17
South West	2.98	1.42	1.55	1.24	0.18	463.76
Wales	3.03	1.46	1.56	1.22	0.17	454.44
Scotland	3.22	1.55	1.67	1.41	0.14	477.37

Source: FES. Report for 1966, HMSO, 1967
[1] Unweighted average of the yearly averages.

TABLE 5.12

Regional Population, Employment, Activity Rates, 1966

	Home Population (Resident) thousands				Employment Thousands	Employees as % of adult population	Percentage Activity Rate by Age Group			
	All ages	0-14	Males, 15-64 Females, 15-59	Males 65 & over Females 60 & over			15-24	25-44	45-64	65 and over
UK:										
Total	54744.1	12830.3	33605.7	8307.9	24065	57.4				
Males	26602.4	6576.7	17496.4	2529.1	15220	76.0	75.2	80.7	86.5	12.4
Females	28141.7	6253.6	16109.3	5778.8	8845	40.4	66.0	36.5	37.7	7.1
North:										
Total	3316.8	810.9	2030.1	475.8	1335	53.3				
Males	1630.9	415.1	1063.3	152.5	884	72.7	84.2	89.6	85.9	19.2
Females	1685.9	395.8	966.8	323.3	451	34.9	66.0	44.0	46.9	10.4
Yorks. & Humberside										
Total	4732.1	1108.0	2903.7	720.4	2111	58.3				
Male	2300.3	568.3	1513.4	218.6	1351	78.3				
Female	2431.8	539.7	1390.3	501.8	754	39.3				
North West:										
Total	6731.9	1607.8	4082.9	1041.2	3034	59.2				
Males	3232.6	824.0	2105.6	303.0	1873	77.8	84.1	88.4	85.1	19.1
Females	3499.3	783.8	1977.3	738.2	1161	42.7	69.2	47.9	53.1	10.3
East Midlands										
Total	3298.5	779.1	2043.5	475.9	1437	57.0				
Males	1633.0	400.1	1082.4	150.5	925	75.0	79.7	83.1	84.2	18.5
Females	1665.5	379.0	961.1	325.4	512	39.8	66.7	41.8	47.6	10.2

West Midlands										
Total	5021.4	197.0	3171.0	653.4	2388	62.4				
Males	2492.8	614.7	1679.4	198.7	1534	81.7	80.3	92.4	89.4	25.1
Females	2528.6	582.3	1491.6	454.7	854	43.9	65.6	46.0	53.7	12.5
East Anglia										
Total	1582.5	350.0	974.0	258.5	615	49.8				
Males	789.8	178.9	525.9	85.0	403	66.0	63.0	75.4	81.5	14.1
Females	792.7	171.1	448.1	173.5	212	33.9	61.4	35.6	41.8	8.0
South East										
Total	17071.9	3755.3	10614.5	2702.1	8068	60.6				
Males	8226.1	1925.6	5497.9	802.6	4994	79.3	79.7	90.9	88.9	22.2
Females	8845.8	1829.7	5116.6	1899.5	3074	43.8	72.3	48.0	53.0	12.1
South West										
Total	3619.0	824.2	2167.8	627.0	1355	48.5				
Males	1763.9	422.2	1144.8	196.9	874	65.1	65.3	77.0	75.9	14.2
Females	1855.1	402.0	1023.0	430.1	481	33.1	59.3	36.7	41.1	7.7
Wales										
Total	2701.2	624.8	1650.0	426.4	1007	48.5				
Males	1323.0	319.1	867.1	136.8	680	67.7	71.2	78.6	78.0	11.7
Females	1378.2	305.7	782.9	289.6	327	30.5	54.5	33.6	36.0	6.2
Scotland										
Total	5190.8	1342.4	3109.6	738.7	2193	57.0				
Males	2489.9	687.3	1580.9	221.6	1369	76.0	77.6	87.6	84.9	17.6
Females	2700.9	655.1	1528.7	517.1	824	40.3	64.2	44.9	46.4	10.1
Northern Ireland										
Total	1478.0	430.9	858.6	188.5	511	48.8				
Males	720.1	221.4	435.7	63.0	317	63.5	61.2*	78.3*	70.3*	9.5*
Females	757.9	209.5	422.9	125.5	194	35.4	64.7*	36.2*	32.8*	5.6*

Source: Abstract of Regional Statistics, (HMSO) 1967
*1965

I.5   Proposals for Reducing Poverty

Major proposals for reducing the degree of poverty (and inequality) fall into the following categories; changes in social security benefits, changes in taxes, minimum wage legislation, and trade union pressure. The advocates of changes in social security benefits usually wish to increase the size of benefits to specific groups (e.g. large families, the aged, the disabled, etc.) but may disagree on the particular group which ought to receive special help, on amounts of additional benefits, on methods of paying for the additional costs, and whether the proposed increase should be selective or non-selective.

The proponents of increased selectivity argue that it is impossible to eliminate poverty as long as equal social benefits are provided to rich and poor alike. If, on the other hand, the government withdrew various benefits from the relatively well-off, more resources would be available to assist the truly needy. Since the largest body of the poor are families with many children (at least half a million dependent children in Britain live in families with an income below national assistance level) most pro-selectivity groups want to pay substantially larger family allowances to families below a certain income level and no allowances to those above a certain level. A variant of this suggestion is to make the size of family allowances vary not only with the number of children but also with the size of family income; i.e. to provide payments-per-child which vary inversely with income size. Some people wish to apply the 'selectivity principle' not only to social security benefits but also to various other types of social benefits and subsidies.

The principal opposition to the selectivity concept comes from those who are opposed to 'means tests'. They claim that means tests are humiliating, that many people would suffer from poverty rather than submit to the degradation of means tests, and that certain benefits should be provided to everyone as a right. Probably the most vocal pressure group for increasing the payments of certain social security benefits—mainly family allowances—on a non-selective basis is the Child Poverty Action Group, who claim that payment for increased allowances must be recovered through the income tax system. But merely to make family allowances taxable for most taxpayers would mean that only a part of the increase would be recovered; however, by cutting income tax relief for children, the whole of the increase might be recovered.[1]

The Negative Income Tax

Historically, economists who believed that it was socially desirable to reduce gross inequality of income tended broadly to favour redistribution through progressive income taxation and through grants to those unable to work. They often frowned upon indirect taxes both because these are sometimes regressive in their income effects and because they may distort the price mechanism. And they supported income redistribution in favour of the poorer income groups in the belief that this would 'maximise happiness' and that greater family income equality would produce greater equality of opportunity for youth. Those who opposed such a redistribution tended to argue that progressive income taxes (or any further progression of taxes) would be harmful to the community because it would reduce incentives, the consequent fall in productivity would reduce national income; and social happiness would not, therefore, be maximised.

There is a growing interest among economists (especially in the US, but also in the UK) in adopting a sort of upside down progressive income tax, the 'negative income tax' to eliminate poverty. The negative income tax is a form of income supplementation based on the system of income taxation.

There are different views as to the best forms of negative taxation; here two are mentioned, namely the 'poverty gap' plan and the 'social dividend plan.[2] In both systems some standard of income is set which is regarded as reasonably adequate. In the 'poverty gap' plan,

---

1   *Poverty*, Child Poverty Action Group, Spring 1967.
2   C. Green and R. J. Lampman, 'Schemes for Transferring Income to the Poor', *IR* February, 1967.

the difference between a person's or a family's actual income and the standard is known as the poverty gap. The plan would reduce or close the gap by paying allowances or 'negative taxes' to the poor; the size of the cash benefits would depend on the size of the family, amount of actual income, etc. In short, a progressive negative tax system could be imposed with the poorest receiving the largest allowances. The 'social dividend' plan would give each family a standard income benefit and then would tax pre-benefit income so that the tax would be less than the benefits for poor families but more than the benefits for families which were not poor. [1]

Both plans use some standard income guarantee, a break-even level of income where the tax liability equals the benefits and a tax rate applied against a tax base. If the break-even level and the negative tax rate is low, then the system would not do much to reduce poverty. However, a 100% negative tax rate would be unworkable for it would mean that some people must work for nothing or else conceal their incomes; thus it would reduce the supply of work effort at low wage rates or earnings levels. Therefore negative tax proposals generally cite a tax rate less than 100%. Still the guaranteed minimum income could also reduce work incentives where it was equal to or higher than actual earnings. [2]

However, if a scheme was designed to preserve the incentive to work, it would represent a solution to the problem of poverty that does not distort the market price mechanism. It could be a universal method of eliminating poverty; and therefore could eliminate the pockets of poverty and the anomalies found under our present social security system. Further as a unitary solution, it would eliminate the many different types of allowances and benefits we have and thereby would provide some savings in manpower and other administration costs. A negative tax scheme could logically be integrated into a progressive income tax system and could achieve greater equity than would be the case in its absence from the system. And lastly, since every adult would need to fill out a tax form, it would remove additional means tests and the need for poor people to apply for assistance. [3]

A National Minimum Wage

In its *Report on the Circumstances of Families*, the Ministry of Social Security found that there were 125,000 families with two or more children in 1966 whose incomes were less than the Supplementary Benefit level for these families although the father was employed full-time. Of these families, less than half (55,000) had only two children. Therefore, there is a considerable number of fathers of large families whose pay is below Supplementary level. A study by Mrs J. Marquand [4] found that there also exists a significant number of male workers in full-time employment in good health and with relatively small families whose earnings also fall below the Supplementary Benefit level.

Knowledge of the existence of a large number of 'low paid' workers has led a number of trade unions, amongst others, to advocate the passage of legislation to establish a legal national minimum wage to eliminate poverty among wage earners. It was precisely this desire to eliminate extremely low wages which led to the passage of the Trade Boards Act, 1909; under this Act trade boards were set up to establish statutory minimum wages in certain trades. This Act was superseded by others and finally by the Wages Council Act, 1959; under the 1959 Act, Wages Councils may be established under orders from the Minister of Labour where there is not adequate machinery for the effective regulation of the pay of any group of workers or where such regulation is likely to cease to exist and consequently where a reasonable standard of pay will not be maintained unless a Wages Council is established. Since the minimum wages of more than 3.5 million workers are regulated by 57 Wages Councils, why are some people advocating in addition a legal national minimum wage?

1   *Loc Cit.*
2   G. H. Hildebrand, 'Second Thoughts on the Negative Income Tax', *IR* February, 1967.
3   E. R. Rolph. 'The Case for a Negative Income Tax', *IR* February, 1967.
4   J. Marquand, 'Which are the Lower Paid Workers?', *BJIR* Vol. 5, No. 3, November 1967.

Not all low-wage earners are covered by Wages Councils. Mrs. J. Marquand found that of the twenty manufacturing industries with the lowest paid workers, fourteen were covered by Wages Councils.[1] The lowest paid workers in these fourteen Wages Councils industries, although receiving their legal minimum wage, were nevertheless below Supplementary Benefit levels, indicating the weakness of the Wages Councils. Also it seems that although there was adequate union organisation in the remaining six lowest paid industries, the unions were not sufficiently strong to raise pay to a 'reasonable' level. Further there are several industries which do not rank as low paid when the distribution of earnings is examined, but which nevertheless have large numbers of low-paid workers. Therefore, the advocates of a legal, national minimum wage would argue that Wages Councils, as presently constituted, do not cover all the low wage earners.

'There is a very strong tendency for manufacturing industries whose lower paid workers are relatively low paid to be industries which are contracting, or at most, expanding more slowly than the average.'[2] It can be expected, therefore, that a national minimum wage may increase the rate of contraction. Some people would be unemployed; and where the adoption of a minimum wage upsets wage differentials, increased pay may have to be given to those workers paid above the minimum to restore former differentials.

Trade Union Pressure and the Share of Wages

One of the aims of trade unionism is to increase the share of wages in the national product. A considerable literature has been written about this form of income redistribution. A study[3] of the share of wages in the long run found that labour's share in Great Britain has been relatively constant, rising from 38.6% in 1870 to only 41.9% in 1950, but the proportion of wage earners among the gainfully employed had gone down substantially. Consequently, wage earners gained more than other income groups. The largest gains occurred during the two World Wars, when full employment raised wages but inflation cut the shares of rent and salaries. According to Phelps Brown and Hart, trade unions forced upwards the share of wages only when they were aggressive and when the employers simultaneously were faced with a 'hard' market so they could not recoup profits easily by raising prices. Once employers were squeezed between aggressive unions and hard markets, they tended to go along at the lower profit margin for a time. However, profit margins rose again in the 'soft' market of the '40s.

Four situations are possible: (1) hard markets and hard unions; (2) hard markets and soft unions; (3) soft markets and hard unions; and (4) soft markets and soft unions. The share of wages tends to gain in the first case and the share of profits in the last, with the other two cases lying in between. These cases may be illustrated as follows: the first case by the period of 'new unionism' starting in 1889, the second by the period after the collapse of unions in 1879, the third by the period after World War II, and the fourth by the period of 1903-5, and 1926 to 1928 after the General Strike.

What has been the situation in recent years? First, let us lump wages and salaries together to see how they fared relative to other incomes. From an index[4] with 1950 as 100, we find that by the first quarter of 1967, the wages and salaries bill rose to 298.8, gross trading profits to 217.3, gross trading surpluses to 346.3, self-employment and rent combined to 233.6 and the total of all domestic incomes to 291.4. The compounded annual rate of increase between 1950 and 1966 shows that while total domestic income increased by 6.7%, income from rent increased by 8.2%, from wages and salaries by 6.9%, from gross trading surpluses by 7.9%, from gross trading profits by 5% and from self-employment

---

[1]   J. Marquand, 'Which are the Lower Paid Workers?', *BJIR* Vol. 5, No. 3. November 1967, p.373.

[2]   *Loc.cit*.

[3]   E. H. Phelps-Brown and P. E. Hart, 'The Share of Wages in National Income', *EJ,* June 1952.

[4]   *SIPEP* No 22, Sept. 1967, Table S.3., p. 4.

by 3.7%. Catching up with the decline in previous years, rent from property increased most rapidly. Income from self-employment increased least rapidly over this period. The percentage share of income from self-employment and rent combined declined from 16.4% of total domestic income to 13.4% in 1966. The share of trading profits of companies also declined from 14.8% of total income in 1950 to 13.6% in 1966. During the same period, the share of wages and salaries increased from 67.1% to 69.5%.[1]

Let us consider the Gross Domestic Product in manufacturing industry from 1956 to 1966 by type of income in millions of pounds. In 1956 the share of wages in manufacturing income was 46.3%; by 1966, this share fell to 44%. On the other hand, the share of salaries increased from 16.9% in 1956 to 21.25% in 1966. Since wage earners are more heavily unionised than salary earners in manufacturing industries and since the share of salaries has increased while that of wages has declined, the redistribution of income cannot be attributed to trade union pressure. Looking at the economy as a whole we find that the share of wages in the national product declined from 48.7% in 1956 to 47.6: in 1966 while the share of salaries has increased from 14.6% to 19.5% during the same period.[2] The share of salaries increased for two reasons: firstly, the number of salary earners relative to wage earners is increasing; and secondly, salary earners have recouped a small bit of their differentials which had narrowed relative to wage earners during the war and immediate post-war years.

From the mid-fifties to the squeeze, although unions have been 'hard', the market has been 'soft'. Also the relaxation of rent controls and the shortage of housing were bound to increase the share of rent from property. The decline in the share of income from self-employment is due to the relative decline in the number of self-employed persons as a result of the growth of corporations, the larger average size of enterprises and farms and the spread of supermarkets.

II.   COLLECTIVE BARGAINING AND INCOMES POLICY

II. 1   The Labour Market Institutions: Trade Unions and Employers' Associations

The British trade union movement, the oldest in the world, is highly diverse in structure because unions developed at different periods of time and reflect different historic environments, needs and beliefs. In addition to local craft unions, national craft and multi-craft unions, and general occupational unions, there exist some industrial unions and a variety of different structural types of white collar and professional unions.

The total number of separate trade unions in the United Kingdom had declined from 1,384 in 1920 to 732 in 1950 and to 574 in 1966. This decline is due largely to amalgamations between unions, a process which has been made easier since the passage of the Trade Union (Amalgamation Act) 1964. Trade Union membership in 1966 was 10,111,000. Of these, there were 390 unions with less than 2,500 members each, including 305 unions with less than 1,000 members and 245 with under 500 members each. These small unions represent 67.9% of the total number but only 2.2% of the total membership. 25.7% of all unions have more than 2,500 but less than 50,000 members each; however, the combined membership of these 'middle-size' unions represents only 16.4% of the total membership of all unions. At the other extreme, the 37 largest unions account for only 6.5% of all unions by number, but their combined membership represents 81.4% of the total membership of all unions. And the 18 largest unions, each with at least 100,000 members, together account for 68.6% of total union membership. Thus, British union membership appears as a pyramid where the vast majority of members are concentrated in a few large unions and the vast majority of unions have relatively few members.

Formed in 1868, The Trades Union Congress acts as the voice and central co-ordinator of the trade union movement. In 1967 there were 169 unions with a membership of

---

[1]   *Ibid*, Table A.4, p. 4.
[2]   *NIBB* 1967, Table 17, p. 21.

8,787,282 affiliated to the TUC. Each year the delegates from affiliated unions met to determine the general policy of the TUC for the coming year and to elect the General Council, the TUC's executive board. The General Council is supposed to carry out the decisions laid down at the Annual Congress, watch legislation affecting labour and promote common action on wages, hours of work, etc., aid unions attacked on any important trade union principle, watch industrial movements and co-ordinate industrial activity, carry on propaganda to help the union movement, and enter into relations with unions in other countries.

The TUC has little formal authority. Its only disciplinary powers are contained in two Standing Orders relating to disputes between affiliated unions and to the conduct of affiliated unions. The Council interferes as little as possible in the domestic affairs of autonomous unions. And neither the General Council's decisions nor those of Congress are binding on affiliated unions.

A new function for the TUC was created with the birth of the government's 'early warning' system on incomes and prices in November 1965.[1] Further, the General Council plays an important role in regard to strikes. Unions are obliged to inform the General Council when they are going to call a strike which may involve large numbers of workers, directly or indirectly. The Council does not intervene in a dispute unless it is requested to intervene by the unions which are on strike. However, the Council may take the initiative to influence a settlement if the negotiations have broken down, if the deadlock is such that other affiliated groups of workers are directly or indirectly involved in a work stoppage, or if wages, or hours, or conditions of work are imperilled.

The General Council also plays a role on a multitude of tripartite bodies composed of representatives of employers' associations, unions and either the government or the public. Consultation between the TUC and the Government is conducted on all sorts of economic, social, industrial, educational, manpower and production problems.

There are three types of employers' associations: trade associations concerned primarily with matters affecting their trade; employers' associations concerned primarily with collective bargaining and industrial relations; and those concerned with both trading and collective bargaining matters. Our interest here is mainly in the second type, and among these there is diversity in structure. Most are organised on an industry basis; some are purely local bodies and deal with a section of one industry, while others are nation-wide in scope and deal with an entire industry. In the main industries, local or regional associations are combined into national federations. There are roughly 1,500 employers' associations dealing with industrial relations matters and about 80 of them are national federations.

The CBI, the confederation of employers' national federations, was formed in 1965 as a result of the application of the nationalised industries and local transport undertakings and the merger of three organisations: the British Employers' Confederation, the confederation of associations and national federations concerned with collective bargaining; the Federation of British Industries which was composed of trade associations; and the British Manufacturers' Association, the federation of small employers. The establishment of NEDC and NBPI and the government's attempt to develop an interrelated plan on wages, prices, profits and productivity exposed to the employers' associations their need to develop a unified policy on trade and labour matters. Like the TUC, it has also agreed to take part in the incomes policy 'early warning' system. And like the TUC, it represents its member organisations to the government and the public, and its representatives sit on a number of government advisory bodies.

II.2   Collective Bargaining

In 1916 the Committee on the Relations between Employers and Employed (the Whitley Committee) urged the formation of Joint Industrial Councils in each industry, composed

---

[1]   See p. 210.

of representatives of the employers' association and trade unions. The Councils were to meet at regular intervals, and would not only consider the terms and conditons of employment within the industry, but also all matters of joint concern. The Committee's report influenced the developments of 'Whitley Committees' in the government services and Joint Industrial Councils in the nationalised industries and in private industries. By 1960 over two hundred Joint Industrial Councils had been established. Most Joint Industrial Councils are both negotiating bodies which consider the terms and conditions of employment in the industry and consultative bodies which discuss other matters; but a few do not negotiate, and a few have little or no consultative functions. Many provide for arbitration when negotiations break down.

In some important industries, such as engineering, shipbuilding, iron and steel, and cotton, no Joint Industrial Councils were established because they had adequate negotiating machinery at the time of the Whitley Committee's reports. For example, national negotiations in the engineering industry occur at *ad hoc* meetings between the Engineering Employers' Federation and the Confederation of Shipbuilding and Engineering Unions if the subject pertains to wages or conditions of the generality of manual workers. If the subject to be negotiated concerns only one or a few unions, then the Federation meets with them. When there is a failure to agree, negotiations break down. There is no agreed procedure to take the issue to arbitration.

In most industries the national negotiations determine national minimum wage rates, but in recent years a few have negotiated minimum earnings guarantees. However, local agreements may provide for improvements in the terms and conditions at works level. Consequently, workers' earnings may increase as a result of changes either in the terms of national agreements or in pay at works level. The difference between the rate of change of earnings and the rate of change of pay contained in national agreements is known as wage drift.

Wage drift may arise in any of the following ways: (1) Management, on its own initiative, may increase employees pay in order to recruit additional labour, to retain its present labour force, or to adjust the wage structure of the firm. (2) Piece-workers' earnings per unit of input may increase when the output-labour input ratio is raised if piece rates are not adjusted or are adjusted inadequately. (3) Works bargaining over piece and time rates may increase actual earnings. Usually, an increase in some workers' earnings sparks off demands for increases by other workers to restore former relativities. (4) Many national agreements provide a single rate for a type of labour (e.g. a process worker) while factory job rates may provide differentials for different gradations of skill for a type of labour (e.g. process worker grade 1, grade 2, etc.). (5) An increase of works-rated skills will lead to wage drift.

The most common form of wage payment is that based on a time-rate. Where a standard time-rate is negotiated in an agreement and is effectively applied, as in the Ford Motor Co. agreement, then it is the employer's responsibility to see that each employee 'does a fair day's work for a fair day's pay'. Many employees object to a completely standardised time-rate because it offers no incentive to a worker to use his talents to the fullest. Consequently, some agreements stipulate what constitutes a 'fair day's work' and pay extra sums when this measured amount of work is exceeded. For example, an agreement made by the National Joint Council for the Mastic Asphalt Industry fixes hourly rates of pay and a schedule of a 'fair day's work of eight hours', i.e. the quantities of work required for a normal day's output from gangs of the normal size. Work performed in excess of the stated quantities is paid at ordinary time-rates, but such payments may not exceed a stipulated number of hours' pay.

About one-third of all employees are paid by the piece or by results. Piece-work rates may either take the form of prices fixed for units of work or of times allowed for units of work. Either of these forms of payment may relate to the work of an individual or to a group. The size of a group may vary from a small gang to a department to the output of the entire firm. Pay may be for straight piece-work, that is, a uniform price per unit of work for the entire output, or of differential piece-work. Under a differential system, rates may be progressive, that is, they increase as output increases, or regressive, that is, they decrease as output increases. Under the time allowance system, when the worker saves time by working at faster speed, the hourly earnings may increase in exact proportion to the increased speed, or the scheme may be arranged to have a progressive or regressive effect. Trade unions prefer straight piece-work systems to differential systems and progressive to regressive differential systems.

In some collective agreements, as in the Lancashire cotton industry, piece-work price lists are applied uniformly throughout the industry. In most agreements piece-workers are guaranteed the basic time-rate as a minimum payment for the period worked. The conditions governing the fixing and changing of piece-rates are usually provided. Also, many agreements provide that piece-rates must be set at a level that would ensure that a worker of average ability is able to earn a specific percentage over time-rates.

Some collective agreements contain 'sliding-scale' clauses which provide for automatic changes in wage rates with changes in the retail-price index. Historically, 'sliding-scale' clauses had been negotiated which tied wages to the price of the product rather than to the retail-price index, e.g. in the coal and textile industries.

Collective agreements provide for the normal weekly hours of work. Usually, the normal work week changes at infrequent intervals. After the Second World War there was a general trend to a 44 or 45 hour normal work week; between 1959 and 1962 to a 42 or $42\frac{1}{2}$ hour normal work week; and since 1964 the movement has been towards a 40 hour work week. The TUC advocates a 35 hour work week.

To reduce the actual numbers of hours worked, collective agreements provide for a higher rate of pay for overtime hours than for normal hours. Usually, overtime pay takes the form of a specific fractional addition to the rate of pay for work done in the normal hours. Often the rate progresses according to the duration of overtime worked. Overtime worked on Saturdays or national holidays usually entitles one to a higher rate than weekday overtime, and Sunday work to a higher rate than Saturday overtime work. Some agreements limit the amount of overtime that may be worked. Overtime may be restricted to a specific number of hours a day, a week or a month, but provision may be made for exceeding the limit under certain circumstances. The number of actual hours worked by women and young people is limited by legislation (principally the Factories Act, 1961), but in practice the number of hours actually worked by women is usually below the normal weekly hours.

In 1950 the International Labour Office adopted Convention No. 100 advocating equal pay between men and women for equal work. Great Britain is one of five countries in Western Europe that has not as yet endorsed this resolution, but equal pay for equal work exists in the Civil Service and in the teaching and most other professions. In much of British industry, women's wage rates are about three-quarters of men's rates, and it has been estimated that implementation of equal pay would cost about £600m a year.

Trade unions have fought for equal pay for equal work; in national agreements in the post-war years, they have either sought for equal absolute increases in wage-rates for male and female workers which reduces their percentage differentials, or for higher percentage increases for women than for men which reduces absolute differentials. In an index of weekly wage rates for manual workers in all industries with 31 January 1956 as 100, men's weekly rates increased from 107.8 in 1956 to 149.8 in January 1966 while women's increased from 104.2 to 155.1 between the same dates. Thus, the rate of increase of female's wage rates has clearly been greater than that of males.

However, a different picture emerges when we consider average earnings. In manufacturing industries, female average weekly earnings expressed as a percentage of men's earnings fell from 53% in 1950 to 48% in 1960 and to 47% in October 1965. It seems that while national collective agreements have tended to narrow the male-female differential in rates, market forces and working hours changes have tended to widen the male-female differential in earnings.

Before the turn of the century there were considerable differentials in the wage rates of craftsmen, not only between counties and wider regions, but also between small villages. As the area covered by collective agreements widened, many of these district wage-rate differentials disappeared. And as national agreements awarded national flat-rate increases in rates and as district negotiations became less frequent, the remaining district wage-rate differentials became relatively less important.

On the other hand, absolute regional differentials in earnings tended to reflect the state of the labour market. To some extent, regional differentials are inter-industry differentials in the sense that the industry composition varies from one area to another; therefore general average earnings would be expected to vary. However, there are considerable regional variations in earnings even in the same industry and for the same type of work.

Since 1880 the differential in wage rates between skilled and unskilled workers has halved in the UK. It has been argued that this narrowing is caused by the growth of union organisation among the unskilled workers, and by the attempts of unions to seek flat-rate increases. On the other hand, some economists believe that the spread of public education has affected the relative supply of skilled and unskilled workers and that this has caused the narrowing. And still others explain the narrowing in terms of the development of egalitarian tendencies in the country generally or in terms of the changes in relative demand for different types of labour.

II.3   Royal Commission on Trade Unions and Employers' Associations

The Royal Commission on Trade Unions and Employers' Associations, appointed in 1965, had not reported at the time of writing this book. There are however a few areas in which the Royal Commission *should* recommend the passage of legislation by Parliament. One such area relates to the rules of trade unions. A trade union's rules are in law a contract of association between union members. However, aside from a few compulsory rules, e.g. those related to political funds, the law is silent about the content of the rules. Under the Trade Union Acts, 1871 and 1876 all *registered* unions (but not unregistered ones) must include rules which provide for certain matters; union's name and objectives; imposition of fines; conditions for 'benefit' entitlement, manner of making or altering rules; investment of funds; periodic auditing of accounts; appointment and removal of trustees, officers and management committees. However, whether other rules are included or excluded, the content of most of these rules is left to the union's discretion.

Professor Cyril Grunfeld wrote:

'The union rules, which define the union's objects, constitute its governing committees and officers and regulate members' relations *inter se,* may in law be shaped freely according to the will of the members. The rule book may be well and thoughtfully drafted or just thrown together. It may be designed to maximise member participation in union government and the accountability of its officials to members, or it may be weighted to favour the exercise and retention of power by a small ruling group. It may try to cover every aspect and contingency of union life in detail or may be confined to the bare essentials'.[1]

If a union violates its own rules, it may be sued for breach of contract by one of its members. But if a union's rules are designed to minimise member participation and to maintain a small clique in power and if the union does not violate these rules, union members have no easy legal means of securing democratic rights. Therefore, it is proposed that legislation be enacted empowering the Registrar of Friendly Societies to draw up model rules which protect the 'democratic rights' of union members and to make the adoption of rules by unions along the lines of the model 'a condition of registration'. However, to make the above proposition viable, registration *should* confer important

---

[1]   C. Grunfeld, *Modern Trade Union Law,* Sweet & Maxwell, London, 1966, p. 55.

benefits on a union; as the law stands today, registered unions have a few minor legal advantages over unregistered ones.

A legal benefit which should be conferred on registered trade unions is the right to recognition by employers and to collective bargaining wherever it has in its membership the majority of workers in any grade in an establishment. As the law stands at present an employer may refuse to recognise a union or bargain in 'good faith'; he also may prevent his employees from joining trade unions by making their signature to the 'document' (a statement in which the employee agrees not to belong to a union) a condition of employment. A recent survey found that the 'major obstruction to the expansion of union membership ' in poorly organised areas of the labour force 'is employers' refusal to recognise unions and their pursuance of policies designed to discourage or prohibit their employees from joining them'.[1] Thus, the legal right to recognition by registered trade unions would actively induce unions to obtain registration.

The Royal Commission may also ask for legal changes in regard to compulsory unionism. A recent survey [2] found one worker in six bound by some form of compulsory unionism. Two out of every five trade unionists are covered by formal or informal closed shop agreements; and in manual occupations, every other trade unionist is in a closed shop. In support of the closed shop, four arguments may be advanced: (1) The existence of non-unionists weakens the unions' position in collective bargaining with employers, and therefore the elimination of non-unionism is desirable. (2) Compulsory unionism reduces membership turnover and allows a union to devote more of its energies to tasks other than recruitment. (3) The closed shop may give union leaders greater power to maintain discipline among the rank-and-file. (4) Since the non-unionist usually benefits from the higher wages and better working conditions won by unions, he should be made to pay for the unions expenses as do all union members.

Three arguments may be advanced against the closed shop: (1) The closed shop infringes on the civil liberties of the individual who has a conscientious objection to joining a union. (2) The expulsion, rightly or wrongly of a union member from a union means that the worker must forfeit his job under the closed shop; such acts give unions too much power over the individual. (3) When union leaders ignore the wishes of their members, members have the right to leave their union. However, since under a closed shop, resignation from a union means forfeiting one's job, the closed shop may hinder the rank and file from taking effective steps to press an undemocratic or irresponsible leadership to mend its ways.

The third argument against the closed shop would become largely redundant if the aforementioned legislation was passed to ensure that the individual union member's democratic rights were guaranteed in the union's rules. However, such a law would offer no protection to the non-unionist whose case was presented in the first and second anti-closed shop arguments. The problem facing the Royal Commission is to propose a law that will not destroy any of the benefits of the closed shop whilst protecting the rights of the non-unionists. A possible solution would be to devise some legal means of 'taxing' or 'fining' the non-unionist a weekly sum equivalent to a union subscription, with the proviso that such sums be contributed to an accredited charity instead of the union.

One area in which legislation may create more financial and industrial relations problems than it might solve is legislation designed to 'punish' strikers in order to reduce the number of man days lost on strikes. The argument in support of such legislation runs as follows. The majority of collective agreements have no termination dates and are not legal contracts. If they were made legal contracts, then strikes called by a union prior to

---

[1]   George S. Bain, *Trade Union Growth and Recognition,* Research Papers 6, Royal Commission on Trade Unions and Employers' Associations, H.M.S.O., 1967, p. 99, para. 243.
[2]   W. McCarthy, *The Closed Shop,* Blackwell, Oxford, 1965

the termination date of the contract would be an illegal breach of contract and the union calling such a strike could be sued for damages. A distinction must be made between 'conflicts of interests' and a 'conflict of rights'; the former is associated with negotiating a new contract, and the latter refers to 'grievances' or conflicts over the interpretation or enforcement of existing contracts. Strikes over conflicts of interests after the termination of an existing contract should be legal. Strikes over a conflict of rights would always be in breach of contract. The government should provide Labour Courts to adjudicate over conflicts of rights. In the post war years in the UK, a larger proportion of strikes are thought to have been due to conflicts of rights than of interests. Most of these strikes of 'rights' are local, are small in terms of numbers of strikers, and are unofficial (i.e. not officially authorized by a trade union). If legislation along the lines described were passed— so the argument runs—the unions would be forced to discipline members who go out on strike in breach of the union contract. Since most of the present day strikes are over 'rights', such legislation would reduce the number of working man days lost due to strikes.

Before considering the arguments against such legislation, some relevant aspects of existing law in relation to strikes should be mentioned. The vast majority of strikes in Britain are probably in breach of the contract of employment. Except in a few occupations such as in the police force, strikes are legal providing the employer receives proper notice. The contracts of Employment Act, 1963 establishes a minimum period of notice of seven days to sever the employment relationship; but the legal period of notice for many employees is longer than seven days. Strikes called without due notice are unlawful and the employer has two civil sanctions: he can take action for damages against all or some of the strikers; he may exercise his right to terminate the employment of those who broke the employment contract. Employers rarely avail themselves of these legal sanctions because of their possible effects on future industrial relations in their firms.

Since the Second World War there has been a growth in the number of collective agreements which contain no-strike clauses, i.e. provisions in which the parties agree not to resort to the strike or lockout until mutually agreed arbitration procedures have been exhausted. 'Where a no-strike clause has become incorporated in the individual contracts of employment of the employees concerned, whether by express incorporation or incor- poration as a customary implied term, such employees will have lost the right to strike before exhausting the agreed procedure'.[1] The civil sanctions available to the employer faced with such an 'unconstitutional strike' are the same as in the cases of strikes called without due notice.

The arguments against additional legislation are, first, that the existing law is adequate. Secondly, the suggested legislation penalizes a union for those strikes called by members which the union does not endorse. It therefore shifts responsibility for disciplining workers from the employer to an innocent third party. Thirdly, the growth in the numbers and use of labour lawyers and arbitrators may be more costly to the economy than the savings incurred from a reduction of strikes—assuming there is a reduction of strikes. In the US, where this proposed system exists, arbitration and labour law have become a very costly business. Fourthly, there is no guarantee that such legislation will reduce the number of man-days lost due to strikes. In the US, while there are far fewer unofficial 'lightning' strikes than in the UK, the number of man days lost due to strikes per head of working population is far greater than in the UK—even though the proportion of trade unionists in the labour force is smaller in the US. If the UK is placed in a league table with all Western European countries which regard the collective agreement as a legal contract, we find that about as many countries suffer from a higher proportion of man days lost than the UK as do those who suffer less. It is probably wiser (but more difficult) for unions and employers to seek those institutional and industrial changes that will lead to a reduction of unofficial 'lightning' strikes than to jump into legislation when the 'cure' may be worse than the 'disease'.

---

[1]   C. Grunfeld, *op. cit.*, p. 324.

H

II.4 The Multiple Objectives of Incomes Policies

Implied in any incomes policy is the basic assumption that government, in addition to its ability to influence changes in wages and salaries through indirect monetary and fiscal measures, also has the ability to influence such changes directly. Acceptance of this assumption, however, does not necessarily imply agreement about the objectives or the desirability of an incomes policy. Nevertheless, whether or not government can directly influence changes in wages and salaries may depend on the kind of changes desired, that is, on the objectives of the incomes policy. Broadly speaking, the objectives examined below have been ascribed to the British incomes policy at one time or another.

One objective is to use an incomes policy as an anti-inflationary device to maintain stable prices by restraining the rate of increase of *total* incomes so that they do not rise faster than the rate of increase of productivity. Empirical studies have concluded that for each rate of increase of productivity, there is a critical level of unemployment; if unemployment falls below this level, pay will increase faster than productivity.[1] Consequently, the purpose of restraining *total* incomes is to alter the critical level of unemployment in the attempt to enjoy both high levels of employment and price stability. However, post-war experiences with voluntary incomes policies in western Europe indicate that under conditions of considerable demand for products, and hence for labour, wage restraint has been unsuccessful in the long run. Over long periods and under high demand conditions, union leaders have been unable to resist the pressures from their rank and file, and employers faced with labour shortages have increased pay to recruit or retain employees and have passed on their increased costs to the consumer. Therefore, those who hold that the chief objective of an incomes policy is to restrain the rate of increase of total incomes in the long run do so because they have faith that some day, by tinkering with the institutions and processes of collective bargaining and methods of wages payments, Western democracies will discover how to alter the critical level of unemployment in order to maintain full employment without inflation.

A modified version of the above objective claims that an incomes restraint policy is a useful tool used in conjunction with monetary and fiscal policies to contain demand during short-run emergency periods, such as a balance of payments crisis. Accordingly, it has been argued that the severity of monetary and fiscal deflationary measures has been reduced by wage restraint, and therefore, crises had been weathered with a lower level of unemployment than would have been otherwise possible. On the other hand, it also has been argued that once wage restraint breaks down and particularly where the economy has again become buoyant, the previously frustrated pressures from rank-and-file union members burst explosively so that the resulting increase in pay is greater than it would have been if it had not followed a period of restraint. Be that as it may, the evidence is inconclusive. A recent study by ECE of post-war incomes changes in western Europe and the UK, in countries with and without incomes policies, with differing policies, and institutitions, economies, and degrees of union strength, claims: 'But on the evidence given here, it seems that differences in the sensitivity of wages to unemployment are more closely associated with the level of unemployment than with any obvious institutional or policy differences.' And again, ' . . . the evidence so far available suggests that in no western European country has the rate of changes in wages—whether conventional rates or earnings—been so immutably determined by external forces that any effort on the part of those concerned to change the response would have been futile. Yet the

---

[1] For example, Professor Phillips holds that if productivity increases at the rate of 2% a year and if the level of unemployment falls below 2½%, wage rates will increase faster than productivity. A. W. Phillips, 'The Relation between Unemployment and the Rate of Change in Money Wage Rates in the United Kingdom, 1862-1957', *Economica,* Nov., 1958. See also R. G. Lipsey, 'A Further Analysis', *Economica,* Feb., 1960. Criticism of the Phillips view may be found in G. G. Routh, 'A Comment', *Economica,* November, 1959. Today, it is frequently held that if productivity increases by 3%, the critical level of unemployment would be 2%.

evidence also suggests that conditions in the labour market—and the rate at which consumer prices have been rising—set limits, in circumstances like those of the past 10-15 years, to the power of those concerned with wage bargaining to influence the rate at which wages increase'.[1]

A third objective is to use an incomes policy as a device to redistribute income in favour of the poorer sections of the community by enabling low-wage earners to receive larger pay increases than high-wage earners. The evidence from countries where this objective has been pursued, e.g. Sweden, indicates that attempts to redistribute income through the machinery of collective bargaining have been largely frustrated by wage drift. Further, a recent study by S. Gupta throws doubt on the desirability of using an incomes policy for redistributing income.[2] This study superimposes on an input-output model of the British economy at 1963 prices the effects of identical percentage pay increases in each industry on prices in each industry and in all industries, on export prices and on the retail price index. These results were then rank correlated with average earnings in each industry. The same percentage pay increase in each industry gave to high-wage earners a larger absolute increase than to low-wage earners. Nevertheless, the pay increases in low-wage industries had a greater impact on prices in the industry concerned, in all industries, on export prices and on the retail price index than did the increases accruing to high-wage earners. Giving tapered pay increases in each industry (i.e. giving larger absolute or percentage increases to lower than to higher wage earners in each industry) would only enlarge these effects since the proportion of low-wage earners is greater in industries with low average earnings than with high average earnings. Since low-wage industries tend to be more labour intensive and to have lower productivity than high-wage industries, these results are not surprising. But the findings do suggest that the policy objective of using the collective bargaining machinery to reduce income inequality will conflict with the anti-inflationary or stabilising objective of an incomes policy. The findings suggest therefore that the goal of redistributing income in favour of the poor had best be pursued through taxation and social-security schemes, perhaps through a negative income tax.

II.5   UK Incomes Policy—A Brief Chronology

There were three attempts to establish an incomes policy in the UK before 1964. Firstly after the 'convertibility crisis' in 1947, the post-war Labour government sought to restrain increases in pay in 1948 and to use its remaining war-time powers to hold back prices. Trade union leaders agreed to support the government, and in response to Sir Stafford Cripps' White Paper dealing with wage restraint, they withheld national negotiations. Consequently, the wage-rate index remained fairly steady; nevertheless, wage drift grew, that is earnings rose faster than nationally negotiated rates as a result of piece-work pay and other unscheduled pay increases at the enterprise level. By mid-1949 and early 1950, unions were already under considerable pressure from their members to abandon wage restraint. Then, when devaluation and the Korean War pushed prices upwards by the end of 1950, union leaders were unable to resist internal union pressures and abandoned restraint.

Secondly, the Conservative government introduced a voluntary and temporary wage 'pause' in 1956; but lacking trade union support, it was not successful. It then set up an advisory body, the Council on Prices, Productivity and Incomes, composed entirely of independent persons, which issued 4 general reports in 1958, 1959 and 1960. Thirdly in 1961, the government again failed to win union support for a wage 'pause'. And in 1962, it established a new independent advisory body, the National Incomes Commission which could make enquiries and issue reports on specific pay agreements referred to it by the

---

[1]   ECE, *Incomes in Post War Europe: A Study of Policies, Growth and Distribution,* UN, Geneva, 1967, Chap. 3, p. 18.

[2]   Lerner, Cable and Gupta (editors), *Workshop Wage Determination,* Pergamon Press, to be published 1969.

government. Lacking union cooperation, NIC was powerless to influence pay movements in private manufacturing.

Then in 1964, the new Labour government secured the support of the TUC and the employers' associations for an incomes policy to complement a policy for a faster rate of growth. In December 1964 both sides of industry and the government signed a joint declaration of intent on productivity, prices and incomes. And in February 1965, the government set up the National Board for Prices and Incomes (which replaced NIC) to implement a prices and incomes policy by examining and reporting on selected cases, referred to it by the government. The NBPI was to review cases of increases in pay or prices, whether proposed or already agreed upon, in the light of a 'norm' and certain criteria proposed by the government.[1]

In April 1965 a White Paper on Prices and Incomes Policy[2] outlined the criteria to be adopted by the Board and by employers and unions in their negotiations. Less regard was to be paid to such factors as comparisons with levels or trends of incomes in other employments, and greater regard was to be paid to an 'incomes norm'. The norm of 3-3½% was set. Exceptional wage increases above the norm were permitted in four types of cases:

> 'where it is essential in the national interest to secure a change in the distribution of manpower (or to prevent a change which would otherwise take place)'; 'where there is widespread recognition that the pay of a certain group of workers has fallen seriously out of line with the level of renumeration for similar work'; 'where there is general recognition that existing wages and salary levels are too low to maintain a reasonable standard of living'; and 'where the employees concerned, for example by accepting more exacting work or a major change in working practices, make a direct contribution towards increasing productivity in the particular firm or industry. Even in such cases some of the benefit should accrue to the community as a whole in the form of lower prices.'

Then in November 1965 the government established a 'voluntary' early warning system,[3] as a prelude to a compulsory one; henceforth, the TUC and employers' associations were to notify the government of pending increases in prices or wages to give the government time to consider these decisions before they were put into effect. The TUC established a special committee to examine pay claims. Unions were expected to refrain from pursuing a claim until they heard the TUC's views, which might take up to five weeks. The TUC referred a small number of important cases to special panels for further discussion with the union concerned. The remainder received the TUC's approval plus a reminder of the criteria of incomes policy. Unions not affiliated to the TUC and employers were to notify the Ministry of Labour of proposed increases.

Between July 1965 and July 1966, Britain's economic difficulties, particularly her balance of payments problem remained the dominant influence on collective bargaining. Nevertheless, and despite efforts to reduce home demand, unemployment continued at lower levels. The percentage unemployed fell from 1.5 in December 1964 to 1.2 in July 1965 to 1.1 in July, 1966. The index of weekly wage rates (1956 = 100) for all industries and services rose from 147.1 in July 1965 to 154.5 in July 1966 while the index of average earnings of all employees (1963 = 100) rose from 114.4 to 121.9 during the same period.[4]

The government eventually introduced strong deflationary measures and in July 1966 a price and wage stand-still.[5] The stand-still was to last for one year: during the first half-

---

1 *Machinery of Prices and Incomes Policy, Cmnd. 2577.*
2 *Prices and Incomes Policy, Cmnd. 2639.*
3 *Prices and Incomes Policy: 'An Early Warning System', Cmnd. 2808.*
4 See Appendix Table 12 p. 245.
5 *Prices and Incomes Stand-still, Cmnd. 3073.*

year, from 20 July 1966 to 20 January 1967, there was a freeze on all prices and all personal incomes; during the second half, from 20 January to 20 July 1967, there existed a period of severe restraint. The implementation of all agreements negotiated on or before 20 July 1966 was deferred for six months. The freeze applied to increases in *rates of pay* and to reductions in working hours, but not to other conditions of service except in so far as they were likely to add significantly to labour costs. However the freeze did not apply to:

(a)   Increases in payments made in compensation for expenditure incurred (e.g. travel allowances);

(b)   Increases resulting directly from increased output, e.g. piece-work;

(c)   Increases genuinely resulting from promotion to work at a higher level, whether with the same or a different employer;

(d)   Increases under normal arrangements for increasing pay with age, as with apprentices or juveniles, or by means of regular increments of specified amounts within a predetermined range or scale.

Then in August 1966, the Prices and Incomes Act 1966 was passed which gave the government compulsory powers to enforce its stand-still and restraint policies. The Act provided a statutory basis for the NBPI Part II contained a compulsory 'early warning' system with penalties for failure to comply and a means of delaying implementation of settlement. Part IV empowered Ministers to make Orders directing that specified prices or pay should not be increased and that unjustified price or pay increases which had been implemented since 20 July 1966 could be reversed; Orders under Part IV were signed 14 times. The Act also provided for the deferment of the dates on which Wages Council Wage Regulation Orders become effective. It protected employers from legal action if they withheld pay increases in accordance with the government's policy. Employers could be fined for paying disapproved pay increases or charging disapproved price increases. Unions could also be fined for inducing employers to contravene an order. Provision was made in the Act to 'activate' the compulsory sections, including the compulsory early warning system only by Order. The government wanted to continue the 'voluntary' incomes policy, but passed this Act so that compulsion could be used if needed. The powers under this Act were to end in August 1967.

A White Paper[1] in November 1966 set forth the policies during the period of severe restraint. The incomes norm was zero, but pay increases were permitted for increased efficiency, for need to improve the living standards of low-paid workers and for acute labour shortages. The operative dates of agreements which were due to be implemented in the first six months of 1967 were deferred to 1 July 1967, unless they satisfied the criteria for the period of severe restraint. The paper drew attention to the adverse economic effects of shortening the intervals between successive pay claims and declared that twelve months should be the minimum period between claims.

There were not many known attempts to countervene the stand-still and restraint policies. In any case, growing unemployment made the government's task easier. Between July 1966 and July 1967 unemployment grew from 1.1% to 2.1% and in August rose to 2.4%; the July and August 1967 totals were the highest for those months since 1940. The index of weekly wages rates for all industries and services (1956 = 100) rose from 154.5 in July 1966, the start of the 'freeze', to 155.6 in January 1967, the start of the period of restraint; during this latter period, it rose to 157.5 in June and then jumped to 160.0 in July 1967 when some of the deferred settlements were paid. The index of average earnings for employees in all industries and services (seasonally adjusted, Jan. 1966 = 100) rose from 103.4 in July 1966 to 105.3 in June 1967 to 106.0 in July 1967; this was a smaller increase than in previous years, partly due to short-time working and partly to the effects of a shorter working week and to the government's policy. However, from

---

[1]   *Prices and Incomes Standstill: Period of Severe Restraint,* Cmnd. 3150.

January 1967 to November 1967 the earnings index rose by 7.3%. In the meanwhile, the retail price index rose from 116.6 in July 1966 to 119.2 in July 1967.

In a White Paper, *Prices and Incomes Policy after 30 June 1967*[1], the government outlined its plans for a return to a voluntary incomes policy. In judging references to it, the NBPI again would rely on the criteria contained in the April 1965 White Paper *(Cmnd. 2639);* the main difference being that under the new criteria, the norm would be zero. The paper repeated the principle (contained in *Cmnd. 3150*) that twelve months should be regarded as the minimum period which should normally elapse between the operative dates of successive improvements for any group of workers, and added that the parties concerned should not seek to make good increases foregone as a result of the stand-still and severe restraint. The Paper made clear that Part IV of the Prices and Incomes Act 1966 would elapse on 11 August 1967. But after noting that the CBI and TUC had urged a return to full reliance on a voluntary policy, the government also made clear that it proposed to activate Part II of the 1966 Act before Part IV lapsed.

On 1 August 1967 the Prices and Incomes Act 1967 became law and contained the provisions mentioned above in *Cmnd. 3235.* From Part II of the 1966 Act, employers must notify the Minister of Labour of claims and employers and unions must notify him of settlements within seven days subject to penalties of £50 for failing to do so. The Act gave the government a delaying power which enabled it to hold up a proposed pay or price increase for up to seven months subject to a reference to the NBPI. In the first month, the government must decide if it intends to refer the case to the NBPI. If a reference is made, then there is a stand-still for three months, or earlier if the NBPI reports earlier. If the NBPI finds against the proposal, the government may then hold it up for a further three months. Then even though the NBPI has found against a proposed pay increase; there is nothing to prevent the retrospective payment of the increases. In short, under the 1967 Act, the government may delay a wage increase, but it cannot prevent the increase from taking place. However, employers who implement a settlement when forbidden under the Act shall be liable on summary conviction on indictment to a fine which shall not exceed £500. Also any union or other person who induces a strike to compel an employer to implement a settlement which is forbidden under the Act's delaying powers could also be fined up to £500.

The TUC disagrees with some details of the criteria in the government's present incomes policy, and adopted its own standards in 'vetting' claims.[2] The TUC regards anyone paid less than £15 a week as a low-paid worker. It therefore urges unions in their wage claims to aim at raising national minimum rates progressively to a level of £15 a week; claims of £1 for workers paid less than £14 a week is compatible with the TUC's incomes policy, providing that the full increases are applicable only to those who are on or near the existing minimum, with tapering increases to those whose current earnings (excluding overtime) are not more than £15 a week. The General Council of the TUC also thinks that the government's criteria governing productivity agreements (see the next section) are too rigid, and in exceptional circumstances will use comparability as a criteria. Where unions can show that there has been a sharp rise in profits or dividends, the TUC will take this into account when assessing claims. It urges affiliated unions to notify it of claims before they are submitted to employers and of settlements as soon as they are reached.

The TUC was also critical of the NBPI's role. The General Council's Report to the 1967 Congress in September states that ' . . . the Government had shown an undue propensity to elevate the board to a much more central role in the development and operation of incomes policy than had originally been envisaged by the TUC when it agreed to the establishment of the board, and the Government should be pressed to

---

[1] *Cmnd. 3235.*
[2] *Incomes Data,* Report 22, May 1967. It should be noted that the TUC's policy is applied to claims, not settlements.

modify their undue reliance on the Board as the chosen instrument of incomes policy'. Subsequently, the TUC and CBI expressed their joint anxiety that the NBPI showed signs of extending into fields that were none of its business, such as fiscal and economic policy.[1]

Nevertheless, after devaluation the TUC General Council reaffirmed its support for the continuation of the incomes policy and accepted that an increase of 3½% in prices as a direct result of devaluations should not be regarded as a justification for increased pay. However, various pressures have built up within the TUC to break with the zero norm. For example, in January 1968 the Confederation of Shipbuilding and Engineering Unions catering for over three million workers applied for a 'substantial increase', and the election of Hugh Scanlon to the Presidency of the Amalgamated Union of Engineers and Foundry Workers may tilt the balance at the 1968 TUC conference to a far more critical approach to the incomes policy.

In the meanwhile, in April 1968, the Government issued another White Paper[2] which presented its policy for 1968 and 1969. It set a ceiling of 3½% per year on all increases in wage and salary earnings. The ceiling applies to all increases in basic pay rates, scales, ranges and allowances, in overtime rates and shift work rates, and in improvements in fringe benefits, normal or standard hours or holiday entitlements. However, it excluded from this ceiling the same exceptions as those stipulated in *Cmnd. 2639*. Twelve months should elapse between the operative dates of successive settlements. The policy should apply to charges and fees of self-employed persons and to company directors 'and others' salaries which are not fixed by collective bargaining.

The White Paper further asserts that company dividends should be limited to not more than 3½% above the amount of ordinary dividends declared in respect of the preceding account year or the account year before that; or where dividends in each of the last two account years were abnormally low, and subject to examination and approval by the Treasury, not more than the amount in respect of an earlier account year. This requirement affects all companies incorporated in the UK with the exception of unit trusts, investment trusts, those close companies which increase distributions to meet the requirements of the Finance Act 1965, and companies wholly owned by other companies where ordinary dividend payments are exclusively inter-company transactions.

II.6   The Criteria of the NBPI

By the end of December 1967, the NBPI had published fifty reports (over half dealt with wages and salaries) including two general reports. The various White Papers and Acts previously mentioned laid down the guidelines which the NBPI was expected to follow. But within this framework, the NBPI's application of the guidelines and its proposals for the future add up to a series of short-run and long-run criteria.

The Low Paid Worker

The NBPI's Second General Report stated:

'The second justification under the Present White Paper[3] for an exception to the nil norm is on behalf of the low paid. We have found this criterion extremely difficult to apply. Clearly anyone whose pay is scarcely above the level of national assistance is low paid. By and large, however, the concept of the low paid is a relative rather than an absolute one: the most that can be said in most cases—and even this is difficult—is that pay is too low, or alternatively too high, in relation to somebody else's. What is at issue, therefore, is the question of differentials. If pay increases are

---

[1]   *Incomes Data,* Report 31, Oct. 1967.

[2]   *Cmnd. 3590.*

[3]   *Prices and Incomes Standstill: Period of Severe Restraint Cmnd. 3150.*

confined to those at the bottom of the scale, there may be no incentive to others to acquire the necessary qualifications and skills needed to supervise them'.[1]

In the reference of the Agricultural Wages Board's proposals, the issues were clear since agricultural workers are among the lowest-paid workers. The agricultural workers' increase was therefore approved.[2] However, complex problems arose when a proposal by the Retail Drapery Wages Council[3] for an increase in the statutory minimum rates by 15s. for males and 12s. 6d. for females was referred to the NBPI. The NBPI conducted its own sample survey among employees in multiple chain stores to ascertain their distribution of earnings, hours and fringe benefits but used the Ministry of Labour's figures for independent drapery shops. The survey revealed a considerable dispersion in earnings and that the majority of drapery workers earned more than their statutory minimum rates. Adult male drapery workers (excluding managers) earned about £4 less than the average earnings of male manual workers generally, but this differential was largely composed of overtime and shift work, payments which the drapery worker did not receive. When male drapery workers were compared with male clerical workers, however, earnings levels were approximately the same. Adult female drapery workers (excluding managers) earned almost as much as female manual workers and over £2 a week less than female clerks. However, a comparison of the distribution of drapery workers' earnings and those in other industries showed that at all levels of earnings below £15 there were larger proportions of male workers in drapery than elsewhere.

The NBPI found that the minority whose pay was no higher than the statutory minimum were among the lowest paid in the country, although the majority were not 'low paid'. Therefore, it proposed that the statutory minimum rates should be raised, but that tapered increases should be awarded giving most to those with the lowest *earnings* and least or nothing to those with relatively higher earnings. The NBPI further proposed a reduction in the size of the wage rate increases proposed by the Wages Councils.

When considering the NBPI report, the Wages Council found that even if it had wanted to do so, its terms of reference prevented it from carrying out the recommendations. A Wages Council may propose increases in the statutory minimum rates; it has no control over rates paid above the statutory minimum and hence, no control over increases applied to earnings. In any case, the Wages Council disagreed with the lower increase recommended and reaffirmed its original decision. Under the terms of the Wages Council Act, 1959, if a Wages Council reaffirms its original decision after it had been referred back by the Minister of Labour, the Minister has no other alternative than to make the new Wages Council Wage Regulation Order. Subsequently, the NBPI referred the problem of the terms of references of Wages Councils to the Royal Commission on Trade Unions and Employers' Associations.

Cost of Living

The NBPI has argued in a number of cases (e.g. in the printers', busmen's, electricity supply workers' and Midland bank staffs cases) that

'an increase in the cost of living does not itself constitute a justification in terms of the White Paper for an acceptable pay increase . . . one of the purposes of the productivity, prices and incomes policy is to bring about greater stability in the cost of living. If the cost of living is rising because earnings are increasing faster than productivity, and if, every time the cost of living goes up, earnings also go up, prices and incomes will chase each other in an endless spiral. We would recom-

---

[1] *Second General Report July 1966 to August 1967.* Report No. 40. *Cmnd. 3394.*
[2] *Cmnd. 3199,* Report No. 28. Jan. 1967.
[3] Report No. 27 *Pay of Workers in the Retail Drapery, Outfitting and Footwear Trades. Cmnd. 3224.* March, 1967.

mend therefore that in future the cost of living should be given less weight than has in the past been customary in the settlement of bank salaries'.[1]

However, when dealing with the problem of pay differentials between London and the rest of the country, of the non-industrial civil service, the NBPI stated:

'In our view, the most appropriate bases for London weighting in the Civil Service and in other employments is that for which London weighting was originally introduced for the Civil Service—namely, to compensate for the higher cost of living in London as compared with the rest of the country'.[2]

It appears that while the NBPI will not recommend a general pay increase on the increased cost of living argument, it is willing to approve an increase of pay to a particular group in an area based on the greater cost of living in that area as compared with other areas. Be that as it may, the TUC has stated on numerous occasions that if the cost of living was permitted to increase rapidly, it would be unable to urge unions to moderate their wage claims.

Labour Shortage

In the light of the government's proposals, the NBPI does not approve of pay increases on the ground that a firm is faced with a labour shortage. It maintains:

'that the desirable course for an employer faced with a tight labour market is to utilise the labour already at his command more economically thus increasing productivity and relating wage costs more closely to productivity. If instead he merely seeks to outbid his competitors, he would be exposed to retaliation from them. This retaliation will negate his initial action and will bring about no increase in productivity'.[3]

In its pre-freeze report on the pay of London busmen, the NBPI refused to approve a pay increase above the 3-3½% norm even though there existed an acute shortage of London busmen, unless the busmen's productivity increased. It claimed:

'In an era of general labour shortage, a pay increase has to be very large if it is to be effective. And a very large increase in pay in a labour intensive industry such as the bus industry, without an equivalent increase in productivity, would hasten its contraction'.[4]

The same formula was applied in the reports on the London Weighting in the Non-Industrial Civil Service (*Cmnd. 3436*), on Fire Service Pay (*Cmnd. 3287*) and on the Salaries of Staff employed by the General Accident Fire and Assurance Corporation Ltd. (*Cmnd. 3398*), amongst others.

On the other hand, the NBPI may have contradicted this formula when dealing with the Pay of the Higher Civil Service (Cmnd. 2822). The gap between Assistant Secretaries and Under-Secretaries has narrowed over the years. The NBPI approved, among other things, of an above-the-norm salary increase for Under-Secretaries of 11.7% or an addition of £550 per annum to a £5,250 salary. The NBPI claimed:

'We consider in the light of this evidence, that the salary structure of the Administrative Class must be improved if the Civil Service is to compete fairly with others for its share of talented people . . . '[5]

---

[1]   *Cmnd. 2839.* para. 28
[2]   *Cmnd.* Nov. 1967, para. 45.
[3]   Report No. 40, *Second General Report July 1966 to August 1967 Cmnd. 3394,* August 1967, para. 15.
[4]   *Cmnd. 3012,* para. 64.
[5]   *Cmnd. 2822,* para. 14, January 1966.

The very large pay increase proposed for Under-Secretaries was in recognition of their greater responsibilities as compared with Assistant Secretaries from whom they are recruited, but above-norm increases were also proposed for other grades. The report suggests there had been a high turnover among Under-Secretaries, but does not give evidence of any shortage of qualified applicants to fill the vacated posts. The proposed increase to Under Secretaries was an addition to their transfer earnings. Since turnover among the other grades is not particularly high and since there is not absolute shortage of recruits to the Higher Civil Service, the proposed increases to these other grades are entirely quasi-rents. Why the Higher Civil Service may compete for personnel while private industry may not, was not stated; nor was it stated why the Higher Civil Service required a pay improvement in order to compete for personnel when it suffered no shortage of qualified recruits.

Inter-Industry Comparability

The NBPI has claimed:

'The social case for special treatment for particular groups of workers who have fallen behind in pay has led to the multiplication of such formulas . . . automatically linking their pay increases to pay increases elsewhere. Most of the formulas are open to criticisms that the choice of some of the comparisons is not easily justified, and the use of wage rates rather than earnings means that the formulas do not guarantee that the pay of the workpeople concerned will in fact be kept in line with the pay of those with whom comparison is made. All of them provide a mechanism for spreading increases in wage rates from one group to another, regardless of the reasons for which the original increases were given . . . For this reason, where such formulas have come to our attention, we have recommended that they should no longer be used'.[1]

However, when dealing with the pay of government employees, the NBPI has had no alternative except to examine whether their pay was comparable with someone else's. For example, the NBPI accepted the findings of the biennial pay body for the Armed Forces which compares the Armed Forces pay with a broad average of pay outside the services.[2] Further, such comparisons have thrown open the question of altering the terms of the Fair Wages Resolution of the House of Commons, 1946, whose purpose was to ensure that workers employed on government contracts or by the government would receive pay comparable with their counterparts in private industry. In determining the pay of Industrial Civil Servants (*Cmnd. 3034*), the NBPI found the Fair Wages Resolution system failed to perform its expected task because comparisons were made of wage rates and not of earnings; the industrial workers in private industry had a large superstructure added to their rates while the industrial civil servants were underpaid and had difficulties in recruiting and retaining staff.

Internal Differentials

The NBPI asserted:

'The Board's general approach to the whole problem of pay has been to try and loosen the relationship between pay within a factory or an industry and the pay thought to be paid elsewhere . . . The Board has instead tried to substitute for this loosened relationship between internal pay and what is thought to be external pay, a closer relationship between internal pay and internal performance'.[3]

In every case where differentials between workers and supervisors had been squeezed

---

[1] Cmnd. 3087, para 62.
[2] Report No. 10 *Armed Forces Pay*, Jan. 1966.
[3] *Cmnd. 3394*, para. 52.

as a result of the former having secured pay increases, the NBPI has recommended similar increases to the latter

The NBPI claims that 'one of the purposes of an incomes policy is to narrow differentials when they are too large, but also to enlarge them where they are too low'.[1] However, the problem remains of the criteria employed to determine what differentials are too wide or too narrow. In the electricity supply industry, the manual and technical workers had received considerable pay increases as a result of their Staff Status and Productivity Agreements in 1964-5. Therefore, the clerical and administrative grades claimed increases because of the effect of the increase of others on their own internal position. The NBPI recognised the clerks were 'disturbed' and approved of the additional 'disturbance' money awarded to them.[2]

In many cases, the NBPI has suggested that pay differentials should be related to the gradations of job evaluation schemes. Job evaluation, when studied carefully and with adequate consultation and negotiation with the workpeople concerned, can produce wage or salary structures in which employees believe their pay differentials are 'fair' even when they are disturbed about their absolute levels of pay. Therefore it is often a useful method of solving internal differential problems. However, a too slavish adherence to a pay structure based on a national job evaluation scheme in a firm with works in different parts of the country may reduce the firm's ability to recruit or to retain certain types of labour in tight local labour markets, i.e. it may reduce management's ability to cope with pay problems produced by external labour market pressures.

Productivity and Pay

The NBPI clearly explained in Report No. 23 its policy on Productivity and Pay during the period of severe restraint in 1967:

'To qualify for an increase above the nil norm both a productivity agreement and a new scheme of payments by results would need careful preparation and would need to meet the following requirements:

(i)   It must be shown that the workers are making a direct contribution towards increasing productivity by accepting more exacting work or a major change in working practices.

(ii)   Forecasts of increased productivity must be devised by the application of proper work-standards.

(iii)   An accurate calculation of the gains and costs must show that the total cost per unit of output, taking into account the effect on capital, will be reduced.

(iv)   The scheme should contain effective controls to ensure that the projected increase in productivity is achieved, and that payment is made only as productivity increases or as changes in working practice take place.

(v)   There should be a clear benefit to the consumer, in lower prices or in improved equality. In some instances, 'lower prices' may mean prices lower than they would have been if the undertaking can prove that factors outside its control would otherwise have led to higher prices.

(vi)   An agreement covering part of a plant must bear the cost of consequential increases elsewhere in the plant, if any have to be granted.

(vii)   In all cases negotiators must beware of setting extravagant levels of pay which would provoke resentment outside.'

The TUC was dissatisfied with these criteria and claimed they were 'a mixture of apparent precision and actual vagueness, the total effect of which might cause negotiators to conclude that productivity bargaining is not worth while'. Some specific points made

---

[1]   *Cmnd. 3394,* para. 52.
[2]   *Cmnd. 3394,* para. 56.

by the General Council were: (a) In some cases such as maintenance work an indirect contribution might have a crucial effect on productivity: 'more exacting work' appeared to be a precise phrase but its meaning was not clear—did it imply greater physical effort, more effective use of effort, or both? (b) Requirements (iii) (iv) and (v) implied that the bargain must be 'hard' in the sense that payment should be commensurate with the value of productivity gains (expressed in unit costs) actually achieved after the effect on capital had been taken into account, and made as they were achieved. In many cases this was not possible simply because the available techniques could not give the required degree of accuracy. Moreover, 'the effect on capital' would depend on decisions about the time over which the cost of new equipment is spread. (c) If the criteria were interpreted too rigidly, they would put out of count those agreements the initial purpose of which is to engender a general atmosphere of co-operation as a necessary preliminary to improving productivity.[1]

In Report No. 36 *Productivity Agreements* in June 1967[2] the NBPI surveyed the value of the productivity agreements referred to it and introduced the new guidelines to govern the acceptability of such agreements in the post-severe restraint period. These guidelines are different from the previous ones in the following respects: wherever the word 'must' is used in the earlier guidelines, the work 'should' is now employed. The fifth criteria is altered to read: '(v) The undertaking should be ready to show clear benefits to the consumer through a contribution to stable prices'. The word 'plant' in criteria (vi) is changed to 'enterprise'. Instead of demanding accurate forward estimates of potential savings based on work study, the new criteria require 'appropriate standards of work study'. In place of insistence on some cost reduction from every agreement it is now said only that a reduction should usually result. The TUC General Council claimed that these changes go 'some way to modify the rigid language used in the earlier report'.[3]

The first criterion that an exceptional pay increase should be given only to those who contribute directly to increased productivity creates anomalies between those who are in a position to increase output and those who cannot. As in the engineering clerks' case, the latter may become disturbed by the effects of the agreement on their relative pay position. However, the NBPI provides for this problem in criteria (vi) in so far as an agreement covering part of a plant must bear the cost of consequential increases elsehwere in the plant, if any have to be granted. But it could come to pass that those who contribute directly to increased productivity become disturbed because while their own increases were based on their working harder, the increases to others were not so based.

Another problem is beginning to arise. In 1964-5, before the formation of the NBPI, a productivity agreement was signed in the Electricity Supply Industry which, in addition to other things, assured management that labour would co-operate with it in changing former manning practices. In September 1967 the NBPI approved an increase for the same workers who entered into another productivity agreement in which they promised to co-operate with management's attempts to introduce work study. The employees claimed that co-operation would be withdrawn if the pay increase was not forthcoming. It seems that management was forced to buy co-operation twice. However, the NBPI felt the employees were justified in their claim because their earnings failed to increase during the intervening years as much as the generality of workers who had not enetered into such agreements.

In addition to encouraging productivity agreements, the NBPI has urged work study and more accurate setting of rates and measurement of work times in incentive payment schemes. In almost all pay references the NBPI has made some suggestion on how to improve labour utilisation; and in almost all the other references suggestions to improve the efficiency of the firm were made. Further, in many pay reports, the Board

---

1   General Council Report: *TUC Report,* 1967. pp. 289-91.
2   Cmnd. 3311.
3   *Op. cit.*

has suggested changes in the actual machinery of negotiation. Whether any or all of the particular suggestions in particular cases are desirable and/or feasible will not be commented upon here. However, it appears that the NBPI has interpreted its terms of reference very widely and assumes for itself an expert knowledge of a very large range of industries and labour markets.

III   HOUSING AND RENTS

III.1 Increasing the Stock of Housing

The government, in its housing programme for 1965 to 1970[1] set itself a target of building 500,000 new houses a year by 1970 in Great Britain to increase our present stock of 17.7 millions of dwellings. It estimated that the country needs about one million houses to replace the unfit ones already identified as slums, up to two million more to replace old houses not yet slums but not worth improving, and about 700,000 to overcome shortages and provide a margin for mobility. In addition, it estimated that we need to build 30,000 houses a year to replace the loss caused by demolition and 150,000 a year to keep up with new households being formed in the rising population.

Is it likely that this target will be reached? To answer this question, let us first look at the increase in house-building since 1965.[2] In 1965, 382.3 thousand dwellings (houses and flats) were completed in Great Britain, of which 213.8 thousand were completed in the private sector and 168.5 thousand in the public sector. These figures rose in 1966 to a total of 385.5 thousand but private dwellings fell to 205.4 thousand while publicly-owned dwellings increased by 180.1 thousand. Dwellings completed increased by 0.9% between 1965 and 1966; but the compound annual rate of increase required to reach the 1970 target from 1965 is 5½% a year. Dwellings completed in the last three-quarters of 1967 (the last available figures) showed a 3% increase over the comparable period in 1966. Although the annual rate of increase of housing completions appears to be rising, it does not seem to be rising fast enough to reach the proposed target.

In any case, the government, as part of its post-devaluation cuts in public expenditure, decided to reduce approved local authority building programmes by 15,000 houses in England and Wales during the next two financial years, 1968-9 and 1969-70. This is unlikely to prevent the total dwellings completed in 1968 being greater than the expected 1967 total for England and Wales of over 400,000. However, what happens after 1968 depends on how fast private housing investment rises. Nevertheless, it is now highly likely that total local authority dwellings built in 1970 in England and Wales will be closer to 220,000 than to the formerly planned estimate of 250,000.

One of the chief limitations in increasing the number of houses built each year is the existing capacity of the construction industry. Roughly 40% of the industry is engaged in the housing sector and about two-thirds of the workers in this sector are engaged in new house-building. Between 1961 and 1964 the annual increase in new house-building averaged about 20,000 a year; but 'this increase was not achieved without considerable overheating of the construction industries and the consequent slowing down of completions owing to shortage of labour and materials'.[3] However, since 1964, while there has been a larger annual increase in new houses completed, the labour force in this sector has tended to decline. The labour force in the construction industry engaged on building new houses declined between 1962 and 1963, increased to a peak of 357,000 operatives in 1964 and then fell to 354,000 in 1965 and to 342,000 in 1966. The greater output per worker is partly a statistical illusion caused by the growth in the application

---

[1] *Cmnd. 2838*, November, 1965.
[2] *Housing Statistics*, Great Britain No. 7, Oct. 1967.
[3] *Cmnd. 2838*.

of industrial techniques in house-building. Industrialised dwellings as a percentage of all dwellings completed by local authorities and new town authorities increased from 14.4% in 1964 to 19.2% in 1965 to 26.3% in 1966.[1] All workers who 'manufacture' houses or parts of houses are not included in the statistics relating to new house-building in the construction industry.

III.2 Improvements to Existing Houses

In addition to building new houses to increase the stock of dwellings, the quality of the existing stock may be improved. 'Improvement' as defined in the Rent Act, 1965, 'includes structural alterations, extension or addition and the provision of additional fixtures or fittings, but does not include anything done by way of decoration or repair'. The government encourages improvement in many ways.

The Housing Act, 1964, assigns to local authorities the duty to inspect dwellings in their districts and to establish improvement areas in neighbourhoods which contain dwellings lacking one or more of the standard amenities but which are so constructed that it is practicable to improve at least half of them to full standard so that they will be fit for human habitation for at least fifteen years. In these areas the local authorities have power to compel landlords to improve their property to full standards. If a tenant gives his written consent to such improvements the authority may give notice to the landlord to improve the dwelling within twelve months. However, if the Rent Bill of December, 1967, is passed, the landlord will be able to increase the rent under controlled tenancies from 8% to 12½% for improvements, but the tenant will have the right to challenge the amount of expenditure on improvements. Where the tenant fails to give his written consent under the 1964 Act, the authority may give notice to the landlord to make certain improvements when there has been a change of tenant. Local authorities are further empowered to compel improvements to a dwelling outside an improvement area if the tenant makes a written request to the authority. From July 1964 to June 1967, work was completed in 1,685 compulsorily improved dwellings and 7,031 preliminary[2] notices were served requesting improvements under the terms of the 1964 Act. Under earlier Acts, approved improvement grants in 1966 were given to local authorities for 30,239 dwellings and to private owners and housing associations for 77,481 or a total of 107,720 dwellings.

A landlord who is liable to incur expenditure in complying with an improvement notice may apply to the local authority for a loan. The 1964 Act also provides for local authority grants to landlords of one half of the cost of improvements subject to an upper limits and under the Housing Subsidies Act, 1967, the government may subsidize conversion or improvements of dwellings let by housing associations or local authorities. The subsidy would be paid for twenty years after the improvements were made and would be equal to three-eights of the cost of the improvements and the expense of acquiring the property. However, the Minister should not pay a subsidy for improvements greater than two thousand pounds for each dwelling.

III.3 Housing Loans

Money loaned for house purchase, that is, a mortgage, is lent on the security of that property. The mortgagee holds the title deeds until the mortgagor pays off the loan. The three main lending institutions on long-term mortgages are building societies, local authorities and insurance companies, of which building societies are clearly the most important (see Table 5.13 below). Banks also lend money for house purchases, but

---

[1] Ministry of Housing and Local Government. *Housing Statistics,* Oct., 1967.
[2] *Housing Statistics,* Oct. 1967.

usually do so either for short-term loans or for up to only 50% of the purchase price and/or only against adequate security other than the house property.[1]

TABLE 5.13

Loans for House Purchase Institutional Sources, UK 1960-66

Numbers of Loans in Thousands

	Advances				Repayment of Principal			
	Building Society	Local Authorities	Insurance Companies	Total	Building Society	Local Authorities	Insurance Companies	Total
1960	558	78	—	636	318	36	—	354
1961	544	107R	—	651R	323	40R	—	363R
1962	618	94	118	830	342	47	57	446
1963	852	119	107	1078	430	60R	73	563R
1964	1,052	195R	132	1379	505	74R	79	658R
1965	965	239R	163	1367	506	86R	73	665R
1966	1,245	122R	147	1514	578	115R	87	780R

Source: Ministry of Housing and Local Government, *Housing Statistics,* Oct. 1967.
Note: R—Revised figure.

'The financial achievement which has enabled over 40 per cent[2] of all families to live in their own house is largely due to the building society movement',[3] claims a contemporary writer. Building society mortgages are usually for twenty to twenty-five years; but longer term mortgages on post-war property and to younger people may be made, as are shorter-term loans on older property. Mortgages are usually arranged so all repayments are made before the age of retirement of the mortgagor who in turn usually agrees to pay a regular sum each year for the period of the loan. A regular instalment, usually monthly, is composed of a changing combination of interest and principal. The interest predominates in the early years, steadily declines, and eventually becomes less than the principal in the total instalment payments. The interest paid can be set off against tax; these tax concessions benefit mortgagors whose incomes are expected to rise over the years, because the cost of the loan is much lower in the early years.[4] The building societies usually make their loan terms competitive vis-a-vis the landlord by setting them in relation to the mortgagor's ability to pay; when interest rates rise, the societies may lengthen the period of the loan to ensure that mortgagors continue to find the terms acceptable.[5] When building societies set rates, the determining factor, asserts Lionel Needleman, is the supply of funds; the demand for housing is not very sensitive to moderate variations in the cost of finance.[6]

Local authorities may borrow funds from the Public Works Loan Board on fixed terms to re-lend for house purchase. Usually the fixed interest rate to mortgagors is about ¼% above the fixed rate that the authority pays to the Board. Nevertheless, each authority sets its own lending terms and practices vary widely. While building societies may consider granting mortgages varying from 70% to 97% depending on the age of property, the most generous authorities may offer 100% mortgages, regardless of age. On the other hand, some authorities are far less generous than building societies.

Life insurance companies grant loans for house purchase on condition that the borrower takes out an endowment policy (which may be of the profit or non-profit variety) as well

[1]   A. S. Merrett and Allen Sykes, *Housing Finance and Development,* Longmans, Green & Co. Ltd., London 1965.
[2]   About 20% of all families own their own home and a further 20% are buying their homes.
[3]   Adela Adam Nevitt, *Housing, Taxation & Subsidies,* Nelson, 1966, p. 30.
[4]   Merrett & Sykes, *Ibid:* p. 32.
[5]   Newitt, *op. cit.*
[6]   Lionel Needleman, *The Economics of Housing,* Staples, 1965, p. 134.

as the loan. The borrower pays a premium on the policy; when the policy matures, it is used to pay off the loan. If the borrower dies before the policy matures, then the loan is paid off out of the death benefits. The borrower pays interest on the loan but does not repay the loan itself. According to Merrett and Sykes:

'Currently 40 per cent of the amount of the endowment policy premiums qualify for income tax relief, . . . plus the whole of the interest payments. As the endowment policy premiums are mainly an indirect form of loan repayment, it means in addition to the subsidy from the tax deductibility a 12½ per cent—15 per cent subsidy . . . is also given on the capital repayments. The latter element of subsidisation is not present in the loan repayments to any other lending institutions . . . '[1]

Another private source of housing finance is housing associations, which operate on a non-profit basis to build houses either for owner-occupation for their own members or for renting. Housing associations are recognized under the various housing acts which also empower local authorities to use them in slum-clearance programmes. To assist housing associations to provide housing accommodation, a Housing Corporation was established under the Housing Act, 1964. The Act gave the Corporation power to make loans to housing associations (subject to Treasury consent), to sell or lease land to associations, to compulsorily purchase land, and to provide housing accommodation in place of a housing association when the latter is experiencing difficulties.

III.4 Housing Subsidies

Local authority housing is heavily subsidized both by the Exchequer and from rates. Between 1956 and 1966 the central government's net housing subsidies to local authorities, public corporations, etc., increased from £76m to £108m per annum. In the same decade local authorities net housing subsidies to their own houses rose from £29m to £82m per annum (see Table 5.14). Thus the housing contribution made by local authorities has increased both proportionately and absolutely faster than the Exchequer's contribution.

One weakness of the Exchequer subsidy system to local authorities arises because different Housing Acts provide different subsidies for dwellings built at different periods. A local authority may pool all its exchequer subsidies and apply the total to all the dwellings in the housing account. Authorities frequently transfer subsidies under older acts for older houses and apply them to newer dwellings. However to bring forward a subsidy, the authority needs to build new houses. Those authorities which are not building new houses continue to receive subsidies for dwellings built at a fraction of the present cost of building even though the tenants may be able to afford to pay an unsubsidised rent. Those authorities which failed to build houses when the cost of building was cheaper may receive a subsidy which fails to bridge the gap between the rent for new houses determined by the market and the rent the new tenant may be able to afford. Consequently, some local authorities have more subsidy than they need and others have less.[2] Rural authorities and new town corporations with a relatively higher proportion of post-war dwellings need to charge higher rents than in urban areas, but incomes in rural areas are generally lower than in urban areas.[3]

Certain anomalies, however, will be corrected. The Housing Subsidies Act 1967 repealed sections of a variety of previous Acts. In place of the repealed sections, the 1967 Act gave the Minister the power to reduce, discontinue or transfer subsidies where the Minister is satisfied that the local authority has failed to discharge any of its duties under the Housing Acts 1957 to 1965.

---

[1] Merrett & Sykes, *Housing Finance and Development*, p. 33.
[2] Merrett & Sykes, *Ibid.*, Chap. 7.
[3] Merrett & Sykes, *Ibid.*, p. 17.

Social problems

TABLE 5.14

Housing Subsidies, UK, 1956-66 (Selected Years) £ million

	1956	1958	1960	1962	1964	1966
Central government						
Permanent housing						
Subsidies to local authorities	60	67	73	78	86	100
Subsidies to public corporations	4	4	6	7	7	8
Temporary housing						
Annuities	8	8	8	2	–	–
less receipts from local authorities	-2	-1	-2	-1	-1	-1
Emergency housing: net payments to						
local authorities	6	3	4	2	2	1
Net subsidies	76	81	89	88	94	108
Local authorities						
Emergency housing						
Expenses less rents, etc.	6	4	4	2	2	1
less receipts from central government	-6	-3	-4	-2	-2	-1
Other housing						
Loan charges	162	198	229	268	320	410
Payments to central government for						
temporary houses	2	1	2	1	1	1
Other expenses	69	74	83	101	116	140
less rents, etc.	-144	-178	-210	-253	-307	-369
less subsidies from central government	-60	-67	-73	-78	-86	-100
Net subsidies	29	29	31	39	44	82
Combined public authorities	105	110	120	127	138	190

Source: NIBB, 1967.

According to Adela A. Nevitt,[1] another weakness of the subsidy system arises because no account is taken of the different rates of interest paid by local authorities on their *total* debt. The current market rate of interest is the same for all authorities, but each authority's total debt is the result of borrowing over many years at different interest rates. 'The length of each loan will be as variable as the interest rate and in any particular year the average interest paid on the total debt is a reflection of past rather than current borrowing'.[2] Until 1967 the same subsidy was given to authorities regardless of their current financial situation. 'This is another causal factor in granting more subsidy than is needed to one authority while granting less than is needed to another'.[3]

Although the historic position cannot be altered, the future position of authorities' housing debts will change. The Housing Subsidies Act 1967 introduced a new basis for calculating the size of Exchequer subsidies to local authorities, development corporations and housing associations. For approved new dwellings the subsidies are the difference between twice the amount of instalments on a 60-year loan at the rate of interest prevailing when the dwelling was completed and what the instalment would have been if it had been calculated at the rate of 4% per annum. The Act also provided for additional subsidies where blocks of flats of four of more storeys are built. The Minister will pay for each of sixty years eight pounds for each four-storeys block, fourteen pounds for each five-storeys block and twenty-six pounds for each six or more storeys.

Assistance for private house purchase is also provided in the Housing Subsidies Act, 1967. The Option Mortgage scheme is designed to help people with moderate incomes who are buying their own houses. Interest on a mortgage is deducted from a mortgagee's income before his income tax is calculated. Mortgagees who pay tax at the full standard rate of 8s. 3d. in the £ get this tax relief at a higher rate than those who pay at only 6s. or

---

[1] Nevitt, *Housing, Taxation & Subsidies,* Chap. 7.
[2] *Loc. cit.* p. 93.
[3] *Loc. cit.*

4s. in the £ and those on low incomes who pay no income tax and get no tax relief. With an option mortgage, the mortgagee would lose the income tax relief, but part of the interest on the loan would be met by a government subsidy. If the mortgagee is entitled to tax relief at 8s. 3d. in the £ on all his interest, he would be better off with tax relief. However, if the mortgagee qualifies for the tax relief on his interest at only 6s. or 4s. in the £ or gets no tax relief, he would normally be better off with an option mortgage and the government subsidy.

III.5 Rents

Before the passage of the Rent Act, 1965, rents in the private sector of housing were (and to some extent still are) chaotic. Rents in over two million houses were controlled at levels fixed by the Rent Act, 1957. These were related to gross values applicable in 1957 and were completely out of step with increases in values since that date. Generally speaking, rent control legislation has failed to consider changing values, and this has caused a decay in the stock of houses for rent in the private sector. As Mr J. P. Macey pointed out, even within the group of controlled properties, there were a great many anomalies as between rents of dwellings which were otherwise very similar in size and amenity.[1] Rents not subject to control were tending to find 'reasonable' levels in areas where there was little excess demand for housing. However, where excess demand existed, a few landlords were charging 'exorbitant' rents and taking advantage of the tenants' lack of security of tenure.[2] The Rent Act, 1965, replaced the Rent Act, 1957, and applied to the tenancy of all dwelling-houses whose rateable value was not more than £400 in Greater London and £200 in the rest of England. The Act established registration areas and within these areas provided for the appointment of rent officers to keep registers of he rents paid under regulated tenancies of dwelling-houses, the particulars with regard to these tenancies and specifications of the houses. The amount to be registered as rent included any sums payable by the tenant to the landlord for the use of furniture or for services; in addition to the rent, the landlord might request the tenant to pay the rates.

The Lord Chancellor and the Minister of Housing appointed rent assessment committees in the registration areas whose duty is to handle appeals cases to determine if a rent is fair. In determining what rent is or would be a fair rent regard is had to the age, character and locality of the dwelling-house and to its state of repair. For the purpose of the determination it was assumed that the number of persons seeking to become tenants of similar dwelling-houses in the locality on the terms (other than those relating to rent) of the regulated tenancy was not substantially greater than the number of such dwelling-houses in the locality which were available for letting on such terms.

A Joint Working Party[3] established to assess 'Fair Rents' under the Rent Act, 1965, welcomed the fact that the Act did not try to lay down any exact method of assessment. 'It provides a flexible method, not tied to any formula, and thus gives scope for judgment and enables the Valuer to take account of the peculiarities of each individual letting. Furthermore, the Act makes it possible to adjust rents in the light of changing circumstances due to the passage of time or to physical changes in a particular property . . . The new legislation recognises that market rents, providing the market is free from Government or other intervention and providing there is a reasonable balance between supply and demand will often provide the best guide as to what is a "fair rent" as between landlord and tenant.'

The Working Party also found that rents in the public sector were not based upon any logical pattern and were often 'unfair' as between one municipal tenant and another,

---

[1]   J. P. Macey, 'Housing Policy and its Implications', *Housing,* May, 1967.
[2]   Joint Working Party Report on 'Fair Rents', *Housing,* March, 1967.
[3]   Established by the Royal Institution of Chartered Surveyors, the Chartered Auctioneers and Estate Agents' Institute, the Chartered Land Agents' Society and the Institute of Housing Managers.

either under the same local authority, or different authorities. 'These differences have nothing to do with the value of the house as a commodity let to the tenant but they arise from historical accidents concerned with the state of each local authority's housing revenue account and other factors'.[1] As mentioned in section III.4, some local authorities receive larger government housing subsidies than they need while others receive less than they need.

Before 1949 local authorities were required to charge rents which were reasonable by comparison with the local rents for working-class dwellings in the locality. The Housing Act, 1949, deleted the reference to working-class families and gave local authorities wider powers and enabled them to provide dwellings for any section of the population. The Act merely required authorities to set a reasonable rent. What does 'reasonable' mean in this context. Basing their conclusions on case law on the subject, the Working Party decided that 'reasonable' means: '(a) Reasonable as between one municipal tenant and another having regard to the location, size and amenity of the dwelling. (b) Reasonable in relation to the burden falling upon the tenant, the ratepayer and the tax payer. (c) Reasonable in relation to the rents of similar privately-owned dwellings occupied by similar groups of people'.[2] However, the Working Party found that few authorities sit down and review their rents from first principles, that the subject of rents gives rise to strong feelings, and that therefore anomalies remain.

At the time of writing it appears that more legislation on rents may be forthcoming.

If the Rent Bill introduced in the House of Lords in December 1967 becomes an Act, it will effect mortgagees and mortgagors of 'controlled'[3] and 'regulated'[4] mortgages. The Bill empowers county courts to mitigate hardship to mortgagors under 'regulated' mortgages. The court may by order limit the rate of interest, extend the time for the repayment of the principal or vary in other ways the terms of the mortgage. Further, under a 'controlled' mortgage sums paid in excess of the permitted rate of interest may be recovered.[5]

In the meanwhile, the passage of the Leasehold Reform Act, 1967, enables tenants of houses held on long leases at low rents to acquire the freehold or an extended lease. Low rent, in this Act, means a rent that is less than two-thirds of the rateable value of the property.

Tables 5.15 and 5.16 show that the popular belief that the relatively worse off sections of the population are housed in local authority dwellings and the financially better off may be found in the private sector is false. Indeed, Table 5.15 shows that there are more households with an income of less than £10 a week who rent unfurnished dwellings in the private than in the public sector. Further, Table 5.16 clearly demonstrates that for households with incomes of less than £40 a week, rent tends to be lower in the private than in the public sector. Only for household incomes of £40 or more is rent greater in local authority unfurnished dwellings than in privately rented dwellings. Of course, these figures do not tell us whether the standard of rented dwellings in the public and private sector for each household income is comparable. However, the figures indicate that to some extent our subsidies to local authorities are benefiting the relatively wealthy and do not benefit many relatively poor families.

---

[1]   *Loc. cit.,* p. 15.
[2]   *Loc. cit.*
[3]   A 'controlled' mortgage is a mortgage to which the Increase of Rent and Mortgage Interest (Restrictions) Act 1920 applied before the passage of this Act.
[4]   A 'regulated' mortgage is a legal mortgage of land which includes a dwelling-house which is subject to a regulated tenancy which is binding on the mortgagee.
[5]   The permitted rate of interest is 6½% per annum or 1% above the standard rate of interest, whichever is the less.

TABLE 5.15

Occupation of Different Types of Dwelling by Household Weekly Income, UK, 1966

	Under £6	£6 but under £10	£10 but under £15	£15 but under £20	£20 but under £25	£25 but under £30	£30 but under £40	£40 but under £50	£50 or more	All households
Local authority rented unfurnished	35	82	98	115	167	159	168	79	52	955
Other dwelling rented unfurnished	60	95	76	121	105	71	88	38	24	678
Rented furnished dwelling	5	7	14	18	24	15	12	6	6	107
Rent-free dwelling	6	12	19	20	17	15	10	6	2	107
Dwelling in process of purchase by occupier	1	7	17	62	116	146	217	97	115	778
Dwelling fully owned by occupier	36	82	99	80	92	72	77	46	65	649
Total (numbers)	143	285	323	416	521	478	572	272	264	3,274

Source: FES, 1967

TABLE 5.16

Average Rent (shillings per week) of Unfurnished Dwellings by Household Weekly Income, UK, 1966

	Under £6	£6 but under £10	£10 but under £15	£15 but under £20	£20 but under £25	£25 but under £30	£30 but under £40	£40 but under £50	£50 or more	All households
Local authority	29.25	33.76	37.48	41.19	44.75	46.20	47.88	47.69	54.87	43.65
Private	20.36	30.50	32.51	31.80	39.66	40.85	46.85	49.98	63.14	36.88
Total (average)	23.63	32.01	35.31	36.38	42.79	44.40	47.52	48.43	57.48	40.84

Source: FES, 1967

REFERENCES AND FURTHER READING

ECE, *Incomes in Post War Europe: A Study of Policies, Growth and Distribution*, UN, Geneva, 1967.

A. S. Merrett & Allen Sykes, *Housing Finance and Development*, Longmans, Green & Co. Ltd., London 1965.

A. A. Nevitt, *Housing, Taxation and Subsidies*, Nelson, London 1966.

Colin Clark and G. Stuvel, (eds.), *Income Redistribution and the Statistical Foundations of Economic Policy*, Bowes & Bowes, Cambridge, 1964.

A. R. Prest and T. Stark, 'Some Aspects of Income Distribution in the UK since World War II', *MS*, Sept. 1967.

Report of Committee on Higher Education, Cmnd. 2154 HMSO, 1963.

Ministry of Social Security, *Everybody's Guide to Social Security*, HMSO, 1967.

NBPI *Reports*

Royal Commission on Trade Unions and Employers' Associations, *Research Reports*.

B. C. Roberts (editor) *Industrial Relations: Contemporary Issues and Perspectives*, Methuen, 2nd edition, 1968.

TABLE A–1

UK De Facto or Home Population[1] 1953–67 Thousands

	United Kingdom			England and Wales			Wales	Scotland			Northern Ireland		
	Total	Males	Females	Total	Males	Females	Total	Total	Males	Females	Total	Males	Females
Census figures													
1951	50,225	24,118	26,107	43,758	21,016	22,742	2,599	5,096	2,434	2,662	1,371	668	703
1961	52,709	25,481	27,228	46,105	22,304	23,801	2,644	5,179	2,483	2,697	1,425	694	731
Mid-year estimates													
1953	50,592	24,317	26,276	44,109	21,206	22,903	2,596	5,099	2,436	2,664	1,384	675	709
1954	50,765	24,401	26,364	44,274	21,288	22,986	2,601	5,104	2,437	2,667	1,387	676	711
1955	50,947	24,510	26,436	44,441	21,389	23,052	2,603	5,112	2,442	2,669	1,394	679	715
1956	51,184	24,645	26,539	44,667	21,517	23,150	2,608	5,120	2,447	2,673	1,397	681	716
1957	51,430	24,779	26,651	44,907	21,648	23,259	2,611	5,125	2,450	2,675	1,398	681	717
1958	51,652	24,889	26,764	45,109	21,744	23,365	2,615	5,141	2,461	2,680	1,402	684	719
1959	51,956	25,044	26,912	45,386	21,885	23,501	2,622	5,162	2,473	2,689	1,408	686	722
1960	52,372	25,272	27,100	45,775	22,097	23,678	2,629	5,177	2,483	2,694	1,420	692	728
1961	52,816	25,534	27,282	46,205	22,353	23,852	2,635	5,184	2,485	2,699	1,427	696	732
1962	53,341	25,854	27,487	46,709	22,660	24,049	2,635	5,197	2,495	2,702	1,435	700	736
1963	53,678	26,038	27,640	47,028	22,834	24,194	2,663	5,205	2,499	2,705	1,446	705	741
1964	54,066	26,254	27,811	47,401	23,044	24,358	2,676	5,206	2,500	2,707	1,458	711	747
1965	54,436	26,441	27,995	47,763	23,227	24,536	2,693	5,204	2,497	2,707	1,469	716	753
1966	54,744	26,602	28,142	48,075	23,392	24,683	2,701	5,191	2,490	2,701	1,478	720	758
1967	55,068	26,778	28,290	48,391	23,562	24,828	n.a.	5,187	2,489	2,698	1,491	727	764

Sources: AAS, No. 103; MDS, No. 262

Note: [1] The de facto or home population relates to people actually in the country (excluding members of H.M. Forces serving overseas, while including Commonwealth and foreign forces in the UK).

TABLE A–2

UK Gross Domestic Product, Expenditure (at 1958 prices) 1952–67. £million

	Consumers' expenditure, durable goods	Consumers' expenditure, non-durable goods and services	Public authorities' current expenditure	Gross domestic capital formation, excluding dwellings	Dwellings	Value of physical increase in stocks and work in progress	Exports of goods and services	Total final expenditure at market prices	Adjustment to factor cost[1]	Imports of goods and services at factor cost	Gross domestic product at factor cost
1952	600	12,255	3,857	1,933	546	65	3,825	23,081	2,192	3,584	17,305
1953	775	12,658	3,962	2,037	711	135	3,985	24,263	2,282	3,867	18,114
1954	924	13,059	3,947	2,246	736	54	4,210	25,176	2,397	4,009	18,770
1955	1,018	13,533	3,832	2,461	689	313	4,470	26,316	2,493	4,413	19,410
1956	897	13,786	3,806	2,644	650	244	4,665	26,692	2,481	4,426	19,785
1957	1,005	13,994	3,751	2,848	621	250	4,784	27,253	2,538	4,537	20,178

1958	1,175	14,211	3,673	2,906	586	111	4,707	27,369	2,655	4,584	20,130
1959	1,409	14,697	3,744	3,094	674	179	4,834	28,631	2,918	4,886	20,827
1960	1,465	15,296	3,824	3,374	758	601	5,107	30,425	3,073	5,478	21,874
1961	1,419	15,737	3,964	3,711	813	335	5,259	31,238	3,109	5,444	22,685
1962	1,501	16,028	4,091	3,660	839	87	5,350	31,556	3,118	5,546	22,892
1963	1,833	16,541	4,153	3,722	857	221	5,580	32,907	3,318	5,753	23,836
1964	2,001	17,077	4,229	4,276	1,087	590	5,789	35,049	3,527	6,291	25,231
1965	1,952	17,445	4,374	4,465	1,110	365	6,065	35,776	3,508	6,371	25,897
1966	1,918	17,854	4,534	4,583	1,075	199	6,282	36,445	3,570	6,503	26,372
1967	2,021	18,141	4,735	4,791	1,171	96	6,276	37,231	3,700	6,878	26,653

Sources: NIBB various: *Preliminary Estimates of National Income and Balance of Payments 1962-67*, Cmnd. 3571; E.T., April 1968.

Note:[1] This represents taxes on expenditure less subsidies, valued at 1958 rates.

TABLE A–3

UK Personal Income, Expenditure and Saving 1952–67

	Personal income before tax						£m	Transfers abroad (net) and taxes paid abroad £m	UK taxes on income (payments) £m
	Total[1]	Wages and salaries	Forces' pay	Employers' contributions	Current grants from public authorities	Other personal income[1]			
1952	12,793	8,230	342	535	911	2,775	8		1,177
1953	13,568	8,700	349	585	1,002	2,932	-6		1,134
1954	14,343	9,310	363	611	1,021	3,038	-4		1,236
1955	15,571	10,210	356	678	1,115	3,212	9		1,330
1956	16,738	11,120	396	746	1,193	3,283	26		1,452
1957	17,652	11,770	392	806	1,252	3,432	28		1,602
1958	18,600	12,135	395	940	1,484	3,646	4		1,696
1959	19,694	12,715	389	993	1,636	3,961	8		1,776
1960	21,205	13,720	393	1,046	1,653	4,393	5		1,991
1961	22,908	14,835	385	1,167	1,802	4,719	1		2,249
1962	24,102	15,610	401	1,263	1,981	4,847	8		2,458
1963	25,497	16,355	419	1,371	2,234	5,118	22		2,510
1964	27,594	17,690	450	1,477	2,369	5,608	31		2,801
1965	29,950	19,000	467	1,667	2,734	6,082	42		3,373
1966	31,715	20,160	513	1,809	2,974	6,259	60		3,684
1967	33,100	20,830	512	1,923	3,355	6,480	74		4,034

Sources: NIBB 1967; *Preliminary Estimates of National Income and Balance of Payments 1962-67,* Cmnd. 3571; E.T., April 1968.

Notes: [1]Before providing for depreciation and stock appreciation.
[2]Before providing for additions to tax reserves.

National insurance and health contributions £m	Total personal disposable income £m	Consumers' expenditure				Balance (personal saving)[2]		Personal saving plus durable consumption
		Durable goods including tax		Other £m	Total £m			
		Amount £m	As % of PDI			Amount £m	As % of PDI	As % of PDI
476	11,132	579	5.20	10,187	10,766	366	3.30	8.51
525	11,915	714	5.99	10,761	11,475	440	3.62	9.61
532	12,579	837	6.65	11,327	12,164	415	3.25	9.90
594	13,638	934	6.85	12,179	13,113	525	3.86	10.71
642	14,618	884	6.05	12,945	13,829	789	5.40	11.45
657	15,365	1,005	6.54	13,594	14,599	766	4.99	11.53
859	16,041	1,175	7.33	14,211	15,386	655	4.08	11.41
897	17,013	1,379	8.11	14,817	16,196	817	4.80	12.91
913	18,296	1,420	7.76	15,586	17,006	1,290	7.05	14.81
1,072	19,586	1,388	7.09	16,529	17,917	1,669	8.52	15.61
1,197	20,439	1,464	7.16	17,502	18,966	1,473	7.21	14.37
1,303	21,662	1,677	7.74	18,464	20,141	1,521	7.02	14.76
1,444	23,318	1,844	7.91	19,648	21,492	1,826	7.83	15.74
1,685	24,850	1,837	7.39	20,995	22,832	2,018	8.12	15.51
1,797	26,174	1,830	6.99	22,314	24,144	2,030	7.76	14.75
1,900	27,092	1,950	7.20	23,218	25,168	1,924	7.10	14.30

TABLE A—4

Great Britain, Working Population, Unemployment etc. 1952–67 Thousands

	Total working population[1] (at June in each year)	Total in civil employment (at June in each year)	Estimated number of employees[2] (at June in each year)	HM Forces and Women's Services (at June in each year)	Registered unemployed (monthly average)	Wholly unemployed, excluding school leavers[3] (monthly average)	Unemployment rate[4] (per cent)	Unfilled vacancies (monthly average)
1952	23,294	22,119	20,800	880	414	325	2.0	275
1953	23,373	22,238	20,880	870	342	313	1.6	274
1954	23,725	22,662	21,190	845	285	266	1.3	329
1955	23,969	22,990	21,460	809	232	209	1.1	405
1956	24,156	23,200	21,700	767	257	226	1.2	357
1957	24,246	23,291	21,850	708	313	289	1.4	276
1958	24,117	23,129	21,820	620	457	402	2.1	198
1959	24,196	23,242	21,944	569	475	433	2.2	223
1960	24,526	23,711	22,326	518	360	337	1.6	314
1961	24,774	24,046	22,624	474	341	305	1.5	320

1962	25,059	24,245	22,944	442	463	419	2.0	214
1963	25,163	24,276	23,064	427	573	502	2.5	196
1964	25,306	24,565	23,209	424	381	362	1.6	317
1965	25,513	24,820	23,417	423	329	308	1.4	384
1966	25,644	24,974	23,554	417	360	323	1.5	371
1967	25,342	24,449	22,828	417	560	512	2.4	250

Sources: SIPEP, September 1967; MDS October 1967; MLG November 1967; MLG April 1968.

Notes [1] The total working population represents the total number of persons aged 15 and over who work for pay or gain or register themselves as available for such work. Part-time workers are counted as equivalent to whole-time workers. Most, if not all, persons registered as temporarily stopped are on the payrolls of employers and included in the number in civil employment. To avoid duplication therefore the total working population is obtained by adding together the figures for HM Forces and Women's Services, men and women on release leave, total in civil employment and registered wholly unemployed; registered temporarily stopped are omitted from the addition.

[2] The figures relate to the total number of employees insurable under the national insurance scheme. They represent the number of employed persons aged 15 and over who work for pay or gain or register themselves available for such work. Part-time workers are counted as equivalent to whole-time workers. In 1965 the MOL reverted to the pre-1959 method of estimation. The figures for 1959–64 have been recalculated on the old basis.

[3] As these figures are annual averages they cannot be simply compared with series taken at June in each year.

[4] The unemployment rate is the number of registered unemployed expressed as a percentage of the estimated number of employees.

TABLE A–5

UK Currency Circulation, Clearing Bank Deposits and Interest Rates 1952–67

	Estimated currency circulation with public (average) £m	London clearing banks' gross deposits (average of monthly figures) £m	2½% Consols, gross flat yield % (average of working days)	Bank Rate % Date of change	New Rate
1952	1,370	6,083	4.23	1952 Mar. 11	4
1953	1,462	6,256	4.08	1953 Sept. 17	3½
1954	1,551	6,495	3.75	1954 May 13	3
1955	1,657	6,454	4.17	1955 Jan. 27 1955 Feb. 24	3½ 4½
1956	1,765	6,288	4.73	1956 Feb. 16	5½
1957	2,842	6,432	4.98	1957 Feb. 7 1957 Sept. 19	5 7
1958	1,905	6,636	4.98	1958 Mar. 20 1958 May 22 1958 June 19 1958 Aug. 14 1958 Nov. 20	6 5½ 5 4½ 4
1959	1,969	6,935	4.82		
1960	2,062	7,236	5,42	1960 Jan. 21 1960 June 23 1960 Oct. 27 1960 Dec. 8	5 6 5½ 5

1961	2,151	7,395[1]	6.20	1961 July 26	7
				1961 Oct. 5	6½
				1961 Nov. 2	6
1962	2,161	7,611	5.98	1962 Mar. 8	5½
				1962 Mar. 22	5
				1962 April 26	4½
1963	2,210	7,971	5.58	1963 Jan. 3	4
1964	2,332	8,550	6.03	1964 Feb. 27	5
				1964 Nov. 23	7
1965	2,483	8,989	6.42	1965 June 3	6
1966	2,637	9,376	6.80	1966 July 14	7
1967	2,700	9,772	6.69	1967 Jan. 26	6½
				1967 Mar. 16	6
				1967 May 4	5½
				1967 Oct. 19	6
				1967 Nov. 9	6½
				1967 Nov. 19	8

Sources: FS various; MDS various

Note:[1] Excluding the business of Lloyd's Bank Eastern branches after December 1960.

TABLE A–6

UK Public Sector: Current Account 1952–66. £million

	1952	1953	1954	1955	1956
RECEIPTS					
Taxes on income	2,170	2,092	2,110	2,287	2,334
Taxes on Expenditure:					
Central government	1,901	1,933	2,041	2,177	2,271
Local authorities[1]	392	433	460	475	556
National insurance and health contributions	476	525	532	594	642
Gross trading income:					
Central government and local authorities	40	63	108	112	122
Public corporations	277	321	354	315	345
Gross rental income	181[3]	214	244	261	297
Interest and dividends, etc:					
Central government	64[4]	49	51	73	81
Local authorities	15	16	17	19	22
Public corporations	27[5]	21	23	31	32
Grants from abroad	120	105	50	46	26
TOTAL	5,663[4]	5,772	5,990	6,390	6,728
EXPENDITURE					
Current expenditure on goods and services[2]	2,894	3,034	3,113	3,171	3,428
Subsidies		365	422	350	359
Current grants to persons	1,393	1,002	1,021	1,115	1,193
Current grants paid abroad		61	65	70	73
Total current expenditure excluding debt interest	4,287	4,462	4,621	4,706	5,053
Debt interest:					
Central government	609	639	637	708	723
Local authorities	45	46	54	62	79
Public corporations	118[4]	118	127	137	126
Total current expenditure	5,059	5,265	5,439	5,613	5,981
Current surplus before providing for depreciation and stock appreciation and additions to tax and interest reserves	604	507	551	777	747
TOTAL	5,663[4]	5,772	5,990	6,390	6,728

Source: NIBB various

Notes: [1] Rates.
[2] Excluding current expenditure on goods and services on operating account of public corporations and other public enterprises.
[3] Excluding rental income of public corporations.
[4] Including payment of interest by public corporations to central government.
[5] Including rental income of public corporations.

1957	1958	1959	1960	1961	1962	1963	1964	1965	1966
2,570	2,704	2,747	2,713	3,066	3,447	3,379	3,523	4,020	4,418
2,351	2,390	2,486	2,620	2,812	2,980	3,034	3,359	3,766	4,243
615	650	714	771	831	916	1,014	1,099	1,232	1,353
657	859	897	913	1,072	1,197	1,303	1,444	1,685	1,797
128	155	164	180	98	73	78	91	99	98
323	340	391	539	645	751	846	931	995	1,038
330	365	398	437	485	517	548	596	667	745
68	77	94	78	95	121	97	100	124	131
26	28	34	37	40	48	52	59	60	67
38	35	38	46	50	51	37	41	50	54
21	3	-	-	-	-	-	-	-	-
7,127	7,606	7,963	8,334	9,194	10,101	10,388	11,243	12,698	13,944
3,585	3,673	3,920	4,164	4,499	4,824	5,083	5,399	5,883	6,391
407	385	369	487	586	600	560	509	564	558
1,252	1,484	1,636	1,653	1,802	1,981	2,234	2,369	2,729	2,973
75	77	82	94	118	121	132	163	178	182
5,319	5,619	6,007	6,398	7,005	7,526	8,009	8,440	9,354	10,104
705	780	774	861	897	878	931	943	969	1,041
101	117	139	164	211	240	269	320	377	429
144	149	159	154	162	170	94	105	120	105
6,269	6,665	7,079	7,577	8,275	8,814	9,303	9,808	10,820	11,679
858	941	884	757	919	1,287	1,085	1,435	1,878	2,265
7,127	7,606	7,963	8,334	9,194	10,101	10,388	11,243	12,698	13,944

I

TABLE A-7

UK Balance of Payments, 1952-67 £ million

	Imports (f.o.b.)	Exports and re-exports (f.o.b.)	Visible balance[2]	Invisible balance: Government military	Invisible balance: Government other	Invisible balance: Private	Current balance	Official capital (net)	Long-Term Capital Account[1]: Private investment (net) Abroad	In the UK	Total	Balance of long-term capital	Balance of current and long-term capital transactions	Balancing item	Balance of monetary movements[1]
1952	3,048	2,769	-279	-12	-49	+503	+163	-20	-127	+13	-114	-134	+29	+66	-95
1953	2,927	2,683	-244	-17	-49	+455	+145	-49	-173	+28	-145	-194	-49	-49	+17
1954	2,989	2,785	-204	-60	-71	+452	+117	-28	-238	+75	-163	-191	-74	+57	+17
1955	3,386	3,073	-313	-67	-71	+296	-155	-62	-182	+122	-60	-122	-277	+121	+156
1956	3,324	3,377	+53	-101	-74	+330	+208	-68	-258	+139	-119	-187	+21	+42	-63
1957	3,538	3,509	-29	-61	-83	+406	+233	+66	-298	+126	-172	-106	+127	+80	-207
1958	3,378	3,407	+29	-126	-93	+537	+347	-50	-310	+164	-146	-196	+151	+64	-215
1959	3,640	3,522	-118	-129	-98	+494	+149	-124	-303	+172	-131	-255	-106	-28	+134
1960	4,141	3,733	-408	-172	-110	+432	-258	-103	-322	+233	-89	-192	-450	+292	+158
1961	4,045	3,892	-153	-198	-134	+490	+5	-45	-313	+426	+113	+68	+73	-34	-39
1962	4,098	3,994	-104	-223	-136	+590	+127	-104	-242	+248	+6	-98	+29	+60	-89
1963	4,370	4,287	-83	-236	-145	+580	+116	-105	-329	+279	-50	-155	-39	-71	+110
1964	5,016	4,471	-545	-267	-165	+575	-402	-116	-406	+148	-258	-374	-776	+45	+731
1965	5,065	4,784	-281	-267	-179	+617	-110	-84	-356	+208	-148	-232	-342	+104	+238
1966	5,263	5,116	-147	-273	-188	+577	-31	-82	-292	+272	-20	-102	-133	-13	+146
1967	5,673	5,023	-650	-258	-191	+585	-514	-54	-363	+391	+28	-26	-540	+220	+320

Sources: ET Sept., 1967; *UK Balance of Payments 1967, Preliminary Estimates 1962-67*, Cmnd. 3571.
Notes: [1] Assets: increase −/decrease +
     Liabilities: increase +/decrease −
     [2] Including payments for US military aircraft and missiles.

TABLE A-8

UK Reserves, Net Liabilities and Overseas Holdings in Sterling 1952-67 (End of Period) £ million

	Gold and Convertible currency reserves	External Liabilities (net) and/or overseas holdings in sterling[1]							
		Total		International organisations		Sterling area countries		Non-sterling countries	
		External liabilities in sterling (net)	Overseas Sterling holdings	Excluding International Monetary Fund	IMF	External Liabilities in sterling (net)	Overseas Sterling Holdings	External Liabilities in sterling (net)	Overseas Sterling Holdings
1952	659		3,786	91	476		2,482		737
1953	899		4,004	91	420		2,715		778
1954	986		4,179	96	380		2,822		881
1955	757		4,045	89	380		2,764		812
1956	799		4,091	87	582		2,730		692
1957	812		3,918	62	583		2,608		665
1958	1,096		3,976	49	574		2,519		834
1959	977		4,212	32	673		2,704		803
1960	1,154		4,432	27	522		2,478		1,405
1961	1,185		4,504	62	896		2,631		915
1962	1,002	3,772	4,106	89	517	2,430	2,675	736	826
1963	949	3,892	—	105	522	2,592	—	673	—
1964	827	4,299	—	110	881	2,591	—	717	—
1965	1,073	4,865	—	104	1,377	2,595	—	789	—
1966	1,107	5,161	—	118	1,538	2,591	—	914	—
1967	1,123	5,350	—	101	1,439	2,442	—	1,368	—

Sources: *ET*, March, 1968; *U.K. Balance of Payments*, 1967.
Note: [1] At the end of 1962 the series 'UK external liabilities and claims in sterling' replaced the series 'overseas sterling holdings'.

I*

TABLE A-9

UK External Trade[1] 1954-67

| | Value of the external trade of the UK (£m) | | | | | Volume Index Numbers 1961 = 100 | | | | Unit Value Index Nos. 1961 = 100 | | | | |
| | Imports[4] (c.i.f.) | | Exports (f.o.b.)[2] | | Re-exports (f.o.b.) | Imports | | Exports | | Imports | | Exports | | Terms of Trade[3] |
	Total	Manufactures	Total	Manufactures		Total (weight = 1000)	Manufactures (weight = 337)	Total (weight = 1000)	Manufactures (weight = 843)	Total (weight = 1000)	Manufactures (weight = 337)	Total (weight = 1000)	Manufactures (weight = 843)	
1954	3,359	679	2,650	2,107	98	73	50	82	79	104	98	91	89	87
1955	3,936	971	2,957	2,392	116	80	62	87	85	108	106	92	90	86
1956	3,944	984	3,226	2,638	143	80	62	91	91	110	107	95	93	87
1957	4,139	1,012	3,374	2,776	130	83	66	93	93	111	100	100	96	89
1958	3,834	978	3,250	2,714	142	84	67	89	89	103	96	99	97	96
1959	4,087	1,127	3,422	2,875	131	90	76	93	92	102	98	98	97	96
1960	4,655	1,523	3,648	3,059	142	101	100	97	97	102	101	100	99	97
1961	4,547	1,531	3,796	3,199	158	100	100	100	100	100	100	100	100	100
1962	4,627	1,556	3,905	3,270	157	103	103	102	101	99	99	101	102	102
1963	4,983	1,702	4,211	3,499	154	107	112	108	106	103	101	104	104	101
1964	5,696	2,160	4,411	3,695	154	119	136	111	111	107	105	106	106	99
1965	5,752	2,254	4,728	3,997	173	120	137	117	117	107	109	108	109	102
1966	5,947	2,471	5,047	4,278	194	122	146	121	120	109	114	112	114	103
1967	6,442	2,844	5,026	4,270	185	132	168	119	118	109	116	114	116	105

Source: ROT, October 1967, April 1968.

Notes: [1] This table is based on the revised figures first appearing in ROT March 1966. These differ from earlier figures because of
    (a) revised estimates for parcel post and
    (b) the inclusion of figures for trade in precious stones and pearls.

[2] Including repayment of lend-lease silver to United States valued at £22.4 million for 1956 and £7.1 million for 1957.

[3] Export unit value index as a percentage of the import unit value index.

[4] The import figures of Table A.9 differ from those of Table A.7 because of the inclusion of charges for insurance and freight. Apart from this, both series will differ because of certain adjustments made for valuation and coverage. A further explanation is to be seen in the 1967 *UK Balance of Payments*.

TABLE A-10

Productivity in UK 1952-67 Index numbers 1958 = 100

	Output per person employed		Output per man hour worked in manufacturing
	Gross Domestic Product	Total Industrial Production	
1952	89	88	88
1953	90	90	89
1954	95	96	93
1955	97	98	97
1956	97	98	96
1957	99	100	99
1958	100	100	100
1959	104	105	105
1960	107	110	110
1961	108	110	110
1962	109	111	113
1963	113	116	119
1964	118	123	126
1965	120	125	130
1966	121	127	133
1967	124	130	137

Source: NIER various.

TABLE A-11

UK Prices 1952-67   Index numbers, 1958 = 100

	Retail prices	Consumer goods and services							
		Total	Food	Drink, tobacco	Housing (incl. rent and rates)	Durable goods	Clothing	All other goods	Services
1952	81.3	83.7	80.6	91.4	72.3	96.5	95.1	84.8	79.2
1953	83.9	85.4	84.3	91.8	76.0	92.1	94.3	84.5	81.3
1954	85.3	87.0	87.3	91.9	78.8	90.6	95.1	85.0	83.2
1955	89.2	90.1	92.6	92.4	81.4	91.8	95.4	88.3	86.5
1956	93.6	94.2	96.4	95.5	84.3	98.6	97.5	93.7	92.4
1957	97.1	97.3	98.6	98.0	89.8	100.0	99.1	97.7	96.6
1958	100.0	100.0	100.0	100.0	100.0	100.0	100.0	100.0	100.0
1959	100.6	100.6	101.2	97.9	105.3	97.9	99.5	99.8	101.7
1960	101.6	101.5	100.7	99.4	108.5	96.9	100.8	100.5	104.0
1961	105.0	104.4	102.2	103.8	113.4	97.8	102.5	104.1	107.9
1962	109.5	108.2	105.7	109.6	119.4	97.5	105.5	107.9	111.7
1963	111.7	109.6	107.5	111.1	127.0	91.5	107.1	109.4	114.2
1964	115.4	112.7	110.4	117.2	133.7	92.2	108.7	112.0	116.6
1965	120.9	117.7	114.2	128.7	142.1	94.1	111.0	116.6	120.7
1966	125.6	122.1	117.8	133.1	150.6	95.4	113.9	120.7	126.0
1967	128.7	124.8	120.0	135.0	156.2	96.5	115.4	122.7	130.9

Source: NIER various.

TABLE A-12

Wage Rates, Earnings and Salaries in UK 1952-67   1955 = 100

	All manual workers[1]			
	Weekly Rates of Wages	Hourly Rates of Wages	Average weekly earnings	Average salary earnings[2]
1952	85.8	85.7	80.9	–
1953	89.8	89.7	85.9	–
1954	93.7	93.6	91.5	–
1955	100.0	100.0	100.0	100.0
1956	107.9	108.0	108.0	107.3
1957	113.4	113.6	113.0	114.8
1958	117.5	117.9	116.9	118.5
1959	120.6	121.1	122.2	126.3
1960	123.7	126.3	130.1	133.4
1961	128.8	134.3	138.0	139.9
1962	133.6	140.5	142.9	147.7
1963	138.4	145.7	148.9	155.8
1964	144.9	153.2	161.8	164.5
1965	151.2	162.9	174.8	178.4
1966	158.3	173.7	185.0	186.1
1967	164.2	180.8	192.3	194.7

Source: SIPEP September 1967, March 1968; MLG April 1968
Notes: [1] The indices of rates of wages relate to manual workers in all industries and services but those for average weekly earnings cover only those in industries included in the Ministry of Labour half yearly earnings enquiries.
[2] October in each year.

Index